British Youth Television

Faye Woods

British Youth Television

Transnational Teens, Industry, Genre

Faye Woods
University of Reading
Reading, Berkshire, United Kingdom

ISBN 978-1-137-44547-6   ISBN 978-1-137-44548-3   (eBook)
DOI 10.1057/978-1-137-44548-3

Library of Congress Control Number: 2016942689

© The Editor(s) (if applicable) and The Author(s) 2016
The author(s) has/have asserted their right(s) to be identified as the author(s) of this work in accordance with the Copyright, Designs and Patents Act 1988.
This work is subject to copyright. All rights are solely and exclusively licensed by the Publisher, whether the whole or part of the material is concerned, specifically the rights of translation, reprinting, reuse of illustrations, recitation, broadcasting, reproduction on microfilms or in any other physical way, and transmission or information storage and retrieval, electronic adaptation, computer software, or by similar or dissimilar methodology now known or hereafter developed.
The use of general descriptive names, registered names, trademarks, service marks, etc. in this publication does not imply, even in the absence of a specific statement, that such names are exempt from the relevant protective laws and regulations and therefore free for general use.
The publisher, the authors and the editors are safe to assume that the advice and information in this book are believed to be true and accurate at the date of publication. Neither the publisher nor the authors or the editors give a warranty, express or implied, with respect to the material contained herein or for any errors or omissions that may have been made.

Cover illustration: © fStop Images - Twins / Getty
Cover design by Oscar Spigolon

Printed on acid-free paper

This Palgrave Macmillan imprint is published by Springer Nature
The registered company is Macmillan Publishers Ltd. London

To mum, dad and Hilary

Acknowledgements

First thanks must go to Rachel Moseley and Richard Dyer at the University of Warwick for teaching me how to be an academic. This book was planned and then later completed in two terms of research leave from the Department of Film, Theatre & Television at the University of Reading. I would like to thank my colleagues' support for this, in particular John Gibbs and Anna McMullan, who carved out space for me as this project reached its conclusion. Across the life of this book, Amy Holdsworth has provided guidance and feedback, both at the proposal stage and at the close, reading probably multiple versions of the same words. Karen Lury also provided valuable guidance at the proposal stage. Several people gave their time, valuable feedback and advice on chapters: Chris Becker, Jonathan Bignell, Cathy Johnson, Amanda Anna Klein, Rachel Moseley, Ally Peirse, Dave Rolinson, Helen Wheatley and Helen Wood. Sarah Currant was my personal librarian, continual support and offered a keen eye in the closing stages. I also want to thank the third-year FTT students of both Contemporary TV Drama and Television and Contemporary Culture across the years. I have tried many of these ideas out on them and have greatly enjoyed all the conversation and laughter. Thanks also to the ladies of the backchannel for their tireless support, laughter and pictures to push me to the finish, and to Chris Porter for always giving me time. Finally to my parents and sister, who sacrificed and supported me over the many years of my education, even though I never ring them enough. Dad made me scholar from those first steps of Fred & Ginger on a Saturday afternoon, and mum and Hils watched them with me.

Contents

Part I Framing   1

1 Made in Britain: Mapping British Youth Television   3
Situating British Youth Television   8
Existing Scholarship   11
Tracing the Roots   15
Structure   19
Notes   20
References   21

2 Branding Youth Space: British Youth Strands and Channels   27
A Brief History of Television's Youth Spaces   31
Terrestrial Youth Strands: T4   33
Commercial Digital Youth Channel: ITV2   35
Public/Private Digital Youth Channel: E4   38
Public Service Digital Youth Channel: BBC Three   46
Notes   57
References   58

Part II Fiction   67

3 British Youth Drama: Space, Place, Authenticity and Intimacy   69
Situating British Youth Drama   71
Misfits: British Youth Drama's First Wave   77
My Mad Fat Diary: Emotional Saturation and Unruly Female Subjectivity   83
In the Flesh: Intimacy, Landscape and Allegory   94
Settling Down, Remaining Disruptive   101
Notes   102
References   102

4 Teen TV Translations: Across the Pond   107
Formats and Globalisation   110
Teen Translations and Permeable National Boundaries   113
Discourses of Authenticity   117
Space and Place   128
Learning Lessons and Finding a Voice   134
Notes   136
References   136

Part III Factual   143

5 Youth Factual: First Person, Peer Address and Interaction   145
Peer Presenter and Personal Investigation   149
Surveilling the Social Media Everyday   153
Squaddie Docs, the Personal and Our War   157
Our World War   170
Agency and Immediacy in Online Factual Content   173
Notes   179
References   180

6	**Structured Reality: Designer Clothes, Fake Tans, Real Drama?**	185
	Glocalising The Hills	190
	Shaping British Structured Reality	200
	Coding Class: Space and Place	205
	Coding Class: Gender	208
	Camp Play and Comic Voice	215
	Notes	220
	References	221
7	**Conclusion: A Short-Form Future?**	225
	The Swiftly Shifting Media Landscape	230
	Youth Channel Identity and Short-Form Content on Digital Platforms	232
	British Youth Voice on YouTube: Beauty Vloggers	237
	'New BBC Three': A British Youth Platform?	243
	Notes	247
	References	247
Index		253

LIST OF FIGURES

Fig. 2.1	An early E4 ident offers a playful shattering of the classic Channel 4 icon	42
Fig. 2.2	2010's 'E4 Bunker' promo	45
Fig. 3.1	*Misfits'* establishing shots set concrete against expanses of water and sky	82
Fig. 3.2	The amateur scribbles conjure Rae's diary onto the screen, layered over action	91
Fig. 4.1	Suburban spaces are at odds with *The Inbetweeners'* attempts at deviant drinking	130
Fig. 4.2	The *Skins* US trailer takes place in a large, brightly lit suburban home	132
Fig. 5.1	Anonymous social graphics layered over transitional shots in *Teens*	155
Fig. 5.2	A helmet-cam captures an IED explosion and its aftermath in *Our War*	169
Fig. 6.1	A shallow depth of field, golden light and pastel-toned grade aestheticise the privileged lifestyles of *Made in Chelsea*	189
Fig. 6.2	*TOWIE* presents Chloe's glamorous excess as comic spectacle within the domestic everyday	209
Fig. 7.1	The top of the new BBC Three homepage showcased the channel's focus on comedy and factual programming, offering shareable links to the BBC iPlayer	244
Fig. 7.2	BBC Three's YouTube channel showcased a range of short-form content, and also advertised the arrival of new drama *Thirteen*	245

PART I

Framing

CHAPTER 1

Made in Britain: Mapping British Youth Television

Three young men – two white, one British-Asian – sit slumped in a bus stop shelter in long shot, surrounded by pouring rain and backed by identikit white-brick terraced houses. The screen splits and the right-hand side fills with a sunlit lakeside, packed with partying, laughing, tanned teenagers clad in shorts and bikinis. We cut to the right as the Brits crane forward and gaze in confusion and wonder at the mirage of American leisure. Their grey-toned, rainy image is framed between slender female dancing bodies saturated with colour. They rise and walk through the dividing border, gasping as they emerge from the rain into the bright sunshine. They smile broadly to each other as they wander through the mass of partying American youth. We cut back to the split-screen long shot to find an elderly couple installed in the bus shelter, an American female voiceover invites the audience to 'Come on over to *Beaver Falls*, new British drama starts 27 July on E4'. Left is Britain: dull, grey, rainy, elderly. Right is America: youth, sunshine, leisure and the potential of sex. The trailer introduces *Beaver Falls* (E4, 2011–2012), a dramedy as 'laddishly' juvenile as the lazily punning title suggests, which follows a trio of British graduates working at a wealthy American summer camp. The trailer sets up a dichotomy between national representations of youth, British mundane realism and American utopian fantasy, suggesting that British youth television was able to breach the divide.

This book offers the first study of contemporary British youth television, mapping a broadcasting eco-system that emerged in the past 15 years through the rise of digital television and its migration across

© The Editor(s) (if applicable) and The Author(s) 2016
F. Woods, *British Youth Television*,
DOI 10.1057/978-1-137-44548-3_1

multiple platforms and screens. Presenting a British counterpart to the US-dominated field of teen TV scholarship, this study examines individual programmes, genres and trends. It considers their social and historical contexts and larger industrial frameworks, tracing commonalities across fiction and factual programming. 'Teen TV' has been used in scholarship as an umbrella term under which some international texts have been included (Davis and Dickinson 2004b); however, I follow Karen Lury (2001) in defining the national field as 'British youth television'. This signals national distinction and reflects British programming's embrace of both teens and twentysomethings, from the school uniforms of *Some Girls* (BBC Three 2012–2014) and *The Inbetweeners* (E4, 2008–2010) to the housemates of *Being Human* (BBC Three, 2008–2013) and *Switch* (ITV2, 2012).

By focusing on the past two decades, this book builds a case study of a significant period of change in British television, an era that Amanda Lotz defines as 'post-network' television in the US (2014) and James Bennett marks as 'digital television' (2011), where 'various industrial, technological, and cultural forces have begun to radically redefine television, yet paradoxically, it persists as an entity that most people still understand and identify as "TV"' (Lotz 2014, 7). This encompasses the growth of digital television in the UK and television's spread across multiple streaming and download platforms, from the BBC iPlayer to Netflix to YouTube, as a medium accessed through a range of devices from DVRs to mobile phones. A revolution rather than a 'death', this is a landscape that encompasses both linear televisual flow and non-linear flexibility, professional and amateur production, where 'digital media are increasingly less "new" and increasingly more "ordinary"' (Lotz 2014, 15). British youth television is directly engaged in the challenges facing the British television industry as it negotiates its position in the international media landscape and chases the proliferated attention of youth audiences. This book traces its journey up to 2015 and contemplates where its future may lie.

This book expands the privileging of the US hour-long drama in previous studies of teen TV (Davis and Dickinson 2004b; Ross and Stein 2008b) to bridge divisions between the academic study of fiction and factual television. By bringing together *My Mad Fat Diary* (E4, 2013–2015) and *Our War* (BBC Three, 2011–2014), *The Inbetweeners* and *The Only Way is Essex* (ITV2/ITV Be, 2010–) in a single study I can chart continuities and thematic concerns across drama, sitcom, reality TV and factual storytelling, identifying British youth television's preoccupations and its structure of feeling (Williams 1977). I build a comprehensive picture of the landscape of British youth television by integrating close analysis of televisual texts – form, aesthetics, tone and representation – with a charting of larger industrial frameworks. Woven through this analysis is the complex relationship with US teen TV, the push and pull of influence and distinction. British youth television follows a long history of the cross-Atlantic flows of pop cultures, blurring yet also defining national identities. Borders are rendered permeable in the age of digital media, with television circulating internationally via streaming platforms, peer-to-peer sharing and remakes. This transatlantic exchange shapes the televisual diet of British youth audiences, which is heavy on US content.[1] It also shapes British youth television's negotiation of its own territory and its relationship with public service broadcasting;[2] at times, it is in thrall to US television, while at others, it is eager to assert its national difference.

The late 2000s saw US television coalesce around the 'millennial' as a target of its teen programming. ABC Family rebranded in 2007 as a millennial-targeted cable channel (Stein 2015) and in 2008 MTV began a large-scale market-research project on the demographic that influenced its programming and branding decisions (Pardee 2010; Stelter 2010). 'Millennial' referred to the demographic born between 1982 and 2004 and combined the lucrative teenage and young adult consumers. It was defined and disseminated by William Howe and Neil Strauss' book *Millennials Rising* (2000) with the help of the influential Pew Research centre (Stein 2015, 3). Louisa Ellen Stein argues that like all generations, the 'millennial' is a discursive construct, crafted by marketers, consultants and industry discourse, an 'evolving, self-defined culture' (2015, 7). In contrast, British industrial discourse has never been as clearly defined around the figure of the millennial, tending to prefer 'youth' as a signifier of the 16–34-year-old demographic.

As Simon Frith argues, 'youth' itself is a discursive construct which in the 1980s 'became a category constructed by TV itself, with no other referent: those people of whatever age or circumstance who watched "youth" programmes became youth' (1993, 64). British press discourse in the 2010s has labelled the demographic Generation Y (Browning 2014; No author 2014), Millennials (Bulkley 2013; Sanghani 2014; Chamorro-Premuzic 2014) and at times Generation Rent to reflect a coming of age during the economic downturn (Osborne 2015). My use of 'youth' over 'teen' or 'millennial' feels both nationally appropriate and positions my study as a continuation of Lury's foundational work. Lury argues that 'youth' is 'not determined by age, but relates to a historical and mediated construction of "youth" or "youthfulness" as an attitude, or a series of traits, habits, and beliefs' (2001, 126). I use youth to describe the demographic category of those aged 16–34 – one used within the television industry – and a televisual construct defined by tone, address and its location within defined youth spaces in the schedule and channel line-up.

It is only in the early years of the twenty-first century that British youth television has found its feet, following sporadic bubbles of youth provision throughout the first 50 years of British television (J. Hill 1991; Osgerby 2004a; Moseley 2007; Lury 2001). It is a form shaped by the narrowcast digital television channels developed by both commercial television and public service broadcasters ahead of the digital switchover in 2012. British television is distinct from the US system that dominates existing discussions of teen TV and is shaped by a blend of public service broadcasting and advertising. It is made up of five main channels that combine publicly owned and commercial broadcasters, which have various levels of public service remit.[3] They range from the licence-fee funded, publicly owned BBC One and BBC Two to the commercially funded and publicly owned Channel 4, to the commercially funded ITV and Channel 5, which maintain minimal public service content. Before the 2012 switchover to digital television, all five main channels were delivered terrestrially, free-to-air. Alongside these sit a swathe of commercially funded cable and satellite channels, with BSkyB, Virgin Media and recently BT competing as the primary distributers of these channels. The first decade of the twenty-first century saw the arrival of a range of digital television channels delivered free-to-air via set-top boxes, with the Freeview platform becoming the dominant distributor. Each of the existing main channels has a parcel of digital 'sister channels', and a range of other digital channels owned by commercial media companies target different niche audiences. Thus, the British system offers five main channels, a range of channels delivered via cable and satellite, and a range of free-to-air digital television channels. The latter is the space of British youth channels.

Public service broadcasting plays a central role in the formation, maintenance and distinctiveness of British youth programming, as the provision of programming for young people (along with children) forms part of the public service objectives set out by the 2003 Communication Act.[4] Yet the importance of public service broadcasting is challenged by the increasing ambivalent attitude towards its value amongst its target demographic (Born 2003; Ofcom 2015). The traditionally low viewing rate of the

16–34-year-old demographic, particularly the younger end of those aged 16–24, makes them important for public service broadcasters and advertising-funded commercial channels alike (with the advertising-funded public service broadcaster Channel 4 straddling both). Their status as hard-to-reach has seen provision for youth audiences form part of the BBC and Channel 4's public service remits, with particular focus on education and citizenship. In turn, their elusiveness combines with a reputation for high leisure spending to make them the most coveted demographic for advertisers. The competition for this portion of television viewers drove the growth and innovation of British youth television.

The media industry pays close attention to the preferences and behaviour patterns of youth audiences as they are seen as indicators of future patterns of consumption. Ofcom research indicated that in 2014, 16–24 year olds viewing of 'live' linear television had fallen to 50 per cent, with the rest of their television delivered through 'over the top' services (streaming and download). The youth demographic's increasing preference for the flexibility of online on-demand platforms such as BBC iPlayer, All4, Netflix and Amazon Instant Video is being presented as evidence of the fast pace of change in the delivery and consumption of television (Ofcom 2015, 19). British youth television forms a focal point for the challenges facing public service broadcasting in the digital era, as competition for all audiences expands across these on-demand and streaming platforms. With the BBC approaching charter renewal in 2016 under a hostile Conservative government and the commercial sell-off of Channel 4 under consideration, public service broadcasting is under attack with an intensity not seen before (even in the 1980s under Margaret Thatcher). The rise of E4 and particularly the trajectory of BBC Three concentrate the tensions between public service broadcasting, entertainment and commercial services in the British television industry. With budget cuts driving the latter's closure as a linear channel and move to online-only status in February 2016, 'New BBC Three' signals a future for British television in line with the shifting consumption habits of its target audience. If, as Apple CEO Tim Cook has proclaimed, 'the future of television is apps' (Jarvey 2015), will the individual channel identities that have played such a key role in British youth television be lost? How will YouTube and Facebook's dominance as digital streaming portals amongst youth demographics affect future British youth television? Is the current breadth of programming a blip, destined to follow the brief flowerings of youth-targeted content in 1950s and 1960s pop programming (J. Hill 1991; Osgerby 2004a), early

1980s teen drama (Moseley 2007) and late 1980s/early 1990s entertainment programming (Lury 2001)? For now, this book highlights an important portion of recent British television, charting the development and consolidation of this national, demographically defined, televisual identity.

SITUATING BRITISH YOUTH TELEVISION

So what is British youth television? Defining 'Britishness' in the short space of this introduction is a fool's errand, as that way stereotypes and reductiveness lies. As this book demonstrates British youth identity is not singular, it contains many different articulations. What I am certain of is the presence of class, which seems to play an inevitable and essential component in cultural representations (Biressi and Nunn 2013) and that public service broadcasting (and its relationship with commercial television) shapes the televisual landscape. Part of the work involved in defining what British youth television *is* involves explaining what it is *not*. For me, Channel 4 programmes such as Shane Meadows and Jack Thorne's *This is England* trilogy (Channel 4, 2010, 2011, 2015) or the crime drama *Top Boy* (Channel 4, 2011–2013), despite their youth casts, are *not* British youth television. Instead, I class these as 'event serials' (Rolinson and Woods 2013) – a category which includes historical epic *The Devil's Whore* (2008) and council estate ensemble *Run* (2013) – airing in short runs on Channel 4 and paratextually framed through discourses of authorship and prestige. Television on Britain's main channels is often *about* youth rather than *for* youth. Outside of the deft explorations of youth concerns and layered long-term representations of evening soap operas (*EastEnders* (BBC One, 1985–), *Coronation Street* (ITV, 1960–), *Brookside* (Channel 4, 1982–2003)), the primetime schedules often see young people 'othered' and framed through social problems. This is particularly illustrated in the over-representation of criminal youth – the dominant representation of ethnic minorities – in dramas such as *Fallout* (Channel 4, 2008), *Top Boy* and *Accused* (BBC One, 2010). As I note in Chapter 3, these mirror British cinema's favouring of representations of inner-city criminal youth and 'Brit Grit' storytelling (Lay 2002) throughout the 2000s. Happily, such representations are slowly being broadened in British youth television via E4's *Youngers* (2013–2014) and *Chewing Gum* (2015–). British youth television is distinct from prime-time programming *about* youth, separate from prestige serials and topical single dramas, existing primarily in youth spaces on digital niche channels.

British youth television is not a genre – it encompasses many – nor would I follow Lury's analysis of youth programming of the late 1980s and early 1990s and call this current iteration a 'sensibility' (2001), as it contains a variety of styles and attitudes. This is television defined by industrially informed borders, a collection of programmes on a particular set of channels, and whilst it displays identity, it is not an identity itself. I choose to term it a 'form', a form of television produced for and about youth audience by British youth channels. It is characterised by interlocking thematic concerns, which this book traces through drama, comedy, documentary and reality TV. What emerges as a central thread is a quest for and assertion of that nebulous, elusive quality of 'authenticity' that is often central to the discourses that surround British youth television (Berridge 2013, 787). It is there in the paratextual shaping of channel identities; in negotiations of social realism, melodrama and affect in youth drama; in a focus on young voices and bodies in the *Skins* brand's transatlantic travels; and in the centralising of personal perspectives in documentary content and the complex negotiation of construction and performativity in structured reality's hail to the savvy reality TV viewer. 'Authenticity' is a culturally deployed construct and is by no means nationally distinct, as MTV's market research highlights its centrality to US Millennials (Pardee 2010). However, it operates here within British filmic and televisual legacies of realism (J. Hill 1986; Caughie 2000), which influence British youth television's industrial discourses and shape its relationship with audiences. As Rachel Moseley notes, British youth drama is underpinned by a 'realist paradigm', connected to its directness of representation and frankness in language use (2015, 39–40). Although I am well aware that televisual 'truth claims' of authenticity are a construct – and hence I return at times to the phrase 'authenticity claims' – I must also recognise their powerful cultural pull. As Sarah Banet-Weiser points out, 'even if we discard as false a simple opposition between the authentic and the inauthentic, we still must still reckon with the power of authenticity – of the self, of experience, of relationships' (2012, 5). We still want to believe.

Why is authenticity so central to youth identity? Psychologist Susan Harter highlights adolescence as a time preoccupied with 'authentic-self behaviour and its converse', which signifies this life stage as a time when the 'search for the true self is of paramount concern'. She suggests this is the result of adolescents' struggle with 'the societal demand that [they] create *multiple selves* associated with different social roles or contexts' (2002, 384), arguing that the attempt to negotiate proliferations of 'selves' creates a 'natural concern over which is "the real me"' (2002, 385). Adolescence is characterised here as a search for and prioritising of the authentic self, which is centralised in British youth television's 'structure of feeling' and its address to teenage and twentysomething audiences. Raymond Williams uses structure of feeling to articulate the emotional relations of a specific time and culture, as the 'felt sense of the quality of life at a particular place and time: a sense of the ways in which the particular activities combined into a way of thinking and living' (Williams 1961). The emotional relations of British youth television prioritise a quest for and assertion of 'authenticity'.

These assertions are prompted by British youth television's industrial context. The cultural connotations of public service broadcasting's paternal and institutional address prompts youth television to emphasise its independence of voice and conscience, presenting itself as true of self. It also positions itself as a nationally distinct variation on imported US teen TV, grounded in British traditions of realism, serving as a reaction to the glossy aesthetic, aspirational glamour, confident verboseness and underlying conservativity of programmes such as *Dawson's Creek*, *One Tree Hill* (WB/CW, 2002–2012) and *The O.C.* (Fox, 2003–2007). This is a distinction in line with ideologies surrounding British traditions of realist-filmmaking which 'has always been promoted in terms of cultural value, pitting the authentic, indigenous culture of "ordinary people" against the Americanised culture of glamour, spectacle, commercialism and more entertainment' (Ashby and Higson 2000, 9). However, this is not to construct an oppositional positioning of British youth television as 'authentic' and US imports as inauthentic; instead, this is a dialogue and negotiation.

This discourse of authenticity seeks to build intimate relationships between text and viewer through a signalling of transparency, banishing fears of didacticism, whether from imported US content (Berridge 2013, 788) or public service broadcasting's 'educational' remit. Yet this transparency is countered by a fundamental ambivalence at play in British youth television, its combination of an affect-driven emotional saturation and pleasure in melodrama with a savvy distance and sceptical gaze on television's construction. Here I build on Lury's identification of the oscillation between cynicism and enchantment at play in late 1980s and early 1990s youth television (2001). Where Lury positioned this play as uneasy (2001, 42), I argue this is now normalised throughout British youth television. This ambivalence also connects with the ambivalent pleasures that Lauren Berlant (2008) identifies in the female subject's relationship with socially denigrated 'feminine' popular culture. The programmes and channels of British youth television are placed in a similarly culturally delegitimated position (Newman and Levine 2011) due to their association with youth, soap opera's melodrama-informed storytelling and reality TV. Berlant usefully suggests that rather than signalling failure, this ambivalence serves as 'an inevitable condition of intimate attachment and a pleasure in its own right' (2008, 181). The ambivalent pleasures of British youth television are something I return to throughout, particularly in relation to structured reality in Chapter 6.

Thus, the operating principles of British youth television are a claim for authenticity and investment in transparency, tied to nationality through televisual traditions of realism and public service broadcasting's (intended) separation from commercial desires. Yet these are filtered through a fundamental ambivalent address, highly invested yet also distant. These accompany a negotiated relationship with US teen TV to conjure the structure of feeling of British youth television.

Existing Scholarship

To talk about British youth television, it is essential to map out the academic coverage of US teen TV, as this forms the dominant academic coverage of contemporary youth and television. British youth television's late development – *Skins* arrived a decade after *Dawson's Creek* – together with its relative lack of (legal) international circulation, has resulted in its absence from the academic corpus of teen TV. This is defined by two edited collections, 2004's *Teen TV* from Glyn Davis and Kay Dickinson and 2008's *Teen Television* from Sharon Marie Ross and Louisa Ellen Stein. Both predominantly cover hour-long dramedies airing on the WB and UPN, although the former augments this with Australian (Dickinson 2004; Douglas and McWilliam 2004) and MTV (Olsen 2004) programming, and the latter with wider historical and industrial analysis (Martin 2008; Turnbull 2008; Ross 2008b). As a result, contemporary youth narratives have been enshrined in scholarship as definitively American and teenage. Both collections do valuable work in setting out teen TV's storytelling, representations, industrial and cultural contexts, with Ross and Stein adding cultures of reception to the mix. Elsewhere teen TV scholarship has largely centred on studies of individual US programmes, from *Dawson's Creek* (Bindig 2008) and *Buffy the Vampire Slayer* (Wilcox and Lavery 2002; Wilcox 2005; Levine and Parks 2007) to *Gilmore Girls*

(WB/CW, 2000–20007) (Calvin 2008; Diffrient and Lavery 2010) and *My So-Called Life* (ABC, 1994–1995) (Byers and Lavery 2007).

Sitcoms, reality TV and MTV's music programming have all made significant contributions to US programming for the teenage market, but academic study is dominated by the WB model of US teen TV. This model is defined by its hour-long dramedies *Buffy the Vampire Slayer* and *Dawson's Creek*, together with the shows that followed in their image (with the industry narrative largely erasing the network's African-American sitcoms). *Party of Five* (Fox, 1994–2000) and *My So-Called Life* formed important precursors; however, by the late 1990s, 'WB programming *was* teen programming from a pop culture standpoint' as much due to the network's marketing as the content of its programming (Ross and Stein 2008a, 15). Louisa Ellen Stein's recent *Millennial Fandom* (2015) has brought the field up to date, broadening the teen TV corpus to include *Glee* (Fox, 2009–2015), *Gossip Girl* (CW, 2007–2011), *Pretty Little Liars* (ABC Family, 2010–). Stein also added online web series and millennial-targeting cable channel ABC Family to frameworks of teen TV.

As Rachel Moseley notes, US teen TV draws from the generic identity of the Hollywood teen film, 'including character types, formal and stylistic elements, settings, spaces, iconography and narrative themes' (2015, 38). From *Dawson's Creek* to *Pretty Little Liars*, US teen TV has been dominated by upper-middle-class, white ensemble dramas with underlying conservative tendencies (Dickinson 2004; Stein 2015). Moseley suggests that this conservatism followed in the wake of ABC's didactic *After School Special* (1972–1997) (2015, 40). It can also be linked to broadcasters' fear of advertisers reprisals over contentious content, as Chapter 4's discussion of MTV's *Skins* illustrates. Former WB executive Susanne Daniels termed the network's programming 'teen fantasies' operating in an 'angsty feel-good milieu'. Rather than referring to genre-hybrids such as *Buffy the Vampire Slayer* and *Roswell* (WB/UPN, 1999–2002), Daniels uses fantasy to signal the utopian pleasures of the WB (Daniels and Littleton 2007, 192), which are evoked by characters' verbal dexterity, their beautiful bodies and their largely white aspirational lifestyles. Here US teen TV mirrors the normalising work of US television as a whole (J. Gray 2008, 158–160), offering lifestyles beyond the reach of much of its audience. UPN's *Veronica Mars* (2004–2007) and NBC's *Friday Night Lights* (2006–2011) were rare in this era in their direct address of class concerns (*The O.C., Gilmore Girls* and *Gossip Girl* are initially structured around class difference, but swiftly assimilate their outsiders into the upper middle class). ABC Family pushes this closer to the foreground in *Switched at Birth* (2011–) and *The Fosters* (2013–) (Kohnen 2015).

WB-informed-teen TV draws on the aesthetic and storytelling traditions of serialised 'quality television' (Feuer 1984; McCabe and Akass 2007). The legitimation this endows counters teen TV's connections with consumer culture and the 'low-brow' status of its feminine melodrama (Ross and Stein 2008a, 8). Melodrama is the core of teen TV (together with a strong strand of comedy); Davis and Dickinson suggest that its programmes 'express key cultural concerns through this model of personal, psychological plight' (2004a, 6). Rachel Moseley notes that teen narratives take seriously the intensity and significance of teenage experience, valuing emotion and constructing an intimacy in their storytelling (2015, 39). Recognising the role of emotional realism in teen TV's melodrama brings complexity to the form's aspirational tendencies. Ien Ang suggests that for the audiences of 1980s US prime-time soap operas, the programmes' glamorous, melodrama-intensive storytelling produced a form of 'realism'. Rather than a physical reality, this was 'the construction of a *psychological* reality' (1985, 47) and US teen TV's pleasures are driven by a similar intertwining of aspirational lifestyles and emotional realism. As Chapter 3 demonstrates, British youth drama develops a complex relationship with melodrama, which is in part informed by its hesitancy towards US teen TV.

Moseley suggests that US teen TV offers a broad address 'in which both engagement with the melodramatic/emotional and knowing distance can be accommodated' (2001, 43), which aligns with Lury's construction of British youth television's ambivalent address. Thus, attempts to delineate British youth television as realism and US teen TV as melodrama (a frequent occurrence in press coverage) obscures structuring connections. As I argue throughout, drawing on Moseley and Ang, together with Miranda Banks' articulation of teen male melodrama (2004), British youth drama operates around its own, ambivalent yet intensely felt, brand of melodrama.

In contrast to teen TV, scholarship on British youth television has remained critically out of focus (Moseley 2007, 184), its absence from the wealth of studies of national television history reflecting British television's scant attention to youth audiences. Scholarship examining British television for younger audiences has been largely restricted to studies of children's programming (Buckingham et al. 1999; Davies 2001), where there is a tendency to look to television history (Oswell 2002) and industry

(Steemers and D'Arma 2012). Beyond this, a cultural studies-led focus on contemporary media has tended to revolve around the 'problem' of young people and television, focusing on regulation, audiences and effects-based outcomes (Buckingham 1993; Livingstone 2002; Osgerby 2004b). Glyn Davis and Kay Dickinson note that across the wealth of cultural studies work on British youth, there is a surprising lack of interest in television. They suggest the form's lack of counter-cultural identity made it an ill fit with the field's investment in youth culture's resistance (2004a, 4). Quests for subversion or resistance in youth television audiences, as Will Brooker's small-scale study of *Dawson's Creek*'s audiences demonstrates (2001), largely come up short. As this book will argue, British youth television's relationship with its audience offers a greater complexity that such models allow.

Amongst the few studies of youth in British television, John Hill (1991) and Bill Osgerby (2004a) both highlight the role of pop music programming in the 1950s and 1960s, whilst Lury (2001) and Moseley (2007) document entertainment and drama programmes of the 1980s and 1990s. Lury positions the youth-programming boom of 1987–1995 as a reaction to changes in the media environment – the arrival of cable and satellite competitors including MTV, combined with Channel 4's public service broadcasting remit to cater for youth – and the rise of the 'Generation X' demographic. During this period, entertainment and music programming targeted at a youth audience developed a distinct aesthetic practice, cultural attitude and viewing sensibility (2001, 17). Lury suggests this viewing sensibility offered an 'uneasy *play* between investment and alienation, between an outsider's distaste and detachment and the insider's investment and knowledge' (2001, 42). Drawing on policy documents and close analysis, Moseley (2007) argues that the small amount of youth drama produced by British television in the early 1980s illustrated cultural and political anxieties, particularly around youth unemployment. She charts how the teenager was discursively constructed as 'a figure in need of information, education and regulation, rather than entertainment' (2007, 185). As Chapter 2 illustrates, this tension between education and entertainment remains part of the discourse surrounding public service broadcasters and youth content. Moseley suggests that *Going Out*'s (ITV, 1981) conjunction of a naturalist agenda and mannered aesthetic has been inherited by contemporary British teen dramas (2007, 195); this prediction is verified in my exploration of British youth drama's embrace of 'social surrealism' in Chapter 3.

Moseley's chapter was published just before *Skins* debuted, and work by Deborah Hunn (2012) and Susan Berridge (2013) has begun to position contemporary British youth television in the academic landscape. Hunn examines *Skins*' assimilation of and antagonism towards the fans of its lesbian romance. Berridge identifies the programme's emphasis of British teenage 'independence, rebellion and nihilism' and its presentation of drug use and casual sex as everyday acts (2013, 786), yet suggests underneath this provocative posture lay conservative ideologies around gender and sexuality. In a recent overview of teen drama, Moseley has suggested that *Skins*' tendency towards tonal unevenness and political irreverence produces an 'unsettling viewing position which typically aids the construction of a believable adolescent world where values and attitudes are not yet fixed' (2015, 43). This unsettled position is teased out in my identification of the ambivalent pleasures of British youth television. Despite these welcome recent developments, there remains a significant gap in academic study that this book will fill. In order to do so, I take Moseley's knitting together of textual, social and industrial analysis as my methodological model. I also take Lury's articulation of the viewing sensibility present in the previous flowering of youth-focused British television, using it as a base on which to develop my own theorising of the structure of feeling and thematic threads of contemporary British youth television.

Tracing the Roots

If British youth television is largely a recent phenomenon, what are its televisual roots? Four areas feed into the development of its voice: teenage drama in children's television, soap opera, music television and reality TV. British youth television is distinct from children's television; however, both exist within the framework of public service broadcasting (Steemers and D'Arma 2012). The BBC and Channel 4 remits both require provision for children – in Channel 4's case 'older children' – and youth audiences. Alongside soap opera, children's television of the 1980s and 1990s offered some of the few representations of teenage life in British schedules. In particular, the serialised, ensemble-led interweaving of issue-based storytelling and comic hijinks that form the foundation of British youth drama's storytelling can be found in the teenage dramas *Grange Hill* (BBC One, 1978–2008), *Byker Grove* (BBC One, 1989–2006) and *Press Gang* (ITV, 1989–1993).

'Teenage drama' (to distinguish it from youth drama) was positioned on the fringes of the children's schedules, in the post-5pm slot on BBC One and post-4.30pm on ITV. This is a transitional space akin to its protagonists' 'in-between' adolescent life-stage. Here they lead into the imported Australian soaps *Neighbours* (Network Ten/Eleven/Seven Network, 1985–) and *Home and Away* (Seven Network, 1988–) that were popular with young audiences (Lury 2001, 15) and the 'youth' slot of 6–7.30pm that followed. These teenage dramas address a younger demographic than British youth television, the older child/younger teen boundary we now term 'tween', with *Wolfblood* (CBBC, 2012–) a contemporary example. *Grange Hill* serves as the urtext of teenage drama, with its early 1980s seasons causing controversy due to their embrace of 'realism' and children's point of view (Jones and Davies 2002). The programme echoed British soap opera in its exploration of public-service-approved social and informational concerns through an intimate and emotional engagement with the personal (2002, 150), a trait central to British youth television. This personalised frame was enabled by *Grange Hill*'s delicate juggling of an address to multiple sub-demographics within in its large 11– 18-year-old comprehensive school ensemble. This multiplicity provides space for a shifting identification for the young viewer whose own identity and point of view is in flux (Ross 2008a, 150–151), which is seen in British youth ensembles from *Skins* to *Misfits* (E4, 2009–2013) to *The Only Way is Essex*.

Press Gang serves as *the* proto-British youth drama, narrowing *Grange Hill* and *Byker Grove*'s large ensembles to older teenagers, with three of its five seasons taking place post-school, where it 'looked like a teen series in need of a new timeslot' (McGown no date). This was signalled by its embrace by Channel 4, where it was repeated it the Sunday evening 'youth' slot whilst still running in the children's ITV schedule. On Channel 4 it sat alongside prestige US import *The Wonder Years* (ABC, 1998–1993), in a slot later home to *My So-Called Life*. Simultaneously positioned as both ITV children's drama and Channel 4 youth drama, *Press Gang* illustrates the tricky status of British teenage drama in the 1990s. The programme followed the staff of school newspaper the *Norbridge Junior Gazette*, a combination of high-flyers and wayward cases on their last chance led by tough 16-year-old editor Lynda Day. Offering teenage characters engaged in aspirational careers whilst still school-bound, its workplace ensemble was dominated by the tempestuous relationship between controlling editor Linda and American troublemaker Spike, which featured complex verbal and emotional jousting. The programme offered capers, mysteries, romances and social issues – darker stories featured drugs, child abuse and firearms – in tightly constructed plots. These intertwined with a strong comic voice whose touches of surrealism pre-echo the social surrealism central to British youth drama. This offbeat comic voice tempered potential slippage into didacticism in the programme's occasional ventures into stark issue-led storytelling. Teenage drama in the children's schedules needed to walk a delicate tightrope, exploring identity and social concerns whilst resisting didacticism, yet smuggling in educational content. As a receptacle for adult culture's protectionist fears and the object of public service remits, children's television must clearly 'mark' its engagement with educational storytelling, with its moral lessons learnt much quicker than in British youth drama.

Outside of children's television, British soap operas *EastEnders*, *Coronation Street* and *Brookside* have consistently offered prime-time space for complex youth representations as part of their larger ensembles. The value of soap's youth representations are identified in Sue Jackson's work on the articulation of young femininities within New Zealand soap (2006) and Chris Barker's study of British teenage audiences' relationship with the genre (1997). *Brookside*'s investment in the lives and language of its youth characters illustrates creator Phil Redmond's ongoing commitment to the documentation of teenage life in British television (Moseley 2007, 187), from *Grange Hill* and *Going Out* to Channel 4's early evening youth soap *Hollyoaks* (1995–). The latter is regrettably the most significant absence of this book, a casualty of the space and time needed to satisfactorily study a soap opera airing each weekday. *Hollyoaks* has long served as a valuable site for Channel 4 to satisfy its public service requirement to offer social and personal educational programming for young audiences, exploring issues from teen pregnancy to mental illness to child abuse. However, soaps also depict the everyday of teenage life, its mundanity, comedy, romance and friendships. The popularity of soaps with youth audiences (Price 2015) has led them to be the focus of experiments with transmedia storytelling. Examples include *EastEnders'* online spin-off *E20* (which also aired on BBC Three, 2010–2011), which was built as a parallel text targeted at youth audiences (Evans 2011, 110–112; Johnson 2012, 151–152), and *Hollyoaks'* ongoing use of social media to engage audiences with high-profile story events. This includes the recent reveal of a long-running whodunnit story on social media platform Snapchat (No author 2015).

With US imports filling out drama and comedy spaces, factual programming largely dominated British television's youth provision until the late 1990s. Channels viewed music programming as a simple way to cater to this demographic (Moseley 2007, 192) and the genre spans the life of British youth television. It stretches from the establishment of the 6pm scheduling slot as a youth space following the dissolution of the Toddlers' Truce in the 1950s (J. Hill 1991) through *Ready Steady Go* (ITV, 1963–1966), *Top of the Pops* (BBC One/Two, 1964–2006), *The Tube* (Channel 4, 1982–1987) and *The Word* (Channel 4, 1990–1995) to Saturday night talent shows such as *The X Factor* (ITV, 2004–). Different channels' attitudes towards their youth audiences are articulated by shifts in aesthetic and audience address, from BBC One's early evening pop institution *Top of the Pops* to Channel 4's raucous late-night entertainment show *The Word*. Music programming has played a defining role in the representation and dissemination of British youth culture: from performers to presenters (Osgerby 2004a, 78–81) to the studio audiences that charted the changing faces, fashions and attitudes of the mass of British youth (Lury 2001, 61–63). Osgerby positions 1960s pop TV shows as reflecting the working-class nature of the British teenage market compared to the dominantly middle-class America teenage figure (2004a, 80), intertwining contrasts of class and nationality that play out through this book.

The 'ordinary' teenage studio audience and the youthful pop stars of these music programmes are blended in the rise of reality-hybrid talent programmes in the 2000s and their shift to the 'ordinary' youth-as-star-performer (A. Hill 2015). The blending of music programming with elements of reality TV (Holmes 2004) in blockbuster talent shows such as *Pop Idol* (ITV, 2001–2003) and *The X Factor* draw strong youth audiences (Price 2015). Outside of Saturday night entertainment blockbusters, reality TV forms the foundation of British youth television, sharing a noisy, boundary-pushing nature that draws media and cultural attention. The low-cost programming of reality TV has supported fledgling youth digital channels as they built identities and audiences. *Big Brother* (Channel 4, 2000–2010/Channel 5, 2011–) overflowed from Channel 4 onto E4, supporting the channel in its early steps. British youth television's audience is the *Big Brother* generation, raised on the game-doc and the celebrity gossip magazines (Holmes 2005) that feed its transmedia narratives. This combination produces a highly media literate audience, hyper-aware of the construction of reality TV (A. Hill 2004), yet searching for transparency and moments of authenticity. This literacy allowed for the development of structured reality charted in Chapter 6, which offered a complex viewing position in its blend of reality and soap opera.

So whilst British youth television is a relatively recent phenomenon, we can trace the roots of its voice in these four areas. On the fiction side, we have the teenage drama within children's schedules – where *Press Gang* served as proto-teen TV – and in soap opera's layered teenage representations, whereas factual has been dominated by the lengthy history of music entertainment and the more recent noisy arrival of reality TV. These roots of British youth television laid down investments and preoccupations that are picked up by the form as it flowers into a wealth of programming in the early decades of the twenty-first century.

STRUCTURE

My mapping of British youth television begins with an industrial narrative, as Chapter 2 establishes the form's framework and situates the channel identities discussed throughout the following chapters. Exploring how the British television industry has developed its address to the 16–34-year-old demographic over the past 15 years, it examines Channel 4's youth strand T4, alongside digital channels ITV2, E4 and BBC Three. The latter two serve as central case studies, with particular focus on channel branding and the role of public service broadcasting, indicating how the industry responded to shifts in competition and viewing practices. Chapters 3 and 4 examine fiction programming, with the former exploring representation, imagery and storytelling in British youth drama. It uses *Misfits* to set out British youth television's negotiated relationship with US teen TV, identifying how national identity was built around space, place and language. Case studies of *My Mad Fat Diary* and *In the Flesh* (BBC Three, 2013–2014) then draw out the role of intimacy, emotion and affect in British youth drama's storytelling. Chapter 4 takes British youth television across the Atlantic, charting the MTV translations of E4's *Skins* and *The Inbetweeners* for the US teen TV market. By analysing the discourse surrounding these attempts to rework British youth television as US teen TV, this chapter highlights the complexities of attempts to define national television identities as absolutes, particularly in a transnational television environment.

The following two chapters look at non-fiction storytelling. Chapter 5 looks at factual programming for youth audiences, focusing on Channel 4 and particularly BBC Three to explore the role of public service broadcasting, the peer address and point of view in documentary content. The intimacy central to Chapter 3's drama programming is also drawn out here in a case study of 'squaddie documentary' series *Our War*. This investigates the role of first-person filming and direct address in the construction of soldier-as-witness in the Afghanistan conflict. Chapter 6 looks to reality TV, examining structured reality's blurring of boundaries between soap opera and reality TV. Case studies of *The Only Way is Essex* and *Made in Chelsea* (E4, 2011–) demonstrate how British youth television assimilated the format of MTV's *Laguna Beach* (2004–2006) and *The Hills* (2006–2010), glocalising the form to suit British audiences and channel identities. The chapter identifies how these programmes' heightened level of construction and performativity address a savvy viewer through a framework of camp and classed identities, drawing out the ambivalent address central to their pleasures. Chapter 7 draws together the overarching themes of the book, briefly considering the role of short-form content and the retention of national identity as television becomes spreadable digital 'content'. Speculating on the future of British youth television, it considers the place of British youth identity in shifting distribution models and a digital landscape dominated by US-based international media companies.

British youth television is made up of a range of genres; like British identity itself, it is not a monolithic form and there are no absolutes; it offers many different types of programming, styles and storytelling. However, by charting the industrial and textual makeup of this eco-system, this book traces thematic concerns and identifies echoes across factual and fiction television. Together these build a picture of British youth television, one of identity, representation, class, industry, scepticism, ambivalence, intimacy and emotion. This book fills a significant gap in the recent academic history of British television; it identifies a group of channels and programmes at the forefront of industrial change; it charts transatlantic relationships and defines national difference; and it gives British youth television its voice.

Notes

1. Audience research conducted by Ofcom in 2014 found that 'younger adults were more likely than older audiences to want variety and a mix of global content, with American programming and comedy in particular being seen as high quality' (Ofcom 2015).
2. Ofcom defines this in its third review of public service broadcasting thusly: 'Parliament defines the broad purposes of PSB as the provision of TV pro-

grammes dealing with a wide range of subjects, of a high standard and catering for as many different audiences as possible. The legislation aims to ensure that content is broadcast which is for the public benefit, rather than for purely commercial purposes. PSB's mission, as captured in the BBC's original Reithian mission: *"to inform, educate and entertain"* remains essentially the same. Crucially, PSB content should be universally available to all citizens' (Ofcom 2015, 1) To this we can add the public purposes of the BBC as set out by the current Royal Charter (set to be renewed at the end of 2016): sustain citizenship and civil society, promote education and learning, stimulate creativity and cultural excellence, represent the UK, its nations, regions and community, bring the UK to the world and the world to the UK and deliver to the public the benefit of emerging communications technologies ('Public purposes' 2015). For the purposes of this book, the mission to inform, educate and entertain is the heart of public service broadcasting.
3. I use this term over 'terrestrial', as all British television became digital following the 2012 switchover.
4. As set out in the 2003 Communications Act, the public service objectives include: the reflection, support and stimulation of the diversity of cultural activity in the UK, including drama, comedy, and feature films; the provision of news and current affairs, facilitating civic understanding and fair and well-informed debate, in and from the UK and from around the world; satisfy a wide range of different sporting and leisure interests; a quantity and range of programming of educational value, dealing with science, religion and other beliefs, social issues, matters of international significance, high quality and original programmes for children and young people; programmes that reflect the lives and concerns of different communities and cultural interests and traditions within the UK; programmes made in the UK, including an appropriate range and proportion of programmes made outside the M25 area ('Communications Act' 2003).

References

Ang, Ien. 1985. *Watching Dallas: Soap Opera and the Melodramatic Imagination*. New York: Methuen.

Ashby, Justine and Andrew Higson. 2000. 'Introduction'. In *British Cinema: Past and Present*, edited by Justine Ashby and Andrew Higson, 1–18. London: Routledge.

Banet-Weiser, Sarah. 2012. *Authentic(TM): The Politics of Ambivalence in a Brand Culture*. New York University Press.

Banks, Miranda J. 2004. 'A Boy for All Planets: Roswell, Smallville, and the Teen Male Melodrama'. In *Teen TV: Genre, Consumption, Identity*, edited by Glyn Davis and Kay Dickinson, 17–28. London: BFI.

Barker, Chris. 1997. 'Television and the Reflexive Project of the Self: Soaps, Teenage Talk and Hybrid Identities'. *British Journal of Sociology* 48(4): 611–628. doi:10.2307/591599.

Bennett, James. 2011. 'Introduction: Television as Digital Media'. In *Television as Digital Media*, edited by James Bennett and Niki Strange, 1–27. Durham, NC: Duke University Press.

Berlant, Lauren. 2008. *The Female Complaint: The Unfinished Business of Sentimentality in American Culture*. Durham, NC: Duke University Press.

Berridge, Susan. 2013. '"Doing it for the Kids"? The Discursive Construction of the Teenager and Teenage Sexuality in *Skins*'. *Journal of British Cinema and Television* 10(4): 785–801.

Bindig, Lori. 2008. *Dawson's Creek: A Critical Understanding*. Lanham, MD: Lexington Books.

Biressi, Anita and Heather Nunn. 2013. *Class and Contemporary British Culture*. Basingstoke: Palgrave Macmillan.

Born, Georgina. 2003. 'Strategy, Positioning and Projection in Digital Television: Channel Four and the Commercialization of Public Service Broadcasting in the UK'. *Media, Culture & Society* 25(6): 774–799.

Brooker, Will. 2001. 'Living on Dawson's Creek Teen Viewers, Cultural Convergence, and Television Overflow'. *International Journal of Cultural Studies* 4(4): 456–472.

Browning, Mark. 2014. 'Learning to Talk to "Generation Y"'. *Broadcast*, 1 July. www.broadcastnow.co.uk/opinion/learning-to-talk-to-generation-y/5073694.article (accessed 19 May 2016).

Buckingham, David. 1993. *Reading Audiences: Young People and the Media*. Manchester University Press.

Buckingham, David, Hannah Davies, Ken Jones and Peter Kelley. 1999. *Children's Television in Britain: History, Discourse and Policy*. London: BFI.

Bulkley, Kate. 2013. 'Tapping into a New Mindset'. *Broadcast*, 18 July. www.broadcastnow.co.uk/opinion/tapping-into-a-new-mindset/5058385.article (accessed 19 May 2016).

Byers, Michele and David Lavery. 2007. *Dear Angela: Remembering My So-Called Life*. Lanham, MD: Lexington Books.

Calvin, Ritch. 2008. *Gilmore Girls and the Politics of Identity: Essays on Family and Feminism in the Television Series*. Jefferson, NC: McFarland.

Caughie, John. 2000. *Television Drama : Realism, Modernism, and British Culture*. Oxford University Press.

Chamorro-Premuzic, Tomas. 2014. 'Are Millennials as Bad as We Think?' *The Guardian*, 24 January. www.theguardian.com/media-network/media-network-blog/2014/jan/24/millennials-generation-gap (accessed 19 May 2016).

Communications Act 2003. www.legislation.gov.uk/ukpga/2003/21/contents (accessed 19 May 2016).

Daniels, Susanne and Cynthia Littleton. 2007. *Season Finale: The Unexpected Rise and Fall of the WB and UPN*. New York: HarperCollins.
Davies, Máire Messenger. 2001. *'Dear BBC': Children, Television Storytelling, and the Public Sphere*. Cambridge University Press.
Davis, Glyn, and Kay Dickinson 2004a. 'Introduction'. In *Teen TV: Genre, Consumption, Identity*, edited by Glyn Davis and Kay Dickinson, 1–16. London: BFI.
———. (eds). 2004b. *Teen TV: Genre, Consumption and Identity*. London: BFI.
Dickinson, Kay. 2004. '"My Generation": Popular Music, Age and Influence in Teen Drama of the 1990s'. In *Teen TV: Genre, Consumption, Identity*, edited by Glyn Davis and Kay Dickinson, 99–111. London: BFI.
Diffrient, David Scott and David Lavery (eds). 2010. *Screwball Television: Critical Perspectives on Gilmore Girls*. Syracuse University Press.
Douglas, Kate and Kelly McWilliam. 2004. '"We Don't Need No Education": Adolescents and the School in Contemporary Australian Teen TV'. In *Teen TV: Genre, Consumption, Identity*, edited by Glyn Davis and Kay Dickinson, 151–165. London: BFI.
Evans, Elizabeth. 2011. 'The Evolving Media Ecosystem: An Interview with Victoria Jaye, BBC'. In *Ephemeral Media: Transitory Screen Culture from Television to YouTube*, edited by Paul Grainge, 105–121. Basingstoke: Palgrave Macmillan.
Feuer, Jane. 1984. 'MTM Style'. In *MTM 'Quality Television'*, edited by Jane Feuer, Paul Kerr, and Tise Vahimagi, 52–84. London: BFI.
Frith, Simon. 1993. 'Youth/Music/Television'. In *Sound and Vision: The Music Video Reader*, edited by Simon Frith, Andrew Goodwin and Lawrence Grossberg, 57–72. Routledge
Gray, Jonathan. 2008. *Television Entertainment*. London: Routledge.
Harter, Susan. 2002. 'Authenticity'. In *Handbook of Positive Psychology*, edited by C.R. Snyder and S.J. Lopez, 382–394. New York: Oxford University Press.
Hill, Annette. 2004. *Reality TV: Audiences and Popular Factual Television*. Abingdon: Routledge.
———. 2015. *Reality TV*. Abingdon: Routledge.
Hill, John. 1986. *Sex, Class and Realism: British Cinema 1956–1963*. London: BFI Publishing.
———. 1991. 'Television and Pop: The Case of the 1950s'. In *Popular Television in Britain: Studies in Cultural History*, edited by John Corner, 90–107. London: BFI.
Holmes, Su. 2004. '"Reality Goes Pop!" Reality TV, Popular Music, and Narratives of Stardom in Pop Idol'. *Television & New Media* 5(2): 147–172.
———. 2005. '"Off-Guard, Unkempt, Unready"?: Deconstructing Contemporary Celebrity in Heat Magazine'. *Continuum* 19(1): 21–38.
Howe, Neil and William Strauss. 2000. *Millennials Rising: The Next Great Generation*. New York: Knopf Doubleday Publishing Group.

Hunn, Deborah F. 2012. '"The Dark Side of Naomily": Skins, Fan Texts and Contested Genres'. *Continuum* 26(1): 89–100.
Jackson, Sue. 2006. '"Street Girl"'. *Feminist Media Studies* 6(4): 469–486.
Jarvey, Natalie. 2015. 'The Future of Apple TV is Far Away (and More Takeaways from Tim Cook's Event)'. *Hollywood Reporter*, 9 September. www.hollywoodreporter.com/news/future-apple-tv-is-far-821546 (accessed 19 May 2016).
Johnson, Catherine. 2012. *Branding Television*. Abingdon: Routledge.
Jones, Ken and Hannah Davies. 2002. 'Keeping it Real: Grange Hill and the Representation of "the Child's World" in Children's Television Drama'. In *Small Screens: Television for Children*, edited by David Buckingham, 141–158. Leicester University Press.
Kohnen, Melanie. 2015. 'Cultural Diversity as Brand Management in Cable Television'. *Media Industries* 2(2): 88–103.
Lay, Samantha. 2002. *British Social Realism – From Documentary to Brit Grit*. London: Wallflower.
Levine, Elana and Lisa Parks (eds). 2007. *Undead TV : Essays on Buffy the Vampire Slayer*. Durham, NC: Duke University Press.
Livingstone, Sonia M. 2002. *Young People and New Media: Childhood and the Changing Media Environment*. London: Sage.
Lotz, Amanda D. 2014. *The Television Will Be Revolutionized*, 2nd edn. New York: NYU Press.
Lury, Karen. 2001. *British Youth Television: Cynicism and Enchantment*. Oxford University Press.
Martin, Jeff. 2008. 'TV Teen Club: Teen TV as Safe Harbour'. In *Teen Television : Essays on Programming and Fandom*, edited by Sharon Marie Ross and Louisa Ellen Stein, 27–42. Jefferson, NC: McFarland.
McCabe, Janet and Kim Akass. 2007. 'Introduction: Debating Quality'. In *Quality TV: Contemporary American Television and Beyond*, edited by Janet McCabe and Louisa Ellen Stein, 1–12. London: I.B. Tauris.
McGown, Alistair. No date. 'Press Gang (1989-93)'. *Screenonline*. www.screenonline.org.uk/tv/id/571944 (accessed 22 May 2016).
———. 2007. 'Teenagers and Television Drama in Britain 1968–1982'. In *Re-Viewing Television History: Critical Issues in Television Historiography*, edited by Helen Wheatley, 184–197. London: I.B. Tauris.
———. 2015. 'Teen Drama'. In *The Television Genre Book*, 3rd edn, edited by Glen Creeber, 38–43. London: Palgrave Macmillan.
Newman, Michael Z. and Elana Levine. 2011. *Legitimating Television: Media Convergence and Cultural Status*. London: Routledge.
No author. 2014. 'Generation Y Takeover: The Issues That Matter to Us and Why'. *The Guardian*, 14 March. www.theguardian.com/lifeandstyle/2014/mar/14/generation-y-takeover-guardian-digital-journalists (accessed 19 May 2016).

———. 2015. 'Best Social Media and Digital Marketing Campaign: Hollyoaks Snapchat: Who Killed Fraser?' *Broadcast*, 24 June. www.broadcastnow.co.uk/home/broadcast-awards/broadcast-digital-awards/best-social-media-and-digital-marketing-campaign-hollyoaks-snapchat-who-killed-fraser/5089672.article (accessed 19 May 2016).

Ofcom. 2015. 'Public Service Broadcasting in the Internet Age'. Ofcom. http://stakeholders.ofcom.org.uk/consultations/psb-review-3 (accessed 19 May 2016).

Olsen, Glyn. 2004. 'Total Request Live and the Creation of Virtual Community'. In *Teen TV: Genre, Consumption, Identity*, edited by Glyn Davis and Kay Dickinson, 112–124. London: BFI.

Osborne, Hilary. 2015. 'Generation Rent: The Housing Ladder Starts to Collapse for the under-40s'. *The Guardian*, 22 July. www.theguardian.com/money/2015/jul/22/pwc-report-generation-rent-to-grow-over-next-decade (accessed 19 May 2016).

Osgerby, Bill. 2004a. '"So Who's Got Time for Adults!": Femininity, Consumption and the Development of Teen TV – from Gidget to Buffy'. In *Teen TV: Genre, Consumption, Identity*, edited by Davis Glyn and Kay Dickinson, 71–86. London: BFI.

———. 2004b. *Youth Media*. Abingdon: Routledge.

Oswell, David. 2002. *Television, Childhood, and the Home: A History of the Making of the Child Television Audience in Britain*. Oxford: Clarendon Press.

Pardee, Thomas. 2010. 'Want to Reach the Millennial Market? Start with Snooki'. *Advertising Age*, 30 November. http://adage.com/article/special-report-me-conference-2010/mtv-reach-millennial-market-snooki/147370 (accessed 19 May 2016).

Price, Stephen. 2015. 'Ratings Analysis: Youth Audiences 16–34s'. *Broadcast*, 2 July. www.broadcastnow.co.uk/features/ratings-analysis-youth-audiences-16-34s/5089986.article (accessed 19 May 2016).

'Public Purposes'. 2015. *BBC*. www.bbc.co.uk/aboutthebbc/insidethebbc/whoweare/publicpurposes/. (accessed 19 May 2016).

Rolinson, David and Faye Woods. 2013. 'Is This England '86 and '88? Memory, Haunting and Return through Television Seriality'. In *Shane Meadows: Critical Essays*, edited by Martin Fradley, Sarah Godfrey and Melanie Williams, 186–202. Edinburgh University Press.

Ross, Sharon Marie. 2008a. *Beyond the Box: Television and the Internet*. Oxford: Blackwell.

———. 2008b. 'Defining Teen Culture: The N Network'. In *Teen Television: Essays on Programming and Fandom*, edited by Sharon Marie Ross and Louisa Ellen Stein, 61–77. Jefferson, NC: McFarland.

Ross, Sharon Marie and Louisa Ellen Stein. 2008a. 'Introduction: Watching Teen TV'. In *Teen Television: Essays on Programming and Fandom*, 3–26. Lanham, MD: MacFarland.

——. (eds). 2008b. *Teen Television: Essays on Programming and Fandom*. Jefferson, NC: McFarland.

Sanghani, Radhika. 2014. 'Happiness Survey: Millennials are the Most Joyous Generation – Telegraph'. *The Telegraph*, 5 August. www.telegraph.co.uk/women/womens-life/11012814/Happiness-survey-millennials-are-the-most-joyous-generation.html (accessed 19 May 2016).

Steemers, Jeanette and Alessandro D'Arma. 2012. 'Evaluating and Regulating the Role of Public Broadcasters in the Children's Media Ecology: The Case of Home-Grown Television Content'. *International Journal of Media & Cultural Politics* 8(1): 67–85.

Stein, Louisa Ellen. 2015. *Millennial Fandom: Television Audiences in the Transmedia Age*. Iowa City: University of Iowa Press.

Stelter, Brian. 2010. 'MTV is Looking Beyond "Jersey Shore" to Build a Wider Audience'. *New York Times*, 25 October, B1.

Turnbull, Sue. 2008. '"They Stole Me": The O.C., Masculinity, and the Strategies of Teen TV'. In *Teen Television : Essays on Programming and Fandom*, edited by Sharon Marie Ross and Louisa Ellen Stein, 170–184. Jefferson, NC: McFarland.

Wilcox, Rhonda. 2005. *Why Buffy Matters: The Art of Buffy the Vampire Slayer*. London: I.B. Tauris.

Wilcox, Rhonda and David Lavery (eds). 2002. *Fighting the Forces: What's at Stake in Buffy the Vampire Slayer*. Lanham, MD: Rowman & Littlefield.

Williams, Raymond. 1961. *The Long Revolution*. London: Chatto & Windus.

——. 1977. *Marxism and Literature*. Oxford University Press.

CHAPTER 2

Branding Youth Space: British Youth Strands and Channels

This chapter explores the structuring framework of British youth television, the strands and digital channels that target the 16–34-year-old demographic. These are the spaces that shape the voice of British youth television. Using industrial analysis, I track the last 15 years of provision, which is a period that saw significant shifts in the British television landscape. Terrestrial broadcasters expanded their reach through niche digital channels and on-demand, and online viewing emerged to change the televisual landscape. With this demographic often seen as early adopters of media and technological change, industrial discourses positioned television itself as under threat in the competition for the attention of youth audiences. Yet, as Simon Frith's discussion of 1980s youth television has shown, concerns over television's place in the youth audience's diverse media attentions is not new. Similar discourses positioned computer games, home video rentals and satellite television's music channels as competitors to terrestrial television in the 1980s and beyond (Frith 1993, 69). Through a series of case studies, this chapter charts how the British television industry has chased and addressed this demographic. It touches on the role of channel branding in digital television, British youth television's assimilation of US teen TV, the place of public service broadcasting in a shifting television environment, and the British television industry's multi-platform responses to shifts in linear and on-demand viewing.

The phased switchover to digital television in Britain took place across the early 2000s and was completed in 2012, facilitated by the popularity of the free-to-air digital platform Freeview, which was launched in 2002

(Johnson 2012, 78). All four of the British terrestrial broadcasters (the BBC, ITV, Channel 4 and Channel 5) expanded their reach through a suite of digital channels accompanied by an ebb and flow of online content. Three of these – BBC Three, ITV2 and E4 – offered a youth-skewing alternative to their parent channel brands. Catherine Johnson argues that 'a strong brand militates against some of the financial risks of moving into such new areas by drawing on the values and consumer relations already established by the core brand' (2012, 95). Each of these digital youth channels was built on the back of audience-drawing repeats of, and companion programming for, its parent channel's hit programmes. These formed the scaffold on which to draw audiences and build original programming. For BBC Three, this was *EastEnders* (BBC One, 1985–) and *Doctor Who* (BBC One, 1963–1989/2005–), for ITV2, this was *Pop Idol* (ITV, 2001–2003), *The X Factor* (ITV, 2004–) and *I'm a Celebrity Get Me Out of Here* (ITV, 2002–), and for E4, this was *Big Brother* (Channel 4, 2000–2010/Channel 5, 2011–).

This chapter's four case studies illustrate different facets of the industrial shifts that have impacted British youth television across the past 20 years. T4 serves as an example of a youth-branded strand on terrestrial television, cohering a mixed schedule across a portion of Channel 4's weekend programming and assimilating US content through interstitial elements and brand identity. A brief glance at ITV2 looks at the commercial sector's address to youth audience,[1] but my primary focus is on British television's two primary public service broadcasters. As Catherine Johnson points out, channels themselves, their identity and schedules have:

> an important function within UK public service broadcasting as a central site through which public service provision is evaluated by both viewers and regulators. The communicative ethos of the terrestrial channels, therefore, has to conform to the values of public service broadcasting, which extends beyond individual programmes to encompass a broader broadcasting ethos. (2012, 173)

E4 offers an example of the progressive refinement of a digital youth channel identity through imported and British programming, and illustrates the role of branding and interstitial content in channel identity. The analysis of the life of BBC Three – which fills a surprising gap in existing scholarship – and its future move to online-only status touches on the BBC's struggle to find its identity in a commercially dominated market. In the process it highlights the tensions between public service remits and a commercially valuable youth audience.

As Chapter 1 noted, the 16–34-year-old audience is hugely valuable to commercial television, yet it is also a demographic that public service broadcasters needed to capture. These are the hard-to-reach, high leisure-spending consumers desired by advertisers and increasingly deserting linear television (Plunkett 2014b; Steel and Marsh 2015). In turn, the remits of public service broadcasting require them to address this audience, where they are particularly valuable in the delivery of areas such as citizenship and education that are largely absent from the commercial market's offerings. This demographic are also the future licence fee-payers and voters who will determine the role of the BBC – and in part Channel 4 – in the televisual landscape. This is a televisual landscape in a complicated relationship with US content, with youth strands and digital channels illustrating British television's attempt to articulate national specificity whilst also negotiating the role of popular US imports.

The period covered here is one of change, one 'characterized by a much greater emphasis on multi-platform engagement with audiences', which Gillian Doyle argues is 'evident in all stages of the television industry – from content production to product assembly to distribution' (2010, 432–433). Youth audiences are viewed as the drivers of shifts in viewing behaviour, together with demands for participation and interaction. BARB's (British Audience Research Board) report on British viewing habits during 2014 showed that 'metropolitan' 16–24-year-old households had the highest rate of broadband without a television set – 12.4 per cent (BARB 2015, 36). Research by regulatory body Ofcom indicated that in 2014, 16–24 year olds' viewing of 'live' linear television had fallen to 50 per cent, with the rest of their television delivered through what the industry terms 'over the top' services (streaming and download) (Ofcom 2015, 19). Television ratings for the first half of 2015 identified a year-on-year drop of 10 per cent amongst 16–34 year olds in linear TV viewing, leading industry magazine *Broadcast* to argue that 'the multi-screen revolution is here' with a fierce 'battle for the soul of young viewers' at its heart (Price 2015). As BARB's 2015 Viewing Report noted: 'It has always been acknowledged that every generation falls out of love with TV in its late teens and early 20s, yet finds its way back as it settles down' (BARB 2015, 35), yet questioned what happens if this first love never blossomed and this journey home never occurs. The story of the last 15 years is British youth television's quest to counter this lovelessness.

Television channels remain a largely under-studied area outside of the wealth of discussions of HBO (Johnson 2007; Leverette et al. 2007) and historical industrial analysis of the BBC and Channel 4 (Born 2003; Brown 2007; Hobson 2008). Julie Light (2004), Cathy Johnson (2012) and Georgina Born (2003, 2011) offer the most significant scholarship on British television channels and this is accompanied by a growing parcel of scholarship on channel branding, idents and associated ephemeral media (Fanthome 2007; Johnson 2012; Grainge 2011a; Grainge and Johnson 2015). A small number of studies have explored US channels targeting teen and youth audiences (Ross 2008; Wee 2008; Marx 2016; Stein 2015), with this analysis joining the range of work on MTV (which is largely limited to its first decade) (Kaplan 1987; Goodwin 1993). British youth channels operate in an aligned but distinctly different television landscape from these latter set of channels, one inevitably shaded by Britain's blend of commercial television and public service broadcasting. Only the five main – formerly terrestrial – UK channels are regulated as public service channels (this, combined with E4's entertainment focus, explains the limiting of youth-focused documentary to Channel 4); however, BBC Three and E4 offer key examples of their respective institution's reach to 16–34 year olds.[2] This in part explains my choice to exclude ITV2 as a significant case study in this chapter – although I do briefly touch on the channel – as well as the absence of non-terrestrial channels MTV UK and Trouble (delivered via cable and satellite rather than free-to-air digital). This is due to the lack of original British content on the latter two channels and my interest in how youth channels serve as flashpoints for British television's negotiation of its public service commitments and commercial desires. In part, then, this chapter offers a contribution to the body of work that considers European public service broadcasting's engagement with youth audiences and its place in the age of social media and on-demand viewing (Doyle 2010; Strange 2011; Dijck and Poell 2015; Vanhaeght and Donders 2015).

Catherine Johnson's *Branding Television* offers television scholarship's most complete industrial analysis of the period covered by this book, charting the development of branding in British and US television. As part of this analysis, Johnson identifies how logos, slogans and trailers work to construct a channel's brand identity (2012, 1) and seek to bind the viewer with the channel. A strong channel identity and audience relationship is particularly important in the digital era's 'attention economy' (Christophers 2008, 248) with its crowded market of platforms, where British youth television fights for the attentions of the 16–34-year-old demographic. Johnson's work forms the conceptual framework for this chapter, together with Karen Lury's study of youth-focused British entertainment programming of the 1980s and early 1990s, in which she identifies an oscillation between cynicism and enchantment (2001, 42). I build on Lury's work to articulate the tone and ideologies of British youth television's channel identities. This chapter looks to the recent past as well as the future, offering a brief history of British television's niche targeting of youth audiences before moving on to short case studies of T4 and ITV2, then continuing on to more substantial case studies of E4 and BBC Three.

A Brief History of Television's Youth Spaces

Looking at some of the approaches to scheduling youth programming in the past can help us understand contemporary television in its state of seemingly perpetual change. As the liminal space between children's and adult programming, the early evening slot has long offered a key space for youth programming. The development of the 6pm slot as a youth slot can be traced back to the 1950s and the end of the 'Toddler's Truce'. This policy required BBC and ITV to suspend broadcasting between 6 and 7pm, allowing children's bedtime and homework to remain undistracted (J. Hill 1991, 91). This freeing of the 6–7pm slot opened the door for the development of new television formats which could be made quickly and cheaply, such as pop music programming for young audiences (J. Hill 1991). These included the BBC's *Six-Five Special* – whose arrival on Saturday 16 February 1957 formally ended the Toddlers' Truce – *Oh Boy!* (ABC, 1958), *Drumline* (BBC, 1959), *Juke Box Jury* (BBC, 1959–57) and *Thank Your Lucky Stars* (ITV, 1961–1966). The scheduling of the generation-defining *Ready Steady Go!* (Associated Rediffusion, 1963–1966) on a Friday evening rather than at Saturday tea-time began a Friday evening music programming tradition that was later taken up by Channel 4's *The Tube* (1982–1987).

The 6pm slot saw further development in the 1980s as a space for BBC Two youth dramas such as *Maggie* (1981–1982) and *Grange Hill* spin-off *Tucker's Luck* (1983–1985). Their scheduling outside of the children's schedule and daytime 'educational' slots positioned these dramas as liminal, with their teenage protagonists facing life choices post-compulsory education (Moseley 2007, 194). The pop programming on BBC One and ITV had needed to address a wider, family audience; however the scheduling of these dramas on the minority channel BBC Two reflected their targeting of a distinctive youth demographic.

Later in the 1980s, the 6pm slot became home to *DEF II*, which gathered a range of programmes aimed at a 16–34-year-old demographic under a branded flow. This was cohered by idents rather than presenters providing links. *DEF II*'s programming often used a fast-paced and deconstructive aesthetic, with presenters displaying the anarchic and irreverent attitude seen in the 'zoo' production style (Lury 2001, 34). This style echoed that of non-terrestrial music channel MTV Europe, which, along with a range of other music video channels, was beginning to offer competition for television's youth market in the late 1980s. Although its UK market penetration was low during this period, MTV's style and form had significant industrial and cultural impact, and was felt to be 'the source of a new kind of television' (Lury 2001, 39). *DEF II*'s programming included current affairs series *Reportage* (1998–1994), alternative travel hybrid *Rough Guide to…* (1989–1999), music show *Dance Energy* (1990–1992) and tongue-in-cheek French pop culture import *Rapido* (1988–1992). These sat alongside North American imports including US fly-on-the-wall documentary *Yearbook* (1991), sitcom *The Fresh Prince of Bel Air* (1990–1996) and Canadian teen drama *Degrassi Junior High* (1987–1989). These imports established US teen TV as a foundation of British youth television schedules (Woods 2013, 17). *DEF II* also had a late-night slot, with late Friday night delineated as a defined 'youth' space on BBC Two and Channel 4, particularly after the arrival of Channel 4's anarchic, controversial entertainment magazine *The Word* (1990–1995). Simon Frith argues that the move from the 'classic youth slot' of Friday early evening to late night with *The Word* formed part of television's reorientation of its youth address from 12–24 'pop viewers' to the more affluent, advertiser-desiring 'young adult 18–34' demographic (1993, 73). British youth television blends these two viewing groups, paying close attention to the 16–24-year-old viewer.

The 6pm slot remained a youth slot on both BBC Two and Channel 4 after the dissolution of *DEF II*. Channel 4 scheduled prime-time US imports such as *Blossom* (1991–1995) and repeats of *Happy Days* (1974–1984) in weekday 6–7pm slots and since its 1995 debut, British youth soap *Hollyoaks* has progressively expanded to be stripped across the week at 6.30pm. BBC Two scheduled Australian soap *Heartbreak High* (Network 10/ABC, 1994–1999) and US teen telefantasy *Buffy the Vampire Slayer* (WN/UPN, 1997–2003) in the 6–7.30pm slot. This scheduling necessitated controversial edits to the latter programme in order to make the prime-time US supernatural drama 'appropriate' for the early-evening slot (as a result it was also given a late night unedited repeat) (Hill and Calcutt 2007). These *Buffy* episodes had previously aired uncut in prime-time on satellite channel *Sky One*, whose schedule was then dominated by US imports and leant towards the 16–34-year-old demographic (Born 2003, 780). *Buffy*'s BBC Two struggles illustrated the problems in assimilating prime-time US teen TV into pre-watershed British terrestrial youth slots. The development of digital youth stations offered a dedicated prime-time space for US teen TV to move into uncensored.

TERRESTRIAL YOUTH STRANDS: T4

Channel 4's youth strand T4 offers an example of a youth supertext – consisting 'of the particular program and all the introductory and interstitial materials ... considered in its specific position in the schedule' (Browne 1984, 588) – embedded within a larger broadcasting schedule. Running from 1998 to 2012, the weekend strand cohered a string of programming intertwined with idents and presenter interaction. T4's early success contributed to Channel 4's youth programming address in the early 2000s. The strand also acted as a precursor to digital channel E4 which targeted the same 16–34-year-old demographic. T4 followed *DEF II*'s construction of a youth supertext through a branded frame and tonal address, blending British and US programming within the larger schedule of a public service broadcaster. However, T4 offered less explicitly 'public service' content than its BBC Two predecessor – no documentary or current affairs – with a mixture of entertainment, reality, sitcom and drama that presaged E4's own blend. At its peak, T4 covered the majority of Channel 4's weekend daytime schedule – 9–2pm Saturday and 9–5pm Sunday. Here it existed both as an overarching structure and in the spaces 'inbetween' its programmes, branded in listings magazines and through logos, idents and studio *mise-en-scène*. Presenter-led segments drew together both British originals and imported US teen TV into a branded 'flow' (Williams 1974) of television, constructing a separate youth supertext within Channel 4's schedule. Industry press described T4 as *Heat* magazine with attitude, 'looking at things with a raised eyebrow', a sceptical stance appealing to 'spunky teenagers' and hungover students (No author 2003a).[3] At its peak, T4 commanded an average 25 per cent share of the 16–34 year-old audience (Hughes 2003) and its practices and scheduling helped establish the attitudes and ideology of British youth television. It signalled a transitional moment in Channel 4's history as television shifted from a broadcast to digital niche mode.

Created by former children's TV presenter Andi Peters, then head of Channel 4's youth programming, T4 was built around the Sunday morning omnibus of UK youth soap *Hollyoaks*. By 2003 it had grown to make Channel 4 the second most-watched terrestrial channel in its slot (No author 2003a). *Hollyoaks* was later joined by British youth programming such as dramedy *As If* (2001–2004) and music programme *Popworld* (2001–2007). The latter served as T4's totemic text, with the sarcastic, mocking interview style of its presenters indicative of the address T4 cultivated. T4 positioned US imports such as *Dawson's Creek* (WB, 1998–2003), *One Tree Hill* (WB/CW, 2002–2012), *The O.C.* (Fox, 2003–2007) and *Smallville* (WB/CW, 2001–2011) at key points in its schedule, echoing Channel 4's primetime showcasing of 'quality' US programming in the 1990s (McCabe 2005; Rixon 2006). The strand's blend of the cutting, distanced pose of *Popworld* and the melodrama-led US teen TV established a tone that blended arch distance and emotional investment within a single brand identity.

Browne argues that scheduling determines a programme's form and frames how it is read by audiences, as well as reflecting 'the work-structured order of the real social world' (1984, 588). T4's weekend morning and lunchtime schedule slot saw the strand regularly labelled as 'hangover TV', 'deliberately designed to appeal to those who have been out wilfully killing brain cells' (O'Neill 2000; McLean 2008). The strand's knowing edge framed its soaps, reality TV and US teen TV as 'guilty pleasures', with any excesses, tensions or perceived artistic failings subsumed to the ironically informed consumption encouraged by T4's presenter address. This framing absolved the viewer of any guilt from watching low-status, delegitimated, teen-led programming.

T4's play between a distanced and engaged persona (Woods 2013, 23) was informed by a shaggy and shambolic 'zoo' aesthetic. This was familiar from Saturday morning children's TV on BBC One and ITV, as well as the 'yoof' programming developed by Janet Street Porter at Channel 4's *Network 7* (1987–1988) and BBC Two's *DEF II* programming strand.[4] A 2000 article in *The Guardian* noted that T4's presenters were allowed a 'great deal of freedom to knock the more ludicrous storylines and characters' (O'Neill 2000) of its programming, which was illustrated in then-presenter June Sarpong's frequently expressed distaste for *Dawson's Creek*'s popular heroine Joey Potter. This was later extended both to Sarpong and Steve

Jones' mocking critiques of the complex family dynamics and melodrama-infused storytelling of *The O.C.* in the segments framing the programme, and the paratextual 'skits' I discuss elsewhere (Woods 2013). This framing saw T4 seek to place itself 'above' its programmes, particularly imported US teen TV, by constructing the presenter and, by extension, the audience as reflexive and savvy (Woods 2013, 24). Taking care to not be mistaken for an 'involved' viewer of texts – one traditionally coded as feminine – and avoiding the culturally subordinate position linked to the role (Ross 2008, 8). In this way, the strand encouraged a detached viewing position that helped to assimilate US teen TV into T4's British youth flow (Woods 2013), illustrating Paul Rixon's assertion that 'some form of interaction is occurring between the cultural import and the pre-existing culture' (2006, 23). The irreverent flow of T4, with its permanently arched eyebrow, sarcastic music programmes and British soap opera, *could* be an uneasy fit with the aspirational lifestyles and melodramatic narratives that characterised the US teen TV produced by WB and Fox in the late 1990s and 2000s.[5] But T4's mockery reduced US teen TV's elevated status as glossy import, smoothing its assimilation into the low-budget British T4 flow (Woods 2013, 24).

By containing the presenters' mockery and gentle critique to the linking segments around the programmes, T4 enabled the US imports to retain their escapist pleasures (Woods 2013, 16). Thus, it offered a dual-layered position of pleasure and ironic detachment, from which the shows were celebrated, yet gently mocked (ibid.). The playful attitude its presenters displayed towards this imported programming signalled T4 as transparent and thus 'authentic' (Woods 2013, 21). This framing and audience address would go on to play a central role in E4's channel identity, which itself would be built upon a foundation of imported US programming, yet retain a strong British youth voice. E4 drew on T4's brand identity and mode of address to attract the 16–34-year-old demographic, with T4 playing a key role anchoring the early years of E4 in a daily branded 4–8pm slot. However, the rise of digital television ultimately led to the cancellation of T4 as the digital youth channel syphoned the audiences and identity of the strand (Rowley 2012).

COMMERCIAL DIGITAL YOUTH CHANNEL: ITV2

ITV's youth provision offers a commercial contrast with that of the BBC and Channel 4 because its public service broadcasting licence contains no youth programming requirement.[6] Thus, the 'premium youth profile'

(Price 2011) of ITV2 serves purely to attract advertising revenue targeting the coveted demographic. This resulted in the development of a populist entertainment- and celebrity-driven channel, one described as 'ITV1's younger, more annoying, funnier sister, who may give you some of her own clothes and make-up, but will also nick yours' (ibid). Where BBC Three and E4's iconographic British youth programmes are comedies and dramas, ITV2's are entertainment programmes – structured reality programme *The Only Way is Essex* (ITV2/ITVBe 2010–) and comedy panel show *Celebrity Juice* (2008–). This bawdy, pop culture panel show presented by comic character Keith Lemon (the alter ego of Leigh Francis) was originally pitched as '*Have I Got News for You* meets *Heat* magazine' (McMahon 2008, 2) and has grown to become the channel's highest rating programme (Kanter 2012). The brash fake-tanned persona of Lemon has strong connections with the pleasure in artificiality and camp displayed by *The Only Way is Essex*, which Chapter 6 explores in detail. *Celebrity Juice*'s coarse, brightly toned, celebrity-driven, topical gossip personifies ITV2; a glittery, gossipy, indulgent entertainment-driven commercial youth channel with a strong degree of self-awareness.

E4 was built from US imports and *Big Brother* and BBC Three relied on spin-offs and repeats of BBC One hits to drive audiences to its original programming. In a similar manner, *Pop Idol*, *The X Factor* and *I'm a Celebrity* built and remain the foundations of ITV2, informing its channel identity. Launched in December 1998 as part of the ill-fated digital service On Digital (Born 2003, 774), ITV2 has long lacked the commissioning budgets for original programmes of its youth channel competitors (No author 2003b). In turn, requirements to repeat its parent channel's family audience-driven programming has at times diluted its youth channel brand (Price 2011). Yet it has drawn relatively strong audiences with its mixture of companion programming and celebrity-driven reality programming. In contrast to BBC Three and E4's support of their public service remits through their development of 'new voices', ITV2 has been built around what then-head of channel Zai Bennett (previous to his tenure at BBC Three) termed 'top talent' (McMahon 2009). This is displayed by the celebrity docusoaps of ex-glamour model and one-woman-brand Katie Price, from *Jordan and Peter* (2005) to *What Katie Did Next* (2009–2011). These programmes offered a mixture of the glamour of Price's celebrity life and the everyday of her family and relationship struggles. Price's docusoaps helped coalesce the channel's identity in the late 2000s, but a changing of the reality TV guard in 2010 saw *The Only Way is Essex* ascend to fill her shoes after she left ITV2 for a lucrative deal with satellite channel Sky Living. *The Only Way is Essex* drew on the hybridising of soap opera and reality TV in MTV's *The Hills* (2006–2010), glocalising the form for a British youth audience. The programme treated its non-celebrity cast's everyday with the aesthetics of a soap opera and was structured through a camp, knowing address to the savvy reality TV viewer that was the core of ITV2's audience.

The Only Way is Essex slid easily into ITV2's 'young and fun' (McMahon 2009) brand identity of girly glamour. This brand was articulated in a 2008 ident that positioned the channel as consumerist, feminine entertainment, displaying an abstract animation of the flowing liquid from a spilt nail varnish bottle intermingling with a cascade of crystals, shoes and sunglasses. A 2010 marketing push built around the phrase 'You know you want to' foregrounded *The Only Way is Essex*, successful teen TV supernatural import *The Vampire Diaries* (CW, 2009–) and *Celebrity Juice*. The teasing phrase framed the channel as a guilty pleasure, as indulgent entertainment, a sexy secret, befitting its low cultural capital. This identity was emphasised by the gossipy conspiratorial tone of its female continuity announcers as they read viewer tweets and Facebook comments during the programme bumpers of *The Only Way is Essex* advert breaks.

ITV2 is currently undergoing a negotiation of its channel identity following the launch of new channel ITVBe in October 2014. This targets an audience of 'intelligent young mums' and *The Only Way is Essex* has been moved to the channel, taking 14 per cent of ITV2's audience with it (Campelli 2015). This has led ITV2 to undergo a reorientation towards a young male audience, driven by sitcom import *Two and a Half Men* (CBS, 2003–2015) and the success of its *The Inbetweeners*-in-Ancient-Rome sitcom *Plebs* (2013–). The channel has also attempted boost its young male audiences by building sketch shows around social media comedians such as Dapper Laughs. The latter's misogyny-filled, 'banter'-driven comedy made him a highly shareable commodity in the boundaryless, unregulated spaces and niche audiences of social media. Yet what ITV2 executives pitched as a 'risque brand of humour' (Ellis-Petersen 2014) saw significant cultural pushback when it was framed as a 'dating advice' programme, particularly within an ITV2 that had long-courted female audiences (Plunkett 2014a). ITV2 provides an example of how a purely commercially driven digital youth channel operates in the UK market. Linked to the populist address of its parent channel, it draws audiences with a celebrity- and entertainment-led schedule, using the resulting low cultural capital to construct itself as a gossipy guilty pleasure, a gendered identity it must now renegotiate.

Public/Private Digital Youth Channel: E4

E4 built on T4's irreverent youth brand and Channel 4's existing connection with youth audiences to construct a 'mischievous and cheeky' (Brittain 2008) channel identity. Launched in 2001 alongside FilmFour, E4 began its life as a hybrid pay channel on satellite and cable. Positioned as a fun, irreverent risk-taker, the entertainment channel is described as 'mischievous' and 'naughty', a place where it was 'Friday night every night' (Brown 2007, 240). As 'a place where you leave your responsibilities at the door' (Parker 2009), this is a channel brand imbued with youthful irreverence. This identity was established from E4's launch night when Sasha Baron Cohen's comic character Ali G, the disruptive 'youth' interviewer, introduced the channel to viewers: 'As we all know, news, documentaries and nature programmes ruin normal telly', he reassured audiences that E4 was 'gonna have none of that crap on' (Khalsa 2011). From the outset, its channel brand offered an oppositional identity, one built around entertainment, with a core audience of 16–34 year olds. However, an E4 executive was careful to identify the channel as speaking to 'people who have the Channel 4 values and attitudes, the young in spirit' (Brown 2000), here illustrating Simon Frith's observation that '"youth" has become a viewing sensibility, a category constructed by TV itself' (Frith 1993, 64); E4 sold youth.

So, what are Channel 4's 'values and attitudes', the 'core values' that E4 (and FilmFour) would exploit to strengthen and extend the Channel 4 brand (Born 2003, 781)? As Susan Berridge notes, a requirement to cater to special interests and minority groups, which included youth, was built into Channel 4's public service remit from its outset in 1982 (2013, 789). As a publicly owned broadcaster funded by advertising through a link with ITV that lasted its first 10 years, Channel 4's initial remit was to experiment and innovate, addressing tastes and interests not catered to by ITV (Ellis 2000, 151–154). The Broadcasting Act of 1990 cut the ties with ITV and made Channel 4 responsible for its own advertising, whilst retaining its remit for innovation, originality and diversity. This shift led the broadcaster to target the commercially valuable demographics of 16–34 year olds and ABC1s. As Catherine Johnson suggests, this required a brand identity that was 'malleable enough to cover the diversity of its programming, and the different identities of its diverse audience' (2012, 91). Born identifies a tension in Channel 4's balancing of a remit for diversity and innovation with a pursuit of a commercially valuable audience, viewing E4 as exacerbating the tensions between 'the universality principle at the heart of PSB' with its need to attract a 'big and diverse audience', and a targeting of a youth demographic (2003, 782). This focus was enshrined by 2010's Digital Economy Act, which included a requirement for Channel 4 to provide 'relevant media content that appeals to the tastes and interests of older children and young adults' (Digital Economy Act 2010). This address to a youth audience is spread across E4 and Channel 4, with the latter taking the documentary and factual content that could impair E4's commercially valuable entertainment brand. This programming bolsters Channel 4's public service output, leaving education and citizenship concerns to creep into E4 by stealth. Channel 4's Annual Review identified *Youngers* (2013–2014) and *My Mad Fat Diary* (2013–2015) as notable Trojan horses (Channel 4 2014, 62) and I pick up the latter's engagement with mental health issues in Chapter 3.

Brand Extension and US Imports

The BBC and ITV's own digital youth channels were still in nascent or unformed states as E4 launched. This meant that satellite broadcaster BSkyB's Sky One served as its closest competitor for the 16–34-year-old market in multi-channel homes, as it offered a similarly entertainment-led, US import-dominated schedule (Brown 2000; Born 2003, 782). Yet Channel 4 was at pains to deny this rivalry, distinguishing E4 as an 'intelligent and youthful' (Brown 2000) channel aimed at its own core audience. Johnson describes E4 as 'a classic example of brand extension, taking the core brand values of Channel 4, but developing them to provide a linked, but different, service' (2012, 92). E4 served as a protectionist venture from Channel 4, expanding its reach and potential income in the new multi-channel age as well as providing generational renewal. The channel was an attempt to ensure Channel 4's future, using 'innovative entertainment' to draw the young audiences that its research had found felt little connection with public service broadcasting (Born 2003, 782). These were also central concerns of and motivations for BBC Three – as I discuss below.

E4's launch sought to position it as a youth-focused entertainment channel, yet its early role was as a pay-TV home for the US imports that were central to Channel 4's identity. These imports had complicated Channel 4's remit to support the British independent sector and as E4 was being developed, it was under pressure from the industry regulator the

Independent Television Council to reduce its reliance on bought-in programming (Rixon 2006, 55). As a hybrid pay channel funded by a combination of cable and satellite subscriptions and advertising, E4 was not under the same restrictions as its parent channel. This allowed it to be built around the acquisition of costly bundled pay- and free-to-air rights for *Friends* (NBC, 1994–2004) and *ER* (1994–2009). In doing so, Channel 4 outbid the deep pockets of BSkyB and challenged the company's monopoly over the most popular US imports (Brown 2007, 238–240).

Airing these NBC hits, together with HBO prestige dramas *The Sopranos* (HBO, 1999–2007) and *Six Feet Under* (2001–2005), up to six months before their terrestrial broadcast helped to grow Channel 4's foothold in the multi-channel landscape. However, with half of E4's first-year budget of £40 million being spent on acquisitions (Brown 2000), this limited the channel's development of British programming (No author 2012). Instead, the dominant British presence on E4 was *Big Brother*, whose second season in the summer of 2001 kept the channel in low-cost programming. A live feed from the house and daily companion show *Big Brother's Little Brother* (2001–2011) helped the channel to double its audience (Brown 2007, 309). E4's oscillation between highbrow US imports and lowbrow UK reality television needed a strong channel brand – one cohered by marketing and idents – in order to reconcile potential tensions.

Finding a British Voice

Whilst they drew the desired 16–34-year-old audience, the heavy financial burden of the US imports and the schedule-dominance of the reality blockbuster stagnated E4's ability to develop the innovative and risky original programming it had been tasked with as part of its role as a 'research and development lab' (Born 2003, 784) for Channel 4. As a result, although E4 had developed a strong brand to reconcile the two halves of its identity, it had not yet truly given voice to itself as a *British* youth channel. Original programming was essential to the development of this voice and steps began to be taken to address this in the latter half of the 2000s. This was facilitated by E4's move in 2005 from a pay-TV hybrid on cable and satellite to an advertising-funded digital channel on free-to-air digital platform Freeview (No author 2004c). Debuting as a 24-hour channel ready for the start of *Big Brother* in May 2005, E4 could now compete on an even playing field with its competitors BBC Three and particularly ITV2, which had nearly doubled their audience share on Freeview

(Reevell 2005). The move paid off and E4 doubled its advertising income by 2006 (Brown 2007, 297).

The Freeview move was followed by a £20 million increase in E4's budget, the most significant step in the development of its British youth voice (Reevell 2005). This enabled a decisive shift towards British youth programming with the channel's first original drama, the zeitgeist-dominating *Skins* (2007–2013) and sleeper hit schoolboy sitcom *The Inbetweeners* (2008–2010). E4's role as the catalyst for British youth television's late 2000s development was compounded the success of zombie satire *Dead Set* (2008) and particularly social realist telefantasy *Misfits* (2009–2013). The latter joined *Skins*, *The Inbetweeners* and BBC Three's *Being Human* (2008–2013) as the defining texts of British youth television. These E4 programmes developed new voices – writers, directors and performers – which then-channel head Angela Jain argued supported Channel 4's public service responsibility (Burrell 2009).

In late 2008, E4 overtook Channel 5 to become the fifth most popular channel for 16–34 year olds, with nearly 50 per cent of its audience coming from the demographic (Rogers 2009). Earlier that year *Skins* became E4's highest-rated programme (Reevell 2008a), a position previously dominated by episodes of *Friends*. This indicated that the US import-dominated E4 of the early 2000s had shifted to a blended British youth space. The loss of *Friends* to Comedy Central in 2011 along with the cancellation of *Big Brother* (only for it to be resurrected on Channel 5) removed key schedule scaffolding. However this opened up further space and budget to develop original British content, including *Made in Chelsea* (2011–) and *My Mad Fat Diary*, consolidating E4's status as a significant voice in the cultural world of British youth. It is important to note that the channel's identity still relies as much on US imports as on British programming, with *Glee* (Fox, 2009–2015) and *The Big Bang Theory* (CBS, 2007–) amongst the channel's most popular programming. Thus, E4 offers a negotiated channel identity that must assimilate this US programming into its British 'voice'. Here branding plays an essential role via idents, adverts and continuity announcers, with interstitial elements building the 'tone of a cheeky child making fun of an older sibling' (Khalsa 2011).

Building E4's Brand

Catherine Johnson argues that a strong brand mitigates against some of the financial risks of digital expansion (2012, 95), with branding essential to both differentiating between channels and unifying them under the parent channel's core values (2012, 93). E4 maintains Channel 4's central qualities – innovation, experimentation and controversy – offering an interpretation which foregrounds 'irreverent fun' (ibid.). Its royal purple icon features an E encased in a number 4, whose soft rounded edges evoke yet distinguish it from the Channel 4 icon's fragmented sharpness. Johnson argues that a channel's branded identity creates a personality for the channel 'over and above its individual programmes' (2012, 126), with the ident functioning as a form of entertainment in itself and the logo serving as a character. The E4 icon is anthropomorphised throughout the years in a series of idents, along with viewer-created 'e-stings' that air in late-night junctions.

E4's channel identity was articulated in one of its early idents featuring the classic Channel 4 icon (Figure 2.1). The icon's multi-coloured fragmented blocks fall to the floor and shatter into a mass of tiny giggling, bounding, multi-coloured E4 icons; a purple icon then leaps to the foreground accompanied by the sound of a raspberry being blown. The classic Channel 4 ident referenced here had been replaced some years earlier (Fanthome 2007); however, this E4 ident drew on the long-standing

Fig. 2.1 An early E4 ident offers a playful shattering of the classic Channel 4 icon

iconography of Channel 4 to demonstrate E4's connection to and distinction from its parent brand. Birthed from a shattered Channel 4, it was presented as a more youthful, anarchic presence.

Since the 2004 refresh of E4's brand identity, the channel's idents have tended to present E4 as a bizarre, ironic or anarchic presence within British landscapes or mundane spaces. Mark Brownrigg and Peter Meech argue that the production of a variety of idents allows them to adapt to the tone of the programming and facilitate genre shifts (2011, 71). The collection of new idents in 2004 featured a lounge-lizard-style band playing bland elevator music, clad in retro purple suits. The band was placed incongruously in deserted British spaces, including a London bus depot backed by a container park and cranes, a deserted low-lit beach, a bingo hall and industrial scrubland. The surreal nature of the juxtaposition positioned E4 as a comic, entertainment oasis in mundane British landscapes, signalling both its national identity and its disruptive presence. A 2008 ident refresh saw a 'typically British scene' of a barn, a beach hut or a hotel transformed into a 'deranged E4 space' (Sweney 2007) through an outpouring of both abstract and everyday animated objects. These signified the chaotic influence of E4, transforming the spaces into surreal wonderlands. This set of idents sought to reflect E4's 'personality' as 'beautifully random, joyously daft and generally not taking things too seriously' (ibid.). The 2013 refresh featured the E4 logo anthropomorphised into Eefer, a slightly-battered, part logo, part robot, with eyes, legs and 'the ability to drink beer through a hatch' (MPC Advertising 2013) – retro-futurist, surreal, yet everyday. Accompanied by a terrier dog and a slightly blank affect, Eefer was featured within British locations: sitting contemplative on Welsh mountain tops, barbecuing in seaside caravan parks and canal-boating along countryside rivers. Each of these three sets of idents seek to establish E4 as a bright, incongruous, wryly knowing presence within locations (particularly 2004 and 2013) marked as British through their mundaneness, tradition or detachment from modernity.

It is within E4's interstitial elements that the pleasurable ambivalence central to British youth television is articulated; where the play between investment and detachment that Karen Lury describes as uneasy in early youth programming (2001, 42) is normalised, shaping the channel's programmes. John Ellis suggests that the 'bits inbetween' programmes are 'a series of distillation of television, and an internal meta-commentary on ordinary TV' (2011, 60). They show how 'television regards itself (its brands)' and 'how it wants its programmes to be read (the trailers)' (ibid.).

E4's trailers strongly articulate how its British viewers should read its programming, through an archness at play in the accompanying voiceover that echoes T4's framing presenters, although here this is offered in an overtly comic manner through the character of 'Voiceover Man', who is aligned with the cheeky, detached nature of E4's channel identity.

Johnson notes that during the 1990s, continuity announcements became more informal and ambiguous, with this change in tone communicating a channel's personality and 'emphasising the connection between viewer and channel' (2012, 125). E4 follows T4 in the construction of an overarching supertext that offers a negotiated relationship with sincerity (Woods 2013, 26), one that is more ambivalent about its US imports than its British originals. E4's distinctive tone and turns of phrase – 'chuffing', 'ruddy hell', 'tellybox' – that appear across interstitial elements and its website are indebted to the parodically bombastic Voiceover Man (initially Patrick Allen and succeeded by Peter Dickson). This character became as much a part of E4's branding as its distinctive purple palate and idents. Voiceover Man's rich, pompous, booming voice connotes British gravitas, yet its over-enunciated, straining tone communicates an excessive investment. When juxtaposed with youth content and offering commentary through comic phrasing (whilst US channel NBC positioned its Thursday night programming as Must See TV, E4 showcases its high-rating US sitcom imports as 'Quite Big Thursdays'), Voiceover Man signified E4's care to display a detached attitude towards its programming. This was most prominent in its US imports, such as a 2008 promo for the season five premiere of *One Tree Hill* that introduced the season's four-year time jump. Over a montage of its glossily beautiful characters, Dickson's rich British tones ponders whether the audience had ever 'thought them lads and ladyfolk looked a tad "mature" to be in school uniform' and explaining that 'one night the writers got wazzed up and decided to set the new series four year in the *ruddy future*'.[7] The trailer positioned its audience as textually aware of the aesthetics and melodrama-led storytelling of US teen TV, rendering its framing within E4 as one of knowing camp. Here E4 extended T4's approach to assimilating US texts into British youth flow.

The centrality of Dickson's voice to E4's brand was highlighted by the channel's 2008 website revamp, which included a section devoted to his cult celebrity with 'a dictionary of his phrases, a "school" in his name and competitions for users to impersonate him' (Brittain 2008). Dickson moved in front of the camera in in promos such as 2010's 'E4

Bunker', which referenced the current media panic around working-class youth-as-threat (which I touch on in Chapter 3). Dressed in a purple suit, Dickson addresses the audience with a microphone amidst a desaturated, apocalyptic vision of 'hoodies' – largely played by dwarves to bring a further surreal edge – destroying a suburban cul-de-sac (Figure 2.2). Accompanied by an orchestral rendering of 'Land of Hope and Glory', Dickson intones that the country was being 'ruddy well knackered' by: 'Hoodie people! ASBO-monkeys pumped full of alco-piddle! And a general abundance of undesirables.' He goes on to offer the 'E4 bunker' as 'a place for your family to hide and watch E4, whilst Blighty goes to the dogs'.[8] As he runs through the new US and British shows airing on the channel, a televisually perfect, excessively-smiling, shiny-haired family lock down the hatches of the bright purple bunker located in the middle of the street, before sitting together on a retro-futurist sofa and laughing with an edge of mania. The promo signified the channel's awareness of the current hyperbolic discourses surrounding British youth from press and politicians – representations with which its audience would be intimately familiar, yet were largely absent from the commercially driven, middle-class leaning E4. It mocked a Little England vision of British youth, signalling E4 as space free from such judgements and fearsome representations. This positioning of its programming squarely as escapist entertainment was fed

Fig. 2.2 2010's 'E4 Bunker' promo

through a knowing, ironic address. Offering an ambivalent play with promotion and brand identity, the promo signalled E4's pleasures without having to sell them sincerely.

Channel brands and the relationships they maintain become more important as channels fight for declining linear audiences (Price 2015). However, as E4's target demographic increasingly moves to on-demand platforms such as All 4, this channel branding becomes erased, subsumed into an overarching Channel 4 'brand'. Chapter 7 returns to this issue when I look at All 4 short-form content. This chapter closes by examining the BBC's move into digital youth television. As Georgina Born notes, although Channel 4 and the BBC are both public service broadcasters, their framing of their respective brand expansions into digital youth channels were distinctly different. Channel 4 positioned its digital spread through discourses of financial stability and entrepreneurialism, whereas the BBC's new digital channels and radio stations were presented as engaging with 'social and cultural utility, universality and particular minority needs' (Born 2003, 794). I focus here on BBC Three's juggling of this public service requirement and a youth address, as well as its projected shift to an online-only channel.

PUBLIC SERVICE DIGITAL YOUTH CHANNEL: BBC THREE

Both E4 and BBC Three operate under the umbrella of public service broadcasters; however, Channel 4's public/private status positions it as an audience and profit-driven company (with these profits reinvested in the corporation), which distinguishes E4 from the licence-fee funded BBC Three. The latter's current remit requires that it informs, educates and entertains its audience with a mixed schedule of news, factual, current affairs, scripted comedy, entertainment and drama, which 'should not shy away from causing debate and controversy' (BBC Trust 2014, 5). The edgy humour and anarchic identity central to a youth audience appeal may be freely available for commercial broadcasters, but at the BBC this must be tempered by fears of censure and scandal (Rushton 2009). BBC Three's position within a publicly funded public service broadcaster brings with it the burden of a hyper-vigilant British press and the taint of responsibility. It must juggle this with a channel brand and youth address that necessitates a presentation of itself as a risk-taking peer (I draw out BBC Three's peer address in Chapter 5's discussion of the channel's documentary output). As *Broadcast* magazine argued, 'a channel emblazoned with the BBC logo –

however it is animated – will never quite be cool' (ibid.). Yet the BBC must maintain the loyalty of 16–34-year-olds, as they are tomorrow's voters and licence fee-payers.

BBC Three has always had to fight for legitimation and acceptance of its public value, and in part serves as a synecdoche of the conflict over the place for and value of public service broadcasting in contemporary society. Dealing with the same battles fought by its parent institution against the rhetoric of commercial competitors and an aggressive political discourse (Born 2011), BBC Three's youth address sees it subjected to further critique. The larger ongoing discourse around the BBC becomes laser-focused around BBC Three due to its niche focus on a small youth demographic rather than the mainstream breadth courted by BBC One and BBC Two. The channel is forever stuck between a rock and a hard place: it must demonstrate its public value through drawing in youth audiences, yet it must also prove its distinctiveness by providing public service content – such as news, documentary and arts – not offered by the commercial market (No author 2002). These challenges contributed to the conflicted birth I chart below and inform ongoing tensions with the market. BBC Three has long received critiques from those outside of its 16–34 target demographic, both from politicians and broadcasting's elder statesmen such as John Humphreys and Jeremy Paxman (Rushton 2010). This discourse draws from an ideology of public service built around legitimation and cultural capital, which conflicted with the noise and potential controversy required of youth entertainment. As channel strategist Stephen Arnell noted 'titles such as F**k Off, I'm A Hairy Woman tended to stick in the mind, certainly of opinion formers who rarely if ever sampled the channel' (2014).

The BBC's constant tensions between the Reithian tenets are most acute in BBC Three, which must balance public service content and the populist pleasures that draw youth audiences, particularly its often-critiqued comedy and factual entertainment (Rushton 2010). BBC Three executives have been engaged in an ongoing push-back against what they viewed as the wilful lack of awareness shown by the press and politicians of the channel's success in factual content (Kanter 2013a) and the attacks on the public value of the channel. Then-channel head Danny Cohen described the latter as 'a kind of chauvinism around young people, a belief that they are less deserving of licence-fee money than anyone else' (Rushton 2010). Young audiences were citizens as much as any Radio 4 listener and were essential to the corporation's future.

E4 is touched on in some television scholarship (Born 2003; Johnson 2012), but BBC Three is strangely absent from the field. This case study serves a dual purpose, mapping the channel's history to correct this absence whilst exploring the tensions at the heart of its existence. It will explore the complicated dance in which BBC Three has always been engaged: drawing the attention of youth audiences to public service broadcasting whilst negotiating the role of entertainment in its output. I consider the struggles of its birth, the ongoing development of its channel identity and the cultural perception of its role as a niche youth channel within a huge, public-owned broadcaster. These concerns were concentrated with the 2014 announcement that BBC Three would cease to exist as a linear channel and would move online as a cost-saving venture (Kanter 2014a). This finally occurred on 16 February 2016, after this book's completion; I briefly outline the ultimate shape of the online 'New BBC Three' on its launch day in Chapter 7. However, here I draw on industry discourse to chart the long progression of plans for 'New BBC Three', as this illustrates both the BBC's relationship with youth audiences and how British youth television was confronting shifts in viewing practices in the 2010s.

Delivering and Delineating BBC Three

> I want to make it very clear we will *always* make ground-breaking drama like *Murdered by My Boyfriend* and *In the Flesh*. We will still give you comedy of the calibre of the *Mighty Boosh* and *Gavin & Stacey* and we will still make documentaries like *Our War* and *Life and Death Row*. We will still champion new talent like Georgina Campbell and James Corden. That is what we do now and what we will always do. (Kavanagh 2015a)

As BBC Three stood on the precipice of crippling budget cuts, a new online era and an uncertain future in mid-2015, its new 'digital controller' Damian Kavanagh sought to clarify talk of the channel's 'closure' in one of a series of BBC blog posts mapping the progress of 'New BBC Three'. This statement serves as a useful marker of the identity BBC Three was attempting to articulate to its viewers, regulators and the industry at large at this point in time. It presented a BBC Three home to risk-taking drama, comedy both surreal and cosy, and serious documentaries, a space for the development of new talent. This selection of texts also handily highlighted the BAFTA-winning content of the channel, positioning BBC

Three as a legitimated space. Conspicuously absent were the imported US animation (*Family Guy* (Fox, 1999–2003, 2005–), *American Dad* (Fox/TBS 2005–)) and factual entertainment (*Snog Marry Avoid* (2008–2013), *Don't Tell the Bride* (BBC Three/BBC One, 2007–)) that were frequently referenced in critiques or press reports on the channel (No author 2005; Rushton 2010; Beaumont-Thomas 2014). This process of legitimation disavows BBC Three's most popular programming from low-status genres in order to define it as a place of cultural value, worthy of the licence fee. Here we see BBC Three presenting itself as a model of prestige British youth television, one that is award-winning, nationally distinct and niche targeted to its market, a channel worth saving – an identity BBC Three had struggled to assert across its life.

BBC Three grew from the ashes of BBC Choice, one of the BBC's early digital channels, which the broadcaster planned to rebirth as a channel targeting 16–34 year olds as part of a package of digital television and radio expansions in 2001. These aimed to drive public take-up of digital television by supporting currently underserved areas, including the arts, science and culture-focused BBC Four, and minority-led radio stations 1Xtra and BBC Asian Network. Faced with criticism from commercial broadcasters over the BBC's targeting of a commercially valuable audience (No author 2004a), Culture Secretary Tessa Jowell held up the government's approval of BBC Three (Satchell 2001). After a year of negotiations, together with market analysis from the ITC, this was finally granted under a revised plan that refocused the channel towards the older, smaller 25–34 demographic, with an emphasis on original British material (80 per cent of its output) and a commitment to breaking new talent (No author 2002). The commitment to original British content distinguished the channel from the import-led E4, which meant it lacked audience-drawing content on which to build its schedules. In turn, its market impact was limited by requirement to offer the news, current affairs, arts, documentary and regional drama that were absent from its advertising-driven 16–34 competitor channels due to their expense and perceived low audience return. This gave the channel a 'considerable challenge to build an audience' (ibid.).

Commencing broadcast in 2003, BBC Three's first year on air saw criticism over its perceived reliance on films and 'BBC bankers' such as *EastEnders* repeats and spin-offs from popular programmes. Yet as channel head Stuart Murphy argued, building on established BBC brands allowed the channel to drive new viewers to original programming, which BBC Three was producing more of than ITV2 or E4 (No author 2004a). Its early years saw it struggle to balance its public service commitments with content attractive to youth audiences. A 2004 review of BBC digital services by the BBC governors critiqued the channel for an over-reliance on BBC repeats and celebrity, relationship and lifestyle programming (No author 2004b). But by 2005 BBC Three drew praise from industry magazine *Broadcast* for asserting itself in a crowded market whilst under nearly constant attack, highlighting its strength of programming, bold commissioning and knowledge of its target audience (No author 2005).

Solidifying Identity and Online Experiments

The year 2007 marked a new phase in the channel's maturation, with Danny Cohen's arrival as channel head (following a year running E4), a push towards the younger end of the 16–34 demographic (Bashford 2007) and the impact of the BBC's 'Creative Futures' initiative. The latter sought to stem the loss of younger viewers to online and multi-channel competitors, in part through developing new entertainment content for BBC Three (Thompson 2007). BBC Three has a strong foundation in comedy, a high risk and development-heavy genre that benefits from the channel's commitment to developing new voices. This produced a range of misfires, but also successes from *Little Britain* (BBC One/BBC Three, 2002–2003) to *The Mighty Boosh* (BBC Three, 2004–2007) and the recently debuted *Gavin & Stacey* (BBC One/BBC Three, 2007–2010). Cohen sought to develop the channel's drama footprint by airing six drama pilots; this resulted in the commissioning of *Being Human*, a supernatural flat share dramedy that saw critical and rating success. *Being Human*, like *Skins* and *Misfits* at E4, illustrated the importance of drama series in the solidifying of youth channel identities. Drama brings cultural legitimation and the potential for an international spread that the cultural specificity of comedy often limits (Chapter 4 discusses examples of this international spread). However, successive budget cuts (Rushton 2009; Kanter 2011) have significantly impacted BBC Three's ability to develop drama series, falling from three to a single series per year (Kanter 2013a). This led to the cancellation of short-lived telefantasies *The Fades* (2011) and *In the Flesh* (2013–2014), both of which would go on to win BAFTAs.

Arguably the success of *Being Human* and *Gavin & Stacey*, alongside a succession of well-received factual content, helped to develop BBC Three's cultural footprint in the late 2000s. This factual content included *Jack: A Soldier's Story* (2008) and *Blood, Sweat and T-Shirts* (2008), which both supported the BBC's remit to 'bring the world to the UK' (BBC Trust 2014, 6), and signalled key factual threads for the channel. The former was an early text in BBC Three's documentation of young soldiers in Afghanistan (discussed in Chapter 5) and the latter catalysed the channel's preference for exploring global issues and labour concerns (here sweatshop and child labour) through immersive factual formats. In contrast to its drama and comedy successes, BBC Three's factual content saw less cultural permeation. Yet this programming signalled the channel's solidifying of its youth voice together with its ability to deliver the tricky tonal balance required of educational content for youth audiences.

BBC Three's audience steadily increased, reaching a 4.2 per cent share of 16–34 year olds in 2008 and beating Sky One in multi-channel homes (Reevell 2008b). In 2008 the channel became the first to stream live through the BBC website, a move which accompanied a brand refresh with a new logo and idents created by Red Bee Media. Red Bee's Charlie Mawer noted that the rebrand sought to counter the channel's low brand recognition amongst its target demographic, where 'it was seen as a bit cold and distant and male and not young enough' (Grainge 2011b, 92). A vibrant deep fuchsia became BBC Three's central colour and new idents featured a lively, surreal, brightly coloured planet. Here, abstract city landscapes and blank expanses were populated by tiny animated figures and dotted with neon tubes, buildings made of television sets, giant lipsticks and a single high-heeled shoe. This rebrand shaded BBC Three with a feminine edge, repositioning the channel as a warm, inventive community that was separated from the rest of the BBC in its own world. This community concept was extended online and into the interstitials, with the website built around interaction and user-generated content, inviting viewers to submit their own continuity announcements to be broadcast on air (ibid.). The user-generated continuity announcements did not last long; however, participation became facilitated by social media and integrated into interstitial spaces. Programme credits and idents were accompanied by continuity announcers reading tweets and Facebook responses to the previous programming – a practice also used by ITV2 – seeking to draw the audience into a gossipy reactive relationship with the channel.

This push to present BBC Three as a distinct, inventive, participatory multi-platform space was in line with recommendations from the Creative Future review. This had warned that the corporation was at risk of 'losing a generation forever', recommending the development of new services through broadband, mobile and interactive platforms to reach younger audiences (Dowell 2006). Cohen positioned 2008's online developments as a 'multi-platform rebirth' which signalled a 'new relationship' between television and the internet (Rushton 2008). Yet this 'rebirth' was short-lived. A 2009 report from the BBC Trust highlighted low awareness of BBC Three's website provision amongst its target audience (BBC Trust 2009, 7) and the following year channel-specific online presences began to be rolled back following the Delivering Quality First review. This saw the BBC move to streamline all its website content and target multi-platform funding towards the iPlayer platform, whilst also refocusing multi-platform and interactive engagement to support event programming (Sweney and Plunkett 2010). However, BBC Three has remained a small-scale vanguard in the BBC's multi-platform strategy, with its website livestream the first step towards iPlayer's livestreaming of all BBC channels. In turn, BBC Three's comedy has had a strong iPlayer presence, with all the channel's sitcoms made available on the platform for seven days before their linear broadcast (Kanter 2013b) and the platform's hosting of the yearly *Comedy Feeds* pilot project (Rigby 2014). These initiates were precursors for the BBC-wide iPlayer 'online first' strategy of online originals and early premieres, which I pick up in Chapter 7.

Death or Rebirth?

In March 2014 the BBC announced its plans to drastically cut BBC Three's budget, close it as a linear television channel and transition it into an 'online-only' channel. These plans were framed as unavoidable, with the corporation faced with a 26 per cent reduction in its budget – £1.5 billion by 2017. It was suggested they would avoid larger cuts elsewhere or 'salami slicing' across all budgets (Kanter 2015a). Yet the figures offered suggested relatively small cost savings against the larger budget hole, as BBC Three's content budget was to be cut by more than £50 million to £25, but £30 million of that saving was to go to BBC One drama and £20 million to BBC Three's running costs (Parker 2014). We see here a continuation of the BBC's practice of diverting budgets for youth-focused content to support mainstream programming – from the 2010 closure of the short-lived BBC Switch brand, which targeted 12–16 year olds with cross-platform content (Plunkett 2010) to the ongoing cuts to the BBC Three budget across its lifetime. The BBC planned for all long-form BBC Three content to be repeated on linear television via the 'bigger stages' of BBC One and BBC Two (Kanter 2014b) and in response to strong press and industry criticism, the £30 million moved to the BBC One budget was pledged to the production of drama for the youth demographic (Kanter 2014c). Yet how niche-focused content that recognised and addressed the specificity of youth experience would be balanced with the broad and diverse concerns of the mainstream channel was unclear.

BBC Three's limited ratings success – a consequence of its remit to experiment and break new talent – together with its delegitimated status and youth demographic made it an easy target for such an attack, as arguably this was as much a political sacrifice as it was a financial one. BBC sources informed *Broadcast* magazine that the sacrifice of BBC Three was preferred over the loss of BBC Four, a key platform for new Director-General Tony Hall's plans to increase the corporation's arts coverage (Kanter 2014a). Industry creatives noted that the political and media establishment were part of BBC Four's core 'upper-middle-class' audience. This was a group the BBC needed onside for licence fee renewal negotiations and who knew how to lobby and turn out to vote (Younge 2014). In contrast, the 16–34 demographic has little if any establishment voice and are largely disillusioned with political decision making. Independent television producer Jimmy Mulville argued that this was a cynical choice targeting 'a demographic that doesn't make a lot of noise' (Gannagé-Stewart 2015a). This was a decision embedded in ideologies of class and age, one that – like the closure of BBC Switch – impacted the very audience that the BBC needed to guarantee its future. BBC Three and young audiences were being sacrificed to prove a point, with some suggesting the move was a strategy to signal to press and politicians what was ahead if the BBC was forced to become a subscription service (Bulkley 2014).

In turn, the discursive repositioning of 'New BBC Three' sought to legitimate the channel in the eyes of the establishment in order to assert its public value. The audience-drawing yet delegitimated forms of factual entertainment and animated comedy were sacrificed in the move online (Wiseman 2014; Munn 2015). Factual entertainment was targeted as a space lacking the opportunity to develop new talent and an ill fit with the 'make you think' and 'make you laugh' guiding principles of 'New BBC Three' (Kavanagh 2015b; Munn 2015). As *The Guardian* pointed out, *Sun, Sex and Suspicious Parents* was 'cruel, funny and crude, and as such – dare we say it – perhaps everything that those holding the purse strings at the Beeb don't hold dear' (Beaumont-Thomas 2014). However, the BBC quietly kept hold of the ratings stalwart *Don't Tell the Bride* and transitioned it to BBC One's feminised light factual 8–9 slot in 2015, before the programme was ultimately let go and picked up by Sky 1 in 2016. This discourse served to position the lithe, digital 'New BBC Three' as a pseudo-prestige space, a worthy subject of public funding.

Admitting that the move came ahead of schedule, the BBC sought to position the 'reinvention' of BBC Three as the biggest strategic decision it had made since the launch of the iPlayer, one whose impact on digital content would echo the streaming service's influence on the on-demand market (Kanter 2014a). As Elizabeth Evans has argued, this discourse offered a contradictory – and incorrect – positioning of 'traditional TV' (as Kavanagh's BBC blogs termed it) as old-fashioned and constraining, 'beholden to regimented and slow schedules'. Yet at the same time the plans privileged the value of linear broadcasting in assurances that BBC Three's long-form content would air on BBC One and BBC Two (Evans 2015). The BBC positioned the move as a pathfinder for both the future shape of the whole corporation and its shifting relationship with its audience (Wiseman 2014), claiming it would 'reinvent public service for the digital world' and drive the digital up-skilling of its workforce (Gannagé-Stewart 2015d). Inevitably the international streaming giants were invoked by both press (Bulkley 2014; Younge 2014) and BBC executives (Kanter 2014c; Price 2014), with both Cohen and then-channel head Zai Bennett suggesting BBC Three needed to learn from Netflix and Amazon, investing in 'fewer but more ambitious shows' (Price 2014) (although it should be noted that BBC Three's annual budget was now less than a one-third of the budget of Netflix's *House of Cards* (2013–)). The move online was presented as mirroring the trajectory of the viewing habits of the channel's youth audience (Kavanagh 2015b). BBC Three content was already seeing significant success on iPlayer, particularly in comedy, with school sitcom *Bad Education* averaging 2 million requests per episode, even in repeats (Price 2014). Award-winning factual drama *Murdered by My Boyfriend* was the most-watched show on iPlayer in June 2014, with two million views (Chapman 2014a), yet most of the channel's factual output saw markedly less views, rarely touching one million (ibid.), illustrating the challenge of reaching audiences.

The decision to move BBC Three online seemed to have been made in haste, as executives could offer little concrete articulation of what the move would entail creatively and financially. This led to uncertainties within the audience and the independent production sector, catalysing campaigns to 'save BBC Three' from 'closure' (Gannagé-Stewart 2015a). The BBC Trust's lengthy review process pushed the planned move online back to February 2016 and frustrations brewed amongst the independent sector over delays in finalising the form and commissioning process of the 'New BBC Three' (Chapman 2014b). The sector's widespread critique of the move indicated the importance of BBC Three to British independent production companies, as original British commissions dominated BBC Three's top 20 programmes amongst 16–24 year olds (Price 2014). However, digital producers largely praised the move (Gannagé-Stewart 2015b), arguing that it reflected the trajectory of 16–24 year olds' online viewing habits (Ackerman 2014), would force producers to learn new skills to engage a young audience 'increasingly disengaged with traditional means of distributing television' (Gannagé-Stewart 2015c) and would offer a place to take risks with new talent, experiment with interactivity and storytelling forms (Younge 2014).

The move reflected the blurring of televisual boundaries happening in online video, with digital media companies (Vice, YouTube) seeking to position themselves as akin to TV channels (Bulkley 2014), YouTube Multi-Channel Networks such as Maker Studios beginning developing programmes for television channels (Farber 2015), and brands such as Red Bull and Coke shifting into content production (Ackerman 2014). Yet there were questions over the strength of the BBC Three brand amongst national and international competition. A BBC Trust review in 2014 argued that despite its remit to build online engagement, BBC Three suffered from low viewer awareness of its online content compared to platforms such as YouTube and the BBC's own iPlayer (Kanter 2014d). Earlier budget cuts had dented the BBC Three brand, with the Trust arguing that cuts to the channel's drama and online content through Delivering Quality First had impacted both BBC Three's reach to its target demographic and their perceptions of the channel's quality. Here we see the importance of drama to the strength and reach of British youth television, and the impact of the BBC prioritising the iPlayer in multi-platform investment.

The first half of 2015 saw plans for the 'New BBC Three' develop at a slow pace (Kavanagh 2014, 2015a, b), with the BBC Trust finally agreeing to the plans in late June in a 'finely balanced' decision. Its report highlighted the potential impact on the BBC's ability to nurture new talent (Gannagé-Stewart 2015c) and the risk of losing of young, diverse and lower-income audiences due inequalities in broadband access (Kanter 2015b). The latter was a welcome recognition of the 'digital gap' that had been absent in the press and industry proselytising over youth and the 'future of television'. July saw 'New BBC Three's finalised £30 million budget revealed – along with a defined focus on 16–24 year olds – to be divided between £10 million for scripted comedy, £10 million for serious factual and £3 million for drama (Gannagé-Stewart 2015d). In a significant move, £6 million was allocated to short-form and digital content to reflect short-form's online dominance (ibid.). New long-form drama, factual and comedy series would debut weekly and monthly on iPlayer, although at this point it was unclear how the BBC Three channel brand would be retained within the dominant brand of the platform. Chapter 7 considers the challenge of retaining the BBC Three channel brand in spreadable short-form content.

The move online to on-demand sees television remediated from a linear television flow to the navigational database of the streaming platform (Bennett 2011, 1), yet a modified form of linearity and flow was retained in Damian Kavanagh's plan for a BBC Three 'daily stream' (ultimately christened the Daily Drop on its launch). This would provide a frequently refreshed online home for the channel on the BBC website, Britain's third most popular site with young people behind Facebook and YouTube (Kavanagh 2015a). This was pitched as a stream of original and user-generated short-form and digital content: 'memes, GIFs, lists, animations, authored pieces from contributors, interviews, and picture galleries' (ibid.). This would include collaborations with the BBC's news and sports divisions, drawing on their innovations in digital content. The emphasis here is on interaction, shareability and a responsive BBC Three, producing content that would spread the channel across its audiences' online spaces. 'New BBC Three' would be an on-demand and platform-agnostic channel offering 'immediacy, a more personalised interactive experience, authenticity of voice and a tone that resonates with young people' (Gannagé-Stewart 2015d). The vision for 'New BBC Three' seemed to collect best practice from the market's digital innovators and link it with the channel's programming strengths; a blend of blockbusting US media companies Buzzfeed and Vice, combined with the scripted comedy and drama that were more costly to develop online – the latter being BBC Three's position of strength. Vice becomes a touchstone in this discourse, with Kavanagh emphasising the company as a model for the short-form factual content that could be central to the channel. This view was supported by his hiring of Vice's former head of development Max Gogarty to lead the channel's short-form division (Kavanagh 2015a).[9] Yet this push towards spreadability needed to be balanced with the risk of sublimating BBC Three content and its brand into powerful international media brands.

This chapter has sketched the youth offerings of British broadcasters, tracing these from terrestrial strands, through the rise of digital television and into an uncertain online future. In charting the life of BBC Three, it has filled a gap in the academic study of the recent history of British television. It has demonstrated how different channels have built distinct identities in pursuit of the same audience demographic. Branding plays an essential role here, serving to connect youth channels to and delineate them from their parent corporations, helping to build audience relationships and smooth the tensions in channels' mixed schedules. This is particularly important in the assimilation of US teen TV, with the divergent identities and representations of the national forms reconciled through T4 and E4's distinct brand identities, which are communicated through interstitial elements. Youth channels have been a space where the struggle over the role and value of public service broadcasting is pushed to the foreground, with BBC Three serving as a synecdoche of the corporation's negotiation of the commercial market together with its remit-required reach and technological innovation.

In an unstable present and an unknown future, the target audiences of youth channels are diffused across a wealth of platforms and entertainment content. This competition is nothing new, but the place of youth channels in an on-demand media landscape is more pressing when press and new media evangelists preach the youth audience's desire for a la carte and perpetually available content. Will these channels' distinctive youth brands become subsumed to the brand identity of their parent channels and on-demand platforms (iPlayer, ITV Player, All 4)? Could youth channels play an important role in British television's long-wavering embrace of digital storytelling and signal the shape of television on the horizon? This book's conclusion touches on some of these concerns. Having established the framework of British youth television, the next chapter moves on to discuss its contents.

Notes

1. ITV is regulated as public service broadcaster; however, it has campaigned to progressively reduce its PSB regulation, which it views as conflicting with its commercial purposes (Fitzsimmons 2009).

2. Ofcom's 2015 review of public service broadcasting recommended Channel 4's public service remit be extended across all its channels and over-the-top services. It remains to be seen whether this will occur (Ofcom 2015).
3. A hugely popular, celebrity-driven entertainment and gossip weekly throughout the 2000s, *Heat* magazine's mastery of a British youth 'voice' and self-reflexive engagement in celebrity (Holmes 2005) is often used as a touchstone in industrial and press articulation of British youth channel's identities.
4. I follow Lury in using 'yoof' to refer to a particular aesthetic and ideology constructed by a set of 1980s and 1990s British programming targeted at the 16–34-year-old demographic. This is distinct from my use of British 'youth' television as a marker of national context.
5. As I discuss in Chapter 3, British youth drama is drawn from traditions of British realism (which includes evening soap opera), distinct from US teen TV's roots in quality popular television.
6. As a profit-driven, commercially funded broadcaster under the pressures of the market, ITV has long campaigned to reduce its now-minimal public service broadcasting commitments (Fitzsimmons 2009). ITV's current public service broadcasting licence requires obligations to provide regional and national news, British-originated programming and a very small commitment to children's (Steemers 2011, 162), arts and religious programming.
7. https://www.youtube.com/watch?v=-Nw_0EJCpSw (accessed 24 May 2016).
8. https://www.youtube.com/watch?v=kQrazhja9tk (accessed 24 May 2016).
9. This was a personnel move indicative of industry flows in the mid-2010s, as public service broadcasters took on experienced digital media executives to shape their short-form engagement, whilst social and digital media companies employed experienced television executives to support their push into television content.

References

Ackerman, Steve. 2014. 'Opponents of BBC3 Move Are in Denial'. *Broadcast*, 7 March. www.broadcastnow.co.uk/opponents-of-bbc3-move-are-in-denial/5068394.article (accessed 25 May 2016).

Arnell, Stephen. 2014. 'BBC3: Coming out of the Shadows'. *Broadcast*, 5 March. www.broadcastnow.co.uk/opinion/bbc3-coming-out-of-the-shadows/5068302.article (accessed 25 May 2016).

BARB. 2015. 'The Viewing Report'. www.barb.co.uk/trendspotting/analysis/annual-viewing-report (accessed 25 May 2016).

Bashford, Suzy. 2007. 'BBC3'. *Broadcast*, 13 September.www.broadcastnow.co.uk/bbc3/121758.article (accessed 25 May 2016).

BBC Trust. 2009. 'Service Review Younger Audiences: BBC Three, Radio 1 and 1Xtra'. www.bbc.co.uk/bbctrust/our_work/services/television/service_reviews/younger_audiences.html (accessed 25 May 2016).

———. 2014. 'BBC Three Service Licence'. www.bbc.co.uk/bbctrust/our_work/services/television/service_licences/bbc_three.html (accessed 25 May 2016).

Beaumont-Thomas, Ben. 2014. 'BBC3 – The Shows We'll Miss'. *The Guardian*, 5 March. www.theguardian.com/tv-and-radio/tvandradioblog/2014/mar/05/bbc3-gavin-stacey-torchwood-summer-heights-high (accessed 25 May 2016).

Bennett, James. 2011. 'Introduction: Television as Digital Media'. In *Television as Digital Media*, edited by James Bennett and Niki Strange, 1–27. Durham, NC: Duke University Press.

Berridge, Susan. 2013. '"Doing it for the Kids"? The Discursive Construction of the Teenager and Teenage Sexuality in Skins'. *Journal of British Cinema and Television* 10(4): 785–801.

Born, Georgina. 2003. 'Strategy, Positioning and Projection in Digital Television: Channel Four and the Commercialization of Public Service Broadcasting in the UK'. *Media, Culture & Society* 25(6): 773–799.

———. 2011. *Uncertain Vision: Birt, Dyke and the Reinvention of the BBC*. London: Random House.

Brittain, Nicola. 2008. 'Content Focus: e4.com'. *Broadcast*, 4 June. www.broadcastnow.co.uk/content-focus-e4com/1482875.article (accessed 25 May 2016).

Brown, Maggie. 2000. 'With Friends Like These...' *The Guardian*, 6 November. www.theguardian.com/media/2000/nov/06/channel4.broadcasting (accessed 25 May 2016).

———. 2007. *A Licence to Be Different: The Story of Channel 4*. London: BFI.

Browne, Nick. 1984. 'The Political Economy of the Television (Super) Text'. *Quarterly Review of Film Studies* 9(3): 174–182.

Brownrigg, Mark and Peter Meech. 2011. '"Music is Half the Picture": The Soundworld of UK Television Idents'. In *Ephemeral Media: Transitory Screen Culture from Television to YouTube*, edited by Paul Grainge, 70–86. Basingstoke: Palgrave Macmillan.

Bulkley, Kate. 2014. 'BBC Is Embracing the Future'. *Broadcast*, 13 March. www.broadcastnow.co.uk/opinion/bbc-is-embracing-the-future/5068550.article (accessed 25 May 2016).

Burrell, Ian. 2009. 'Is This a Magic Formula to Attract Young People Back to Television?' *The Independent*, 7 December. www.independent.co.uk/news/media/tv-radio/is-this-a-magic-formula-to-attract-young-people-back-to-television-1835376.html (accessed 25 May 2016).

Campelli, Matthew. 2015. 'ITV2 Takes a Hit from ITVBe'. *Broadcast*, 23 April. www.broadcastnow.co.uk/news/itv2-takes-a-hit-from-itvbe/5086876.article (accessed 7 September 2015)

Channel 4. 2014. 'Channel Four Television Corporation Report and Financial Statements 2013'. Channel 4 Television Corporation.

Chapman, Alexandra. 2014a. 'BBC3 Eyes Factual Dramas'. *Broadcast*, 21 August. www.broadcastnow.co.uk/news/commissioning/bbc3-eyes-factual-dramas/5076431.article (accessed 28 October 2015).

———. 2014b. 'BBC3 Seeks Online Ideas'. *Broadcast*, 23 October. www.broadcastnow.co.uk/broadcasters/bbc3-seeks-online-ideas/5078908.article (accessed 25 May 2016).

Christophers, Brett. 2008. 'Television's Power Relations in the Transition to Digital: The Case of the United Kingdom'. *Television & New Media* 9(3): 239–257.

Digital Economy Act 2010. www.legislation.gov.uk/ukpga/2010/24/section/22 (accessed 25 May 2016).

Dijck, José van and Thomas Poell. 2015. 'Making Public Television Social? Public Service Broadcasting and the Challenges of Social Media'. *Television & New Media* 16(2): 148–164.

Dowell, Ben. 2006. 'BBC Reaches out to New Generation'. *The Guardian*, 25 April. www.theguardian.com/media/2006/apr/25/newmedia.broadcasting (accessed 25 May 2016).

Doyle, Gillian. 2010. 'From Television to Multi-platform Less from More or More for Less?' *Convergence: The International Journal of Research into New Media Technologies* 16(4): 431–449.

Ellis, John. 2000. *Seeing Things: Television in the Age of Uncertainty*. London: I.B. Tauris.

———. 2011. 'Interstitials: How the "Bits in Between" Define the Programmes'. In *Ephemeral Media: Transitory Screen Culture from Television to YouTube*, edited by Paul Grainge, 59–69. Basingstoke: Palgrave Macmillan.

Ellis-Petersen, Hannah. 2014. 'YouTube Star Dapper Laughs Lands His Own ITV2 Dating Show'. *The Guardian*, 30 July.www.theguardian.com/media/2014/jul/30/youtube-dapper-laughs-lands-itv2-dating-show (accessed 25 May 2016).

Evans, Elizabeth. 2015. 'Public-Service Streaming: BBC Three and the Politics of Online Engagement'. *Antenna*, 21 May. http://blog.commarts.wisc.edu/2015/05/21/public-service-streaming-bbc-three-and-the-politics-of-online-engagement (accessed 25 May 2016).

Fanthome, Christine. 2007. 'Creating an Iconic Brand — An Account of the History, Development, Context and Significance of Channel 4's Idents'. *Journal of Media Practice* 8(3): 255–271.

Farber, Alex. 2015. 'Maker Studios Plots Push into TV'. *Broadcast*. March 12. www.broadcastnow.co.uk/news/maker-studios-plots-push-into-tv/5084130.article (accessed 25 May 2016).

Fitzsimmons, Caitlin. 2009. 'ITV Prepared to Set £35m Cap on PSB Programming'. *The Guardian*, 29 January. www.theguardian.com/media/2009/jan/29/itv-psb-programming-grade (accessed 25 May 2016).

Frith, Simon. 1993. 'Youth/Music/Television'. In *Sound and Vision: The Music Video Reader*, edited by Simon Frith, Andrew Goodwin and Lawrence Grossberg, 57–72. London: Routledge.

Gannagé-Stewart, Hannah. 2015a. 'Indies Voice Concerns about BBC3 Bid'. *Broadcast*, 27 March. www.broadcastnow.co.uk/news/indies-voice-concerns-about-bbc3-bid/5085805.article (accessed 25 May 2016).

———. 2015b. 'Analysis: BBC3's Digital Future'. *Broadcast*, 2 July. www.broadcastnow.co.uk/news/analysis-bbc3s-digital-future/5090016.article (accessed 25 May 2016).

———. 2015c. 'Damian Kavanagh, BBC3'. *Broadcast*, 26 August. www.broadcastnow.co.uk/features/damian-kavanagh-bbc3/5091982.article (accessed 25 May 2016).

———. 2015d. 'BBC3 Given Greenlight to Move Online'. *Broadcast*, 30 June. www.broadcastnow.co.uk/news/bbc3-given-greenlight-to-move-online/5089935.article (accessed 25 May 2016).

Goodwin, Andrew. 1993. *Dancing in the Distraction Factory: Music Television and Popular Culture*. London: Routledge.

Grainge, Paul, ed. 2011a. *Ephemeral Media: Transitory Screen Culture from Television to YouTube*. London: BFI.

———. 2011b. 'TV Promotion and Broadcast Design: An Interview with Charlie Mawer'. In *Ephemeral Media: Transitory Screen Culture from Television to YouTube*, edited by Paul Grainge, 87–101. Basingstoke: Palgrave Macmillan.

Grainge, Paul and Catherine Johnson (eds) 2015. *Promotional Screen Industries:* Abingdon: Routledge.

Hill, Annette and Ian Calcutt. 2007. 'Vampire Hunters: The Scheduling and Reception of Buffy the Vampire Slayer and Angel in the United Kingdom'. In *Undead TV : Essays on Buffy the Vampire Slayer*, edited by Elana Levine and Lisa Parks, 56–74. Durham, NC: Duke University Press.

Hill, John. 1991. 'Television and Pop: The Case of the 1950s'. In *Popular Television in Britain: Studies in Cultural History*, edited by John Corner, 90–107. London: BFI.

Hobson, Dorothy. 2008. *Channel 4 : The Early Years and the Jeremy Isaacs Legacy*. London: I.B. Tauris.

Holmes, Su. 2005. '"Off-Guard, Unkempt, Unready"?: Deconstructing Contemporary Celebrity in Heat Magazine'. *Continuum* 19(1): 21–38.

Hughes, Penny. 2003. 'C4 Farms out T4 Strand to At It'. *Broadcast*, 1 May. www.broadcastnow.co.uk/c4-farms-out-t4-strand-to-at-it/1116455.article (accessed 27 May 2015).

Johnson, Catherine. 2007. 'Tele-Branding in TVIII: The Network as Brand and the Programme as Brand'. *New Review of Film and Television Studies* 5(1): 5–24.

———. 2012. *Branding Television*. Abingdon: Routledge.

Kanter, Jake. 2011. 'BBC3 Braced for Salford Move and Drama Cuts'. *Broadcast*, 6 October. www.broadcastnow.co.uk/bbc3-braced-for-salford-move-and-drama-cuts/5033008.article (accessed 25 May 2016).

———. 2012. 'Dan Baldwin, Talkback'. *Broadcast*, 17 May. www.broadcastnow.co.uk/features/interviews/the-producer/dan-baldwin-talkback/5041950.article (accessed 27 May 2016).

———. 2013a. 'Zai Bennett, BBC3'. *Broadcast*, 7 February. www.broadcastnow.co.uk/features/interviews/zai-bennett-bbc3/5051533.article (accessed 25 May 2016).

———. 2013b. 'BBC3 to Debut All Comedy on iPlayer'. *Broadcast*, 30 July. www.broadcastnow.co.uk/bbc3-to-debut-all-comedy-on-iplayer/5058777.article (accessed 25 May 2016).

———. 2014a. 'BBC Eyes Online-Only Future for BBC3'. *Broadcast*, 5 March. www.broadcastnow.co.uk/bbc-eyes-online-only-future-for-bbc3/5068278.article (accessed 25 May 2016).

———. 2014b. 'BBC3 to Review its Genre Mix'. *Broadcast*, 13 March. www.broadcastnow.co.uk/bbc3-to-review-its-genre-mix/5068544.article (accessed 25 May 2016).

———. 2014c. 'Cohen: BBC One Drama Budget Boost Aimed at Youngsters'. *Broadcast*, 14 March. www.broadcastnow.co.uk/cohen-BBC1-drama-budget-boost-aimed-at-youngsters/5068638.article (accessed 25 May 2016).

———. 2014d. 'Trust: BBC3 Lags behind Online Rivals'. *Broadcast*, 17 July. www.broadcastnow.co.uk/trust-bbc3-lags-behind-online-rivals/5075316.article (accessed 25 May 2016).

———. 2015a. 'Danny Cohen Defends BBC3 Plans'. *Broadcast*, 11 June. www.broadcastnow.co.uk/news/danny-cohen-defends-bbc3-plans/5089263.article (accessed 25 May 2016).

———. 2015b. 'Unpicking the "Finely Balanced" BBC3 Decision'. *Broadcast*, 30 June. www.broadcastnow.co.uk/news/unpicking-the-finely-balanced-bbc3-decision/5089936.article (accessed 25 May 2016).

Kaplan, E. Ann. 1987. *Rocking Around the Clock: Music, Television, Postmodernism and Consumer Culture*. London: Methuen.

Kavanagh, Damian. 2014. 'Blazing a Trail for New BBC Three'. *About the BBC*, 10 December. www.bbc.co.uk/blogs/aboutthebbc/entries/fa632091-9a8c-304e-a479-e054dc368c47 (accessed 25 May 2016).

———. 2015a. 'BBC Three: Where We Are'. *About the BBC*, 26 June. www.bbc.co.uk/blogs/aboutthebbc/entries/c9a425fb-df7b-454e-b83b-34a139acc4e2 (accessed 25 May 2016).

———. 2015b. 'BBC Three: What We've Been up to'. *About the BBC*, 12 August. www.bbc.co.uk/blogs/aboutthebbc/entries/aff22c20-b7cd-4e1f-ac92-363fdd1037ed (accessed 25 May 2016).
Khalsa, Balihar. 2011. 'E4: A Decade of TV Innovation'. *Broadcast*, 20 January. www.broadcastnow.co.uk/e4-a-decade-of-tv-innovation/5022545.article (accessed 25 May 2016).
Leverette, Marc, Brian L. Ott and Cara Louise Buckley (eds) 2007. *It's Not TV: Watching HBO in the Post-Television Era*. Abingdon: Routledge.
Light, Julie J. 2004. 'Television Channel Identity: The Role of Channels in the Delivery of Public Service Television in Britain, 1996–2002'. PhD thesis, University of Glasgow.
Lury, Karen. 2001. *British Youth Television: Cynicism and Enchantment*. Oxford University Press.
Marx, Nick. 2016. 'Expanding the Brand Race, Gender, and the Post-Politics of Representation on Comedy Central'. *Television & New Media* 17(3): 272–287.
McCabe, Janet. 2005. 'Creating "Quality" Audiences for *ER* on Channel Four'. In *The Contemporary Television Series*, edited by Michael Hammond and Lucy Mazdon, 207–223. Edinburgh University Press.
McLean, Gareth. 2008. 'What Makes the Best Hangover TV?' *The Guardian*, 24 October. www.theguardian.com/culture/garethmcleanblog/2008/oct/23/hangover-tv-t4-e4 (accessed 25 May 2016).
McMahon, Kate. 2008. 'Bennett Lines up ITV2 Celebrity Panel Show'. *Broadcast*, 31 July. www.broadcastnow.co.uk/bennett-lines-up-itv2-celebrity-panel-show/1773651.article (accessed 25 May 2016).
———. 2009. 'Zai Bennett, ITV Digital Channels'. *Broadcast*, 2 September. www.broadcastnow.co.uk/zai-bennett-itv-digital-channels/5005139.article (accessed 25 May 2016).
Moseley, Rachel. 2007. 'Teenagers and Television Drama in Britain 1968–1982'. In *Re-Viewing Television History: Critical Issues in Television Historiography*, edited by Helen Wheatley, 184–197. London: I.B. Tauris.
MPC Advertising. 2013. 'E4 Brand Refresh'. *MPC Advertising*. www.moving-picture.com/work/e4-brand-refresh (accessed 25 May 2016).
Munn, Patrick. 2015. 'ITV2 Agrees Fox Deal for Seth MacFarlane's Animated Series; Takes Exclusive Rights to "Family Guy" & "Bordertown"'. *TVWise*, 23 March. www.tvwise.co.uk/2015/03/itv2-agrees-wide-ranging-fox-deal-for-seth-macfarlanes-animated-series-takes-exclusive-rights-to-family-guy-bordertown (accessed 25 May 2016).
No author. 2002. 'Ratings Analysis – Choice the DCMS Still Has to Make'. *Broadcast*, 10 May. www.broadcastnow.co.uk/ratings-analysis-choice-the-dcms-still-has-to-make/1142606.article (accessed 25 May 2016).
———. 2003a. 'Trade Talk – Summers' Day'. *Broadcast*, 8 May. www.broadcastnow.co.uk/trade-talk-summers-day/1117147.article (accessed 25 May 2016).

———. 2003b. 'Spin-offs to Rule on ITV2'. *Broadcast*, 11 December. www.broadcastnow.co.uk/spin-offs-to-rule-on-itv2/1131356.article (accessed 25 May 2016).

———. 2004a. 'Interview: Stuart Murphy – A Happy First Birthday for BBC3?' *Broadcast*, 16 February. www.broadcastnow.co.uk/interview-stuart-murphy-a-happy-first-birthday-for-bbc3/1088593.article (accessed 25 May 2016).

———. 2004b. 'BBC3 Criticised by Governors'. *Broadcast*, 13 May. www.broadcastnow.co.uk/bbc3-criticised-by-governors/1093111.article (accessed 25 May 2016).

———. 2004c. 'Channel 4 to Take E4 onto Freeview'. *Broadcast*, 16 December. www.broadcastnow.co.uk/channel-4-to-take-e4-onto-freeview/1103197.article (accessed 25 May 2016).

———. 2005. 'BBC3 Defies its Critics'. *Broadcast*, 30 June. www.broadcastnow.co.uk/bbc3-defies-its-critics/1026584.article (accessed 25 May 2016).

———. 2012. 'Digital Strategy – Will C4 Stick to its Digital Guns?' *Broadcast*, 11 January. www.broadcastnow.co.uk/digital-strategy-will-c4-stick-to-its-digital-guns/1134813.article (accessed 25 May 2016).

Ofcom. 2015. 'Public Service Broadcasting in the Internet Age'. http://stakeholders.ofcom.org.uk/consultations/psb-review-3 (accessed 25 May 2016).

O'Neill, Phelim. 2000. 'The Weekend Starts Here'. *The Guardian*, 19 July. www.theguardian.com/media/2000/jul/19/tvandradio.television1 (accessed 25 May 2016).

Parker, Robin. 2009. 'Angela Jain, E4'. *Broadcast*, 24 September. www.broadcastnow.co.uk/angela-jain-e4/5005968.article (accessed 24 May 2016).

———. 2014. 'BBC3 Budget Cut in Half by Move Online'. *Broadcast*, 6 March. www.broadcastnow.co.uk/bbc3-budget-cut-in-half-by-move-online/5068363.article (accessed 25 May 2016).

Plunkett, John. 2010. 'BBC Confirms Plans to Axe 6 Music and Asian Network'. *The Guardian*, 2 March. www.theguardian.com/media/2010/mar/02/bbc-6-music-asian-network (accessed 25 May 2016).

———. 2014a. 'Vine Star Dapper Laughs is Not Laughing Anymore after ITV Turn-Off'. *The Guardian*, 17 November. www.theguardian.com/media/2014/nov/17/dapper-laughs-itv-turn-off-vine-vlogger (accessed 12 November 2015).

———. 2014b. 'Ofcom Report Identifies Emerging "Generation Gap" in Young People's TV Viewing'. *The Guardian*, 15 December. www.theguardian.com/media/2014/dec/15/facebook-tv-radio-ofcom-media (accessed 26 May 2016).

Price, Stephen. 2011. 'Time for ITV2 to Emerge from its Sister's Shadow'. *Broadcast*, 23 June. www.broadcastnow.co.uk/news/analysis/time-for-itv2-to-emerge-from-its-sisters-shadow/5029054.article (accessed 25 May 2016).

———. 2014. 'Has BBC3 Fulfilled its Remit?'. *Broadcast*, 24 April. www.broadcastnow.co.uk/features/has-bbc3-fulfilled-its-remit/5070914.article (accessed 25 May 2016).

———. 2015. 'Ratings Analysis: Youth Audiences 16–34s'. *Broadcast*, 2 July. www.broadcastnow.co.uk/features/ratings-analysis-youth-audiences-16-34s/5089986.article (accessed 25 May 2016).

Reevell, Philip. 2005. 'Ratings – Will Launching on Freeview Change the Fortunes of E4?' *Broadcast*, 6 June. www.broadcastnow.co.uk/ratings-will-launching-on-freeview-change-the-fortunes-of-e4/1025442.article (accessed 25 May 2016).

———. 2008a. 'Behind the News: BBC3 and BBC4 vs E4 and More 4'. *Broadcast*, 11 June. www.broadcastnow.co.uk/behind-the-news-bbc3-and-bbc4-vs-e4-and-more-4/1543875.article (accessed 25 May 2016).

———. 2008b. 'Ratings: Digital Focus: BBC3'. *Broadcast*, 13 August. www.broadcastnow.co.uk/ratings-digital-focus-bbc3/1797654.article (accessed 25 May 2016).

Rigby, Sam. 2014. 'BBC Three to Debut 9 Comedy Pilots on iPlayer for Comedy Feeds'. *Digital Spy*, 20 June. www.digitalspy.com/tv/news/a579131/bbc-three-to-debut-9-comedy-pilots-on-iplayer-for-comedy-feeds (accessed 25 May 2016).

Rixon, Paul. 2006. *American Television on British Screens: A Story of Cultural Interaction*. Basingstoke: Palgrave Macmillan.

Rogers, Jon. 2009. 'E4 Overtakes Five with Younger Viewers'. *Broadcast*, 6 January. www.broadcastnow.co.uk/e4-overtakes-five-with-younger-viewers/1959428.article (accessed 25 May 2016).

Ross, Sharon Marie. 2008. 'Defining Teen Culture: The N Network'. In *Teen Television: Essays on Programming and Fandom*, edited by Sharon Marie Ross and Louisa Ellen Stein, 61–77. Jefferson, NC: McFarland.

Rowley, Alison. 2012. 'Channel 4 Axes T4 Brand'. *Digital Spy*, 12 October. www.digitalspy.co.uk/displayarticle.php?id=430400 (accessed 25 May 2016).

Rushton, Katherine. 2008. 'BBC3 Launches Multi-platform Rebirth'. *Broadcast*, 22 January. www.broadcastnow.co.uk/bbc3-launches-multi-platform-rebirth/525166.article (accessed 25 May 2016).

———. 2009. 'BBC3: Search for the Secret of Youth'. *Broadcast*, 18 June. www.broadcastnow.co.uk/bbc3-search-for-the-secret-of-youth/5002614.article (accessed 25 May 2016).

———. 2010. 'Danny Cohen, BBC3'. *Broadcast*, 25 February. www.broadcastnow.co.uk/features/interviews/danny-cohen-bbc3/5011235.article (accessed 25 May 2016).

Satchell, Luke. 2001. 'Jowell Knocks Back BBC3'. *Broadcast*, 13 September. www.broadcastnow.co.uk/jowell-knocks-back-bbc3/1181813.article (accessed 25 May 2016).

Steel, Emily and Bill Marsh. 2015. 'Millennials and Cutting the Cord'. *New York Times*, 3 October. www.nytimes.com/interactive/2015/10/03/business/media/changing-media-consumption-millenials-cord-cutters.html (accessed 25 May 2016).

Steemers, Jeanette. 2011. 'Little Kids TV: Downloading, Sampling and School TV Experiences of the Digital Era'. In *Television as Digital Media*, edited by James Bennett and Niki Strange, 158–78. Durham, NC: Duke University Press.

Stein, Louisa Ellen. 2015. *Millennial Fandom: Television Audiences in the Transmedia Age*. Iowa City: University of Iowa Press.

Strange, Niki. 2011. 'Multiplatforming Public Service: The BBC's "Bundled Project"'. In *Television as Digital Media*, edited by James Bennett and Niki Strange, 132–157. Durham, NC: Duke University Press.

Sweney, Mark. 2007. 'E4 Refreshes its Branding'. *The Guardian*, 10 December. www.theguardian.com/media/2007/dec/10/channel4.advertising (accessed 25 May 2016).

Sweney, Mark and John Plunkett. 2010. 'BBC: 80% of Licence Fee to Be Spent on Programmes'. *The Guardian*, 2 March. www.theguardian.com/media/2010/mar/02/bbc-cuts-strategic-review (accessed 25 May 2016).

Thompson, Susan. 2007. 'BBC3 Appoints "Teen Guru"'. *Broadcast*, 16 August. www.broadcastnow.co.uk/bbc3-appoints-teen-guru/124136.article (accessed 25 May 2016).

Vanhaeght, Anne-Sofie and Karen Donders. 2015. 'Moving Beyond the Borders of Top-Down Broadcasting: An Analysis of Younger Users' Participation in Public Service Media'. *Television & New Media*, 21 July. doi:10.1177/1527476415595871.

Wee, Valeria. 2008. 'Teen Television and the WB Television Network'. In *Teen Television: Essays on Programming and Fandom*, edited by Sharon Marie Ross and Louisa Ellen Stein, 43–60. Jefferson, NC: Macfarland.

Williams, Raymond. 1974. *Televisions: Technology and Cultural Form*. London: Fontana.

Wiseman, Andreas. 2014. 'Features & Formats at Risk from BBC3 Online Move'. *Broadcast*, 10 December. www.broadcastnow.co.uk/broadcasters/features-and-formats-at-risk-from-bbc3-online-move/5080884.article (accessed 25 May 2016).

Woods, Faye. 2013. 'Teen TV Meets T4: Assimilating *The O.C.* into British Youth Television'. *Critical Studies in Television* 8(1): 14–35.

Younge, Pat. 2014. 'The BBC's Online Gamble'. *Broadcast*, 6 March. www.broadcastnow.co.uk/the-bbcs-online-gamble/5068359.article (accessed 25 May 2016).

PART II

Fiction

CHAPTER 3

British Youth Drama: Space, Place, Authenticity and Intimacy

This chapter explores the representations, imagery and storytelling of British youth drama and sitcom, identifying how this programming bears the influence of US teen TV yet seeks to assert a distinct national identity. Programmes such as *Skins* (E4, 2007–2013), *My Mad Fat Diary* (E4, 2013–2015), *Glue* (E4, 2014), *Being Human* (BBC Three, 2008–2013), *Misfits* (E4, 2009–2014) and *In the Flesh* (BBC Three, 2013–2014) draw on the ensemble melodramas or supernatural mythologies of US teen TV, but refract them through narratives clearly grounded in British space and place, filtered through the overarching tonal sensibility and structure of feeling of British youth television.

British youth drama developed in part by defining itself in opposition to its US counterpart, which, as Chapter 1 noted, has tended towards depictions of aspirational lifestyles and a lingering underlying conservativity. In service of the discourses of 'authenticity' central to British youth television's sense of self and its audience relationships, this drama and comedy displays a pleasure in its frank attitude towards 'explicit' content – swearing, sexuality, drink and drugs. This is combined with a tendency towards emotional bleakness and a fondness for the mundane everyday. Displays of comic excess and bacchanalian freedoms – most clearly articulated in E4's

---

An expanded version of the analysis of *Misfits* is published in *Journal of British Youth Television* Volume 12, Issue 2 as 'Telefantasy Towerblocks: Space, Place and Social Realism Shake-Ups in *Misfits*'.

Skins, *The Inbetweeners* (2008–2010) and *Misfits* – play into British youth drama's affective register. Across British youth television, these bodily excesses – which we might frame as a comic pleasure in disgust – are balanced on a sliding scale with an investment in emotion and intimacy, a drawing close that connects with the melodrama inherent in explorations of the intensity of youth experience (Banks 2004). The centrality of melodrama indicates the commonalities between the US and British forms, a transatlantic cross-fertilisation that, as Rachel Moseley notes, problematizes tendencies to divide up the US as fantasy and UK as realism (2015, 41).

Charting the trends and influences within British youth drama and comedy, I position this programming within British televisual legacies and chart shifts as the form has matured. In outlining and defining the field, I group all scripted programming – including comedy-drama and sitcom – under the term 'British youth drama' for convenience. The three case studies used here are all hour-long dramas with strong comedic strands (with *Skins* and *The Inbetweeners* discussed in the following chapter alongside their US translations on MTV). The first third of the chapter identifies the foundations and tendencies of British youth drama using *Misfits* to highlight some key concerns of this programming. A central text within the first wave of British youth drama, this E4 telefantasy chronicles a group of young offenders on community service who develop superpowers after being struck by lightning in a mysterious fantastical storm. Through *Misfits* I plot British youth drama's tonal address and demonstrate how it simultaneously evokes and distances itself from US teen TV, highlighting an investment in space, place and language. Two case studies from the second wave of British youth drama then explore the form's shift from a tendency towards ambivalent detachment to a stronger engagement with emotion and intimacy. *My Mad Fat Diary* offered the first significant representation of female voice in a field dominated by white male identity, using narration and aesthetics to produce subjectivity and an intimate address in its charting of a teenage girl's struggle to live with mental illness. *In the Flesh* continues *Misfits*' presentation of the telefantasy youth as 'other', following uncanny, medically recovered zombies as they face resistance on their re-integration into a Northern village. I consider the programme's uncanny landscapes and bodies within British youth drama's investment in space and place together with the mundane domestic. Both these programmes' investment in emotion and intimacy demonstrate the second wave of British youth drama's confidence in itself and its variety of storytelling; it is no longer at pains to display its ambivalence and detachment in order to distinguish itself from US teen TV.

SITUATING BRITISH YOUTH DRAMA

Televisual representations of youth are not limited to youth programming; as Sharon Marie Ross and Louisa Ellen Stein note, it is 'important to acknowledge that teens and teen themes are represented on television beyond the televisual spaces distinctly named (or overtly branded) as teen' (2008, 5). Representations of British youth appear across the British schedule, from soap operas to crime dramas to event serials; however, this is often within a framework of youth-as-social-issue, from the 2008 storyline surrounding Whitney's abuse in *EastEnders* (BBC One, 1985–), to the investigation of a videoed gang rape on *Law & Order: UK* (episode 6.5 'Line Up', ITV, 2009–), to the range of single dramas or serials exploring gang crime (*Fallout* (Channel 4, 2008), *Top Boy* (Channel 4, 2011–2013), *Accused* (2.2 'Mo and Sue's Story', BBC One, 2010–2012)). If we remove soap opera from the equation – as Chapter 1 argued, soap offers significant and rich representations of teen and twentysomething characters – these are primarily prestigious event serials: 'authored' texts with a social or political message about the state of the nation, separated from the everyday schedules. This is often television 'about' youth, a gaze from outside, of the social observer. To take up Glen Creeber's dividing of *Shameless* (Channel 4, 2004–2013) from the cultural tourist of 'traditional' social realism, British youth drama offers a view of life from within (2009, 433).

Creeber's arguments around social realism are useful for identifying British youth drama's televisual lineage, helping to parse its difference from US teen TV. As this book demonstrates, there are influences and commonalities across the two national forms; however, they grow from different televisual foundations (although arguably nuances are involved). In common with much US network television, teen TV tends to normalise white (upper) middle-class lifestyles and values (Gray 2008, 158–160), favouring a glossy aesthetic and aspirational lifestyle narratives, albeit with a strong spine of emotional realism. Matt Hills (2004), Valerie Wee (2008) and Ross and Stein (2008) have noted US teen TV's connections to discourses of 'quality television'.[1] The latter identifies teen TV's 'combination of self-referentiality, prolonged seriality, and genre mixing' as features shared with quality television (2008, 10). These elements are found in much of British youth drama as it draws significantly from US teen TV;

however, this programming sits clearly within British televisual traditions of (social) realism (Caughie 2000; Cooke 2003). Youth drama offers itself as a realist alternative to the imported US teen TV representations that had previously dominated British youth television spaces. In doing so, it continues ideologies surrounding British traditions of realist-filmmaking, where the 'authentic, indigenous culture of "ordinary people"' is pitted against an Americanised culture of 'glamour, spectacle, commercialism and more entertainment' (Ashby and Higson 2000, 9). Whilst these latter elements are nearly all part of British youth television – with entertainment programming forming a central spine of digital youth channels – British youth drama set out to assert its difference as an indigenous, 'authentic' form compared to the glamorous, aspirational US form.

For example, the national specificity of *Misfits* was a central point in industrial and press discourse, which sought to highlight both the universality and localness (Dunleavy 2009) of its take on a genre familiar from US teen TV. Channel 4 executives described the programme as 'a very British, very funny take on superheroes' and 'a refreshingly honest take on British teenage life' (Parker 2008), whilst its creator Howard Overman explained how he sought to create something 'uniquely British' (Donaghy 2009). Overman cited the domestic comedy and national specificity of *Shaun of the Dead* (2004) as an influence in his 'very British take on the superhero genre' (Nissim 2009). This discourse sought to distinguish *Misfits* from BBC Two's current US import *Heroes* (NBC, 2006–2010), which also featured ordinary people discovering they had superhuman powers. We see here how discourses of national distinction are used to position this new blossoming of original British youth drama (with *Skins*, *The Inbetweeners* and *Being Human* appearing across a span of three years).[2] Teen TV forms the unspoken 'other' within the *Misfits* promotional discourse, with 'Britishness' and 'refreshingly honest' being used as markers of authenticity. These play into the E4 channel brand and allude to *Misfits'* difference from the glossy aspirational tendencies of E4's US imports (*The O.C.* (Fox, 2003–2007), *One Tree Hill* (WB/CW, 2003–2012) and *90210* (CW, 2008–2013). Whilst British youth television still owes a significant debt to teen TV, these discursive constructions of 'authenticity' and realism (to read 'honesty' in a storytelling sense) operate to assert national televisual distinction.

British youth drama can be situated loosely within televisual traditions of social realism, particularly recent shifts identified in cinema (Hill 2000; Monk 2000) and television. Most notably, the increased integration of melodrama into British soap opera's social realism (Geraghty 2006) and the storytelling and aesthetic shifts employed by two Paul Abbot series, *Clocking Off* (BBC One, 2000–2003) and *Shameless* (Cooke 2005; Creeber 2009). In particular, we can align British youth drama with the 'heightened realism' or 'social surrealism' that Creeber charts in contemporary film and television (2009, 429). *Shameless*' depiction of its riotously dysfunctional working-class community on a 'sink' estate serves as a prime example of this rendering of social realist stories through dynamic aesthetics and a sense of the comic and melodramatic surreal. Creeber suggests that the programme re-interpreted the working class of traditional social realism, 'explicitly rejecting the tendency to define "the social" purely in terms of universal societal ideals' and instead presenting a subjective experience (2009, 436). *Shameless*' view from within, together with its vibrant stylised aesthetic and fantasy elements (2009, 436), runs throughout British youth drama. This programming displays a similar comic impulse, moral ambiguity and – most prominently in the first wave – bacchanalian pursuit of pleasure (*The Inbetweeners* derives its comedy in part from its teen protagonists' failure in their quest for said pleasure). *Misfits* shares *Shameless*' blending of its 'othered' underclass representations with surreal comedic excess.

In contrast with state-of-the-nation 'event' serials and single dramas such as *Top Boy, Fallout* and *Run* (Channel 4, 2013) – which share its housing estate setting and ethnically diverse cast – *Misfits* does not seek to explicitly engage with cultural concerns surrounding British youth. Creator Howard Overman noted the programme's 'social-inclusion subtext', but argued that he resisted assigning a 'message' to the drama (Donaghy 2009). The discourse surrounding E4's commissioning of *Misfits* played down its social angle, seeking to highlight the programme's new voices, in order to build on the success of *Skins* and *The Inbetweeners* and assert E4 as a home for original content. British youth drama often engages with social issues – the programmes discussed in this chapter touch on social exclusion, mental illness and immigration – but this is primarily in service of its investment in a skewed vision of teenage and twentysomething life. Where the spectacle of youth is a cause of concern in youth-as-issue narratives, here the spectacle of youth is the source of pleasure. Favouring comedy drama with strong strands of melodrama, British youth drama's tonal address is built on a comic bluntness and pleasure in excess, which plays off a desire for 'authenticity', whether this be through forms of speech, a focus on mundanity or humiliation, the desire for rebellion or an intensity of emotion. The latter utilises the 'emotionally saturated expressions' (Geraghty 2006, 228) of melodrama, reflecting the insecurity of adolescence and twentysomething life as, to borrow Geraghty's description of the soap community, 'a world that is darker and more precarious than before' (ibid.).

Early Steps

As British youth drama only fully blossomed in the 2000s, the form is not old enough to offer the multiple cycles of programming found in US teen TV; however, two distinct waves can be identified since the debut of *Skins* catalysed the form in 2007.[3] Prior to this, programming for British youth from the 1950 to the 1990s was largely limited to entertainment programming (Lury 2001; Moseley 2007), with the 1990s boom in US teen TV imported to fill gaps in fiction programming. However, fragments can be identified across the 1980s and 1990s, which laid the groundwork for the boom in programming facilitated by the maturation of digital youth channels in the 2000s.

In the 1980s, the BBC Two 6pm slot was home to youth-focused programming including Scottish drama *Maggie* (BBC Two, 1981–1982) and *Grange Hill* (BBC One, 1978–2008) spin-off *Tucker's Luck* (BBC Two, 1983–1985); the liminal status of the 6pm slot was befitting of the post-16 world of these dramas, as it distinguished them from the children's schedule. Alongside *Maggie,* Rachel Moseley highlights the largely forgotten Phil Redmond drama *Going Out* (ITV, 1981), which was hidden away in ITV's night-time schedules due to industry reorganisation and ITV's lack of a comparative 'youth' scheduling space (2007, 195). All three dramas dealt with teenagers working out their place in the world during the bleak years of Thatcherism, choosing whether to stay in education or seek elusive employment in a landscape of limited opportunities. Moseley suggests that British youth drama in this period illustrated the social anxiety surrounding teenagers as a result of increased unemployment and perceived anti-social behaviour (2007, 190), concerns which echo through British youth drama up to the present day.

Channel 4 had a strong grasp of the youth audience throughout the 1980s and 1990s, with music and entertainment programming dominating its provision (Lury 2001). Isolated fragments of scripted programming did appear in its evening schedules across the 1990s, primarily twentysomething ensemble sitcoms. These offered quirky combinations of everyday life and the surreal distinct from the social realism of the earlier post-16 dramas. From music industry satires *A Young Person's Guide to Becoming a Rock Star* (Channel 4, 1998) and *Boyz Unlimited* (Channel 4, 1999) to slacker flat-share *Spaced* (Channel 4, 1999–2001), these built inventive comedy from their blending of the mundane lives of their protagonists with edges of fantasy. The first real murmurings of British youth drama's coalescing form and aesthetic came with comedy dramas *As If* (Channel 4, 2001–2004) and *Sugar Rush* (Channel 4, 2005–2006). These documented their teenage protagonists' lives through inventive visual styles, bright colour palates and fast-paced editing. *As If*'s investment in youth point of view and occasional single-character episodic focus was inherited by *Skins* as a central narrative device. With the 10pm E4 slot not yet developed as a British youth drama space, *Sugar Rush*'s exploration of the romantic and sexual awakening of a teenage lesbian saw it confined to the edges of Channel 4's evening schedule. In contrast, the more conventional relationship-driven ensemble drama of *As If* fit comfortably within a Sunday lunchtime T4 slot on Channel 4 and an early evening E4 slot.

The liminal 6–7pm slot on Channel 4 became home to weekday soap opera *Hollyoaks* (Channel 4, 1995–), created by Phil Redmond. As the architect of the channel's first soap *Brookside* (Channel 4, 1982–2003), BBC One children's drama *Grange Hill* and *Going Out*, Redmond is a key presence in the history of British youth television (Moseley 2015, 40). *Hollyoaks* serves as a repository for much of Channel 4's public service address to youth audiences and after the cancellation of *Brookside* became the channel's flagship soap, anchoring the evening schedule. Set in the upscale city of Chester, close to Liverpool, the programme progressively expanded its focus from its initial ensemble of 16 year olds to include a local university and the wider community. Its bright, dynamic aesthetic, young attractive cast and increasing use of score and non-diegetic popular music (absent from other British soap operas) were arguably influenced by Australian imported soap operas *Neighbours* (Seven/Ten, 1985–) and *Home and Away* (Seven, 1987–). Airing directly after the BBC One and ITV children's television strands, these soaps' sunny locations, attractive teenage characters and white middle-class suburban settings offered an aspirational contrast with British soap opera's largely urban communities together with their combination of social realism and comedy. These formed part of larger swathe of imported Australian drama (Douglas and McWilliam 2004) that aired in children's television and the BBC Two

6pm youth slot, including teen drama *Heartbreak High* (Ten/ABC TV, 1994–1999).

Outside of US and Australian imports, high school or college narratives were a relative rarity in British schedules throughout the 1990s and early 2000s. Where high school was central to US teen TV storytelling, British school stories were largely confined to the younger demographics of children's television drama. The community focus of British soap opera did not allow it to follow its prominent teenage characters to their schools like the Australian soaps did. However, the British boom catalysed by the success of *Skins* and *The Inbetweeners* has produced a range of dramas and comedies focused around school life and beyond.

Plotting the Field

Skins and *The Inbetweeners* depicted groups of 16–18 year olds at school-based 'sixth forms' or further-education colleges, covering the space between compulsory education and university in the UK. This mirrored US teen TV's tendency to introduce protagonists in their sophomore and junior years of high school, from *Dawson's Creek* (WB, 1998–2003) to *Veronica Mars* (UPN/CW, 2004–2007) to *Gossip Girl* (CW 2007–2011). The introduction of protagonists around the age of 16 allows programmes to follow a period in which identities begin to coalesce and adulthood beckons. *Skins* renewed its cast every two years as each cohort graduated and *The Inbetweeners* concluded after three series when its protagonists finished school, allowing their casts to remain eternal adolescents. The success of *The Inbetweeners* highlights the significant role of sitcom in British youth television (whereas US teen TV is dominated by the hour-long melodrama), which is partially the result of BBC Three's remit-assigned role to develop new comic talent. A string of BBC Three sitcoms – including *Coming of Age* (2007–2011), *Bad Education* (2012–) and *Some Girls* (2012–2014) – followed *The Inbetweeners*' school setting, together with its fondness for profane and crude comedy. These were joined by wealth of ensemble comedies focusing on the delayed adolescence and stumbling maturation of early twentysomethings, including the long-running *Two Pints of Larger and a Packet of Crisps* (BBC Three, 2001–2011), *Grownups* (BBC Three, 2006–2009) and *Lunch Monkeys* (BBC Three, 2008–2011). Stories of young couples cut their rom-com sweetness with an earthy coarseness in long-distance love story *Gavin & Stacey* (BBC Three, 2007–2010) and the minimalist mundanity of *Him & Her* (BBC Three, 2010–).

Alongside sitcom, the other key trend in British youth drama blends melodrama and telefantasy (Johnson 2005), here influenced by the wealth of US telefantasy from *Buffy the Vampire Slayer* (WB/UPN, 1997–2003), to *Smallville* (WB, 2001–2011), to *The Vampire Diaries* (CW, 2009–). Satellite channel Sky One, which imported a range of US telefantasy programming including *The X-Files* (FOX, 1993–2002) and *Buffy*, sought to targeted *Buffy*'s youth and crossover cult audience in its British supernatural boarding-school drama *Hex* (2004–2005). Although it was a relative failure, *Hex* was a forerunner for the late 2000s strand of British youth telefantasy, that includes twentysomething flatshare comedy dramas *Being Human* and *Switch* (ITV2, 2012) (which also share DNA with the BBC Three twentysomething sitcoms). The success of *Being Human*'s mismatched gothic trio of ghost, vampire and werewolf helped solidify British youth television as a form. Together with *Skins, The Inbetweeners* and E4's first venture into telefantasy in *Misfits*, it coalesced the first wave of British youth drama.

As British youth drama has developed since the mid-2000s, two waves of programming can be identified, which are distinct from the ongoing ripple of sitcoms of the late 2000s and early 2010s (which produced few impactful texts outside of *The Inbetweeners, Him & Her* and *Some Girls*). This first wave established the dynamics, tone and tastes of the field, solidifying channel brands and verifying the audience for original British drama following the dominance of imported US teen TV. The second wave is formed of programmes commissioned after this first set of hits, most notably *The Fades, In the Flesh, My Mad Fat Diary, Fresh Meat* (Channel 4, 2011–2016), *Youngers* (E4 2013–2014) and *Glue*. Secure in their audience and national identity, this second wave had the confidence to develop form, tone and storytelling in different directions. *Misfits* offers an illustration of some of the key concerns of British youth drama: its push-and-pull relationship with US teen TV, the construction of national distinction through space, place and language, as well as its investment in the everyday and mundane. The programme also demonstrates the tonal address of the first wave, which invests strongly in a detached ambivalence in order to assert its distinction from the US form.

MISFITS: BRITISH YOUTH DRAMA'S FIRST WAVE

Misfits' high concept 'ASBO superheroes' (Donaghy 2009), its urban setting and ethnically diverse ensemble demonstrated E4's intent to diversify the normalised middle-class identity offered by its US imports, *Skins* and

The Inbetweeners, a process later continued with *Youngers* and *Chewing Gum* (2015–). *Misfits*' creator Howard Overman originally pitched the group as having Saturday jobs at a department store, which E4 rejected as making the characters 'middle class' (Simpson 2010). Overman reworked his protagonists as 'the least likely, most unheroic group I could find' (Donaghy 2009), drawing on the figures of the chav, hoodie and Scottish Ned which populated British media and political discourse in the late 2000s. Here press and politicians painted images of uncontrolled and disrespectful 'feral' underclass youth, constructed as objects of concern and fear – representations that later formed the centerpiece of the public discourse swirling around the English riots in the summer of 2011. Youth served as symptoms of 'broken Britain', a Conservative Party catchphrase that could 'fit different definitions depending on what the major worry of the hour is – youth crime, teenage pregnancy or anti-social behaviour' (Gentleman 2010). In re-imagining his protagonists outside a middle-class milieu, Overman drew on televisual legacies and landscapes of working-class struggle. Yet the stronger representational pull comes from this discourse of British working-class and 'underclass' youth as threat; perhaps troublingly, to make *Misfits*' teen superheroes working class, they must be positioned as *anti*-heroes.

Misfits' ethnically diverse characters come from various backgrounds and locations – from high-rise towers to semi-detached houses – across the sprawling estate (filmed in Thamesmead in south-east London). Their status as young offenders positions them as rule-breaking delinquents, impulsive and back-chatting, lacking respect and self-control. Yet despite their criminal records, hard partying and disrespect of authority, these are not the fearsome youth of the tabloids or recent British cinema (*Kidulthood* (2006), *Harry Brown* (2009) and *Ill Manors* (2012)). Their crimes are petty (theft, drug possession, drink driving and property damage) and their superpowers ultimately unearth a fundamental decency. Come season two, the faceless hoodie figure so demonised by media panics is taken up and rewritten as a superhero figure.

This conflation of adolescent alienation and the fantastical 'other' has a strong legacy in the genre hybridity of US teen TV, from *Buffy the Vampire Slayer* and *Smallville* to *The Vampire Diaries* and *Teen Wolf* (MTV, 2011–). Rachel Moseley points out that many teen dramas 'deal with questions of difference, otherness, increased power and the impact of these on personal and community relationships', which are often explored through the motif of supernatural power, giving 'the sense that to be a teenager is to be not quite human' (2001, 43). E4 had a proven audience for teen telefantasy in its long-running US import *Smallville*, a teen TV take on the origins of Superman. *Smallville*'s small-town middle-America setting and morally virtuous hero allowed *Misfits* to assert its British identity through its difference from its US predecessor. Clark Kent's rural roots and later his big-city metropolis offered a starkly different visual palate from the grey London concrete of *Misfits*. He also offered a prime example of the 'alienated, emotional and sympathetic [protagonists], attempting to make the right choices as they struggled towards adulthood' prevalent on *Smallville*'s home network WB (Ross and Stein 2008, 19). British youth drama's first wave sought to distinguish itself from US teen TV by constructing its characters almost in opposition to this WB model: as cynical, morally ambiguous and selfish. Superman's altruistic persona and elaborate mythology sits at odds with these homegrown superheroes' lack of social engagement, their carelessness and tendency towards self-preservation. Rebecca Feasey suggests that teen TV works as an educational tool, offering 'resourceful and respectful adolescents to act as role models for future generations of young people' (2008, 47). In contrast, the heroic measures of the *Misfits* gang are often achieved by accident or through self-interest rather than altruism. People get accidentally killed along the way, including – in what becomes a running joke – a range of probation workers. This offers a murkier morality than US teen TV's superpowered protagonists. Chapter 4 touches on the skewed morality of British youth television in conflict with the norms of US teen TV in its discussion of the reception of *Skins US* (MTV1, 2011).

Despite their disparities, connections *can* be made between *Misfits* and teen TV telefantasy. The meteor storm that brings Clark Kent to earth as a child and whose rocks are responsible for the town's strange phenomena is mirrored in the freak electrical storm that bestows superpowers on the *Misfits* gang and other residents of the estate. Overman has highlighted the influence of *Buffy the Vampire Slayer* (Donaghy 2009), and its literalising of the high school as hell metaphor is echoed in the connection of the gang's powers to their personalities and fears. Like the shy girl who literally fades from view in *Buffy*'s 'Out of Mind, Out of Sight', *Misfits*' introverted loner Simon feels ignored, so his power of invisibility literalises this anxiety (although it also works to compound his slightly creepy voyeuristic tendencies). Kelly is concerned about what others think about her – partially the result of her 'chav' identity,[4] a label that she resists due to its underclass connotations in British culture – so she gains the ability to read other's thoughts; yet as Buffy discovered in 'Earshot', this power also exposes her to how others view her. Thus, British youth drama's connections with US teen TV offer a complex interweaving – a push and pull – rather than a purely oppositional relationship.

Space, Place and Specificity

Alongside these links with US teen TV, we can place British youth telefantasy within British children's television's traditions of the gothic and telefantasy (Peirse 2010; Wheatley 2012). Alison Peirse and Helen Wheatley both identify a focus on British landscapes and imagery, combined with an interest in the domestic and everyday, with particularly British suburban and urban spaces rendered uncanny (2010; 2012). Wheatley suggests a group of 1970s ITV gothic children's dramas made and set in Bristol use their distinct regionality to enhance their 'ordinariness' (2012); this remains a central concern of British youth drama's pleasure in mundanity and strong sense of place. Cups of tea, a Curly-Wurly chocolate bar, the high street catalogue shop Argos, pints at the pub, concrete tower blocks and semi-detached suburbia are the order of the day. Humour is drawn from the everyday, yet the familiar can also become unknown.

British youth drama's strong sense of place, particularly a regional, domestic and ordinary space, resonates with the 'local London' identified by Charlotte Brunsdon. This is a working-class, realist London (Brunsdon 2007, 76), 'a London that is lived', a space of the 'the ordinary and the quotidian, the unspectacular', of small narratives and everyday life (2007, 57). Utilising the production cultures of London and the south-west – although rarely the east or north, outside of the Salford-produced *In the Flesh* – British youth drama asserts its locational particularity. This includes the south-east London Thamesmead estate of *Misfits*, *Switch*'s coven of twentysomething witches living in the trendy London neighbourhood of Camden, and the versatile Bristol, home to the surreal everyday of *Skins* and rendered gothic in the first two seasons of *Being Human*. This rooting of British youth drama in regionality often serves to signify an ordinariness which grounds both elements of telefantasy and the blend of heightened melodrama and touches of the surreal found in *Skins*. The mundane urban spaces, the everyday 'local London' where the protagonists of *Misfits* are forced to engage in menial tasks, become the backdrop for the strange and fantastical. Here we see the influence of *Shaun of the Dead* (2004), which Charlotte Brunsdon suggests 'must establish its absolutely undistinctive local … before this can be transformed by the appearance of the zombies' (2007, 58).

Like *Shaun of the Dead* and fellow social-realist tower block fantasy *Attack the Block* (2011), *Misfits* offers a low-key spectacle, rooted in the unstable, transforming bodies of youth and depicted through minimum special effects. This is the result of low budgets, yet it also maintains the verisimilitude of these social realist spaces. These could not take much rupture without breaking free from their cultural connotations and genre conventions – the tie to 'the real' that is so important for British youth drama's sense of self. Catherine Johnson suggests that representing the fantastic 'demands the negotiation of a dialectical position, simultaneously depending upon and disrupting the generic and socio-cultural expectations at work in the text' (2005, 148). *Misfits* depends on its British urban landscapes familiar from film and television's social realist narratives of the underclass; these assert its 'authenticity'. However, it disrupts these signifiers of the 'real' – the brutalism of housing estates, the grey of the concrete and the sky – by making them strange. The overcast, rainy British skies are here made spectacular by the electric storm that bestows the gang's powers, whilst the domestic, social realist world of the estate is rendered uncanny.

Helen Wheatley identifies the uncanny as 'located in the moments … in which the familiar traditions and conventions of television are made strange' (2006, 7–8) *Misfits* utilises spaces that signify alienation and oppression throughout British culture, where the concrete walkways, deserted overlooked squares and cramped flats of council estates offer an undertow of threat. Here, tower blocks form a 'striking visual symbol' for alienation, a persistent social and economic inequity (Burke 2007, 178). Yet *Misfits'* cinematography and production design construct the sprawling Thamesmead estate as a stylised social realist space, a familiar yet unfamiliar world. They exploit concrete's 'semiotic liquidity' (Burke 2007, 179) to render Thamesmead's 1960s Brutalist architecture as both futuristic and derelict – a social realist space rendered skewed and uncanny to match our protagonists' shifting bodies and scrambled sense of self. Gone is the conventional oppressive soundscape of housing estates across film and television, with their car alarms, screaming babies and thumping bass leaking from poorly insulated flats. Instead, the *Misfits* estate is often eerily empty; walkways, streets and the community centre itself show little evidence of a community. The estate is presented as an open space of stark bleak beauty; centred on the expanse of the Southmere lake, this is a landscape full of unexpected angles and textures where collections of establishing shots set concrete against expanses of water and sky (Figure 3.1). Thus *Misfits* reworks the landscapes of British social realism as uncanny spaces to serve

Fig. 3.1 *Misfits*' establishing shots set concrete against expanses of water and sky

its telefantasy of transfigured youth bodies and identities. Yet these spaces rich with televisual resonance of realism also serve to ground its fantastical narratives in a strong sense of regional space that serve to assert its British 'authenticity'.

Speech and Authenticity

One of the devices through which British youth television marks its difference from US teen TV and connotes its 'authenticity' is through its language. Verbal dexterity is a defining feature of US teen TV, with Feasey suggesting its 'performers converse in an intelligent, knowing and emotional manner' (2008, 47). Yet the protagonists of British youth drama often lack the loquaciousness and emotional intelligence demonstrated by the protagonists of programmes like *The O.C.*, *Veronica Mars* and *Gilmore Girls* (WB/CW, 2000–2007). Instead, Britishness is more often marked by bluntness, a creative use of profanity or a fondness for scatological or sexual stories. Charlotte Brunsdon suggests that 'local London' guarantees authenticity through a textual strategy where 'London vernacular speech, particularly of male characters, is dominated by obscenity. The sound of everyday London life is "Fucking this and fucking that"' (2007, 83). From the almost lyrical crudity of the tales told by Nathan (and later

Rudy) to the comically blunt Kelly and the way her Midlands accent rolls the word 'wanker' around her mouth, *Misfits*' 'authenticity' is communicated through a facility with bad language. When a conservative Christian indoctrinates local youth into her evangelical cult through mind control – 'you don't have to behave like this, you can be so much better' – the 'turned' *Misfits* are marked by their clipped precise neat language that matches their conservative, buttoned-up physical transformations (episode 1.6).

The verbal style of British youth television is partially the result of freedoms accorded by scheduling. *The Inbetweeners, Misfits* and *My Mad Fat Diary* were assigned a 10pm slot on E4 and were not repeated before the 9pm watershed, giving them greater scope for sexual content and language.[5] The comical foul mouth of British youth drama is far from the 'superlative emotional sensitivity and a deep desire to do good in the world' that Miranda Banks finds in US teen male melodramas, which she notes are 'arguably characteristics as foreign to the typical teenage boy as are their superhuman powers' (2004, 17). British youth drama grounds itself in this 'typical' boy, who is centralised in its privileging of male point of view (and the dominance of white male writers), compared to US teen TV's strong variety of female leads and voices. I discuss language and masculinity further in the following chapter and now move on to consider a text that sought to counter this privileging of male point of view – a programme that drew on this language of blunt comedy and lyrical crudity to explore female voice and subjectivity.

My Mad Fat Diary: Emotional Saturation and Unruly Female Subjectivity

British youth television's first wave, illustrated here by *Misfits*, simultaneously held its audience at a distance and pulled them into a tight emotional embrace, in the ambivalent oscillation central to British youth television. This tendency sought to define the programming in opposition to the invested, melodrama-led storytelling common to US teen TV, despite or perhaps because of the two forms' commonalities. I now move on to explore in depth how the second wave eased this detachment and investment in excess as it became more secure in its own identity, a confidence displayed in intimate, emotion-led storytelling. At the same time, it maintained British youth drama's distinctive blending of televisual traditions of realism with the pleasurable excesses of melodrama and comedy. *My Mad Fat Diary* and *In the Flesh* serve as case studies of some of the tendencies and shifts occurring as British youth drama matured in this second wave. These programmes allow me to explore the structure of feeling (R. Williams 1961) of British youth drama, displaying the emotion and intimacy that I sense has taken a step to the foreground in the second wave. Both maintain features established in the first wave – *Skins'* subjectivity and intertwining of comedy and melodrama, *Being Human* and *Misfits'* teen telefantasy and sense of place – yet shift to a softer key with less investment in self-conscious excess or aspirational debauchery. Both *My Mad Fat Diary* and *In the Flesh* offer a sharing of self and a physical and emotional closeness, built through an intimate connection with their solo protagonists in contrast to the ensembles that had previously dominated the form. In her study of millennial television and fandom, Louisa Ellen Stein finds a 'celebration of high emotion', or 'feels' in these spaces – particularly the social media platform Tumblr – which she suggests signify a cultural shift (2015, 8), one which builds an intimate collective around public celebration of emotion previously considered private (2015, 156). For Stein, this fandom-based 'millennial feels culture combines an aesthetics of intimate emotion … with an aesthetics of high performativity, calling attention to mediation' (2015, 158). The second wave's embrace of emotion and melodrama ties to this millennial freedom with 'feels' (with both *My Mad Fat Diary* and *In the Flesh* having significant Tumblr-based fandoms) that pushes against the ambivalent address of British youth television. Yet, at the same time, they display playful performativity in their heightened aesthetics and strong comic voice, blending with melodrama, comedy and realism to retain the distinctiveness of British youth television.

My Mad Fat Diary follows 16-year-old Rae Earl as she begins her recovery from a breakdown and suicide attempt. She leaves the safe space of a psychiatric hospital and returns to her mundane life with her single mother, tentatively rebuilding her relationship with childhood best friend Chloe whilst concealing her mental health issues from her new friends. The programme is adapted from Rae Earl's bestselling memoir, which chronicled the everyday lusts and boredoms of her teenage life in 1989. These were confided in the pages of her teenage diary, where they intertwined with her slide into mental illness and hospitalisation for anxiety and an eating disorder. The adaptation privileged emotion and affect over a translation of the book's storyline, building a new fictional story from the skeleton of Earl's framing diary, her health issues and hospitalisation, and shifted the narrative to 1996. Yet the adaptation retained her distinctive narrational tone, comic turn of phrase and hormonal obsessions.[6]

British youth television exists in a perpetual present, so *My Mad Fat Diary* served as an unexpected period drama. By updating Earl's memoir to 1996, the programme caught the 1990s revival gaining pace in 2010s pop culture, driven by fashion trends and a resurgence in electronic dance music, whilst also evoking nostalgia in the older edges of E4's target demographic. In positioning Rae as a music connoisseur clad in a Stone Roses t-shirt, the programme drew on the mid-1990s peak of Britpop and British indie music's cultural dominance in order to embed music into its storytelling, serving as the melos to its melodrama.

My Mad Fat Diary's centralising of a solo female protagonist serves as a contrast to the white male-dominated ensembles of British youth television's first wave. Some female characters did break through the teenage boy blockade to resonate with audiences – *Skins*' Emily and Naomi (Hunn 2012), *Misfits*' Kelli and to a lesser degree Alisha – but Rae is E4's first solo female protagonist. The programme is fundamentally structured around a singular female point of view and offers an intimate connection with the mind of a teenage girl. Weaving emotion into the fabric of its storytelling in order to tie its audience tightly to Rae's perspective, it offers an intimate address constructed through an aesthetic saturated with affect. Affect here 'functions as a collective energy that initiates and sustains gatherings of people or ideas' (Garde-Hansen and Gorton 2013, 31), one that binds the viewer to Rae's intimate emotional space through the tactile closeness of the physical and aural expression of her interiority and emotions. Rae's diary entries form the programme's voiceover, its scribbles and notes are written across the screen; we lapse into her fantasies of sexual dominance and fragments of her childhood memory flit amongst present events. The programme has a strong focus on physicality and touch, built on Rae's disgust over her 'mad, fat' body. She tearfully describes life outside the psychiatric unit as 'smashing up all your senses' and her skin as feeling itchy with embarrassment after strangers see her in a bikini; she tells her diary that happiness is 'fizzy like cherry cola and tingles like kisses on my neck'. Her love interest Finn traces his finger over her thigh in secret communications and the diary scribbles that are layered onto the screen are tactile and amateur, leaving physical traces of her thoughts.

The 'emotional saturation' of melodrama is a central element of *My Mad Fat Diary*'s exploration of Rae's perspective. This plays into the structure of feeling prominent in the second wave of British youth drama, offering an emotion-led experience that is 'a pivotal means by which the individual and the cultural are seamlessly interwoven and simultaneously produced' (Pribram 2011, 41). In foregrounding touch, physicality and the intimate address of female voice, the programme interweaves this structure of feeling with British youth television's public service commitment, producing an affective experience of adolescence and mental illness.

Femininity and Unruliness

My Mad Fat Diary was not the first depiction of teenage mental illness on E4, as *Skins* explored teenage mental illness at multiple points across its run, using its single-character episodic focus to evoke female interiority. Cassie's delicate spaciness is intertwined with her eating disorder in seasons one and two, whilst season four charts Effie's descent from blank nihilism to mental breakdown and season six suggests instability bubbles under Frankie's suddenly reckless behaviour. However, Rae is distinct from the girls of *Skins* both in her ongoing narrative centrality and her size. *My Mad Fat Diary* disrupts its predecessor's tying of mental illness to a delicate white femininity whose emotional fragility often went hand in hand with a self-destructive hyper-sexuality.

The storytelling and aesthetic of *My Mad Fat Diary* structures an intense audience alignment with a protagonist who has potential to be 'othered' due to her size and mental illness. Rae is large and loud; clad in baggy jeans and t-shirts, she jokes with the boys, yet struggles with a desire for normative femininity, envious of her friend Chloe's ease at being 'a girl', yet also contemptuous of her. When Rae tries to perform her version of normative femininity in episode 1.3 – wear a skirt, be quiet, don't be funny, drink Lambrini – the labour of suppressing her true self sees her simmer with frustration, compounded by suffering a 'mega period'. Amidst sharp quick cuts of the mouths and faces of the raucous teenage boys surrounding her in the cafe, the camera tracks in on a canted angle of her silent bored face as she slowly drops her head back in pain and frustration before snapping out of her daze to challenge Chop for calling her by her masculine nickname 'Raemundo'.

With her robust physicality and blunt verbosity, Rae combines vulnerability with comic wit, serving as both melodramatic heroine and unruly woman. In her discussion of Sue Ellen from prime-time US soap opera *Dallas* (CBS, 1978–1991), Ien Ang suggests that a tormented personality and frustrating narrative situation are at the core of the melodramatic heroine (2008, 237). Behind its pose of edgy, nihilistic cool, the foundation of *Skins* is melodrama and it often uses self-destructive femininity to create narrative stakes. Effie serves as its defining melodramatic heroine, her blank inscrutability combining with her sex appeal to render her as the broken bird in need of (male) rescue. Rae offers a different iteration of the melodramatic heroine: she is tormented by her psyche and frustrates her therapist Kessler – and the audience – through her resistance to verbalising her emotional fragility and her self-destructive actions caused by her body issues. Yet her force of will and sharp wit disrupt the model of delicate, sexual, teenage melodramatic heroines built by *Skins*.

Rae is rendered as melodramatic heroine through her emotional sensitivity, paralysing anxiety, self-disgust and self-destructive behaviour, yet her loud blunt nature and comic wit also position her as an unruly woman. Kathleen Rowe Karlyn argues that the unruly woman unsettles social hierarchies, due to being 'too fat, too funny, too noisy, too old, too rebellious' (1995, 19). Rae exhibits unruly physicality – 'Her body is excessive or fat, suggesting her unwillingness or inability to control her physical appetites' (1995, 31) – and demonstrates verbal unruliness: 'Her speech is excessive in quantity, content, or tone' (1995, 31). Her unfurling overflowing monologues – shared occasionally with girlfriends, but primarily with her diary and the audience – often navigate the intensities of her sexual desires, the listing of lusts and the descriptions of her fantasies. The space of the diary and the fantasies of sexual dominance she conjures within its pages fulfil the role Ien Ang's assigns to melodrama's fantasy; providing a safe space 'of excess in the interstices of ordered social life where one has to keep oneself strategically under control' (2008, 243).

Rae's narration contributes to *My Mad Fat Diary*'s centralising of physicality and affect through its descriptions of the physical enactments of her lust: Archie is described as 'Gushington central' and she wants to sink her teeth into Finn's 'delicious arse'. With Rae's unruly desire compounded by the camera's lingering gaze or the layering of the image with her lustful annotations, the boys of *My Mad Fat Diary* are read as objects. Rae's verbalising of hormonal lust is little heard in televisual teenage *girls*, whose sexual desires are more often bound by social convention, presenting desire-as-romance. Yet an articulation of sexual appetite is central to many British televisual teen *boys*, where a swaggering detailing of desire is central to (often false) assertions of masculinity; thus, Rae's unruliness upsets gendered standards. Her key unruly power is her verbal articulacy and comedic vibrancy – 'She makes jokes, or laughs herself' (Karlyn 1995,

31) – with her quick wit deployed in her power battles with her mother. Whilst Chloe envies Rae's wit and the power it brings her in the friendship group, Rae struggles with its contribution to her status as 'one of the lads'. When labelled as such by Finn, the phrase echoes across the soundscape and the screen darkens down in an iris, isolating Rae in her realisation that her humour negates her gender (episode 1.1).

Where the adult unruly woman derives rebellious, confrontational power from the 'disruptive spectacle' of her physicality, Rae's debilitating anxiety is built in part from her inability to realise this power as a teenage girl. She is consumed with self-loathing drawn in part from her unruly body and mind; she wrestles with her desire for normative femininity and male approval, and fears her unruly mind will result in rejection. The programme's central tension is her struggle to reconcile her performance of confidence and comedic verbosity with the anxiety and darkness that can threaten to overwhelm her. In defining the unruly woman, Karlyn separates out melodrama and comedy, suggesting that melodrama depicts purity whilst 'comedy, with its exaggerations, hyperbole, and assault on the rational, depicts those of danger' (1995, 5). Karlyn sets victimisation and tears against resistance and laughter (1995, 4); however, *My Mad Fat Diary* blends the two forms to illustrate the psychological conflict that Rae must work through.

Melodrama and Subjectivity

Melodrama serves as a central mode of narratives built around the intensities and introspection of teenage experience (Banks 2004), as exhibited in US teen TV's combination of emotional realism and aspirational lifestyles from *Dawson's Creek* to *The O.C.* to *Gossip Girl*. *My Mad Fat Diary* is indicative of British youth drama's intertwining of British traditions of realism with the pleasurable excesses enabled by both melodrama and comedy, weaving together the respective oppressiveness and playfulness of the forms. This draws on both the 'social surrealism' Glen Creeber identifies in contemporary British social realism's shift to subjectivity (2009) and the blending of social realist traditions with melodrama that Christine Geraghty charts in the soap opera *EastEnders*. The latter's use of melodrama to 'present a world that is darker and more precarious than before, to represent indeed a society under siege' (2006, 227) is an apt evocation of the teenage condition and particularly Rae's struggle to live with mental illness.

Melodrama's thematic connections to repression and isolation are central to *My Mad Fat Diary*'s exploration of the destructive effects of anxiety. By interweaving Rae's psychological unrest with the romance fantasy of her winning of lust-object Finn – and her later rejection of the relationship due to her insecurities – the programme constructs the emotional journey that Ang argues is central to viewers' enjoyment of melodrama's 'tragic structure of feeling' (2008, 237). Geraghty analyses *EastEnders*' recent shift towards an engagement with melodrama, which she suggests serves to communicate emotionally saturated experience within its social realist soap mode. Here Geraghty identifies a 'greater emphasis on symbols, settings, camera work and lighting that help to express inner emotion' (2006, 227). A similar process occurs in *My Mad Fat Diary*, with the emotionally saturated experience of Rae's inner world communicated through heightened aesthetic devices. Her voiceover, the diary text scribbled over and notating the screen, and her fantasies and fragments of memory are all layered over a relatively mundane aesthetic familiar from British drama's naturalism. This melodrama aesthetic is intertwined with a strong comedic voice similarly built through an overflow of emotion and physicality: unruly lust, blunt wit and flights of fantasy. The audience's empathic engagement is driven by this affective communication of Rae's psychological isolation, emotional conflict, comic frustrations and lustful intensity.

My Mad Fat Diary builds this intensity through its binding of the viewer with Rae's perspective – one suffused with the everyday desires, jealousies and frustrations of teenage girlhood, but augmented by darker obsessions and anxieties. Rae's diary serves as a structuring device and as a filter for the viewer's experience, naturalising her narration as interior monologue bleeding from the page, facilitating the comic flights of fantasy that break into the otherwise naturalist aesthetic. We are aligned with the diary and become Rae's confidantes; closed down to her point of view, we are tied tightly to her emotional responses, centralising affect in storytelling. We may be able to force a gap – part of the programme's emotional impact lies in our awareness of the self-destructive nature of her behaviour – but the programme refuses to release us from Rae's experience.

Two moments take us outside Rae's perspective: episode 2.5 has Archie relay the break-up of the friendship group to Rae, accompanied by a flashback, and Rae reads Chloe's diary in episode 2.6. The latter offers the most important external perspective as here we re-experience preceding narrative events from Chloe's perspective, accompanied by her own diary narration, and with shifts in dialogue and action. This episode highlights both Rae's and Chloe's unreliable narration, the self-involvement of adolescence, with Rae disputing Chloe's interpretation – 'That's not what happened' – in her own voiceover. But reading Chloe's experiences leads Rae to become increasingly unmoored from her own subjectivity, questioning her own reading of events and pushing herself into self-destructive actions due to her guilt over her actions as presented from Chloe's perspective. So, whilst we do experience Chloe's point of view, this is always filtered through and returned to Rae, who uses it as ammunition for her own shame.

My Mad Fat Diary's suturing of the viewer into the intensity of Rae's confessional narrative aligns with two notable televisual teen forerunners. The diary form evokes Adrian Mole – the diarist protagonist of Sue Townsend's series of bestselling comic novels that were adapted for British television in the 1980s – whilst the centralising of female voice aligns with the influential US teen TV vanguard *My So-Called Life* (ABC, 1995). The latter blended teenager Angela Chase's stories with those of her parents, yet foregrounded Angela's point of view through her narration. Rae's diary shares the intimacy, yearning and confusion exhibited in Angela's narration along with its unreliability, its presentation of 'subjective experiences rather than objective truths' (Murphy 2007, 169).

By tying *My Mad Fat Diary*'s aesthetic to the intimacies and blunt freedoms of the diary, the programme gives Rae complete power over the depiction of the narrative. Her voiceover can pause action to comment on or annotate the screen with doodles; notating, modifying, emphasising or even blocking images; and layering the action with her point of view, presenting it as taking place within the diary's pages. Together with Rae's narration, the amateur scribbles conjure the diary onto the screen, the imprecise scrawl is tactile, it has presence (Figure 3.2). At times, this provides comic commentary aimed at both herself and others, pausing to provide or emphasise a punchline; her mum is given a moustache and devil's horns in the midst of an argument, an ejaculating cock and balls is scrawled over the Pepperami sausage Rae is handling during a lustful voiceover monologue about Archie. The scrawls also serve to aestheticise Rae's self-hatred: the screen fills with circular staring faces when she is forced into the street in swimwear after a shop fire alarm, rendering her tiny in the middle of the frame; doodles of food crowds down the screen when she struggles with eating in public, telescoping the medium shot down to her face isolated within the expanse of the frame; angry scratches cover a long shot of her after she binge eats. At their darkest, the scribbles

Fig. 3.2 The amateur scribbles conjure Rae's diary onto the screen, layered over action

make tactile, weighty, the blocking of connection taking place in Rae's consciousness. They construct a filter in the plane between the viewer and the action, loading it with her self-loathing and making it inescapable.

These annotations and doodles form part of a range of aesthetic devices used to explore Rae's consciousness, including point of view camera, moments of fantasy, fragments of memories and the use of pop music as score. A forbidden kitchen cupboard glows golden; Rae unzips her skin like a fat suit and steps out with a perfect body; a lusted-after PE teacher offers himself like a Greek statue in a ray of light with javelin in hand. Snatches of gold-tinted childhood memories of playing with Chloe in a field of waist-high summer grass or giggling at the top of a set of stairs augment their present-day relationship, which shifts on uncertain ground. The use of digital effects to reveal a protagonist's interiority links with Greg M. Smith's reading of *Ally McBeal*'s (FOX, 1997–2002) use of the device to visualise 'inner states: feelings, thoughts [and] fantasies' as akin to 'film melodrama's expression of subjectivity' (2007, 50).

Rae's subjectivity is often communicated through a melodrama-infused heightening of aesthetic via composition, score, colour and sound. Episode 1.3's closing scene sees Chloe and Rae snuggled together in Chloe's candle-lit bedroom after her abortion, listening to Oasis' Knebworth concert on the radio. In this intimate moment, with its soft light, comforting cushions and giggles, Rae stiltedly confesses her illness and suicide attempt – 'I hurt myself' – to a tearful Chloe in a series of tight close-ups. This is underscored by an uncomfortable angular extended guitar solo and rolling male vocal emanating from the radio, compounding the long pauses and painful emotions. Their conversation is interrupted by a phone call from Chloe's boyfriend and she leaves Rae to rush to him. Left alone in her spiralling anxiety at Chloe's reaction and abandonment, Rae's interiority is indicated through a montage of layered cross-fades: extreme close-ups of her tearful eyes, her fingernails digging into hands, flickering candles and the scrap of paper holding her therapist's phone number. A discordant guitar – a recurrent score motif signalling her emotional distress – is pulled forward in the audio-mix as the next song in the Oasis set rises in an oppressive wall of drums and guitar chords. This leads into the vocalist's repeated refrain 'I can't tell you the way I feel/Coz the way I feel is oh so new to me', here translated from its romantic roots to emphasise Rae's fear over the effect of her confession and the fractured intimacy of the moment.

When we revisit this scene from Chloe's perspective in episode 2.6, with her diary painting her reaction to Rae in a more positive light, the scene plays out in medium shots and the aesthetic is notably flat and plain. Thus, *My Mad Fat Diary*'s aestheticising of Rae's emotion illustrates Kristyn Gorton's argument that emotion can be viewed as an aesthetic quality, constructed in televisual texts via language, characterisation, shot selection and framing, facilitating audience interpretation (2009, 72). The diary scribbles and moments of subjective aesthetic serve to aestheticise Rae's emotions, visualising affect – be it joy, passion, disgust or shame. Her scribbles signify the emotional intensity she struggles with on top of the everyday – *My Mad Fat Diary*'s otherwise mundane aesthetic – communicating the adolescent overflow of emotion that makes melodrama the key form of teen-focused television texts, although here Rae's struggle with anxiety and dark thoughts constantly threaten to swell the emotional overflow into an overwhelming torrent.

Aestheticising Emotion

These elements serve to aestheticise Rae's consciousness, providing a televisual manifestation of emotion that communicates her physical experience, drawing the audience close – at times uncomfortably so. By enveloping us in Rae's perspective as she works through her anxieties, lusts and frustrations, *My Mad Fat Diary* creates a lack of breathing space for the viewer, heightening its affective experience. To draw on Kristyn Gorton's reading of Elspeth Probyn, it encourages Rae's emotions to be 'felt and enacted by our bodies' (2009, 65). The programme makes Rae's emotions tactile by filtering action through the intimate speech and imagery shared only with her diary, causing the viewer to be drawn in, to participate in her lust, shame, frustration and disgust. The 'catchy' (Probyn 2005) nature of these emotions are compounded by the aestheticising and intimate vocalising of Rae's insecurities and anxiety.

Whilst it does communicate pleasure – particularly in the intimate moments Rae shares with Finn – *My Mad Fat Diary*'s intensely emotion-based structure of feeling is most powerful in its evocation of shame and, to an extent, disgust – Rae's shame at her 'fat' 'mad' body, at her excess of body and emotions, at her mental fragility, her struggle to control her panic attacks and her secret breakdown. Probyn argues that shame 'illuminates our intense attachment to the world, our desire to be connected with others' (2005, 4). Rae's shame over her struggles with mental health relates to her 'fear of contempt and abandonment' (Probyn 2005, 3) if her secrets were exposed to her friends, and this builds the viewer's intense attachment with her. The intimate nature of the television text and the empathic connection built by the programme's focus on Rae's interiority encourage the proximity that Probyn suggests shame makes us feel (2005, 4). Rae performs these emotions for the diary – they are etched on the screen, but shared only with the viewer.

This aesthetic draws the audience in, yet it serves to isolate Rae within the diegesis. *Ally McBeal* sees Ally's fantastical subjectivity leak out to infect others in her diegetic world, with Smith suggesting that the narrative world becomes warped to reflect her sensibility (2007, 59). However, *My Mad Fat Diary*'s layering of Rae's subjectivity through voiceover and overlay effects allows the experience of other characters to remain intact. Whilst she controls the telling of the story, Rae feels that she has no such control over her life and that no one within the narrative can fully share her experience or perspective, emphasising the isolating effect of mental illness. It is only through verbalising her emotions, sharing them with others, can she begin to break through.

My Mad Fat Diary offers E4's first full exploration of female voice, interweaving melodrama and comedy to centralise emotion and intimacy. It holds its audience tight through its aestheticising of affect, tying us to Rae's subjectivity as it unfurls the fantasies, fears and frustrations of her journey towards self-acceptance. The centralising of intimacy and emotion in the second wave of British youth drama continued in *In the Flesh*'s use of teen telefantasy to explore the zombie as 'outsider'. It is here used to communicate the affective intensity of Kieren's return from the undead in an uncanny hybrid-zombie body and the isolation of his return to his hometown.

In the Flesh: Intimacy, Landscape and Allegory

I now pick up two key threads explored in this chapter – *Misfits'* telefantasy teens in British landscapes and *My Mad Fat Diary*'s intimate focus and emotional intensity – to discuss *In the Flesh*, British youth drama's take on the post-9/11 zombie narrative. Having already explored vampires, werewolves and ghosts in *Being Human,* superheroes in *Misfits*, witches in *Switch* and *The Fades'* wraithlike ghouls and angels, the last uncharted territory for British youth telefantasy was the zombie. Enjoying a huge post-9/11 cultural renaissance, the figure appeared across British film horror and comedy in *28 Days Later* (2002) and *Shaun of the Dead*, graphic novels and US cable television in *The Walking Dead* (AMC, 2010–), and summer blockbusters in *World War Z* (2013). Yet how could this undead figure, unthinking and unfeeling, moving in indistinguishable masses and violently conquering post-apocalyptic cities, be positioned within the small-scale of British youth drama, a space defined by explorations of emotion and intimacy, its intertwining of melodrama and social realism, and its fondness for the mundane?

In the Flesh depicts a world ostensibly recovered from a now-contained 'undead' rising and dealing with the re-integration of medically 'cured' zombies into society (termed 'rotters' in the programme) four years after the conflict. The programme's intimate focus on uncanny telefantasy bodies in mundane regional domestic spaces offered a departure from the libertarian post-apocalyptic zombie worlds that had dominated US screens. In contrast to those narratives, where the power of the police or military is largely absent, *In the Flesh* explored the impact of state intervention on zombies, asking what happens *after* the social breakdown so fetishised in these films (Sconce 2014, 108) is controlled.

In the Flesh speculates on the morality of medicating the undead and returning them to their former lives through the figure of Kieren, a teenager who had previously taken his own life only to be revived as a 'rotter' during The Rising. With his death-drive medically controlled, his consciousness restored, and having been 'rehabilitated' through group therapy in a government treatment facility, he is designated a sufferer of Previously Deceased Syndrome (PDS). Tortured by flashbacks to the murder he committed in his 'rotter' state, he is returned to his parents care in his hometown of Roarton, an isolated village in the north of England and staunch with anti-rotter sentiment. His battle with guilt and social prejudice builds a narrative that blends two of Linda Williams' body genres (1991): the violent excess of horror and the emotional excess of melodrama. In line with other second wave British youth drama, this constructs a zombie narrative focused on the intimate and emotional. Working within the established framework of the telefantasy teen as 'other' – emphasised through the social prejudice story-thread – *In the Flesh* situates the supernatural within British spaces that evoke both the uncanny and the mundane.

Like *Shaun of the Dead*'s combination of zombie fantasy and the British suburban mundane, *In the Flesh* depicts a tentatively maintained everyday of village life, one whose curtain-twitching nosiness and whispered gossip poses a potential mortal threat. The violence of The Rising and the local resistance to government assimilation policies are signalled by the padlocked and police-taped church graveyard and the anti-rotter graffiti daubed across the village and countryside. The camouflage-clad local vigilantes of the Human Volunteer Force (HVF) offered the village's only protection during The Rising and are reluctant to relinquish their heroic status in the new era of assimilation. They serve as the zombie narrative's morally corrupt human forces – particularly in their leader Bill – unthinking, relentless and more brutal than the monsters themselves (J. May 2010, 289).

In its intimate take on the zombie narrative, *In the Flesh* replaces the unyielding mass with isolated individuals that provoke sorrow rather than fear. The PDS sufferer is a figure of exclusion and melancholy rather than threat, returned to a world that has already mourned their death. Kyle Bishop frames the zombie as an uncanny, unnatural shell of a former human, a 'walking corpse' lacking the consciousness needed for a psychologically complex protagonist (2006, 201). However, as Sconce notes, 'much as the structural positions of cowboy and Indian reversed during the course of the western, we now increasingly root for the zombies' (2014, 97). The current post-9/11 zombie cycle kicked off by *28 Days Later* has now reached the stage of zombie-protagonists,[7] including zombie rom-coms *Warm Bodies* (2013) and *Life After Beth* (2014) and French television series *The Returned* (Canal+, 2012–). Bishop contrasts the zombie with the ghost and vampire's position of the romantic 'undead', arguing that as its rotting brain offers no real emotional capacity, it is technically 'dead' (2009, 20). *In the Flesh*'s medicated PDS sufferers are rendered as post-zombies: technically dead yet fully conscious, physically mobile and emotionally complex. Kieren is therefore positioned as the more romantic 'undead', as one of its 'sympathetic protagonists and misunderstood heroes' (ibid.). His passivity and trauma make him a reluctant hero, which links him with the skewed, stumbling take on the telefantasy hero offered by *Being Human* and *Misfits*.

Uncanny British Landscapes

Just as *Misfits'* uncanny tower blocks place telefantasy within spaces grounded in British realist traditions, the fictional isolated village of Roarton evokes stories of Northern grit from the 1960s British New Wave through to *Brassed Off* (1996) and *Red Riding* (Channel 4, 2009). These are stories told through their characters' relationship with the often-bleak beauty of Northern landscapes, those which Andrew Higson argues make 'a claim for a *surface realism*, an iconography which authentically reproduces the visual and aural surfaces of the "British way of life". The "authenticity" of place and character' (1996, 136). Like *Misfits*, *In the Flesh* utilises spaces culturally imprinted as social realist in order to assert the regional 'authenticity' of its supernatural tale. Where post-apocalyptic zombie narratives often delight in the ravaged blankness of abandoned city space, *In the Flesh* positions itself in rural space, with its village sat within windswept moors. This is an eternal, natural space both beautiful and unforgiving, one rendered as uncanny through the horror-tinged narrative and the memory of past trauma from The Rising. We are introduced to the village with a pan across a landscape of desolate fog-wreathed moors, with a stone bridge over a gentle stream daubed in red 'beware rotters'. Roarton bears the scars of its supernatural past: the village feels half-dead, with 'missing' posters still fluttering in the sharp winds and pro-HVF graffiti scarring buildings. Its potentially picturesque rural qualities are undone by the sense of loss and fear that lingers in the village's decimated population. Presented in a drained colour palate of browns and greys, its inhabitants are clad in dated, muted clothing styles, as if arrested in a past state by the events of The Rising.

This is land with memory, an uncanny 'landscape suffused with a sense of profound and sometimes apocalyptic anxiety; it is also a landscape of a comprehensive dispossession and vacancy' (Hutchings 2004,

29). Here the programme draws on British film and televisual traditions exploring the threat within rural communities and their wild landscapes, from *The Wicker Man* (1973) to *An American Werewolf in London* (1981). Hutchings suggests that 'abandoned or alienating landscapes and cityscapes articulate, usually in a coded way, a variety of social fears and anxieties' (2004, 34). The moors resonate with British rural horror, of folk tales, of insularity and self-protection; Roarton's controlling fists of religion and vigilantism evoke the potential of mob rule. The village's isolation is established through extreme long shots from its hilled outskirts, offering 'That Long Shot of Our Town from That Hill', 'a shot which lures the eye across the vast empty space of a townscape' (Higson 1996, 138). The composition here links the viewer and Kieren as outsiders, as he is connected with these uncanny wild landscapes rather than the village's hostile community. Trudging down dirt paths in long shot, isolated in expanses of landscape, he avoids the potential dangers of the village; he returns to the site of his rebirth, the cordoned-off graveyard set at the edge of the village against hills and sky, preferring the 'people-free rural landscapes' that are 'rendered alienating through their bleakness' (Hutchings 2004, 34) over the domestic spaces he is uneasily placed within by his parents. Connections here can be traced with moments of rural escape and freedom by urban youth in British cinema from *Ratcatcher* (1999) to *This is England* (2006). Yet the moors of *In the Flesh* remain stark and uncanny, like Kieren himself. The PDS sufferers are 'othered' by their medically maintained inhuman physicality. They bear the scars they died with: sliced wrists, stapled face wounds, a stomach crowded with portals for medication. They are instructed to cover their unsettling blank eyes with contacts and conceal decayed faces with thick camouflage make-up to enable them to 'pass' as living. Yet this also renders them uncanny, skin slightly too beige, lips and face homogenised, a parody of their former living selves.

National Identity and Allegory

These uncanny landscapes combine with a depiction of institutional order to support British youth drama's nationally distinct take on telefantasy. The zombie re-integration is shaped by nationalised state care and a social desire to maintain routine in the face of seismic change. The evoking of a British 'stiff upper lip' and an attempt to maintain calm in the face of disaster frames the three online paratextual shorts – *Keep Calm and Avoid the Undead* (2013) – released prior to *In the Flesh*'s premiere. Here transmedia storytelling provides backstory for The Rising in the form of animated government information films. Their performance of ineffectual officiousness, comically at odds with the supernatural threat, parodies the 'duck and cover' advice given under the threat of nuclear war. They utilise infographics and silhouettes to calmly deliver government instructions to the populace as the supernatural threat of the 'rotters' progressively grows across the three shorts.

The dominant image of British institutions in season one is of order and bureaucracy: gun-wielding soldiers and barbed wire contain and process the medicated mass of shuffling, passive PDS sufferers at the treatment facility. Reintegration proceeds officiously through routines and processes, medication and group therapy, the latter echoing Rae's mental health group therapy in *My Mad Fat Diary*, reading Kieren's zombie state as a psychological breakdown. Kieren's fears of his fragile emotional state and prejudiced hometown are brushed over by doctors and therapists; these symbols of institutional care ignore the complex morality and emotional impact of the policy in deploying the government's quick fix of medication and 'community care'. Once integrated back into society, government regulation comes largely from the soft state of the NHS through Shirley's caring yet bumbling district nurse. She distributes advice leaflets (whose blandly upbeat yet institutional design and colour palate evoke NHS imagery), runs support groups and advises family members on the strict rules for medicating PDS sufferers. The clinically caring bureaucratic script Shirley uncertainly delivers in Kieren's family living room is at odds with the gaping open wound of the medical shunt in his neck and the violence of the injection she amateurly demonstrates for his parents.

The assimilation of these 'othered' bodies into an unwelcoming society draws out the zombie's long-worn allegorical function, its role as a political statement on the present rather than a prediction of the future (Sconce 2014, 97). Here the allegorical function of the zombie serves British youth drama's public service-led engagement with social concerns. Like the sympathetic rom-com zombie protagonists Chera Kee reads as symbolic of miscegenation (2014), PDS sufferers are presented as unjustly feared and subjected to prejudicial treatment, serving as an allegory for British cultural panics over immigration. This allegory is brought to the fore in season two's introduction of the anti-PDS political party Victus, whose grassroots single-issue political platform resonates with the 2014 rise of the 'Eurosceptic' UK Independence Party (UKIP). Roarton evokes the economically ravaged white working-class communities exploited by the anti-immigration policies of UKIP, fermenting fear and prejudice. In turn, the Victus-driven oppressive monitoring of PDS sufferers and the creation of a forced-labour programme strongly evoke both the Conservative government's constrictive monitoring of benefits claimants and the controversial 'workfare' programmes for the unemployed (Coote 2014; Butler 2015).

Emotion and Domesticity

Season two's expansion of its storytelling out to the village as a whole paints this immigration allegory with broad brushstrokes; however, season one's more intimate domestic focus concentrates on the PDS trio of Kieren, his former best friend/boyfriend Rick and his new friend Amy. The immigrant allegory is here layered with sexuality and mental illness, as British youth drama's interest in the 'othered' state of the supernatural teen is explored through the queered zombie body (Elliot-Smith 2014) and interwoven with domestic conflict. Kieren's outsider identity had preceded his 'rotter' status due his artistic nature and intimate relationship with Rick, who abruptly left for the army and ceased contact under the influence of his domineering father. When Rick 'returns', his father – now the militant leader of the HVF – is unable to acknowledge that his heroic soldier son who was killed in action yet miraculously returned to him is a PDS sufferer. In turn, this refusal to recognise Rick's undead state is aligned with his homophobic denial of Rick and Kieren's relationship.

Kieren's story interweaves the zombie narrative with mental illness, as Rick's romantic abandonment and his death in combat had led to Kieren's suicide, infusing the storytelling with an undertow of sorrow and fear. The pain caused by this act permeates his family on his return, requiring them to reorientate themselves after four years of grief. The stigma of mental illness is read onto the PDS-sufferer body, with Kieren's devoted and caring parents seeking comfort in domestic ritual as a way to avoid both his suicide and his undead state. On his first night home, he humours his well-meaning parents' tentative request that he join them at the dinner table despite his inability to consume food or drink. His resulting pantomiming of eating compounds the oddness of this uncanny supernatural boy within the everyday domestic space. Here the programme constructs a minimalist melodrama – riddled with an absurd comedy – from his parents' attempts to conceal their trauma over their son's return in this undead state through a loving parody of their former family routine. The epic scale of a worldwide zombie Rising – we only see the British situation, yet Rick was 'found' in Afghanistan – is here recast as domestic drama. In line with British youth telefantasy's rooting within realist traditions, the conflict over assimilation is rendered as intimate domestic strife, with Kieren's sister's HVF membership layering the antagonism of the village's lingering prejudice onto family conflict.

Season one charts Kieren's processing of his guilt over both his unwanted resurrection and the murderous acts he committed within his community in his rotter state. His coming to terms with his PDS identity – signified by a removal of his contacts and make-up – is aligned with an emergence from the darkness of mental illness and his family's confronting of their grief over his suicide. *In the Flesh* is permeated by guilt, grief and dread, foregrounding affect and emotion. The PDS sufferers' hybrid state complicates the blank mindless zombie of convention, a figure 'immune from neurosis' or emotion (Sconce 2014, 96). Kieren's medication restores his emotional intelligence; his innate sensitivity signalled by his artist skills, his delicate physicality, his queer identity and outsider status. Unexpectedly reunited, he and Rick snatch glimpses and moments of whispered, hesitant, romantic confession. Kieren's perspective is blended with that of other village inhabitants – particularly in season two – but the programme centralises his interiority through the 'emotionally saturated expressions of melodrama' (Geraghty 2006, 228).

The programme's focus on intimacy, intensity and physicality – the latter in the body horror of the 'rotter' – has strong links with the interiority of *My Mad Fat Diary* and Rae's struggle with her own mind. Rae's pleas to remain in the security of the psychiatric hospital align with Kieren's pleas to the treatment centre doctor that he is not psychologically prepared for assimilation. Both protagonists blend emotional sensitivity and vulnerability with a sharp wit; Kieren's depression and wrenching flashbacks to his rotter state echo Rae's battles with sensory overload and dark thoughts. Kieren struggles with his new identity; riddled with guilt and grief, he projects a medicated otherworldly blankness, an 'other' his parents attempt to slot back into his former life in a bid to suppress their own grief. The body horror of his 'rotter' acts punctures his present blankness with sense-memory flashbacks to his ravenous past. *In the Flesh* here blends horror with the melodrama of youth drama, drawing on the affective qualities of Linda Williams' 'body genres' (1991); their visceral embodiment of sensation. Shot through with saturated blacks and greens, Kieren's memories are intensely physical with blood, viscera and brains, shocking amidst the desaturated palate of his current surroundings. His family home signals domestic middle-class mundanity with its drab white synthetic cladding and beige interiors, his mother's apron and her oatmeal coloured jumpers, continuing British youth drama's investment in ordinary, domestic spaces to signify its authenticity through markers of realism, with these grounding its telefantasy narratives.

In the Flesh takes up British youth drama's locating of telefantasy narratives in a strong sense of place, situating uncanny bodies in domestic spaces and connecting them to landscapes that hold memories of British rural horror. In blending the body genres of horror and melodrama, it constructs an intimate focus on Kieren's interiority, displaying this second wave of British youth drama's centralising of emotion.

Settling Down, Remaining Disruptive

British youth drama will always be shaped by its relationship with US teen TV, with which it is intricately entangled; however, it no longer needs to push so hard against its predecessor. The embrace of intimacy and emotion-led storytelling seen in its second wave – alongside a continuing deployment of fantastical dramas and bawdy comedies – demonstrates a comfort and confidence in itself as a nationally distinct form. The first wave of British youth drama sought to define itself clearly in opposition in order to divest itself from the imported US melodramas that had dominated British youth schedules. The emotionally articulate US protagonists and aspirational lifestyles were countered by a quest for 'authenticity'. This was exhibited in British youth drama's pleasure in the mundane everyday and its grounding of narratives in regionally distinct spaces, ones often layered with resonances of televisual social realism. Programmes loudly asserted their British independence, embracing blunt language, boundary-pushing comic excess, moments of fantasy and the surreal, together with a nihilistic pursuit of bacchanalian freedoms. Yet melodrama remained essential to the storytelling of British youth drama, requiring these excesses and a quest for authenticity to be held together in an ambivalent address. As British youth drama's identity became more secure, new programmes displayed a range of styles, forms and voices – although white male protagonists and writers still dominated. The second wave of British youth television more openly embraced melodrama and centralised emotion in its structure of feeling. This facilitated a shift towards intimate and emotion-led storytelling, a closeness and delicacy, contributing a new breadth of affect to the televisual traditions of realism and the view of youth from within, those elements so central to the need to retain an 'authentic' British youth voice. Building its own blend of melodrama, comedy and realism, British youth drama established a secure space for itself in British youth television, welcoming in a greater range of voices, storytelling and tones to this televisual landscape.

Notes

1. For discussion of this term, see Jane Feuer (1984), Robert Thompson (1997), and Janet McCabe and Kim Akass (2007)
2. See the following chapter for analysis of similar processes of distinction occurring around *Skins* and *The Inbetweeners*.
3. See Hunn (2012), Berridge (2013) and Woods (2016) for further discussion of the programme, along with the following chapter.
4. Chapter 6 further discusses British discourse surrounding the figure of the chav.
5. Woods (2013) discusses the content restrictions of US teen TV and different places within the UK schedule.
6. I thank Hannah Andrews for this observation.
7. This stage occurred in the Romero cycle with Romero's own *Return of the Living Dead*'s 1985 introduction of sentient zombies, with growing zombie sentience a theme throughout subsequent Romero films.

References

Ang, Ien. 2008. 'Melodramatic Identificiations'. In *Feminist Television Criticism: A Reader*, edited by Charlotte Brunsdon and Lynn Spigel, 235–246. Maidenhead: Open University Press.

Ashby, Justine and Andrew Higson. 2000. 'Introduction'. In *British Cinema: Past and Present*, edited by Justine Ashby and Andrew Higson, 1–18. London: Routledge.

Banks, Miranda J. 2004. 'A Boy for All Planets: Roswell, Smallville, and the Teen Male Melodrama'. In *Teen TV: Genre, Consumption, Identity*, edited by Glyn Davis and Kay Dickinson, 17–28. London: BFI.

Berridge, Susan. 2013. '"Doing it for the Kids"? The Discursive Construction of the Teenager and Teenage Sexuality in Skins'. *Journal of British Cinema and Television* 10(4): 785–801.

Bishop, Kyle. 2006. 'Raising the Dead'. *Journal of Popular Film and Television* 33(4): 196–205.

———. 2009. 'Dead Man Still Walking'. *Journal of Popular Film and Television* 37(1): 16–25.
Brunsdon, Charlotte. 2007. *London in Cinema: The Cinematic City since 1945*. London: BFI.
Burke, Andrew. 2007. 'Concrete Universality: Tower Blocks, Architectural Modernism, and Realism in Contemporary British Cinema'. *New Cinemas: Journal of Contemporary Film* 5(3): 177–188.
Butler, Patrick. 2015. 'Review of Benefit Sanctions Urged Amid Concern over Regime's Effectiveness'. *The Guardian*, 26 July. www.theguardian.com/society/2015/jul/26/benefit-sanctions-review-urged-amid-concern-over-regimes-effectiveness (accessed 25 May 2016).
Caughie, John. 2000. *Television Drama : Realism, Modernism, and British Culture*. Oxford University Press.
Cooke, Lez. 2003. *British Television Drama: A History*. London: BFI.
———. 2005. 'The New Social Realism of *Clocking Off*. In *Popular Television Drama: Critical Perspectives*, edited by Jonathan Bignell and Stephen Lacey, 183–197. Manchester University Press.
Coote, Anna. 2014. 'Help to Work? Britain's Jobless are Being Forced into Workfare, More Like'. *The Guardian*, 28 April. www.theguardian.com/commentisfree/2014/apr/28/help-to-work-britains-jobless-forced-workfare-unemployed (accessed 25 May 2016).
Creeber, Glen. 2009. '"The Truth is out There! Not!": *Shameless* and the Moral Structures of Contemporary Social Realism'. *New Review of Film and Television Studies* 7(4): 421–439.
Donaghy, James. 2009. 'Faster than a Speeding Joyrider … Misfits Gives Asbo Teens Superpowers'. *The Guardian*, 7 November. www.guardian.co.uk/tv-and-radio/2009/nov/07/misfits-e4-superhero-sci-fi (accessed 27 May 2016).
Douglas, Kate and Kelly McWilliam. 2004. '"We Don't Need No Education": Adolescents and the School in Contemporary Australian Teen TV'. In *Teen TV: Genre, Consumption, Identity*, edited by Glyn Davis and Kay Dickinson, 151–165. London: BFI.
Dunleavy, Trisha. 2009. *Television Drama: Form, Agency, Innovation*. Basingstoke: Palgrave Macmillan.
Elliot-Smith, Darren. 2014. 'Gay Zombies: Consuming Masculinity and Community in Bruce LaBruce's Otto; or Up with Dead People (2008) and LA Zombie (2010)'. In *Screening the Undead: Vampires and Zombies in Film and Television*, edited by Leon Hunt, Sharon Lockyer and Milly Williamson, 140–158. London: I.B. Tauris.
Feasey, Rebecca. 2008. *Masculinity and Popular Television*. Edinburgh University Press.

Feuer, Jane. 1984. 'MTM Style'. In *MTM 'Quality Television'*, edited by Jane Feuer, Paul Kerr and Tise Vahimagi, 52–84. London: BFI.

Garde-Hansen, Joanne, and Kristyn Gorton. 2013. *Emotion Online: Theorizing Affect on the Internet*. Basingstoke: Palgrave Macmillan.

Gentleman, Amelia. 2010. 'Is Britain Broken?' *The Guardian*, 31 March. www.guardian.co.uk/society/2010/mar/31/is-britain-broken (accessed 27 May 2016).

Geraghty, Christine. 2006. 'Discussing Quality: Critical Vocabularies and Popular Television Drama'. In *Media & Cultural Theory*, edited by James Curran and David Morley, 221–232. London: Routledge.

Gorton, Kristyn. 2009. *Media Audiences: Television, Meaning and Emotion*. Edinburgh University Press.

Gray, Jonathan. 2008. *Television Entertainment*. London: Routledge.

Higson, Andrew. 1996. 'Space, Place, Spectacle: Landscape and Townscape in the "Kitchen Sink Film"'. In *Dissolving Views: Key Writings on British Cinema*, edited by Andrew Higson, 133–156. London: Cassell.

Hill, John. 2000. 'From the New Wave to "Brit-Grit": Continuity and Difference in Working-Class Realism'. In *British Cinema: Past and Present*, edited by Justine Ashby and Andrew Higson, 249–260. London: Routledge.

Hills, Matt. 2004. 'Dawson's Creek: "Quality Teen TV" and "Mainstream Cult"?' In *Teen TV: Genre, Consumption, Identity*, edited by Glyn Davis and Kay Dickinson, 54–67. London: BFI.

Hunn, Deborah F. 2012. '"The Dark Side of Naomily": Skins, Dan Texts and Contested Genres'. *Continuum* 26(1): 89–100.

Hutchings, Peter. 2004. 'Uncanny Landscapes in British Film and Television'. *Visual Culture in Britain* 5(2): 27–40.

Johnson, Catherine. 2005. *Telefantasy*. London: BFI.

Karlyn, Kathleen Rowe. 1995. *The Unruly Woman: Gender and Genres of Laughter*. Austin: University of Texas Press.

Kee, Chera. 2014. 'Good Girls Don't Date Dead Boys: Toying with Miscegenation in Zombie Films'. *Journal of Popular Film and Television* 42(4): 176–185.

Lury, Karen. 2001. *British Youth Television: Cynicism and Enchantment*. Oxford University Press.

May, Jeff. 2010. 'Zombie Geographies and the Undead City'. *Social & Cultural Geography* 11(3): 285–298.

McCabe, Janet and Kim Akass. 2007. 'Introduction: Debating Quality'. In *Quality TV: Contemporary American Television and Beyond*, edited by Janet McCabe and Kim Akass, 1–12. London: I.B. Tauris.

Monk, Claire. 2000. 'Underbelly UK: The 1990s Underclass Film, Masculinity and the Ideologies of "New" Britain'. In *British Cinema: Past and Present*, edited by Justine Ashby and Andrew Higson, 274–287. London: Routledge.

Moseley, Rachel. 2001. 'The Teen Series'. In *The Television Genre Book*, edited by Glen Creeber, 41–43. London: BFI.
———. 2007. 'Teenagers and Television Drama in Britain 1968–1982'. In *Re-Viewing Television History. Critical Issues in Television Historiography*, edited by Helen Wheatley, 184–197. London: I.B. Tauris.
———. 2015. 'Teen Drama'. In *The Television Genre Book*, edited by Glen Creeber, 3rd edn, 38–43. London: Palgrave Macmillan.
Murphy, Caryn. 2007. '"It Only Got Teenage Girls": Narrative Strategies and the Teenage Perspective of *My So-Called Life*'. In *Dear Angela: Remembering My So-Called Life*, edited by Michele Byers and David Lavery, 165–180. Lanham, MD: Lexington Books.
Nissim, Mayer. 2009. '"Misfits" is "Wry Take on Superheroes"'. *Digital Spy*, 11 November. www.digitalspy.co.uk/tv/s145/misfits/news/a186340/misfits-is-wry-take-on-superheroes.html (accessed 28 May 2016).
Parker, Robin. 2008. 'E4 Commissions Asbo Superhero Drama'. *Broadcast*, 16 October.
Peirse, Alison. 2010. 'A Broken Tradition: British Telefantasy and Children's Television in the 1980s and 1990s'. *Visual Culture in Britain* 11(1): 109–124.
Pribram, E. Deidre. 2011. *Emotions, Genre, and Justice in Film and Television: Detecting Feeling*. Abingdon: Routledge.
Probyn, Elspeth. 2005. *Blush: Faces of Shame*. Minneapolis: University of Minnesota Press.
Ross, Sharon Marie and Louisa Ellen Stein. 2008. 'Introduction: Watching Teen TV'. In *Teen Television: Essays on Programming and Fandom*, edited by Sharon Marie Ross and Louisa Ellen Stein, 3–26. Lanham, MD: Macfarland.
Sconce, Jeffrey. 2014. 'Dead Metaphors/Undead Allegories'. In *Screening the Undead: Vampires and Zombies in Film and Television*, edited by Leon Hunt, Sharon Lockyer and Milly Williamson, 95–111. London: I.B.Tauris.
Simpson, Paul. 2010. 'Howard Overman: Gently Does it'. *Total Sci Fi*, 13 December. http://totalscifionline.com/interviews/5888-howard-overman-gently-does-it (accessed 28 May 2016).
Smith, Greg M. 2007. *Beautiful TV: The Art and Argument of Ally McBeal*. Austin: University of Texas Press.
Stein, Louisa Ellen. 2015. *Millennial Fandom: Television Audiences in the Transmedia Age*. Iowa City: University of Iowa Press.
Thompson, Robert. 1997. *Television's Second Golden Age: From Hill Street Blues to ER*. Syracuse University Press.
Wee, Valerie. 2008. 'Teen Television and the WB Television Network'. In *Teen Television: Essays on Programming and Fandom*, edited by Sharon Marie Ross and Louisa Ellen Stein, 43–60. Jefferson, NC: Macfarland.
Wheatley, Helen. 2006. *Gothic Television*. Manchester University Press.

———. 2012. 'Uncanny Children, Haunted Houses, Hidden Rooms: Children's Gothic Television in the 1970s and '80s'. *Visual Culture in Britain* 13(3): 383–397.

Williams, Linda. 1991. 'Film Bodies: Gender, Genre, and Excess'. *Film Quarterly* 44(4): 2–13.

Williams, Raymond. 1961. *The Long Revolution*. London: Chatto & Windus.

Woods, Faye. 2016. 'My Generation(s): Cycles, Branding and Renewal in E4's Skins'. In *Multiplicities: Cycles, Sequels, Remakes, Spin-Offs, and Reboots in Film and Television*, edited by Amanda Ann Klein and R. Barton Palmer, 240–259. Austin: University of Texas Press.

CHAPTER 4

Teen TV Translations: Across the Pond

British youth television is intricately intertwined with US teen TV, with its original drama in part developing its voice through a dialogue with imported US texts. But this is not a one-way relationship, as the US 2011–2012 television season debuted three adaptations of British youth drama's first wave. *Skins* (E4, 2007–2013), *The Inbetweeners* (E4, 2008–2010) and *Being Human* (BBC Three, 2008–2013) were translated by basic cable channels MTV and Syfy, and became part of a long history of transatlantic televisual flow. Here we see the US market attempting to assimilate British programmes that, as the previous chapter demonstrated, were closely bound to national televisual identity through space, language and storytelling. Exploring the messy swirl of discourse surrounding these transatlantic translations serves to further define British youth television, as it offers a rich source for the exploration of disjuncture and difference between American and British youth representations. As a result, I focus on the two MTV translations over Syfy's *Being Human* (2011–2014), as the latter was assimilated into the channel's telefantasy norm rather than defined as a youth text. In examining the critical and industrial discourse surrounding *Skins US* (MTV, 2011) and *The Inbetweeners US* (MTV, 2012),[1] I identify how British youth drama was received, reworked and assimilated into US cultural representations and televisual expectations of youth narratives.

Like NBC's 2003 translation of BBC sitcom *Coupling* (BBC Two/BBC Three 2000–2004) analysed by Kevin Sanson, these are 'television series whose American remake is inseparable from an acute awareness of its British original' (2011, 42). The discourse surrounding British youth television as imports and translations highlights the difficulty of defining national absolutes, with transatlantic borrowings and influences drawn to the surface. Yet it also highlights how markers of British youth drama's 'authenticity' were drawn from production practices, connotations of British television's realism and the deployment of language, bodies and spaces. These authenticity claims[2] are held in tension with the traditions and ideologies of both teen TV and the storytelling of US television as a whole.

Different terms are used interchangeably across academic discussions of scripted format flow; although 'remake' and 'adaptation' are the most prominent, I prefer 'translation'. British to US television translations have no real linguistic justification, which suggests that the imperative is a cultural and industrial barrier. Christopher Hogg argues that 'translation' recognises these programmes as a series of variations that make a programming brand accessible and comprehensible to different markets (2013, 122). 'Translation' also signifies how audiences' media literacy can allow an understanding of multiple versions and fluency in multiple media markets (2013, 130). British consumers and press are fluent in US culture and thus need no translation, whereas British culture is conceived of (whether correctly or not) as 'foreign' to a US mainstream population, as suffering a cultural discount. Fluency in British cultural products thus serves as a form of cultural capital in the US, with British originals accessed via cable broadcast and online peer-to-peer flow. Hogg's framing of 'each nation-based textual variant as intact and in dialogue, contributing to an overarching meta-text' (2013, 127) chimes with my own discussion of the *Skins* programme brand. I position the generational renewal of its cast every two years as cycles – variants within an overarching brand – situating the US translation as a further cycle (Woods 2016). Yet tensions occur when a national variant is judged to not offer sufficient translation for its cultural context, as I will demonstrate.

British youth television's pull–push relationship with US teen TV speaks to the long-standing intertwining of the two national televisions. Jeffrey Miller traces the history and influence of British television in the US, suggesting that from the 1960s onwards, popular British imports bore the influence of Americanisation, 'remaking and remarketing ... American genres that had already made their way to Britain, frequently with the assistance of American money' (2000, 12). The messiness and contestation found in the discourses surrounding the US translations of

British youth drama speak to this unbalanced yet reciprocal relationship and ongoing attempts to negotiate national identity through televisual texts. These translations illustrate Kevin Sanson's assertion that television formats are 'potential sites of articulation, congestion, and community' (2011, 39). However, this book's overarching concerns with national identity, ideologies of 'authenticity' and the role of space and place are somewhat at odds with his assertion of the futility of attempting to reconcile 'an increasingly transnational media space with traditional frameworks, perspectives and assumptions about culture and its "authentic" connections to space and place' (2011, 40). British imports and translations were discursively framed as 'not Teen TV', as foreign – sometimes to their benefit, sometimes not – producing national televisual distinctions that trouble Sanson's blurring of boundaries. As this chapter demonstrates, the transatlantic boundaries between teen TV and British youth television are permeable, but at the heart of this relationship are potentially irreconcilable tensions. Whilst British youth drama bears the influence of the US form, it is fundamentally structured in opposition to it; as MTV discovered, assimilating it *back* into teen TV proved difficult.

Tales of transnational television trade have until recently been focused on factual and entertainment formats; however, there is a growing body of scholarship on the global flow of scripted formats (Lavigne and Marcovitch 2011; Sanson 2011; Hogg 2013; Chalaby 2015). This chapter seeks to avoid some of the tendencies of the latter work, particularly the slip into the comfort of comparative analysis or the narrativising of press and fan discord that can deaden productive explorations of translation. It attempts to dip its toe into these areas whilst avoiding falling into step, beginning with a brief journey through some existing scholarship surrounding formats, transnational television trade and translation to identify key concerns. In a bid to avoid comparative analysis (which can limit arguments to same-but-different and produces a uniformity across multiple accounts; Lavigne and Marcovitch 2011), I will then explore some overarching thematic concerns in the industrial and press discourse around the MTV translations of *Skins* and *The Inbetweeners*. Authenticity claims were central to this discourse; MTV presented 'authenticity' as the framework for an attempted redefinition of its channel identity that accompanied its venture into original scripted programming. I chart how authenticity claims were central to the reception of British youth drama as both import and translation, and how this discourse sought to assimilate the programmes into existing American narratives of teenage life. Exploring the discourse surrounding *Skins US*, I identify how production processes and a foregrounding of youth voice and bodies were positioned as 'proof' of these claims and became the programme's downfall. I then use bodies and masculinity to define national difference, viewing *The Inbetweeners* through comic traditions of masculinity, which bridges into a discussion of space and place. Exploring in the role of suburbia in *The Inbetweeners* and the shifts that assimilated its MTV translation into the national imaginary of teenage experience, I then identify how Canadian locations served to compound the 'foreignness' of *Skins US* and undermine its authenticity claims. I conclude by noting how these ultimately unsuccessful British translations contributed to the coalescing of MTV's nascent scripted programming voice.

Formats and Globalisation

The US has long been the dominant partner in transatlantic television flows; however, the mid-1990s saw a boom in the international trade of television formats that originated in Europe, with the UK a sizeable producer (Chalaby 2012, 37). A format is 'a show that can generate a distinctive narrative and is licensed outside its country of origin in order to be adapted to local audiences' (Chalaby 2011, 296). Format trade allows broadcasters to manage risk, using television that brings with it proven success from its home markets. It also saves on development costs, facilitating cost-effective productions, whilst also producing the local content preferred by television audiences. Chapter 6 further explores factual format flow through British structured reality's glocalising of US reality television.

The boom in format trade in the late 1990s catalysed a rise in scholarship chronicling these trade routes, which was predominantly focused on factual and entertainment formats. Globalisation is a central concern of format scholarship, blending the study of trade and industry with social and political concerns in order to bring complexity to earlier assertions of cultural imperialism (Schiller 1971). 'Glocalisation' recognises the identification of audiences as both global and local (Robertson 1992), with the tendency of local audiences to prefer 'culturally proximate' television offered as a 'local counterbalance to the global popularity of American culture' (Hogg 2013, 120). British youth television schedules construct a blended Anglo-American identity through their combination of imported US teen TV and original British programming, targeting viewers who are both 'global and local' (Hogg 2013, 115). American youth culture becomes assimilated into global youth culture through transnational popular culture flows. However, this is not mirrored in the US, where imported British youth television airs outside of niche-focused youth cable channels (MTV, CW or ABC Family) on BBC America, although recent years have seen digital streaming platforms such as Hulu bring British youth imports to televisual spaces frequented by youth audiences. The industrial barrier to the import of UK originals into US prime-time schedules comes from both the scale and success of US domestic production and the disjunction between British programmes and US time-slot and season structure. Instead of importing British youth programming, MTV developed local translations of two of E4's successful programme brands, producing 'glocalised' versions of British scripted formats in order to assimilate the form into US teen TV.

Skins and *The Inbetweeners* formed part of the growth in scripted format trade since the mid-2000s (Lavigne and Marcovitch 2011; Sanson 2011; Hogg 2013; Chalaby 2015): from soaps and telenovelas, to drama, comedy and structured reality. Perhaps the highest-profile case was streaming platform Netflix's $100 million translation of BBC One's political thriller *House of Cards* (1990–1995), which served as the flagship for its move into producing original programming. Chalaby connects the rise in scripted translations since the mid-2000s to the expansion of the US market for drama (2015, 6) caused by the arrival of new providers – cable channels and streaming platforms – and existing channels shifting into drama to build their markets. MTV's translations of *Skins* and *The Inbetweeners* formed part of the channel's push into drama programming after decades of reality TV dominance. This growth in scripted format trade has seen an increasing transparency, with translations recognising the increasingly globalised consumer. Unscripted formats (Chalaby 2012) and earlier British to US scripted translations such as Norman Lear's 1970s sitcoms (Miller 2000) downplayed their foreign-sourced status, but systems of media convergence have led to heightened viewer and press awareness of original source texts (Sanson 2011; Hogg 2013). As my analysis demonstrates, the translation became a central part of the industrial discourse surrounding the MTV series' and the channel's marketing of *Skins US*.

Chalaby notes that scripted formats carry substantial risk as the cultural sensitivity of comedy and drama requires a 'reactualizing' of a script for a new audience (2015, 4): in contrast to the superficial engagement offered by unscripted shows, drama must resonate more deeply with viewers (2015, 5). As melodrama and emotional realism are central to the storytelling of both British youth drama and teen TV, this emotional connection makes their translation particularly precarious. Scripted format trade also undermines the authenticity claims central to both British youth television's sense of self and the discourse surrounding *Skins US*, as it highlights television's status as a commodity or brand. This can undermine the – at times intense – emotional connection teen narratives seek to build with their audiences.

Despite these challenges, scripted format trade persists due to its dual benefits of cost-effectiveness and risk management (Chalaby 2015, 5). Drama buyers can view existing shows and acquire formats with proven ratings success, and channels can save on the time and expense of developing a new show by buying both ready-made scripts and a production bible. The latter can detail a programme's premise and key characters, together with detailed production information including marketing and the shooting schedule (Chalaby 2015, 14). Existing script libraries create production efficiencies; however, they often result in early episodes strongly echoing or reproducing the original text. The lack of creative translation here becomes a central element of press and viewer critique. This is particularly resonant with texts that already exist as imports in the market, as both *Skins* and *The Inbetweeners* had aired on cable channel BBC America prior to their translation. Here they formed part of a long history of British imports into the US market, from cult genre programming such as *The Prisoner* (ITV, 1967–1968) and *Doctor Who* (BBC One, 1963–1989/1996–) (Miller 2000; Hilmes 2012) to the range of prestige programming favoured by public service broadcaster PBS. The latter's preference for genres such as natural history programmes and period drama (Hilmes 2012; Knox 2012) positioned British imports as niche high culture embedded with cultural capital, aligned with a demographic elite. These connotations of cult and high culture linger, even now British imports have spread beyond PBS onto cable channels and streaming services. Cult and prestige form a central part of the brand identity of BBC America (Becker 2007) and inform digital platform Hulu's touting of its streaming of acquired British comedy and youth drama with their profanity intact (Rose 2012). The latter identifies language as a key marker of British imports' authenticity, which was illustrated in the reception of British youth drama.

With the increasing absorption of British independent production companies into powerful international 'super-indies' (Chalaby 2010), US translations are increasingly produced at least in part by the international arms of the original production company. Both *Skins US* and *The Inbetweeners US* gave British producers access to a US market historically resistant to British imports in prime-time and allowed the original creative team to retain a degree of control over their intellectual property. *The Inbetweeners US* was left largely in the hands of US creatives; however, *Skins US* saw creator Bryan Elsley maintain a highly publicised showrunner role, constructed as the brand's 'author' through industrial and press discourse (Rochlin 2008; Widdicombe 2011). Both programmes offered a prime example of televisual translation's 'commercial exploitation of a pre-tested televisual brand', assimilated into the new cultural context of US teen TV, seeking to appeal both to 'viewers who are familiar with the antecedent version and those who are not' (Hogg 2013, 123).

Teen Translations and Permeable National Boundaries

The translation of scripted formats constructs a contradictory reinforcing and permeation of national boundaries; it facilitates transnational trade, yet produces a discursive focus on national distinctions in press and fan reception (Sanson 2011; Hogg 2013). Sanson suggests that the visible transnational circulation of television formats – whether as originals or translations – muddles geographical and cultural distinctions (2011, 40). Cultural boundaries become less constructed by geographical placement and 'more of a contextually specific formation based on personal choice' (2011, 50). Permeable boundaries are facilitated by the proliferation of peer-to-peer sharing online, which breezes past national boundaries in the transnational circulation of original programmes. This enables a British viewer to subsist entirely on a diet US programming consumed immediately after its US airing, and many US audiences to experience British youth television before it arrives through traditional import streams or is transformed by translation.

So, why translate these British youth dramas? What value do they offer for their cable destinations? *Skins* and *The Inbetweeners* traveled from niche digital channel E4 to niche cable channel MTV, greenlit to serve the latter's demographics and brand identity. The translations formed part of the channel's concerted push into original drama and comedy in the early 2010s after years as a reality TV powerhouse. The *Skins* brand offered some of the same ingredients found in the channel's success in reality

TV, from *The Real World* (1992–) to *Jersey Shore* (2009–2012): illicit youth behaviour, the resulting interpersonal conflict and the attention-drawing cultural controversy that followed. This was that aligned with its noisy, edgy youth-focused brand (Stelter 2010). *Skins US* debuted on the same night as Syfy's translation of *Being Human* and a few weeks after Showtime's translation of Channel 4's raucous underclass comedy drama *Shameless* (2004–2013), prompting critical ruminations on the impact and effectiveness of US translations of UK hits (Ryan 2011; Zoller Seitz 2011a; Sepinwall 2015).

The British originals benefited from some form of name recognition within US industrial and critical circles as they had already aired on cable channel BBC America. *Skins* aired in Summer 2008 and was the channel's first imported youth programme (Rochlin 2008), with *The Inbetweeners* following in early 2010. The summer of 2009 had also seen *Being Human* air alongside *Doctor Who* and *Torchwood* in a triptych of British telefantasy. Here we see programming from the Channel 4 family assimilated into the BBC brand in the US, bringing with it the 'rhetoric of hip quality' on which BBC America was building its brand identity (Becker 2007). This brand identity of 'hip quality' was built 'around risk, realism and refinement' and derived from cultural connotations of British programming. This sought to separate the channel from the US network model of 'commercial, conservative, mass-oriented aims' (2007, 284). BBC America's importing of British youth drama served two of those Rs – risk and realism – which were derived from these programmes difference from US teen TV, particularly in their language and sexual content. BBC America here serves as a 'shop window' for potential translations, whilst also developing the programmes' 'cult' viewing status and critical cache. This status was also fed by their circulation via peer-to-peer flows and Channel 4 enabling *The Inbetweeners* and *Skins* to be streamed internationally via YouTube for a period of time.

The teen ensemble melodrama of *Skins* echoed US teen TV such as *Dawson's Creek* (WB 1998–2003) and *One Tree Hill* (WB 2003–2012), yet loudly asserted its difference with tonal swings between the mundane everyday, surreal comedy and dark melodrama. Following a group of 16 year olds through their last two school years in the south-west city of Bristol, the boredom of teenage routine is eased by leisure time spent partying, casually (yet ostentatiously) consuming a range of pharmaceutical substances and engaging in casual sex, tempestuous relationships and identity formations. With BBC America bound by basic cable content restrictions, *Skins* aired in an edited version, with nudity pixelated (contrary to later press claims, *Skins* only features adult nudity), profanity bleeped (Rochlin 2008) and sex scenes and drug use reduced (Kronke 2008; Lawrence 2008). In the move across the Atlantic, *Skins* expanded its audience from E4's niche 16–34 target demographic to the wider address of BBC America, which was reflected in the latter's marketing. Where E4's promotional imagery featured the cast in post-partying, blank-eyed tangles of bodies, BBC America offered clean-cut promotional portraits, with the fully-clad cast grouped arm-in-arm, grinning, against a white backdrop.

BBC America's promotion offered a notably unthreatening vision of British youth, but *Skins US* drew heavily on the original's controversial reputation. MTV sought out the programme 'specifically for its boundary-pushing content' (Itzkoff 2011), as part of the channel's bid to reinvent itself for its 18–24-year-old audience following the cancellation of its structured reality hit *The Hills* (2006–2010). The British independent producers Company Pictures and Stormdog maintained creative control, producing the programme and retaining Bryan Elsey as showrunner. The translation maintained the production methods that formed central elements of its programme brand in the UK; these asserted its 'authenticity' through a foregrounding of youth 'voice'. The translation publicised its search for new young American writers (Hibberd 2010), its use of group of 'teen advisors' (Widdicombe 2011) and its cast of teenage newcomers (Itzkoff 2011). Premiering the same night as Syfy's *Being Human*, *Skins US* drew an audience of over three million – which dropped by half in its second week (Moraes 2011) – along with a storm of controversy, and was cancelled after a single season.

E4's first original sitcom, *The Inbetweeners* chronicled the naive, foul-mouthed exploits of four suburban sixth-form boys in the cringe-comedy mode. Blazer-clad public schoolboy Will is forced to attend the local comprehensive after his parents' divorce; faced with contemptuous mockery in the school halls, he ultimately bonds with anxious Simon, compulsive liar Jay and clueless Neil. Between childhood and adulthood, nerds and the popular crowd, the 'inbetweeners' futilely chase some semblance of cool: attempting to buy alcohol, pursue disinterested girls and deal with quizzical parents. Pegged as the 'anti-Skins' (Hall 2009), both critics and creatives sought to distinguish the sitcom's everyday mundanity and humiliations from its predecessor's aspirational glamour. *The Inbetweeners* developed into E4's biggest ratings success, reaching 4.2 million by its third and final season (Allen 2010). The programme was followed by a film spin-off that was a huge sleeper hit and was followed by a similarly high-grossing sequel. *Skins* was an awkward fit with BBC America, but *The Inbetweeners* aligned smoothly with the cult status of the cable channel's previous comedy selections: both contemporary comedy imports – *The Office* (BBC Two/BBC One, 2001–2003), *Coupling* – and its classic comedy reruns – *Fawlty Towers* (BBC Two, 1975–1979), *Monty Python's Flying Circus* (BBC One/ BBC Two, 1969–1974). Like *Skins*, the sitcom saw its – considerable – profanity bleeped and its teenage male nudity pixellated.

MTV ordered *The Inbetweeners US* in 2011 as part of its *Skins US*-led scripted programming push. This followed an earlier attempt by US network ABC to developed a translation in 2008, which had never made it to pilot stage (Parker 2008). Their negative experience with ABC led creators Ian Morris and Damon Beesley to recruit a US showrunner to adapt and run the translation, with their production company Bwark Productions serving as co-producer. After the failure of *Skins US*, MTV was still struggling to establish its scripted voice and *The Inbetweeners US* debuted to a varied critical response and low ratings. Like *Skins US*, it was cancelled after a single season (Andreeva 2012).

When *Skins US* debuted in January 2011, E4's *Skins* had already cycled through two casts and was about to debut a third. So MTV's translation could be framed as a local variant, a further cast cycle generation within the overarching programme brand (Woods 2016). This framing aligns *Skins US* with Hogg's positioning of US translations as 'variant' on a programme's brand – as pieces within a larger meta-text (2013, 125), as 'textual formation rather than reinscription' (2013, 127). However, the tightness of the translation in early episodes of *Skins US* problematises a reading of 'variance'. Press claims of virtual 'shot-for-shot' translation are inaccurate, yet the pilot and many other episodes align closely to original scripts and story beats. There was some creative variance, as the gay male character Maxxie was replaced with lesbian Tea, yet the reordering of this story from fourth to second episode prompts a suspicion that this move was intended to produce further hypable controversy. Critics also framed the shift as a conservative action, offering the potential titillation of a teenage lesbian and normalising *Skins'* chronicling of Tony's transgressive flirtation with Maxxie (Sepinwall 2015; VanDerWerff 2011).

MTV sought to a build confrontational and disruptive youth voice for its new scripted content and it did so by drawing on a British form, one defined in reaction to the US teen TV, the same programming MTV wanted to distinguish itself from. Both translations aired in a post-10pm timeslot on MTV due to their TV-MA ratings – for over-18 audiences – for scenes of sex and drug taking in *Skins US* and language in *The Inbetweeners US*. This mirrored the British scheduling, yet contrasted with the 8–10pm scheduling of teen TV across US television, helping to position MTV's new scripted programming as 'edgy' alternatives to their competitors. However, the language, drug taking and sexuality of these translations were markedly curbed compared to the British originals. This lead to profanity and risk-taking behaviour becoming discursively positioned as a marker of British distinction, with the *New York Times* suggesting that the only limitation on *Skins'* E4 broadcast was 'the prohibition of two particular swear words' (Itzkoff 2011). Whilst they were reduced in translation, this language and risk-taking behaviour – markers of British 'authenticity' – in turn connected with behaviour and ideologies present in both MTV reality programming and its legacy of music videos. This supported the channel's quest to loudly assert its difference from its teen TV competitors – one facilitated by the budgetary efficiency of translation's production process (saving money on the development, piloting and scripting of new programming) and drawing on programme brands already in (limited) cultural circulation.

DISCOURSES OF AUTHENTICITY

As Chapter 3 demonstrated, constructions of 'authenticity' operating around representation, space and language are central to British youth drama's sense of self. This folds the programmes into long-standing articulations of British television's difference in the press and industrial discourses that surround imports and translation (Miller 2000; Sanson 2011). In the 1970s, Norman Lear had huge success with his translations of British sitcoms *'Till Death Do Us Part* (BBC One, 1966–1975) and *Steptoe and Son* (BBC One, 1962–1974) as *All in the Family* (CBS, 1971–1979) and *Sanford and Son* (NBC, 1972–1977). Jeffrey Miller suggests the British sitcoms facilitated Lear's search for a new engagement with 'realism' in the American sitcom and his attempt to capture social change (2000, 139–168). This is echoed in MTV's use of British youth drama translations to reposition itself around the successes of *Teen Mom* (2009–2012) and *Jersey Shore* (2009–2012) after the cancellation of *The Hills*. This move chased shifts in the ideologies of the channel's millennial audience identified by its own ethnographic research, with the *New York Times* claiming 'under the new guard, flashy reality shows are out ... and a new buzzword, "authenticity," is in' (Stelter 2010).

Miller argues that *All in the Family* held back from the violent attacks on the heart of the nuclear family that were central to the comedy of '*Till Death Do Us Part* (2000, 148). This aligns with press critiques charging that MTV's US translations pulled back and softened their content for the US market (Franklin 2011; Peterson 2011; Genzlinger 2012). For Miller, Lear's sitcom translations illustrate the 'complex ways in which cultural utterances shape the assimilation of transnational televisual texts' (2000, 155). Lear successfully reworked British markers of realism into the embedded ideologies of the US family sitcom, but there were messier, more disruptive results when British markers of realism and the authenticity claims of British youth drama meet the cultural norms of US teen TV. The US press evoked conventional signifiers of British realist storytelling in order to categorise these programmes' British difference, both as BBC America import and MTV translation. For example, 'gritty' is used to describe *Skins* on BBC America – indicating British drama's unsparing nature, which 'requires viewers to tolerate a high level of discomfort' (Franklin 2011) – and in translation on MTV. *Skins US* is contrasted with US teen TV due to its 'gritty settings and stories that are impossibly sad' (Weiss 2011) and is described as 'a sassy, gritty tour through teenage wasteland' (Moore 2011). 'Gritty' is a simplistic yet evocative short-hand for traditions of realism, conjuring up greyness, irritation, dirt, discomfort – grit in an eye or a knee wound, sharp and hard. More common is the descriptive 'authentic', which is connected to both traditions of British realism and teenage experience.

I have argued elsewhere that the *Skins* programme brand is built around the combination of its storytelling, representations and production process (Woods 2016). This combination is central to MTV executive Liz Gateley's articulation of the British programme's value, praising its 'unusually authentic stories', which she ties to 'the unique writing and casting process'. She stated her desire for the translation to preserve the 'authenticity of the British version' whilst speaking to American youth (Hibberd 2009). The *Skins* origin story was endlessly repeated in British press discourse (Woods 2016) and framed the programme on its arrival on both BBC America and MTV. This production process and its centralising of youth voices were positioned as the foundation of the programme's brand identity of 'authenticity'. The creation myth sees experienced television writer Brian Elsley have his television pitches critiqued by his then-19-year-old son, Jamie Brittain, who suggests he write about teenagers, and from there the pair developed *Skins* (Pile 2007; Widdicombe 2011).

Brittain based characters on his friends and built a 'writing room' of young writers and teenage advisors (distinct from British television's tendency towards writers working solo or in pairs) 'in order to keep the language and plots authentic' (Wiseman 2010). By season three, it was reported that the average age of a *Skins* writer was 21 (Armstrong 2009).

The centrality of youth voices to *Skins*' authenticity claims extended to its cast, which contrasted with US teen TV's tendency to favour twentysomething actors to play teenage roles for production, creative and aesthetic purposes. *Skins* touted the youth of its largely unknown cast, renewing the line-up every two seasons as the characters left high school. Each cast cycle blended professionals with amateurs sourced from open castings, with these 'real' teenagers feeding *Skins*' authenticity claims in terms of age, voice and body. This aligns the programme with long-standing narratives positioning non-professional performers sourced from open calls and street encounters as central to the authenticity of social-realist-informed cinema in the US (*Kids* (1995)) the UK (*Fish Tank* (2009)) and France (*Girlhood* (2014)).

Kevin Sanson argues that NBC executives foregrounded the autobiographical nature of the British sitcom *Coupling* in order to position the channel's translation of the programme within a discourse of creative innovation and authenticity, in turn legitimating its sexual content (2011, 45). The aligning of *Skins*' 'authenticity' with youth voice and body – alongside the autobiographical experience of its writers and teen 'advisors' – is replicated in the production process of *Skins US* and well-publicised in press discourse. The youth of its cast and their recruitment through open calls is noted throughout reviews and profiles (Itzkoff 2011; Gilbert 2011; Lowry 2011; Moore 2011), whilst a *New Yorker* article observes a meeting of the teen advisors, who vet scripts in order to 'insure the same authenticity as the British version' (Widdicombe 2011). This serves to legitimate the programme's wealth of sex, drugs and creative profanity as 'authentic' teenage experience, seeking to protect the programme against charges of exploitation or glamorisation.

Elsley repeatedly asserted his creation's 'authenticity', arguably unfairly claiming that prior to *Skins,* televisual teens were 'either dying of a drugs overdose because they have been f***ed by their father or they are impossibly bland' (Pile 2007). Here he elevated *Skins* above his simplistic constructions of social-realist-informed British drama and imported US teen TV. This comparative discourse is maintained in US critics' encounters with British youth drama in import and translation.

Here critics distinguish the programmes from US teen traditions, yet also aid their assimilation by evoking texts familiar to US viewers.

Assimilation and Distinction

Critics softened the 'foreign' difference of British youth drama by framing it as an alternate take on an American teenage original; universality, familiarity and distinction intertwine in a transatlantic dance. The young British *Skins* writers are positioned as echoing or upsetting the tropes, characters and storytelling of US teen narratives (Derakhshani 2008; Gray 2008; Lawrence 2008). The universality of hormonal teen boy humiliation is signified by noting *The Inbetweeners'* debt to the gross-out teen film, from *Porky's* (1981) to *American Pie* (1999) and *Superbad* (2007) (Weisman 2009; Lowry 2010; Smith 2010; Gilbert 2012). Yet its Britishness is positioned as lending freshness and innovation to this reworking of US tropes (Goodman 2012). National distinctions marking British television's 'authenticity' are articulated, yet this critical discourse ultimately positions British youth drama as a new accent on an essentially American teen.

British youth drama is also made familiar by aligning it with US teen texts already legitimated as 'authentic' within cultural and critical discourse. Both iterations of *The Inbetweeners* are linked to cult teen TV show *Freaks and Geeks* (NBC, 1999–2000) (Gilbert 2012), whilst controversial independent film *Kids* is evoked in discussions of *Skins* and its MTV translation (Kronke 2008; Gilbert 2011; Stuever 2011). On its BBC America debut, *The Inbetweeners'* British writers name-checked *Freaks and Geeks* (Weisman 2009) and the *Hollywood Reporter*'s Tim Goodman suggested the British show evoked the NBC series 'only with less naiveté and a relentless enthusiasm for graphic sexual references and truly inspired swearing' (2012). This comparison confers prestige by aligning *The Inbetweeners* with a cult text little-watched on its broadcast, but long-praised for its authentic depiction of teenage experience and unflinchingly observed comedy of teenage humiliation. The link also helped to define the unfamiliar social status of British schooling for a US audience. In turn, the critical discourse around *Skins* employed *Kids* to frame both versions of the programme within the parameters of Larry Clarke's controversy-stoking, cinema-verite-styled portrait of unsupervised, hyper-sexualised, nihilistic US teenagers (Carr 2011; Gilbert 2011); a film that saw its own storm of critical debate around its status as realistic, authentic, sensationalistic or exploitative (Perren 2012, 119). *Kids* is used to identify *Skins'* difference from US teen TV and is often evoked to explain the affect both iterations prompted in adult viewers – 'an empty and ruined feeling' (Stuever 2011) akin to that prompted by the 'grungy, icky, utterly depressing film' (Kronke 2008).

British imports and translations were more often framed by what they were not – US teen TV; this discourse asserts national televisual distinctions, troubling Sanson's assertion of translation's blurring of boundaries (2011, 40). Critics often followed Elsey's lead in structuring *Skins'* depiction of teenage experience in opposition to teen TV, in the process rendering the US form as 'inauthentic'. The CW network had rolled out its Parents Television Council-baiting 'OMFG' promotional campaign for season two of *Gossip Girl* (CW 2007–2011) in the summer that *Skins* debuted on BBC America (Lawrence 2008). This campaign combined with *Gossip Girl*'s place in the cultural zeitgeist (Pressler and Rovzar 2008), leading the programme to serve as the central comparison to both the import and the MTV translation (Kronke 2008; Marcus 2011; Gilbert 2012). This comparison with *Gossip Girl*'s glamorous melodrama of super-rich Manhattan teenagers heightened the reading of *Skins* as British 'realism', despite the strong presence of melodrama, fantasy and social surrealism (Creeber 2009) in its storytelling and aesthetic. *Skins* executive producer Charlie Pattinson asserted that MTV's US translation would be the 'absolute opposite' of *Gossip Girl* (Hibberd 2009). *Skins US* was described as 'more graphic and less softened with melodrama and romantic play' (Gilbert 2011) than CW's teen programming; their tendency towards glamorous lifestyles were contrasted with the MTV show's depiction of teens as 'sad, lonely and disturbed' (Marcus 2011). British youth drama's connotations of realism – themselves produced in opposition with US teen TV – were mobilised to articulate *Skins US'* difference. This supported MTV's positioning of its venture into scripted programming as part of an 'authentic' channel rebranding. This was constructed by distinguishing its new teen drama voice from CW's established identity as purveyor of teen TV; itself derived from predecessor WB's tendency towards aspirational, melodrama-infused teen dramedies.

Yet under the surface, there were commonalities in *Skins'* and *Gossip Girl*'s iterations of teen melodrama. The latter's long-term serialised narrative worked to contain and undercut the glamorous decadence and sexual experimentation that had so scandalised conservative pressure group the PTC. It ultimately constructed these as emotionally empty acts that destroyed relationships and caused regret, in line with the conservative ideologies at the heart of US teen TV (Wee 2008; Stein 2015). Similarly, Susan Berridge suggests that underneath its assertions of nihilism and parent-baiting indulgence in sex, drink and drugs, the embedded ideologies of *Skins* were fairly conservative, particularly around its gendering of sexual freedoms (2013). However, the *Skins* brand's foregrounding of teenage debauchery led questions of morality and consequences to be central to US discourses surrounding both the BBC America import and the MTV translation. Critics argued that in contrast to other 'boundary-pushing teen dramas' on US television, *Skins* offered no moral centre (Lawrence 2008) and had 'no moral lessons to impart' (Derakhshani 2008). This absence of moral consequences was positioned as central to the show's 'authenticity' and its desire to distinguish itself from teen TV's conservative norm (Stuever 2011). In an interview prior to the debut of *Skins US*, Elsley defined the 'edginess' of the *Skins* brand as the result of its 'teen-centric morality' (Widdicombe 2011), continuing the connection of the 'authenticity' of the programme's risk-taking behaviour to its teen 'voice'. Yet later, when the show's depiction of underage sex led to claims of child pornography (as I discuss below), Elsley backtracked to claim his protagonists as '"intensely moral" young people just trying to figure out life' (Ryan 2011).

The consequences of rule-breaking and risky behaviour *were* present in *Skins*, but tended to be delayed until the darker second season of each cast cycle (Woods 2016). So the swaggering, controlling Tony is hit by a car in the season one finale and spends season two recovering from a brain injury, attempting to rebuild the friendships he progressively destroyed over the course of the previous season. Season four sees Effie institutionalised with a mental breakdown, following the abdication of responsibility and manipulative nihilism she displayed in season three. *Skins US*'s direct translation of this narrative structure was a key point in the controversy surrounding the show, as it conflicted with US network television's narrative and ideological expectations. As critic Mo Ryan (2011) suggested, US audiences were trained to expect faster and more severe comeuppances, particularly for younger characters. MTV executive David Janollari explained to the *New York Times* that the production caused tensions with the channel's Standards and Practices department as it countered industry expectations for the immediate ramifications of teenage drug taking and illicit behaviour (Itzkoff 2011).

In the UK, critics recognised the hype of *Skins'* anarchistic excess, with Boyd Hilton noting that alongside its authenticity claims, its success lay in its depiction of 'teenagers in a quite glamorous, visually appealing way' (Frost 2011). In a British context, the programme's combination of realism and excess is clear; here it forms part of the modified social realism that Chapter 3 positioned as central to British youth television, a 'heightened realism' or 'social surrealism' (Creeber 2009, 429). However, in the US, British televisual connotations of realism combined with the discursive centralising of youth 'voice' in *Skins'* production processes; this coded the programme brand – in both its imported and translated state – as one of realism and 'authenticity'. When positioned in a US televisual landscape familiar with the representations and ideologies of teen TV, this led directly to the moral panic over the programme's content. It should be noted that many US critics were quick to temper reads of *Skins* as realist, pulling out the aspirational fantasy in the brand. The British import was described as 'an escapist fantasy in which teens carried themselves like seen-it-all rock stars' (Zoller Seitz 2011b) and an 'over-the-top' guilty pleasure (Kronke 2008), whilst *Skins US* was a teen fantasy and 'well-imagined dreamscape' (Moore 2011). Thus, the *Skins* brand was not too distant from its teen TV surroundings, despite the realist connotations of its British roots.

The authenticity claim central to the *Skins* brand is largely constructed discursively, read on to both the import and the translation through industrial and critical discourse. I move now to distinctions that have physical manifestations in US translations of British youth drama, identifying how the centralising of teen 'voice' in the *Skins* 'authentic' programme brand is extended to the teenage body in performance. Exploring the role of bodies, and by extension masculinity, in the articulation of national difference, I highlight how nudity served as a symbol of British television's permissiveness in the reception of *Skins US*. I then move my discussion of the masculinities of British youth and teen TV to *The Inbetweeners*, examining the emasculated British teenage male and national comic tendencies.

The Problems of Young Bodies

The well-publicised sourcing of performers for *Skins* and *Skins US* via open casting calls positions the teenage non-professional body as 'authentic'. When combined with the recasting of the *Skins* ensemble every two years, we can identify a centralising of youthful bodies – particularly in contrast with the twentysomething actors of US teen TV (Deggans 2011; Ostrow 2011) – as a key marker of the programme's brand. However, it is important to note that both programmes still operate within dominant standards of televisual physicality, with casts largely displaying normative femininity and masculinity. *Skins* places a premium on imperfections and the unformed, echoing British realist televisual traditions, with bodies presented as unkempt and faces often free of make-up or with it unartfully applied. However, as the seasons progress, the *Skins* cast's artful bedragglement does tip towards a fashion-spread louche glamour. On translation to MTV, critics noted a shift to more conventionally US 'telegenic' beauty standards (Deggans 2011; Moore 2011); *Skins'* bodily authenticity is modified by the translation's partial assimilation into teen TV norms.

As they are censored on US screens, British youth drama's profanity and bodily display – enabled by its 10pm, post-watershed timeslot in the UK – becomes discursively constructed as a marker of its authenticity. BBC America's broadcast of *Skins* pixelated its nudity, bleeped swear words and trimmed sex scenes, leading press coverage to contrast this with (misleading) claims of E4's allowance of full-frontal nudity. British television is presented as 'chock-full of nudity' (Lawrence 2008) and a space where full-frontal nudity is 'not uncommon' (Shen 2011); the free-to-air E4 is described as a pay-TV channel (perhaps due to subscription cable's sexual and verbal freedoms in the US) 'that doesn't censor for content, language or nudity' (Derakhshani 2008). *Skins* certainly lingers on partially clothed teen bodies and is particularly fond of underwear-clad girls (the male gaze is strong); however, these framings are deceiving as the frontal *Skins* nudity is all adult: the female neighbour Tony watches during the opening moments of the first episode, the teacher Chris chances upon in the changing rooms, the headless female body on Tony's duvet cover. The minimal teen nudity present is partial, male and comic, with Chris shot from behind as he trudges naked down the street after being locked out of his house in episode 1.4. Yet national distinctions are made through a framing – on both sides of the Atlantic – of British television as permissive, in contrast to US conservatism. Thus, the everyday frankness of *Skins'* British bodies serves as a marker of distinction amongst teen narratives, akin to US subscription cable channel's prestige nudity from *Masters of Sex* (Showtime, 2013–), to *Outlander* (Starz, 2014–), to *Game of Thrones* (HBO, 2011–).

The intertwining of bodily display and profanity with authenticity claims and the potential for controversy was embedded in the US industrial narrative surrounding MTV's translation. MTV executive Liz Gateley claimed the translation would 'preserve the authenticity' of the E4 show, yet confirmed the channel would not show nudity and would limit certain swear words (Hibberd 2009). However, the 'authenticity' of the teenage bodies of *Skins US* resulted in the defining controversy of its short MTV life – a controversy compounded by the production tendencies of translations, as its early episodes lacked deviance from the original's storylines and imagery. The PTC had branded *Skins US* 'the most dangerous show for children ... ever seen' (Jarvis 2011), a claim made partially on the basis of a viewing of the British show. This expected and useful piece of prepublicity – promising teenage drinking, drug taking and sex acts for the MTV audience – was superseded a few days after *Skins US* first aired by a front-page article in the *New York Times*. This claimed that MTV executives were concerned the show could violate federal child pornography statutes due to its use of actors under the age of 18 (Stelter 2011).

Stelter connected the concerns to episode 1.3, which repeated the comic storyline from episode 1.4 of *Skins* that depicted the inconvenience of Chris' viagra-induced erection and depicted him naked from behind in the street. The article highlighted the Justice Department's definition of child pornography, which included 'any visual depiction of a minor engaged in sexually explicit conduct' and the assertion that 'a picture of a naked child may constitute illegal child pornography if it is sufficiently sexually suggestive' (Stelter 2011). The scenes in question involved a 17-year-old actor; however, television critics who had previewed the episode stated confusion over any pornography concerns. They noted the non-sexual content of the scenes and their connection to an emotionally bleak storyline of parental abandonment (Gray 2011; Lacob 2011). Yet in quoting the Justice Department's definitions, the *New York Times* connected the 'concerns' over potential child pornography with the programme's use of young actors and depiction of teenage sexuality (despite a marked reduction in this in *Skins*' translation to the US). The 'child pornography' label lit a cultural fire, stoked by rhetoric from the PTC and its renewed campaign targeting advertisers; discussion of the show moved from newspaper and website reviews to opinion columns, breakfast shows and talk radio. The trade press gleefully catalogued the string of companies dropping their advertising as the season progressed, whilst British press discourse focused on assertions of American prudery (Jarvis 2011; Walker 2011). Here we can see how the *Skins* programme brand of 'authentic' teenage experience, built from its blending of teenage bodies and boundary-pushing content linked to the voices of young writers and advisors, on translation created insurmountable tensions with US culture's complicated relationship with teenage sexuality.

National Distinction Through Models of Masculinity

Teenage male bodies and articulations of masculinity play a central role in British youth drama's showcasing of its national distinction. These operate in contrast with the models of masculinity dominating US teen TV, as articulated in Miranda Banks' description of the aesthetic pleasures of the alien teenagers of *Smallville* (WB/CW, 2001–2011) and *Roswell* (WB/UPN, 1999–2002). Here hardened masculine bodies combine with vulnerable emotional softness to produce 'the new idol for a contemporary audience: strong on the outside, soft in the middle' (Banks 2004, 24). Grown men play teenage boys whose 'soulful eyes, full, pink lips, their dark tousled hair, and their voices filled with adolescent convictions … are worthy of teen fantasies' (2004, 23). British youth drama sees a physical and emotional shift from the US teen masculinity model, instead offering boys who are largely physically unimposing and displaying an investment in the failures of masculinity, often played by actors closer to their teenage years than the twentysomethings of US teen TV, with bodies that reflect this. The sex-obsessed and wittily foul mouthed boys of *Skins*, *The Inbetweeners* and E4's telefantasy *Misfits* (2009–2014) are often awkward and clueless. Tony, the protagonist of the first cast cycle of *Skins*, displays a commanding charisma and self-regard; however, the bragging swagger of *Misfits*' Nathan and *The Inbetweeners*' Jay are positioned as coarse and comically untruthful. The dominant image of masculinity in British youth drama sees a swerve away from the US teen male melodrama's object of desire, its investment in 'tragic beauty of the innocent, yet sexualised hero' (Banks 2004, 19) and privileging of the thoughtful, obedient boy (2004, 17).

The naive, selfish, foul-mouthed boys of *The Inbetweeners* are distant from this teen TV model of masculinity; their lack of power and stumbling pursuit of 'cool' place them within British sitcom traditions of underwhelming and ineffectual masculinities. These are comedies built around men struggling with social status, from *The Likely Lads* (BBC, 1964–1966), to *Men Behaving Badly* (ITV/BBC One 1992–1998), to *Peep Show* (Channel 4, 2003–2015). Both *Skins* and *The Inbetweeners* chronicle the exploits of 16-year-old A-level students, but where the *Skins* cast are clad in trendy casual clothing at a separate sixth-form college, the latter's liminal status as high school sixth-formers infantilises them as uniform-clad 'schoolboys'. Embedding *The Inbetweeners* boys amongst younger high school students allows them to be humiliated by mocking insults from children and teachers alike in cramped school corridors, with blazer-clad Will welcomed to his new school by catcalls of 'Briefcase Wanker'. The programme often builds its gross-out comedy around physical humiliations involving male nudity and the exposing of awkward, slight frames. A clueless Will attempts sex with Charlotte with his body rigid as a board, Simon stands naked and delirious with hypothermia on a boat with only a sock to cover his modesty and Neil blasély wanders a changing room naked after his clothes are stolen.

The Inbetweeners' fondness for emasculating its middle-class teenage boys with humiliation and grotesquery positions it within British traditions of cringe comedy, yet it also has transnational roots. When broadcast on BBC America, US reviewers aligned the British import with US traditions of gross-out teen comedy. In turn, these filmic legacies saw *The Inbetweeners US* fit securely into the comic history of emasculated white suburban boys, from *Porky's* 'failure of the male sexual quest' to *American Pie*'s 'suburbanisation of teenage sexuality' (Speed 2010, 820). Reports of MTV's development of the translation prominently noted the involvement of the casting agents who assembled *The Hangover* (2009) ensemble, positioning the boys within contemporary cinematic trends in man-child comedies of bodily excess (Andreeva 2010). In crossing the Atlantic, the boys were moved from 16-year-old sixth-formers to 14-year-old freshmen, closer to children than adults. This lessened both their desire to strive for masculine maturity and the emasculating nature of the humilities heaped upon them, naturalising any boyishness in the quartet's physicality together with their need to be chauffeured from house parties by their parents. *The Inbetweeners US* retained key comedic beats and iconography images from the British original – Simon's yellow car, his vomiting on the brother of a crush, his borrowing urine-filled trainers from a homeless man – but the translation settled into familiar routes, fitting *too* smoothly into an existing model of US comedy masculinities. As a result it erased the distinction produced by the British original's offer of familiar coming-of-age tales 'spun with wiry and foul-mouthed Brits', which 'polished over the parts where the familiar themes were played out' (Goodman 2012). *The Inbetweeners US* disappears too smoothly into the mass of the comedic norm, with its reworking of British scripts not the only element of weary familiarity; the translation's imagery of an identikit suburban teenage life embedded the programme in the cultural consciousness of American coming-of-age tales.

SPACE AND PLACE

As Chapter 3 argued, regional space and place contributes to the identity and storytelling of British youth drama. On translation to the US, these scripted formats are assimilated into the spaces of teen TV and the teen film, particularly the pull of suburbia – the central locale of the teen film – and its normalising upper-middle-class identity. Early episodes of *The Inbetweeners US* and *Skins US* keep close to original story outlines, recreating familiar jokes, beats and iconography; however, the spaces change around them. This constructs an uncanny experience for the viewer familiar with both. National distinctions are here produced through iterations of space, particularly the shifting meanings of suburbia in the translation of *The Inbetweeners* and the use of Canada to 'double' for US locales in *Skins* due to budgetary concerns. Here the national specificity of American space and place is troubled by Toronto doubling for an unnamed East Coast 'rust belt' city. The resulting combination of British and Canadian 'foreignness' impacted the show's critical reception, impairing its authenticity claims.

British Suburbia

The Inbetweeners' compatriots in British youth drama's first wave – *Skins, Being Human* and *Misfits* – are all embedded in variants of city spaces, from Bristol's spacious Georgian and Edwardian terraces to the stark concrete spaces of unnamed council estates. In contrast, the comedy of teenage manners draws on sitcom traditions and cultural connotations of the middle-class mundane, positioning the teen quartet's fruitless quest for sex and status in the most 'uncool' location possible: suburbia. England is a suburban nation with over half of the country living in suburbs of some kind (Clapson 2005, 65), spaces where *The Guardian*'s Will Dean claims 'nothing ever happens' (2009), which present a 'conformist squadron of Barratt estates told apart only by the cars on drives' and whose air of entrapment and daftness lends itself to comedy (ibid.). The suburbs were a symbol of entrapment for the angry young men of British cinema's 1960s New Wave, the 'feminized jaws of domestic containment' taming their working-class defiance through marriage (Medhurst 1997, 250–251). Yet the suburbs settle into the British sitcom's comedy of manners: from *The Good Life* (BBC One, 1975–1978) and *Butterflies* (BBC Two, 1978–1983) to *Grandma's House* (BBC Two, 2010–2012) and *Friday Night Dinner* (Channel 4, 2011–). These comedies of suburbia are built from the striving for propriety and challenges to middle-class values.

The Inbetweeners introduces Will as a class interloper, cast out of his upper-middle-class private school by his parents' divorce, uncomfortably dropped into a comprehensive school and a boxy detached new-build on an anonymous housing estate.³ Will is the definitive suburban little-Englander, defined by his adherence to rules and maintenance of status. *The Inbetweeners* are trapped socially and spatially in the middle: of the school's social strata, unable to reach popular status, yet not nerdy enough for outcasts; as sixth-formers between childhood and adulthood; and as suburbanites, between town and country. Their location defines their limitations and freedoms: their restricted lives of parks and lifeless house parties carefully monitored by parents, and their fruitless quests to get served alcohol in local pubs. Chauffeured by their parents, escape is brought by access to their own car – Simon's emasculating bright yellow hatchback – yet visits to London, the seaside and countryside only bring disaster.

The suburbs play a key role in articulating the ordinariness of *The Inbetweeners*, a world 'as far away from the bacchanal world of *Skins* as you could get' (Dean 2009). Its creators claim they resisted the encouragement of television executives to 'set it in central London and [have] the kids all take drugs and go to raves the whole time' (Morris 2010); instead, they drew on their own suburban upbringing, its uniformity and – they hoped – universality. Suburbia is not regional, but residential, marked in both cinema and television by its placelessness (Vermeulen 2014). Although I argue throughout this book that British youth television is notable for its locational specificity, *The Inbetweeners* is distinguished by its nowhereness; filmed in north-west Greater London, its indistinguishable standard-build housing estate could be anywhere and every town.

The council estate proliferates across British film and television screens, loaded with class-based signifiers; however, the late twentieth-century commercially built housing estate with its winding streets and boxy, standardised houses is less well represented. Instead, the middle-class mundanity of televisual suburbia is dominated by the more picturesque images of inter-war semi-detached bay-windowed streets. The new-build estate of *The Inbetweeners* offers the variations upon the norm that facilitate the 'complex and subtle signifiers' of inter-class difference that Roger Silverstone suggests suburbia offers 'for those who can read the signs, delicate statements of style and status ... reinforced within the house by the nuances and idiosyncrasies of decoration and material culture' (1997, 7). Will and his mother have 'downshifted' to a relatively new, comparatively spacious detached house, built in light yellow brick with her sportscar in the paved front drive, whereas Neil's house is a smaller, older, dark brown brick semi-detached house that Jay claims smells 'like poor people'.

The home lives of *The Inbetweeners* are dominated by the narrow boxy spaces of mundane, suburban living rooms; with their dated glass television stands, fading wallpaper borders, pleather sofas and ornamental plants. These environs are distinctly at odds with the boys' numerous failed attempts at deviant drinking (Figure 4.1). Parents are rarely far away, monitoring 'crap' Friday-night house parties that are some distance from the raucously destructive parties of *Skins* (episode 1.4). Over-dressed teenage girls perch on sofas in over-lit, sparsely populated living rooms, eyeing the boys warily and kitchens are fruitlessly searched for rogue alcohol. Notably, MTV's translation reorders episodes to position the boys' disastrous trip to a city club (episode 2.4) as its third episode, foregrounding aspirational adventures over the mundane everydayness of the suburban house party.

Fig. 4.1 Suburban spaces are at odds with *The Inbetweeners'* attempts at deviant drinking

US Suburbia

Where *The Inbetweeners'* suburban setting marks out its distinction in British youth drama, on translation to MTV, it slides securely into the familiarity of the national imaginary of suburbia. It also sees an aspirational class shift defined through space, in line with that identified by Miller in the Norman Lear sitcoms. There *Till Death Do Us Part* moves from the Garnett's cramped London terrace to the Bunkers' Queens, New York detached family home in *All in the Family* (2000, 145); the move to LA sees the dark cramped hovel of *Steptoe and Son* become a 'sunny single-family dwelling' in *Sanford and Son* (2000, 152). Miller identifies the Bunker's residence as aspirational for both the American and British working-class alike, as the transatlantic move comes with an elevation of class circumstance. *The Inbetweeners* is translated into the normalised (largely upper-) middle class of film and television suburbia and its particular role in teenage narratives.

As Tim Vermeulen points out, 'there are few genres that know their way around the suburb as well as the teen film' (2014, 135), suggesting the genre is 'particularly well attuned to the nuances and possibilities of the suburban vernacular' (2014, 166). *The Inbetweeners US* aligns with the suburbanisation of teenage sexuality in *American Pie* and its embedding of the teen sexual quest within the family home (Speed 2010, 834). This translation moves *The Inbetweeners* to a spacious, sun-drenched Florida suburb with expansive square-footage, detached homes and country clubs – a world where school buses replace the parental pick-up as the emasculating transport mode. The comedy derived from the spatial containment of new-build suburban living rooms is no longer valid in these wide open-plan kitchens and living rooms. However, American suburbia still offers a class stratum, from Neil's mini-mansion to Jay's front yard dotted with trashcans and spare tyres.

American suburbia and the spatial shift of translation are displayed in the first trailer for *Skins US*. With the 'Skins party' a central part of the programme brand (Woods 2016), this three-minute trailer mirrored that of the British original. The British trailer loudly asserted the programme's presence, depicting a debauched, destructive teenage party using an aesthetic akin to the titillating, soft-core porn-tinged style of the controversial fashion photographer Terry Richardson. The British trailer was located in a family home repurposed as the backdrop for teenage hedonism; the bright light of the camera seeks out teen bodies in a series of darkened rooms in a furious montage of pills, booze and make-out sessions. The protagonists are picked out amongst the crowd, dazed and blank eyed in close-up, ecstatic in dance, partially clothed and tumbling in a mess of limbs onto floors and beds in wider shots. *Skins US* offers a similar debauched party, here presented in reverse, following Michelle backwards from her collapse next to trashcans in a grassy suburban front garden whilst a siren wails. She moves back through a raucous party whose air is filled with a haze of smoke; bodies tumble onto sofas and into bedrooms, pills are chased with alcohol poured directionlessly over mouths. Yet this location is a large, brightly lit suburban house, with a columned double-height living room and galleried upper floor (Figure 4.2). *Skins US* is thus introduced within an aspirational classed space distinct from the ill-defined darkened space of the original *Skins* trailer. This clearly defines the suburban home as the space of wanton teenage destruction, signifying the transatlantic universality of adult fears of the interloping teenage hoard, yet also placing this British-inspired 'realist' narrative comfortably within the identifiable upper-middle-class spaces of US teen narratives.

Canadian Doubling

At the close of the *Skins US* trailer, the familiar *Skins* logo appears with a faded American flag fluttering inside, signalling its maintenance to the original programme brand and its status as an 'open' US translation. *Skins US*'s blended development process decoupled connections between place

Fig. 4.2 The *Skins US* trailer takes place in a large, brightly lit suburban home

and identity, producing a 'syncretic form' (Sanson 2011, 43) that muddled the claims of national distinction central to its articulation of 'authentic' American teenage experience. The US translation was produced by the US arm of a British indie, retained the British Elsley as showrunner, and used a young US writing team and teen advisors; it was shot in Canada with an American and Canadian cast of non-professional actors. This British-Canadian-American blend produces a piece of US teen TV that multiple US critics identified as 'foreign' (Franklin 2011; Stuever 2011; VanDerWerff 2011). The production efficiencies of translation caused early episodes to align closely with the British original's story beats and dialogue (Deggans 2011; Gray 2011; Ryan 2011), which prompted mockery from *GQ magazine*, which claimed: 'We've met undercover narcs who express themselves in more realistic teen slang' (*GQ* 2011). This foreign placelessness undermined *Skins US*'s careful maintenance of its programme brand's markers of authenticity.

The original intention was to set and film the show in Baltimore, with MTV and Company Pictures holding focus groups in the city to develop ideas (Hibberd 2009). As a port city with a racially diverse population, Baltimore could provide the 'grit' and connotations of realism – through the televisual legacy left by HBO's crime serial *The Wire* (2002–2008) – that the *Skins* brand promised. In *The Guardian*, Latoya Petersen connected the lost potential of Baltimore and US television's discomfort around class to *Skins US*'s struggle to translate the unspoken class concerns embedded in the British original:

> A hotbed of post-industrial decline, the city would have been a heady choice – the city boasts white working-class enclaves as well as black working-class neighbourhoods and hundreds of different ethnic and racial territories bracketed by the wealthier Baltimore County. Originally, producers eyed Baltimore's diversity as a reason to shoot the series [there]; the gritty urban landscape would have allowed *Skins*' treatment of class issues to shine. (Peterson 2011)

Instead, *Skins US* ended up being shot as a 'mobile production' (McNutt 2015) in the Canadian city of Toronto, a space that doubles for many different US cities across film and television. *Skins US* was not alone here as a system of tax incentives, production ecologies and the quest for particular varieties of locations beyond that of Los Angeles sends a large percentage of US television to use stand-in locations (2015). For example,

The Good Wife (CBS, 2009–2016) shot New York for Chicago, *Mad Men* (AMC, 2007–2015) shot Los Angeles for New York, whilst Vancouver has played a range of American locations for *The X-Files* (Fox, 1993–2002) and *Supernatural* (WB/CW, 2005–).

Skins US sought to channel associations with British (and perhaps 'prestige' pay cable) 'realism', evoking *Skins'* flat light and scruffy aesthetic. However, in contrast to the spatial distinctions of *Skins'* Bristol location, shooting Toronto for an unnamed American city resulted in *Skins US* lacking a sense of place, which US critics suggested disrupted the programme's connection with the viewer. Both Nancy Franklin of the *New Yorker* (2011) and Todd VanDerWerff at the *A.V. Club* (2011) argued the lack of locational specificity and 'the effort to make things feel like every-city' (ibid.) removed essential contextual circumstances for characters' adolescent experiences, their discontents and dysfunction. Critics argued that this missing of sense of place conflicted with the show's assertion of realism and authenticity. Franklin noted that 'even though MTV touts the series as a frank look at teen-age life today, I had the over-all sense that the show was not entirely real' (Franklin 2011); the *Washington Post*'s Hank Stuever asserted that 'you would think a show such as "Skins," which brags about its realism, wouldn't feel so fake and ... Canadian' (2011). Open translations and the cost-saving economies of their production processes often lead to such charges of insufficient glocalisation. This discourse echoed that which surrounded NBC's *Coupling*, which Sanson notes expressed 'a desire for more attention to the socio-cultural specificities of space and place' (2011, 48). The claims of realism and authenticity embedded in the *Skins* brand – and British youth drama itself – are intimately tied to space and place, so these are complicated by the unmoored locational issues of *Skins US*.

Learning Lessons and Finding a Voice

British youth drama's embedding in national traditions of realism, its sexual content and its profanity are all outward manifestations of its difference from established US teen TV storytelling and representations. However, MTV found that the intimate connections built through a programme brand so embedded in authenticity claims were not easily translated. *Skins US* saw it attempt to translate some of the ingredients of its success in reality TV, namely illicit youth behaviour and the resulting interpersonal conflict, into a new scripted voice. These qualities served as markers of 'authenticity' within British traditions of televisual realism; however, the murky morals they offered could not be easily assimilated into the careful dance with morality expected of US teen TV. Translation made appealing economic sense for an MTV looking to create its own scripted identity from scratch. *Skins* and *The Inbetweeners* align with its own noisy, disruptive, channel identity and its fondness for 'edge' and controversy. British youth drama is constructed in part in opposition to US teen TV and MTV attempted engage this opposition to assert its own difference from its competitors. Yet, the economics and production process of translation produced episodes of *Skins US* that were too strongly aligned to the original (Deggans 2011; Gray 2011) and not sufficiently glocalised for its US audience.

The gulf between *Skins'* hedonistic social surrealism and teen TV's aspirational melodrama was perhaps too far to breach, but *The Inbetweeners US* presented a smoother assimilation into representations familiar from the sexual misadventures of the teen film's suburban male. However, the restrictions of basic cable weakened the creative profanity that US critics deemed central to the original's comic pleasures – 'bus turds' lacked the comic ring of 'bus wankers'. This lead to a lack of distinction from existing US teen storytelling, with MTV failing in its bid to assert the edgy 'authentic' difference of its new embrace of original scripted programming. The cases of *Skins US* and *The Inbetweeners US* illustrate that transatlantic influence is not unidirectional, yet also highlights the national specificity of British youth television; British youth drama may bear the influence of US teen TV, but it is not easily assimilated back into the form.

In the summer of 2011, *Teen Wolf*, MTV's second original scripted series, debuted much more quietly than *Skins*. This programme also built on the safety of an existing teen property, although this was a 1980s teen film (*Teen Wolf* (1985)) that potentially offered even less built-in awareness for US millennials than a British youth drama. *Teen Wolf* shares only the name of its filmic precursor, as its aesthetic, storytelling and representations operated securely within the existing teen TV telefantasy model. Its male protagonists' bodies and characterisations map clearly onto the sensitive supernatural heroes identified by Miranda Banks (2004). The success of *Teen Wolf* – currently in production for its sixth season – signalled that MTV's progress in scripted originals lay in adherence to national television norms. However, the channel's failed British youth translations *did* contribute to its mapping of its distinctive place in the crowded teen TV market, helping to refine its scripted voice. This is most clearly seen in the critically well-received high school comedy *Awkward.* (2011–2016), which displays a casual attitude towards teen sex and drinking. It also utilises profanity – although this is bleeped – in an attempt to capture the rhythms of teenage speech. Yet the bright-coloured aesthetic, wry tone and aesthetically appealing performers of *Awkward.* operate within established models of US teen TV. Overall, these failed translations of British youth drama produced a reinforcing of national distinctions via their transatlantic televisual encounters, particularly through language, bodies, space and place. The difficulty in articulating 'authentic' televisual teen identities when blending national forms highlights the complexity of the relationship between British and US television – that in an era of blurred televisual borders, geographical distinctions are not so easily breached.

Notes

1. As both these MTV programmes go by the same names as the British original, I add the 'US' to help distinguish between the two national iterations. This is also how *The Inbetweeners* translation was presented when imported to E4.
2. I purposely echo documentary's 'truth claims' in this phrasing, as authenticity is not inherent but an ideal – it is conjured discursively and through the connotations of particular textual properties.
3. I use 'housing estate', as well as the term 'new build' here to signify the privately built estates built over the turn of the millennium. These are distinct from both the social housing of the council estate and the traditional British semi-detached suburban street.

References

Allen, Shane. 2010. 'The Secret to Comedy Success'. *Broadcast*, 29 October, 22.
Andreeva, Nellie. 2010. 'MTV Greenlights "Inbetweeners" Pilot'. *Deadline*, 27 September. http://deadline.com/2010/09/mtv-greenlights-inbetweeners-pilot-70379 (accessed 25 May 2016).
———. 2012. '"The Inbetweeners" Cancelled by MTV after One Season'. *Deadline*, 28 November. http://deadline.com/2012/11/inbetweeners-cancelled-mtv-378817 (accessed 25 May 2016).
Armstrong, Stephen. 2009. 'Loyalty Points'. *The Guardian*, 11 May. www.guardian.co.uk/media/2009/may/11/branding-tv-shows (accessed 25 May 2016).
Banks, Miranda J. 2004. 'A Boy for All Planets: Roswell, Smallville, and the Teen Male Melodrama'. In *Teen TV: Genre, Consumption, Identity*, edited by Glyn Davis and Kay Dickinson, 17–28. London: BFI.

Becker, Christine. 2007. 'From High Culture to Hip Culture: Transforming the BBC into BBC America'. In *Anglo-American Media Interactions, 1850–2000*, edited by Joel H. Wiener and Mark Hampton, 275–294. Basingstoke: Palgrave Macmillan.

Berridge, Susan. 2013. '"Doing it for the Kids"? The Discursive Construction of the Teenager and Teenage Sexuality in Skins'. *Journal of British Cinema and Television* 10(4): 785–801.

Carr, David. 2011. 'MTV's Naked Calculation Gone Bad'. *New York Times*, 23 January. www.nytimes.com/2011/01/24/business/media/24carr.html (accessed 25 May 2016).

Chalaby, Jean K. 2010. 'The Rise of Britain's Super-Indies: Policy-Making in the Age of the Global Media Market'. *International Communication Gazette* 72(8): 675–693.

———. 2011. 'The Making of an Entertainment Revolution: How the TV Format Trade Became a Global Industry.' *European Journal of Communication* 26(4): 293–309.

———. 2012. 'At the Origin of a Global Industry: The TV Format Trade as an Anglo-American Invention'. *Media, Culture & Society* 34(1): 36–52.

———. 2015. 'Drama without Drama: The Late Rise of Scripted TV Formats'. *Television & New Media*, 1–18 doi: 10.1177/1527476414561089.

Clapson, Mark. 2005. 'Cities, Suburbs, Countryside'. In *A Companion to Contemporary Britain: 1939–2000*, edited by Harriet Jones and Paul Addison, 59–75. Oxford: Wiley-Blackwell.

Creeber, Glen. 2009. '"The Truth is out There! Not!": *Shameless* and the Moral Structures of Contemporary Social Realism'. *New Review of Film and Television Studies* 7(4): 421–439.

Dean, Will. 2009. 'Hedgy Comedy'. *The Guardian*, 28 March. www.theguardian.com/culture/2009/mar/27/comedy-television (accessed 25 May 2016).

Deggans, Eric. 2011. 'Two Countries Divided by Common TV Shows'. *St Petersburg Times*, 16 January, 2E.

Derakhshani, Tirdad. 2008. 'Real Brit Teens, No Moral Lessons'. *Philadelphia Inquirer*, 21 August, sec. City-D, E1.

Franklin, Nancy. 2011. 'Anything Goes'. *New Yorker*, 28 February, 76.

Frost, Vicky. 2011. 'The Return of Skins'. *The Guardian*, 25 January. www.guardian.co.uk/tv-and-radio/2011/jan/25/the-return-of-skins#ixzz2UgFhnbr0 (accessed 25 May 2016).

Genzlinger, Neil. 2012. 'Not-So-Lovable Teenage Losers, the Translation'. *New York Times*, 20 August, C1.

Gilbert, Matthew. 2011. 'Two British Series Cross Pond to Varying Success'. *Boston Globe*, 17 January, G6.

———. 2012. 'MTV's Refreshing Take on High School Geekery'. *Boston Globe*, 20 August, G3.

Goodman, Tim. 2012. '*The Inbetweeners*: TV Review'. *Hollywood Reporter*, 17 August. www.hollywoodreporter.com/review/inbetweeners-tv-review-363406 (accessed 25 May 2016).
GQ. 2011. 'Dear "Kiddie Porn" Peddlers at MTV'. *GQ* 81(4): 166.
Gray, Ellen. 2008. '"Skins": Teen Angst, Brit-Style'. *Philadelphia Daily News*, 13 August, 32.
———. 2011. 'We're Clothing "Skins" in Controversy, But it's Not Porn'. *Philadelphia Daily News*, 24 January, 39.
Hall, Julian. 2009. 'The Inbetweeners: The Latest Teenage Pick'. *The Independent*, 27 March, 34–35.
Hibberd, James. 2009. 'MTV Shows its Many "Skins"'. *Hollywood Reporter*, 24 August. www.hollywoodreporter.com/news/mtv-shows-skins-88019 (accessed 25 May 2016).
———. 2010. 'MTV Taps Three Young Writers for "Skins"'. *Hollywood Reporter*, 13 July. www.hollywoodreporter.com/news/mtv-taps-three-young-writers-25460 (accessed 25 May 2016).
Hilmes, Michele. 2012. *Network Nations: A Transnational History of British and American Broadcasting*. Abingdon: Routledge.
Hogg, Christopher. 2013. 'Cracking the USA? Interpreting UK-to-US TV Drama Translations'. *New Review of Film and Television Studies* 11(2): 111–132.
Itzkoff, Dave. 2011. '"Skins" on MTV Will Soon Have its Debut'. *New York Times*, 3 January. www.nytimes.com/2011/01/04/arts/television/04skins.html (accessed 25 May 2016).
Jarvis, Alice-Azania. 2011. 'Cult British Teen Drama Shocks the Americans'. *The Independent*, 22 January, 12–13.
Knox, Simone. 2012. 'Masterpiece Theatre and British Drama Imports on US Television: Discourses of Tension'. *Critical Studies in Television* 7(1): 29–48.
Kronke, David. 2008. 'The Kids Aren't All Right in BBC "Skins"'. *Los Angeles Daily News*, 17 August. www.la.com/ci_11395419 (accessed 25 May 2016).
Lacob, Jace. 2011. 'This is Not Kiddie Porn!' *Daily Beast*, 20 January. www.thedailybeast.com/articles/2011/01/20/skins-is-not-kiddie-porn-mtv-show-breaks-no-child-pornography-laws.html (accessed 25 May 2016).
Lavigne, Carlen and Heather Marcovitch (eds) 2011. *American Remakes of British Television: Transformations and Mistranslations*. Plymouth: Lexington Books.
Lawrence, Christopher. 2008. ' "Skins" Pushing Boundaries of Teen Drama – Like Really'. *Las Vegas Review-Journal*, 17 August, 3J.
Lowry, Brian. 2010. 'The Inbetweeners'. *Variety*, 17 January. http://variety.com/2010/tv/reviews/the-inbetweeners-1117941901 (accessed 25 May 2016).
———. 2011. 'Skins'. *Variety*, 17 January. http://variety.com/2011/tv/news/skins-1117944298 (accessed 25 May 2016).
Marcus, Ruth. 2011. 'Not Scared of "Skins"'. *Washington Post*, 9 February, A19.

McNutt, Myles. 2015. 'Mobile Production: Spatialized Labor, Location Professionals, and the Expanding Geography of Television Production'. *Media Industries* 2(1): 60–77.

Medhurst, Andy. 1997. 'Negotiating the Gnome Zone: Versions of Suburbia in British Popular Culture'. In *Visions of Suburbia*, edited by Roger Silverstone, 240–268. London: Routledge.

Miller, Jeffrey S. 2000. *Something Completely Different: British Television and American Culture*. Minneapolis: University of Minnesota Press.

Moore, Frazier. 2011. 'MTV's "Skins": A Raw, Entertaining Drama Where Teens are in Charge, for Better or Worse'. *Associated Press Newswires*, 14 January, 3.41pm

Moraes, Lisa de. 2011. 'Creator Bares All to Try to Save MTV's "Skins": It's "Intensely Moral"'. *Washington Post*, 25 January. www.washingtonpost.com/lifestyle/style/creator-bares-all-to-try-to-save-mtvs-skins-its-intensely-moral/2011/01/25/ABJMh2D_story.html (accessed 25 May 2016).

Morris, Iain. 2010. 'Inbetweeners Creator Admits He's Will, and His Co-writer is Jay (with a Bit of Simon)'. *The Guardian*, 11 September. www.theguardian.com/tv-and-radio/2010/sep/11/inbetweeners-iain-morris-damon-beesley (accessed 25 May 2016).

Ostrow, Joanne. 2011. '"Skins" Peels Back the Layers of Teen Angst'. *Denver Post*, 14 January. www.denverpost.com/ci_17079625 (accessed 25 May 2016).

Parker, Robin. 2008. 'Formats & Deals – US Eyes *The Inbetweeners*'. *Broadcast*, 24 October, 9.

Perren, Alisa. 2012. *Indie, Inc.: Miramax and the Transformation of Hollywood in the 1990s*. Austin: University of Texas Press.

Peterson, Latoya. 2011. 'US Remake Lobotomised Skins'. *The Guardian*, 19 January. www.theguardian.com/commentisfree/2011/jan/19/mtv-skins-us-remake-class (accessed 25 May 2016).

Pile, Stephen. 2007. 'The Naked Truth about Being Young'. *The Telegraph*, 20 January. www.telegraph.co.uk/culture/tvandradio/3662644/The-naked-truth-about-being-young.html (accessed 25 May 2016).

Pressler, Jessica, and Chris Rovzar. 2008. 'The Genius of Gossip Girl'. *New York Magazine*, 21 April. http://nymag.com/arts/tv/features/46225 (accessed 25 May 2016).

Robertson, Roland. 1992. *Globalization: Social Theory and Global Culture*. London: Sage.

Rochlin, Margy. 2008. 'A Show Written for the Young by the Young'. *New York Times*, 17 August, 19.

Rose, Lacey. 2012. 'Hulu to Stream UK's Foul-Mouthed Comedy "The Thick of It" Uncensored'. *Hollywood Reporter*, 18 July. www.hollywoodreporter.com/news/hulu-stream-uks-foul-mouthed-351169 (accessed 25 May 2016).

Ryan, Mo. 2011. '"Skins" Creator Defends the MTV Show's Morals, But What about the Edgy Drama's Other Problems?' *AOL.com*, 25 January. www.aoltv.com/2011/01/25/skins-mtv (accessed 25 May 2016).

Sanson, Kevin. 2011. 'We Don't Want Your Must-See TV: Transatlantic Television and the Failed "Coupling" Format'. *Popular Communication* 9: 39–54.

Schiller, Herbert. 1971. *Mass Communications and American Empire*. Boston, MA: Beacon Press.

Sepinwall, Alan. 2015. 'Review: Syfy's "Being Human" & MTV's "Skins"'. *HitFix*, 17 January. www.hitfix.com/blogs/whats-alan-watching/posts/review-syfys-being-human-mtvs-skins (accessed 25 May 2016).

Shen, Maxine. 2011. '"Skins" Deep; MTV's New Series More Tame Than it Looks'. *New York Post*, 4 January, 61.

Silverstone, Roger. 1997. 'Introduction'. In *Visions of Suburbia*, edited by Roger Silverstone, 1–25. London: Routledge.

Smith, Kyle. 2010. 'Street 16 Party'. *New York Post*, 25 January, 83.

Speed, Lesley. 2010. 'Loose Cannons: White Masculinity and the Vulgar Teen Comedy Film'. *Journal of Popular Culture* 43(4): 820–841.

Stein, Louisa Ellen. 2015. *Millennial Fandom: Television Audiences in the Transmedia Age*. Iowa City: University of Iowa Press.

Stelter, Brian. 2010. 'MTV Is Looking Beyond "Jersey Shore" to Build a Wider Audience'. *New York Times*, 25 October. B1

———. 2011. 'A Racy Show with Teenagers Steps Back from a Boundary'. *New York Times*, 20 January, A1.

Stuever, Hank. 2011. 'In "Skins," Teens' Good Times are a Grown-Up's Nightmare'. *Washington Post*, 17 January, C5.

VanDerWerff, Todd. 2011. 'Skins: "Tony"'. *A.V. Club*, 17 January. www.avclub.com/tvclub/skins-tony-50109 (accessed 25 May 2016).

Vermeulen, Timotheus. 2014. *Scenes from the Suburbs: The Suburb in Contemporary US Film and Television*. Edinburgh University Press.

Walker, Harriet. 2011. 'The Kids are All Right'. *The Independent*, 31 January, 12–13.

Wee, Valeria. 2008. 'Teen Television and the WB Television Network'. In *Teen Television: Essays on Programming and Fandom*, edited by Sharon Marie Ross and Louisa Ellen Stein, 43–60. Jefferson, NC: Macfarland.

Weisman, Jon. 2009. '"Occupation" to Hit BBC America'. *Variety*, 29 July. http://variety.com/2009/biz/news/occupation-to-hit-bbc-america-1118006672 (accessed 25 May 2016).

Weiss, Joanna. 2011. 'Between Expectation and Rebellion'. *Boston Globe*, 30 January, A10.

Widdicombe, Lizzie. 2011. 'Expert Witnesses'. *New Yorker*, 10 January, 25.

Wiseman, Eva. 2010. 'Teenagers: Under Their Skins'. *The Guardian*, 19 December. www.guardian.co.uk/society/2010/dec/19/teenagers-under-their-skins (accessed 25 May 2016).

Woods, Faye. 2016. 'My Generation(s): Cycles, Branding and Renewal in E4's *Skins*'. In *Multiplicities: Cycles, Sequels, Remakes, Spin-Offs, and Reboots in Film and Television*, edited by Amanda Ann Klein and R. Barton Palmer, 240–259. Austin: University of Texas Press.

Zoller Seitz, Matt. 2011a. '"Shameless": American TV's Problem with Class'. *Salon*, 8 January. www.salon.com/2011/01/08/shameless_remake (accessed 25 May 2016).

———. 2011b. '"Skins"' Salacious Teen Thrills'. *Salon*, 18 January. www.salon.com/2011/01/18/mtv_skins (accessed 25 May 2016).

PART III

Factual

CHAPTER 5

Youth Factual: First Person, Peer Address and Interaction

In 2014, faced with its closure as a linear channel, a move to online-only and a significant budget cut, BBC Three commissioned the large-scale, month-long 'Defying the Label' season for 2015. This sought to 'challenge the views of [its] savvy audiences whilst questioning perspectives and attitudes towards young disabled people in the UK today' (No author 2015). Encompassing 15 programmes examining life for young British people living with disability, 'Defying the Label' followed the success of earlier factual seasons 2013's 'It's a Mad World'[1] and 2014's 'Crime and Punishment'.[2] The season included three-part observational documentary *The Unbreakables: Life and Love on Disability Campus* (2015), peer-presented documentaries *Me and My New Brain* (2015) and *The Ugly Face of Disability Hate Crime* (2015), current affairs programme *The World's Worst Place to Be Disabled* (2015) and 'factual drama'[3] *Don't Take My Baby* (2015). The seasons debuted just over a month after the BBC Trust agreed the proposal to close the channel (Gannagé-Stewart 2015a) (a process outlined in Chapter 2) and in the face of the Conservative government's hostile Green Paper, which launched an exploration of the future of the BBC (Plunkett 2015). This was BBC Three's biggest factual season yet and it served to assert the channel's value in the public sphere in an uncertain time, foregrounding its provision of documentary programming targeting youth audiences, a rarity across the schedules. Youth-focused documentary is largely absent from discourses surrounding British youth television and US teen TV due to the dominance of drama, comedy and reality programming in provision for this demographic. The significant production of youth-focused documentary is one of the distinctions of the British system (with MTV's documentary series *True Life* (1998–) one of the only US offerings) due to British youth television's roots in public service broadcasting.

The interests, imagery and worldviews presented in this factual content construct an image of British youth (or broadcasters' preferred image of British youth), one framed by a liberal humanist agenda and shaped by emotional engagement. The challenge for this programming is to present social, political and health-based concerns outside of traditional educational spaces and without showing its institutional hand. This delicate balance is reached by producing documentary programming that centralises youth voice and point of view within emotion-led storytelling. Educational content also expands beyond the televisual, with interactive online platforms offering an intimate address and opportunities for individualisation. Youth documentary's focus on access and the first person across a range of subject matters ties into this book's tracing of the role of 'authenticity' in British youth television's sense of self.

This chapter explores British youth documentary through a series of case studies of BBC Three and Channel 4 factual content. Through these we can trace an investment in intimate, first-person storytelling, offering peer-led experiences of social and personal concerns, both at home and abroad. I begin with a short discussion of BBC Three's 'peer investigation' documentary form, then explore Channel 4's attempt to depict the teenage everyday through *Teens* (2015). This documentary used a 'digital rig' to layer social media communications onto observational footage. Both of these sections set up storytelling and technological themes that connect with the primary case study of this chapter, the Afghanistan war documentary *Our War* (BBC Three, 2011–2014). This series of single documentaries formed part of BBC Three's long-running documentation of young British soldiers' experiences in the conflicts in the Middle East. The programme engages with BBC Three's preference for documentary read through the personal, illustrated here in the use of self-filmed footage and soldier-as-witness. I then offer a brief analysis of how *Our War* influenced the channel's contribution to the BBC's commemoration of the First World War in factual drama *Our World War* (BBC Three, 2014). I close with Channel 4's multi-platform factual content, exploring the extension of its factual provision beyond the televisual text, where an investment in the intimate, youth voice and peer-led content frames interactive content.

These case studies illustrate the dominance of the personal across British youth factual content and particularly in BBC Three documentary. Within the latter, this is seen in the dominance of the autobiographical journey; access to youth voices excluded from society (through health, crime or poverty) through observational series; and the proliferation of self-filmed footage across a range of documentary forms. This investment in the first person connotes an intimacy and access that continues British factual television's fascination with the confessional and the video diary (Dovey 2000). Jon Dovey's *Freakshow* serves as a useful frame for my analysis as his discussion of British factual television of the 1990s identifies tendencies that remain central to youth factual, particularly in the confessional aspects of the autobiographical journey and the use of self-filmed footage across this programming. Technological developments have made social media self-documentation part of the everyday of youth experience, with the direct address of YouTube vloggers a key media form (Burgess and Green 2009). Dovey and Mandy Rose connect this internet-led proliferation of 'vernacular video' to the camcorder-confessional turn in 1990s British factual television and the BBC's *Video Diaries* (1990–1999) and *Video Nation* (1993–2001) projects. They argue that the form acts as 'demotic, promiscuous, amateur, fluid and haptically convenient, [using] technologies at hand and in the hand' (2013, 365). Self-filmed footage (a term I prefer over 'vernacular video' to indicate its spread beyond video diary forms) offers 'a set of practices that have come to be characterised by naive attachments to indexicality, or 'zero degree simulation" (ibid.), connoting transparency and participant control in the documentation of youth experience. Yet, as my analysis demonstrates, the connotations of transparency brought by *Our War*'s soldier-filmed footage are countered by the strongly mediated nature of its documentary narrative.

BBC Three dominates this chapter because it plays *the* central role in British youth-focused factual programming. This has become central to its channel identity and its distinction from ITV2 and E4, and is showcased in the positioning of factual programming as a central pillar of the channel's move to an online-only platform (Kavanagh 2014). This investment is shaped by the channel's remit to 'bring younger audiences to knowledge-building factual content by tackling relevant topics in ways that feel different, original and interesting to them' (BBC Trust 2014, 4) as well as supporting the BBC's overall remit to 'bring the UK to the world and the world to the UK' (2014, 6). As Chapter 2 explained, press and political critiques of BBC Three foreground the channel's delegitimated reality and lifestyle programming, yet factual programming is embedded at the heart of the channel's schedule. In contrast, the 'entertainment' focus of E4 sees the channel dominated by drama, comedy and reality, with no space for factual content. Instead, a relatively small amount of youth-focused documentary, such as *Don't Blame Facebook* (Channel 4, 2013), *On the Edge and Online* (Channel 4, 2015) and *Underage and Gay* (Channel 4, 2015), is currently restricted to the edges of prime-time on Channel 4.

BBC Three documentaries take three dominant forms: observational series, presenter-led current affairs 'investigations' and what I term the 'personal exploration' single documentary. Observational documentary series primarily chronicle youth excised from society and their interaction with institutions; these use multi-stranded ensemble storytelling to explore the experiences of young offenders, teen mental illness or a further education college for those with physical disabilities (*Kids Behind Bars* (2011); *Don't Call Me Crazy* (2013); *The Unbreakables* (2015)). The channel's current affairs documentaries are built around youthful presenters who offer a peer address: Cherry Healey explores the British youth everyday – parenting, binge drinking and first-time homebuying – at times through an autobiographical lens[4]; whilst Stacey Dooley covers internationally focused topics including child labour, religious fundamentalism and the drug trade.[5] Personal investigation single documentaries explore social issues through an autobiographical focus, with the presenter serving as both guide and social actor. These feature both celebrity and peer presenters; pop star and *The X Factor* (ITV, 2004–) judge Tulisa Contostavlos reflects on her teenage experience of caring for a disabled parent and meets other young carers in *Tulisa: My Mum and Me* (2011), whilst former young offender Natalie Atkinson explores whether prisons offer sufficient rehabilitation to young prisoners on short sentences in *Banged Up and Left to Fail?* (2014). These documentaries reflect Jon Dovey's observation that 'forms of factual programming structured around first person experience as a way of knowing can be seen as part of the spread of a generalised sociality in which individuality, local specific knowledges, and "emotional intelligence"' are valorised' (2000, 159). Here complex social, political and health-related issues are refracted through the personal, framed as a journey towards knowledge with a peer guide.

These three dominant documentary frames allow BBC Three to commission low-budget, quick-turnaround documentaries on topical issues alongside longer-term 'prestige' projects such as *Our War* or the institutionally focused observational series. However, the dominance of these frames can also limit the opportunity for innovation and experimentation in BBC Three's factual programming. Working within relatively traditional investigation, journey or observational structures, these documentaries prioritise a straightforward approach to their subject. This neglects BBC Three's potential as a space for challenging or risk-taking television, although, as Chapter 2 highlighted, this position is perpetually in tension with its role as a heavily scrutinised BBC platform. Documentary on BBC Three is positioned safely as a distinctly civic form, operating within historic constructions of documentary as a social agent, speaking 'to the viewer as citizen, as a member of a social collective, as a putative participant in the public sphere' (Chanan 2008, 16). The channel's public service status means its documentary programming is framed as an institutional product, yet as this chapter explores, its address to a youth audience and rigorous focus on the personal is built on an assertion of authenticity and transparency. As a result the negotiation of institution, authenticity and transparency, alongside the role of the individual and the public sphere, produce the central tensions of BBC Three documentary programming.

Peer Presenter and Personal Investigation

BBC Three documentaries place personal testimony, an immersion in embodied experience and a search for meaning and connection above expert viewpoint, foregrounding 'individual subjective experience at the expense of more general truth claims' (Dovey 2000, 25). This distinguishes BBC Three content from sister channel BBC Four, which is dominated by quirky, often eccentric expert presenters in its arts, history and science documentaries. BBC Three's 'peer presenters', whether celebrity or amateur, serve as a combination of a proxy for the BBC Three youth audience and a trusted peer advisor. Positioned as amateur investigators, they are set at only a minor remove from the audience – the 'guide from the side' rather than the 'sage from the stage' (Gray and Bell 2012) – offering an intimate address and accessibility in order to avoid 'talking down' to the youth audience.

The channel's current affairs series – from *Stacey Dooley Investigates* (2009–) to *Cherry Healey: Old Before My Time* (2013) to *Reggie Yates: Extreme South Africa* (2013) – are built around youthful yet experienced presenters who act as peer proxies. They oscillate between a position as an impartial observer and invested advocate, within narratives built around interpersonal interaction with young social actors. Here subjective experience is prioritised over 'expert' opinion; Dooley stands in the frozen Detroit night with a young homeless transgender woman working as a prostitute (*Stacey Dooley in the USA: Homeless in Detroit* (2014)), while Yates helps insert a chest drain into a stabbing victim in a Cape Town ER whilst interviewing both doctor and patient (*Reggie Yates' Extreme South Africa: Knife Crime ER* (2013)). Dooley's and Yates' international travels offer BBC Three's own interpretation of the foreign correspondent-fronted immersive reporting of Channel 4's *Unreported World* (2000–) strand or the multi-platform reportage offered by media company *Vice*. The latter's fascination with international lives of extremes of risk and violence – *Inside North Korea* (2011), *Cables from Kabul* (2013) – is evoked by the framing introductions of each of Yates' *Extreme South Africa* and *Extreme Russia* (2015) episodes. These offer a fast-paced, choppily edited montage of news archive charting each country's violent history; however, Yates' presenting style seeks a companionable connection with his subjects distinct from *Vice*'s ever-present potential of slippage into gonzo journalism. In contrast to the expert foreign correspondents of *Unreported World*, BBC Three's current affairs narratives highlight the presenter's own journey of knowledge, built around an inquisitive, empathic intimacy.

Throughout *Knife Crime ER*, Yates positions the doctors, patients and local youth as his peers, often turning to the camera to reflect with admiration or sadness on what he himself was doing at their age. Yates has been a television and radio presenter since his late teens, but he works to connect his own youth growing up in the council estates of south London and his Afro-Caribbean roots (such as his experience with African Pentecostalism) to those he encounters in hardship or struggling with social pressures, particularly young black men. He takes care to reiterate his – and by extension the British audience's – relative ignorance and privilege in comparison. For example, he notes that at 26, the age of the junior doctors treating hundreds of knife crime injuries in a single weekend, his priority was keeping his trainers clean. The *Extreme South Africa* series is framed as the journey of an outsider, one seeking to discover how the end of apartheid 'affected people like me', and it opens with Yates noting how restrictive his movements as a black man would have been under the regime. However, his ongoing reiteration of his status as privileged interloper is softened by his ability to relate to his subjects as fellow young black men, slipping easily into colloquialism not present in his prime-time presenter speech. These encounters are facilitated by his ease and skill as an interviewer developed through years of live broadcasting encounters with the general public.

The role of the peer presenter – professional or amateur – and the intimate relationship they seek to construct with both the social actors they encounter and the audience at home are facilitated by the physical, structuring and storytelling presence of experienced self-shooting producer-directors. Both *Knife Crime ER* and *Reggie Yates Extreme Russia: Teen Model Factory* (2015) are filmed, produced and directed by highly experienced documentary and current affairs director Ruhi Hamid, whose work throughout the developing world and in conflict zones is characterised by its access and construction of intimate relationships with social actors. Hamid also directed *Women, Weddings, War and Me* (2010) for BBC Three, working with amateur peer presenter Nel Hedayat, and has highlighted the skills needed to nurture and shape amateur presenters in order to facilitate their subjectivity:

> I tailored a journey for Nel to take that would reveal and unfold to her the often shocking stories of women's lives in Afghanistan. As Nel was not an experienced reporter I had to bring out the best in her to react on a human level yet at the same time apply some analysis and find ways to relate what she was experiencing for a BBC Three audience. ('Ruhi Hamid - Producer/Director' 2015)

The documentary director serves here as the invisible intermediary facilitating the encounters and intimate engagement of the amateur peer presenter.

These programmes' use of amateur and celebrity peer presenters to frame social and political concerns through autobiographical experience and emotional connections draws on confessional television's offer of 'insight into the social body' (Dovey 2000, 111). Built around the presenter as subject, witness and investigator, these documentaries are often constructed as a form of 'speaking the self', revealing a personal truth and a mission to understand it – for example, Tulisa's remembrances of her experiences as a young carer and her exploration of the support offered to other young carers or Professor Green's revealing of the impact of his father's death in order to discuss the 'taboo' of male suicide. Here the celebrity peer presenter is positioned as someone affected by the documentary's topic, with their confessional 'self-naming' positioning the programme as their journey 'toward proclaiming a selfhood that is part of a group identity' (Dovey 2000, 111), moving them from the elevated status of celebrity to the position of peer.

Personal exploration documentaries offer varying levels of director intervention – whilst the celebrity peer presenter is clearly offered as both author and witness, amateur peer presenter-led programmes will vary. At times, these presenters drive the narrative and structuring narration with little interaction with the off-camera director. This is seen in *Banged Up and Left to Fail?*, which follows student and former youth-offender Natalie as she investigates her strong belief in the justice system's responsibility to provide more rehabilitation opportunities for young offenders. At points in this documentary, Natalie explains the isolation and fear she felt when she was transferred to adult prison after turning 18. In these sections her narration is accompanied by sparsely illustrated animations, further embedding emotion-led autobiography in its documentary storytelling. Other amateur-led 'personal explorations' feature a greater level of director interaction and external narrators, as seen in snowboard instructor Charlie Elmore's retracing of the steps of her recovery from a traumatic brain injury in *Me & My New Brain* (2015), as she seeks to bring attention to the invisible disability. Although this documentary is built around the amateur peer journey, the presence of both the off-camera directorial voice and a professional narrator – both male voices in the journey of a young women – serves to highlight the status of the documentary encounter, the 'negotiation between filmmaker and subject' (Bruzzi 2006, 199). Here the 'My' of the title and BBC Three documentary's centralising of the autobiographic and subjective are held in tension with the director's choice to retain their interaction and guidance. Such choices position the peer presenter as 'the speaking subject speaking within the frame of somebody else's version of their biographical narrative', serving only as a social actor rather than '"writ[ing] themselves" in autobiographical mode' (Dovey 2000, 110). However, this particular interaction is also arguably a production necessity caused by BBC Three's embrace of the amateur presenter and, in Elmore's case, her disability.

These personal journey and current affairs documentaries construct stories and investigations outside the boundaries of the everyday. Meanwhile, other documentary series invest in an intimate display of the teenage everyday. A pair of Channel 4 documentaries – *The Secret Life of Students* (2014) and *Teens* – seek to explore interpersonal relationships and interiority using a surveillance technology that promises a similar transparency as that invoked by BBC Three's first-person address.

Surveilling the Social Media Everyday

A 17 year-old-girl stands in a quiet corner of a school field to the right of frame, twisting her body in delighted anxiety as she talks to camera, running through the torture of how to end a text to a boy to thank him for a letter that made her feel 'sparkly and bubbly'. As she runs through her choices, the text is overlaid on the image, filling the left of the screen; it taps speedily through her contemplations of what each could mean: full stop, exclamation mark, different permutations of kisses and a variety of emoji faces until it lands on her final choice. The scene of a teenager sharing her romantic experiences with a questioning observational documentary maker is a familiar one across both film and television documentary. The particular aesthetics of this moment from *Teens* illustrates how this series attempted to represent the everyday of a generation whose daily life also unfolds in the digital sphere and for whom sharing of intimacy digitally is the norm. *Teens* and its predecessor *The Secret Life of Students* can be understood as developments of observational documentary's ongoing, impossible quest to fulfil its ideologies of immediacy and transparency through technological innovation (Bruzzi 2006, 74–80), here through the use of a 'digital-rig' developed by documentary production company Raw TV.

The production discourse surrounding these programmes positioned the digital rig as the next step on from the fixed-rig system that had come to dominate Channel 4's observational documentary series in the mid-2010s ('Programme Information: Teens' 2014). Building on the surveillance aesthetic and production process embedded in *Big Brother* (Channel 4/Channel 5, 2011–) the fixed-rig documentary places remote-controlled cameras in domestic – *The Family* (Channel 4, 2008–2010) – and institutional – *One Born Every Minute* (Channel 4, 2010–), *Educating Essex* (Channel 4, 2011) – spaces. These feed into and are controlled by a live gallery, with the system enabled the absenting of the cameraperson in a quest to minimise the appearance of on-the-ground intervention. Raw TV took the fixed-rig system's connotations of immediacy and transparency into the digital realm, augmenting conventional interactive observational footage with a digital communications monitoring system. Here the documentary participants consented to use specially modified mobile phones (Beckett 2014), which run a programme that collects voice calls, text messages, Twitter updates, Facebook and Tumblr posts, WhatsApp and Snapchat messages, videos, photographs and internet search history

24 hours a day (Ip 2014). *The Secret Lives of Students* collected 200,000 pieces of communication over its four-month filming period following a group of freshers at Leicester University – effectively producing two sets of rushes. These were collated and selectively aligned in the finished programme, with social media communications and internet searches layered over observational footage. Channel 4 claimed that Raw TV's 'digital rig' allowed 'unprecedented insight into the teenagers' hidden online lives, [allowing] the filming teams to react instantly to moments of drama as they unfold digitally and in the real world' ('Programme Information: Teens' 2014), suggesting that *Teens* offered a further step in providing intimacy, access and transparency in youth documentary.

WhatsApp messages and tweets hang in mid-air over the documentary footage, strings of text messages track down the screen and clouds of text surround a participant's head. This extra layer of storytelling made claims to 'enhance and subvert the documentary actuality' ('Programme Information: Teens' 2014), with the digital rig offered as a way to explore the intimacies of interpersonal relationships – *The Secret Life of Students* opens with the question 'Ever wanted to look inside someone else's phone?' – offering to expose what is hidden. The promise of transparency through 'authorised eavesdropping', *Big Brother*'s surveillance gaze within everyday life, is facilitated by the 'democratization of surveillance in the interactive era' (Andrejevic 2004, 322). This is supported by the benign attitude of the millennial generation to digital surveillance and their ease with sharing intimacies virtually.

The digital rig could capture intimate confessions and track webs of connections, yet *The Secret Life of Students* struggled with how to bring visual dynamism to static imagery of teenagers interacting with their phone whilst social graphics (to group this collection of texts, tweets, status updates and WhatsApp messages under a single term) are layered upon them. *Teens* develops this aesthetic, at times interweaving social graphics into the participants' physical space, with teenagers walking in front of or through the graphics which unfold around them. This serves to bring physical weight to virtual worlds: words can crowd down on teenage figures, closing down space as they are tapped onto the screen, communicating the weight of an important text message, a longed-for or feared phrase. An unfolding text message thread can unfurl beside a figure – bringing sociality to a static image – or a flood of Twitter comments can oppressively descend on a lone individual. In episode 1.1 the camera follows behind Jess as she walks home after the 'No More Page Three' debate she organised has descended into chaos and her own tears. With her head in the bottom right of the screen, she is surrounded by and walks through gossiping tweets and texts about her actions and the event – 'She's actually mad', 'I'm so gutted I missed it', 'Apparently she cried', 'Anyone who doesn't like page 3 is because you fat and bun [sic]' – a physical manifestation of her wading through the weight of social media judgement.

Teens seeks to bring aesthetic variety and movement by decoupling social graphics and phone calls from the moment of their production. Instead, they are often layered over tracking shots of subjects walking suburban streets (sometimes with phone in hand), engaged in silent domestic activity or staring directly into the camera. This suggests an ever-present layer of communication and a digitally shared stream of consciousness. Transitional sequences see strings of largely anonymous social graphics appear in the skies of long shots of suburbia and school spaces, offering these as fragments of multiple teenage consciousness, the universality of teenage anxieties (Figure 5.1). The documentary returns to sequences where its participants gaze up from brightly coloured pillows into the camera as it tracks across a series of these overhead shots with social graphics appearing around their heads. These sequences conjure the intimacy of the teenage bedroom and the non-verbal expression of concealed emotion, with the digital sphere as a confessional space.

Fig. 5.1 Anonymous social graphics layered over transitional shots in *Teens*

This communication of interiority through graphic overlay evokes E4 drama *My Mad Fat Diary* (2013–2015), yet there the affective layering and annotation of imagery was solely the possession of Rae, with the audience privy to anxieties and confessions committed only to her diary. These digital-rig documentaries depict teenage thoughts shared with others – individuals, friendship groups or crowds of strangers – across different social platforms. They offer multi-layered conversations as participants slips easily between different audiences, from a text to a tweet to a group message to a status update. This multiplicity is a constant challenge for the documentary makers as the need to construct compelling, linear stories out of a web of interaction requires the sifting of a sea of data to isolate texts and tweets from multi-layered feeds – isolating moments from the density of these communication flows. As a result, they fall back on stories of relationship struggles, gossip and social status – subjects common across youth drama, comedy and reality TV – depicting the digital sphere's augmentation of these evergreen concerns.

Unlike fixed-rig documentaries, these programmes retain the strong presence of director interaction in order to draw out intimacies, challenge behaviours or collect individual observations into universal teenage anxieties. Interviews in *Teens* often tease out, contextualise or 'explain' individuals' social media actions – the impact of a single favourited tweet or an unanswered text, the delicate social graces of these virtual worlds. This facilitates *Teens'* attempts to make connections across the emotions and anxieties of its ensemble, those confided to friends or offered up to the virtual universe, from fitting-in to body issues, schoolwork to sex. Communicating both the universality of teenage experience and the depth of feeling amongst its subjects, the digital social landscape exposes the nuances and delicacies of the teenage psyche.

I now move on to *Our War*, the primary case study of this chapter, which uses soldier-filmed-footage and interview to foreground personal perspectives and immersive imagery in its documenting of young soldiers' experiences in the Afghanistan conflict. This analysis builds on the case studies of peer-presenter and digital-rig documentaries, exploring how the series centralises self-filmed footage to build a narrative that foregrounds youth 'voice'. Using the technological innovations of helmet-cams and mobile phones brought on tour, *Our War* builds a series of narratives charting the British forces' involvement in the Afghanistan conflict. This self-filmed footage services the documentary's construction of itself as a transparent, 'uncensored' document of war 'through the eyes' of young soldiers. This is supported by its presentation of young soldiers as storytellers and witnesses, their faces and words interweaving with their self-filmed footage shot in combat and at rest. This builds an intimate picture of the British experience of war, a rigorously personal vision that evacuates the complexity and controversy of the British forces' occupation.

SQUADDIE DOCS, THE PERSONAL AND *OUR WAR*

Outside of news channels, BBC Three has become one of the UK's most consistent documenters of the British military's engagement in the Middle East conflicts. The experiences of British soldiers (both in and after Afghanistan) joins poverty, criminality and health as recurring themes across the channel's documentary output. 'Squaddie docs' (as I term them) are dominated by the observational mode with strong interactive tendencies. They document both the spectacular and the everyday of soldiers' daily lives in programmes such as *Jack: A Soldier's Story* (2008), *Girls on the Frontline* (2010), *Young Soldiers* (2011) and a carefully managed presentation of Prince Harry's military service in *Prince Harry: Frontline Afghanistan* (2013). These documentaries centralise the voices and personal experiences of young soldiers whose daily lives are shaped by complex historical and political forces. The 'negotiation between filmmaker and subject' (Bruzzi 2006, 199) attempts to tease out intimacy and emotion from behind masculine and institutional facades, particularly in documentaries probing the impact of war after service ends, which include *Jack: A Solder's Story, My Boyfriend the War Hero* (2010) and *Life After War: Haunted by Helmand* (2013). Here squaddie docs overlap with BBC Three's interest in youth mental health and disability, as the channel's investment in young soldiers aligns with its interest in young people's engagement with institutions. These are primarily criminal and medical institutions and include observational documentary series such as *The Lock Up* (2011–2012), which follows life in a police youth custody suite in Hull, and *Don't Call Me Crazy*, which focuses on a specialist youth psychiatric unit.

The three-episode first season of *Our War* was commissioned to mark the ten-year anniversary of the British forces' engagement in Afghanistan in 2011, with a second season of three episodes following in 2013. A final 90-minute special *Our War, Goodbye Afghanistan* (2014) looked back across the war as the British forces prepared to withdraw from Helmand province. Susan Carruthers has suggested that 'digital cameras have become an essential piece of 21st Century kit' (2006) for the armed forces and *Our War* is built around soldiers' personal footage filmed on the front lines, claiming to present the conflict 'through their own eyes'. With the cooperation of the Ministry of Defence and British soldiers, producers gained access to footage they frame as 'uncensored',[6] predominantly filmed between 2006 and 2009, from low-res cameraphone images to high-tech DV cameras mounted on soldiers' helmets. I explore how this footage's embodied nature – snapping with the soldier's head to search for the location of a gunshot, juddering as he runs to reach an injured colleague – serves to offer a first-person experience of battle.

Our War's use of 'technologies at hand and in the hand' (Dovey and Rose 2013, 365) plays into British youth television's quest for authenticity, as self-filmed footage offers (naive) connotations of transparency, of 'zero degree simulation' (ibid.). This footage is woven into densely constructed narratives that focus on one or two platoons per episode, chronicling either a particular mission or charting a tour. Here the soldier-filmed footage of life on patrol and in camp is contextualised and given narrative by retrospective interviews, diary extracts, photography and maps, structured by a gruff, blunt voiceover from Yorkshire actor Shaun Dooley. The narration's omniscient viewpoint and sonic similarity to the largely working-class male soldiers sews the ensemble of soldier-as-witness subjectivities together into a clearly defined mission-narrative. Anita Biressi and Heather Nunn suggest that video diaries offer the potential to undermine binary oppositions between 'evidence and experience, objectivity and subjectivity, the public and the private' (2005, 74). *Our War* holds these binaries in tension, with its self-filmed footage and collaging of young soldiers voices producing claims that it was 'direct, unmediated and utterly immersive: war as it's never been seen before on TV' (Barr 2011), that it offered 'war reporting in its purest form … told – quite literally – from the combatant's point of view. No actual reporters are required' (Hill 2014). The self-filmed footage is presented as 'authentic' war document, yet it was encased in a documentary that negotiated 'the polarities of objectivity and subjectivity' (Bruzzi 2006, 46) in its construction of its war stories.

Our War's focus on immersive, personal experience and youth point of view aligns the programme with BBC Three's documentary and factual output. It offers a valuable case study of the channel's preference for documentaries that focus national social concerns and limited engagement with global events through the lens of personal experience. This investment in the personal and the soldier as peer-guide through the conflict is extended by formal and aesthetic elements which attempt to produce an embodied experience of conflict, connoting transparency, intimacy and authenticity within what is ultimately a highly mediated documentary narrative.

Documenting Soldiers at War

BBC Three's squaddie docs can be situated within a consistent ideological thread within war stories where a rigorous focus on the personal, and a desire not to demonise soldiers (Aufderheide 2007, 59), reins in any politicised or historicised perspective of war. *Our War*'s centralising of the soldier's experience aligns it with the 'noble grunt' strand within the war film (*Platoon* (1986), *Casualties of War* (1989)) and the 'grunt's eye view' documentary (*A Face of War* (1967), *Gunner Palace* (2004)). Tony Grajeda notes that the grunt's eye film – from Vietnam to Iraq – tends to offer a 'representation of the U.S. soldier as a figure of overflowing empathy' with a focus on 'individual stories of suffering and tragedy' (2007, 1).

BBC Three's squaddie docs follow the swathe of US 'grunt documentaries' produced in the early years of the Iraq War, which Pat Aufderheide suggests were the result of new filmmaking technologies and the increased access offered by embedding policies (2007, 60). In a trilogy of articles in *Cineaste*, Susan Carruthers charts three waves of Iraq war documentary: the observational view from the ground (2006), the testimonies against the war (2007) and the wounded veteran doc where Iraq exists a traumatic flashback (2008). The observational view and the aftermath of war dominated the rigorously personal address of BBC Three squaddie docs, as British television largely confined the second wave to current affairs programming. *Our War* tells strongly emotional stories of death and heroism on the frontline of Afghanistan, echoing the grunt film's focus on soldiers' trauma, where 'death – witnessing the death of friends, fear of the imminence one's own death, and the killing of others – provide[s] the material for the drama' (Hochberg 2013, 45). The series shed light on a war that had long since moved away from the news headlines, at a time of 'Afghanistan fatigue' (Hill 2014), yet its personal focus offered a depoliticised view of Afghanistan for the BBC Three youth audience.

Our War sought to 'reach an audience who, like many of the soldiers themselves, were still at school when the events of 9/11' catalysed British forces' invasion and occupation of Iraq and Afghanistan (Barr 2011). The opening episode 'Ambushed' deftly sketches out a potted history of 9/11 and the resulting conflicts through voiceover and montaged media archive, with the naive youth audience mapped onto the young soldier-subjects as they speak of experiencing 9/11 hazily as schoolboys (episode 1.1). The programme's narratives are concentrated on the later, more deadly years of the conflict from 2006 to 2009, when British engagement in the Helmand province increased significantly in the face of renewed Taliban forces. This period also offers greater availability of footage as digital recording technologies had become miniaturised and pervasive. The focus on this period also serves to preserve the youth of its interviewees, allowing them to mirror the BBC Three audience and facilitating *Our War*'s construction of the soldiers as 'our boys'. The youth of its subjects is highlighted throughout the series (although older, battle-hardened troops have a stronger presence in season two) with stories regularly foregrounding men barely out of their teens, platoons in their first experience of conflict and the first deaths suffered. The programme offers up youthful camera-friendly, upper-class officers and their gruffer thirtysomething sergeants, yet it is the voices of younger, scrappier, less eloquent working-class soldiers that dominate – 'our boys' coming of age through war.

BBC Three narrows its exploration of Iraq and Afghanistan down to the personal experiences of British squaddies, only occasionally addressing life in these occupied territories. One such rarity was 2010's *Women, Weddings, War and Me*, which focused on young women's experiences in Afghanistan through a 'personal exploration' narrative of a young British-Afghanistani woman returning to Afghanistan. *Our War*'s recognition of any Afghan point of view was kept rigorously paratextual, with its companion website offering a small collection of video diaries and testimonies from young Afghans documenting daily life in and outside of the conflict, alongside animated shorts which gave further historical contextualisation. These paratextual shorts extended the series' emphasis on the personal, but their absence from the documentary itself politicised *Our War* through this lack of voice, particularly when combined with the 'othering' of the people of Afghanistan through the soldiers' point of view. In documenting ten years of conflict, *Our War* rarely brings the viewer into contact with the inhabitants of this occupied land outside of briefly glimpsed casualties of crossfire, hesitant shadows in doorways, snatches of locals questioned for intelligence and smiling children plied with sweets on 'hearts and minds' missions. As Debra Ramsay notes, eradicating 'non-combatants from the spaces of war … supports the perception that it is possible to wage war "cleanly"' (2015, 112). Thus, *Our War*'s absenting of civilians helps to obfuscate the British force's role as occupiers.

'Our': *Institutional Voice and Personal Perspective*

Each episode of *Our War* opens with an introduction that signals institutional cooperation, with Dooley intoning over a montage of spectacular self-filmed footage: 'Now the MoD and the young soldiers have allowed us to use that footage to tell their extraordinary stories.' This framing works to corroborate the programme's footage as a verified, authentic source, positioning personal footage as war document or evidence. *Our War* continues 'the post-Vietnam military management of information involving conflict zones' (Grajeda 2007, 3), maintaining a strong institutional voice that is held in tension with the programme's attempts to position its narratives as personal perspectives. Executive producer Colin Barr sought to downplay the influence of the Ministry of Defence on the production team's access to footage and the choice of stories they told (Barr 2011). In turn, the Ministry's own press release was careful to frame the footage as soldiers' 'personal cameras' ('BBC Documentary to Show Helmand through Soldiers' Eyes' 2011). This stance is compounded by narration that often frames its soldier-filmed footage as an intended souvenir, thus denying any institutional voice in the stories told.

Our War's self-filmed footage forms part of a long history of soldiers documenting their wartime experiences, from diaries in the Nineteenth Century Napoleonic wars (Duvdevani 2013) to the video cameras of Iraq and Afghanistan. The proliferation of soldiers' personal digital recording in the latter conflicts – footage shared across social media, often outside official boundaries and narrative frameworks (Anden-Papadopoulos 2009; Christensen 2009) – made these 'wars for the digital age' (Duvdevani 2013, 281). Delphine Letort suggests that advances in technology have democratized filmmaking, increasing soldiers' agency in the production of war images (2013, 1). However, this agency is questionable in *Our War*, as the footage used may belong to soldiers, but these are military operations and parts of the footage were held in the archives of the Ministry of Defence (Rose 2011). Telling military stories requires military cooperation, with Barr highlighting the Ministry of Defence's role as gatekeeper for this footage in season one (2011). However, by season two, the production discourse sees Barr reposition this involvement and he is careful to deny any editorial access – perhaps wary of inferences of control. Instead, the Ministry of Defence is framed as a permeable layer of executive oversight only operational in cases of security – 'they can red flag it and we discuss it and they then have to prove their case' (Creamer and Barr 2012).

This discourse of the Ministry's burden of 'proof' seeks to assert the programme makers' authority over institutional control and align them with the soldiers' voices and recordings. Within this production discourse, Barr (2011) foregrounds ethics with regard to the selection of footage (mentioning beheadings and dead children in the mass of footage viewed by researchers) together with the rolling consent process involving both soldiers and their families throughout production (Creamer and Barr 2012; Rose 2011). This discourse aims to frame *Our War*'s truth claim as a sensitive and authentic war document.

This discourse of care surrounding the representation of young soldiers' experience aligns the programme with the tendency of the 'grunt doc' to 'valorize the warrior only to eclipse the war itself' (Grajeda 2007, 2). *Our War* rarely offers any political questioning outside the central moral quandary of war, 'the generic conclusion that war is hell' (Aufderheide 2007, 60), presenting a continuation of the grunt film's soldier-as-victim narrative (Aufderheide 2007; Grajeda 2007; Duvdevani 2013). Like the 'grunt film', the programme constructs an implicit argument for 'the inherent virtues of soldiering and its attendant values of courage, honor and sacrifice' (Grajeda 2007, 2). By interweaving the embodied footage of helmet-cams with soldier interviews that serve as witness testimony, the programme constructs a primary narrative of brotherhood, the troop of professional soldiers within a defined mission leaving no man behind.

Questions *do* linger in individual episodes, of overstretched and ill-equipped British forces, of poor command decisions and friendly fire, decisions made and deaths suffered in the chaos of battle. An officer's diary read in voiceover muses existentially on the worth of war and fears of battle (episode 2.3, 'The Lost Platoon'). Broken voices, taut lips, blank stares and tears crack through veneers of masculinity as death and terror is recalled, with the ghost of post-traumatic stress disorder (PTSD) lingering in the soldier interviews. However, *Our War*'s care to communicate 'respect' for the military and soldiers' families sees the traces of dark anger and grief folded away inside the neat corners of 'heroism' by episodes close. Military actions are presented without question of the British forces' role in Afghanistan, with narratives primarily chronicling missions to defend locations, maintain control or draw the Taliban's attention to allow rebuilding work to occur. In framing the British forces as carrying out heroic measures in foreign lands and closing down the war itself so closely to the personal experience and point of view of the soldiers, the programme constructs a clean-cut narrative of 'us and them'. The Taliban's ability to hide in close quarters and plain sight facilitates their presentation as the unseen, invisible enemy, rarely glimpsed in soldier footage. Episode 2.2, 'Into the Hornet's Nest', sees one officer comment that the planned mission was 'real boy's own stuff', with the nostalgic edge of this phrase bleeding into the episode's aesthetic, the maps frequently used to plot the platoon's movements being given an aesthetic of aged archive, blemished and fading at the edges. The phrase also links the mission – a 'noble' one, drawing enemy fire away from the construction of a vital road link – to the last 'good fight' of the Second World War.

Sensitive and politically cautious, *Our War* distracts from its lack of political voice with its visceral embodiment of soldier experience – a spectacle whose affective impact is built around its focus on the personal, the communication of intimate experiences of conflict. The programme name itself is a concentration of ideology and point of view, binding the viewer to the soldier in the experience of war. It serves as reminder that this often-ignored war is 'ours' as a BBC Three demographic and as a nation, the moral weight of the defining war of this generation. *Our War* draws out the structure of feeling Grajeda identifies as 'empathic nationalism' (2007, 3); rather than highly trained fighters, these are presented as 'our' sons, brothers, fathers – 'boys', not men. The programme works to simultaneously highlight its subject's boyishness – noting the youth of platoons and soldiers' lack of experience of combat – and their own construction of themselves as professional soldiers, their care to represent in interview 'the values they aspire to – courage, dignity under pressure, manliness' (Aufderheide 2007, 60). *Our War* presents Afghanistan as half 'boy's own' adventure and half a haunting stripping of boyish innocence.

Embodied Camera

The programme's centralising of soldier-filmed footage – helmet-cams, mobile phones and video cameras – draws on the connotations of the 'video-diary' and first-person address as a 'jargon of authenticity' (Arthur 1993). The video diary foregrounds subjectivity:

> Everything about it, the hushed whispering voiceover, the incessant to-camera close-up, the shaking camera movements, the embodied intimacy of technical process, appears to reproduce experiences of subjectivity. We feel closer to the presence and process of the film-maker. (Dovey 2000, 57)

Facilitated by the miniaturisation of digital video technology, small digital cameras can be strapped to a soldier's helmet or vest, with this footage – both personal and institutional – appearing across social media and even enabling the prosecution of a British marine for murder (Morris and Norton-Taylor 2013). The aesthetics of the first-person camera connote immediacy and transparency; as Dovey and Rose note, the 'grammar of this vernacular is characterised by affect, intimacy, desire and display' (2013, 367) and when strapped to the patrolling soldier, it provides an embodied image. *Our War* frames this soldier-cam footage as laying the Afghanistan war bare, its rawness and jittery nature providing all the markers of the observational camera's truth claims and its 'troublesome notion of "purity"' (Bruzzi 2006, 75), despite the documentary heavily mediating this footage.

Press and promotional discourse tended to present the sensory engagement of helmet-cams and body-cams as a pure vision of war, providing an unrivalled access, an innovative technological advancement in documentary's ability to communicate 'a soldier's eye view'. This helmet-cam is not a direct eye view through the sight of a weapon, but it is an embodied camera; swaying, wrenching, juddering with bodies in action, trudging in single file in ditches, carefully stepping to clear improvised explosive devices (IEDs) from paths, scrambling to the ground under fire, running to reach to an injured colleague, swinging to catch the source of a sound. The helmet-cam captures action as it unfolds, in a modification of observational documentary's conventional following-camera, its positioning on the helmet sutures us into experience as it obscures the wide viewpoint for the focus on the gun, the enemy and the fellow men. Duvdevani draws on Bill Nichols' 'endangered gaze' to understand such soldier-filmed footage. Nichols positions the 'endangered gaze' as that captured under personal risk, with the camera testifying 'to the delicate balance struck between preserving the life of the camera-person and recording the risks undertaken by others whose fate resides beyond the scope of filmic intervention' (1992, 84). *Our War*'s helmet-cam footage blends the cameraperson and subject, observer and intervenor, producing an autobiographic endangered gaze: the scramble on an exposed rooftop position to search out the location of the rattling gunfire of the enemy, the burst of shocked laughter at a sudden bomb blast, the shouted, swearing commands muffled by helmet movement, the edge of panic or adrenaline-soaked excitement clear. Aligning us with the soldiers' bodies and the panic of action, the compact digital video cameras which take the viewer on patrol simultaneously place us in the space of action yet limit our vision. Trapped into the perspective of a single soldier, action largely happens off-camera, out of range or in the flash of an eye.

Yet the filming camera and soldier-cam are not fully converged, as whilst this soldier-filmed-footage is our only direct vision of action 'on the ground', the documentary moves the view up and out to computer-generated maps and intercuts with interview. The maps stake out positions and plot a platoon's mission, identify IEDs or show soldiers' positions relative to the enemy. The interview camera returns to the faces and memories of the soldiers themselves, combining with the maps and voiceover to fill out an omniscient view of the wider action. This omniscience builds clear narratives from the chaos and confusion of battle, providing dramatic dynamism – with Dooley intoning 'little did they know...', 'what the sergeant was about to...' – and the emotional force of potential tragedy.

Our War's combination of maps and helmet-cam footage evokes the medium through which its target youth audience perhaps primarily experience war, albeit a mediated construction: the first-person shooter video game, particularly the blockbuster Second World War series *Call of Duty* (2003–) and its spin-off series *Modern Warfare* (2007–). These are games whose audience reach dwarfs that of a BBC Three documentary, with releases of new games from the franchise exceeding 'opening weeks for cinematic blockbusters in terms of promotion, scale, and initial profits' (Ramsay 2015, 100). Debra Ramsay positions the *Call of Duty* games within the mediated narrative of the Second World War, illustrating how game introductions and 'cut scenes' draw on and play with modes such as television documentary in their historical framing and use of archive (2015, 101). *Our War* flips this relationship, evoking the embodied experience of war-based first-person shooters and their narrativising of conflict as entertainment in a television documentary about war. This produces a circularity – a televisual documentary which echoes the aesthetics of a medium that itself seeks to partially echo war film and television narratives.

Ramsey argues that games such as *Call of Duty: World of War* offer historic wartime events 'experienced directly by the gamer' rather than filtered via the secondhand perspective of characters (2015, 104). The embodied view of *Our War*'s helmet-cam, together with its framing of a weapon within its gaze when on patrol, connects with Ramsay's discussion of the gamer's representation as an arm or weapon: 'Whatever the mode of play, the world of the game is viewed over the barrel or through the sights of a weapon' (2015, 106). However, where the *World of War* avatars are never seen beyond their weapon, *Our War* centres its narrative as much on the faces of its soldiers as the gun. It builds its account by integrating the direct experience of the footage with the perspective of the soldiers captured in it. Their interviews talk us, beat by beat, through the events in the footage and we constantly return to their almost-direct or fallen gaze as evidence of their trauma.

This helmet-cam's intimate focus – compounded by its interweaving with emotional soldiers describing the injury or death of colleagues – could serve to obscure the official voice of the military. Duvdevani suggests that soldiers' autobiographical use of digital video camera could present a new point of view, one distinct from military correspondences and film units: 'that of the regular soldier, who is not necessarily committed to national ideology and discourse' (2013, 280). However, as I have already discussed, *Our War*'s 'autobiographical' soldier-cam footage is positioned within a larger documentary narrative shaped by a directorial voice and institutional framing. This footage primarily offers morale-raising banter in camp, professional control on patrol and panicked reactions in the chaos of battle or an injury. Rare is the video diary footage of a soldier's perspective on war itself – with fragments of philosophical or political concerns largely the preserve of upper middle-class officers' written diaries and letters home. Instead, perspective is largely the preserve of the retrospective interviews which frame this footage.

Like the US Iraq documentary *The War Tapes* (2006), *Our War*'s editing of soldier-filmed footage into a narrative of war by the filmmakers challenges its claims to autobiography and intimacy (Letort 2013, 28). In 'ordering the real' from fragmentary, polyphonic narratives (O'Flynn 2012, 148–149) of injured colleagues, IED blasts and enemy fire, *Our War* streamlines multiple perspectives through voiceover, maps and a strong narrative structure. John Ellis argues that recordings and photographs 'suffer from an excess of potential meaning. What they often lack is any direction for the attention of the viewer', suggesting that 'The physical frame needs an intellectual frame' (2000, 70). The jittery aesthetic of helmet-cam and camp-based video footage serves as a marker of its 'authenticity'; however, their fragmentary and confusing nature necessitates the framing of the footage through retrospective interview, which fills out the limited viewpoint of the helmet-cam and places it within a defined narrative. Soldier-filmed footage is contextualised and made coherent by retrospective interviews filmed long after the action, in domestic spaces or the masculine institutional spaces of the officers' mess.

Testimony and Witness

Our War's 'truth claim' is constructed from two levels of witness – the 'present' of the soldier-cam and the soldier interviews that report their direct experience – often through a very close eye-line match which approximates direct address. Like *The War Tapes,* this use of retrospective interview could emphasise 'the time gap between what is seen and what is verbalized afterwards' (Letort 2013, 19), playing with the distance of memory and the events of war (2013, 21). However, *Our War* works to blur this gap: in interview, the soldiers are simultaneously removed from, yet held within, this past; they primarily speak in the past tense, but the footage places their witness in its present. The matter-of-fact nature of these interviews, their simultaneous detail yet distance and their use of military language works to frame the action with an 'official' voice. This is accompanied by stories of bonding and banter that serve the soldiers' self-presentation of a casual 'laddish' masculinity that couples with their professional skill, a self-presentation which fractures in emotionally fraught moments, creating a 'void that signifies the lingering sense of trauma' (2013, 29).

Kari Anden-Papadopoulos highlights the documentary impulse of soldiers' recording of traumatic war experiences, suggesting that: 'To photograph is a way of externalizing experience, to fix the present into an object that you can refer back to' (2009, 932). Yet *Our War* does not share the dark, violent imagery of enemy combatant death that Anden-Papadopoulos found on social media. The potential of such footage is implied paratextually in a press interview, where Barr discusses the trauma training the production team had to undergo, along with therapeutic discussion, in order to psychologically deal with the hours of collected footage they sifted through (Barr 2011). This suggests that soldiers had captured more disturbing material than was included in the series. We do see injured, prone bodies of soldiers captured by helmet-cams, glimpsed in obscured fragments as panicked colleagues struggle to treat them in the field. 'The Lost Platoon' (episode 2.3) tells the story of a young commanding officer fatally injured on patrol, with his injured body spoken of but never seen as it is carried back to camp through drainage trenches under enemy fire. On reaching camp, the helmet to which the camera is strapped is thrown to the floor as its owner attends his senior officer, the camera capturing the audio against a static shot of a sandy gravelled floor; ragged gasps of the officer certain of his death – 'I'm going down' – interweave with the shouts of his men struggling to keep him conscious as they wait for a delayed helicopter. This discarded camera offers an obscured view; however, multiple witness testimonies from interviews, together with Dooley's narration, fill out the narrative both on the ground and at base.

The relatively bloodless *Our War* does not offer the gruesome trophy pics that Anden-Papadopoulos discusses US soldiers displaying on message boards, and showcases little of the gleeful destruction Christian Christensen describes in YouTube music videos. The latter depict 'troops engaged in violent battle, with deaths and casualties either implicitly suggested or explicitly shown' (2009, 205). Instead, the death of the enemy – the unnamed 'other' – often happens matter-of-factly, positioned as retribution for attacks on 'our boys' or for the death of a colleague. This occurs nearly always at a distance, a precision bombardment of missiles, a plume of smoke, a long-range sniper accompanied by a whoop of satisfaction. Anden-Papadopoulos points out that to display 'close-ups of destroyed human bodies is to disrupt the cultural fiction of war as a hygienic and honorable enterprise (and thereby antithetical to the interests of the US government propaganda machine)' (2009, 933). *Our War*, whilst documenting the panic of battle and the wrenching emotional toll of conflict on soldiers and their families, aligns with this image of war as 'hygienic and honorable'.

With the fragmented, obscured views of events presented by the helmet-cam, the weight of communicating the complex emotions and psychology of soldiers at war falls on the interview, which serves as witness testimony. We don't see the bodily result of IED explosions, although one helmet-cam shot does capture a soldier amidst a blast; clouds of debris fill the screen and settle to reveal an impact zone and the soldier's cries as he claws at its edge (Figure 5.2). Instead, retrospective interviews see soldiers describe blown-off or dangling limbs, offered in faltering phrases. Deaths come off-screen after the helmet-cam has captured frantic efforts to save colleagues and return them to base. Where the helmet-cam witnesses the adrenaline of war and the chaos of battle, the interview serves as the primary witness of trauma.

Early episodes of *Our War* show soldiers directly reacting to footage in interview, often recalling events in split screen with footage. Season two refines this aesthetic to present interviews as witness testimony through the use of very close eye-line matches that connote direct address (here an avoidance of the look to camera signifies a soldier's trauma). The official tone and straightforward military language of the officers – class and rank is clearly signified in both accent and in tone of address – serve

Fig. 5.2 A helmet-cam captures an IED explosion and its aftermath in *Our War*

the documentary's position as document. This dual function as an institutional document and a first-person experience leads the interviewees of *Our War* to oscillate between their institutional position – a care to present Afghanistan as a site of professionalism, doing your job – and their role as witness and victim, and the presentation of Afghanistan as a site of trauma. The interviews place the soldiers in 'home' spaces distant from military action, although the composition isolates them in medium close-ups with shallow depth of field, leaving backgrounds largely defocused.

Talking the viewer through the action, the soldiers recall the immediacy, panic, excitement and terror of battle. Parents of fatally injured soldiers take up the story from their own experience, painting in the story 'back home' as one of fragmentation and obscured views. Time for reflection is allowed at each episode's close, where the men – having recounted harrowing events – often sit quietly within their emotions, the performance of masculinity cracked to reveal the haunted boys inside. Each episode paints the familiar story of the grunt's war tale – war on the frontline is hell, but 'our boys' remain heroes. Lieutenant Bjorn Rose, whose letter to a deceased soldier's parents provides the structuring device for 'Ambushed' (episode 1.1), framed this interview experience and its prompt to talk through events as therapeutic (Rose 2011). In its first-person mode and personalised expression of war, the documentary becomes positioned as both war document and therapeutic, commemorative action.

Our War utilises advances in camera technology to present a visceral experience of war from the point of view of young soldiers who mirror the BBC Three target audience. This leads to a closing down of the Afghanistan conflict to the personal focus preferred by BBC Three's factual programming. This rigorous focus on the personal, together with its centralising of the youth of its soldiers, leaves little space for a politicised exploration of the conflict. *Our War* appears late in the Afghanistan conflict, yet its retrospective narrative focuses on the height of the conflict. This centralises empathic nationalism rather than political contextualising or critique, other than questions of the morality of war itself and its bodily and psychological costs. *Our War* replays the boredom, excitement and chaos of war for an audience who more typically experience it through a games console, yet through its use of direct-address soldier witness, it brings home the broken effect of this in the faces of its young interviewees. The lingering psychological impact of war is highlighted in these interviews, yet the embodied camera's enclosing of us in physical experience also communicates the excitement and adrenaline of war. *Our War* operates around a contradictory positioning of the young solider as hero-yet-victim, continuing the 'prevailing discourse on "The War on Terror"' (Letort 2013, 30). War *happens to* these soldiers – they are casualties of battle and its trauma is derived from their experience, not their actions. *Our War's* helmet-cam offers impressions of immediacy and transparency, but ultimately constructs a war carefully framed into an institutionalised, tightly woven narrative of heroism and comradeship that leaves little space for the challenging of prevailing ideologies.

Our World War

Our War's position as a commemorative commission to mark the tenth anniversary of British troops in Afghanistan, together with its focus on interview-as-testimony, connects it with the use of oral history and soldiers' personal documentation of war in remembrance programmes about conflict: from *Band of Brothers* (HBO/BBC, 2001) and *The Pacific* (HBO, 2014) to *Our World War* (BBC Three, 2014) and *The Great War: The People's Story* (ITV, 2014). The empathic nationalistic embedded in narratives of the two World Wars is thus extended to the contemporary servicemen.

Our World War formed part of the BBC's wide-ranging, year-long commemoration of the centenary of the outbreak of the First World War. It continued BBC Three's ventures into factual drama – *My Murder* (2012) and *Murdered by My Boyfriend* – and built on the success of *Our War*. Executively produced by the latter's producer Colin Barr, the dramas were produced by experienced docudrama producer Sue Horth and drew from archive research and personal testimony. Derek Paget and Steven Lipkin note that the 'war sub-genre of docudrama has provided apparently limitless opportunities for reflections of, and interventions in, past and current geopolitical debate' (2009, 94). *Our World War* echoes *Our War*'s youthful squaddies in an exploration of young men in battle, connecting the two conflicts. Working with a significantly reduced budget compared to the commemorative drama programming of BBC One and BBC Two, *Our World War* drew on the aesthetics of *Our War* to construct an intimate experience of battle (Horth 2014). Three single dramas covered the span of the conflict: following professional soldiers on the first day of the war at the Battle of Mons; a 'Pals' battalion of volunteers at the Battle of the Somme, in a narrative which explores desertion; and conscripted soldiers fighting via the new innovation of tanks at the Battle of Amiens at the close of the war.

Drawing on *Our War*'s basis in oral testimony, *Our World War* is at pains to highlight its basis in soldiers' own voices, illustrating Paget and Lipkin's suggestion that 'historical-event history' and its connections to oral testimony have had a profound influence on docudrama (2009, 95). Built around soldiers' diaries and letters home, each episode closes with a contemporary segment featuring the archive document itself. This acts to verify the drama that has proceeded it as an intimate, personal perspective grounded in youth voice, proposing itself as both 'archive and performance' (Paget and Lipkin 2009, 106). This centralising of oral history and soldier as witness appeared throughout the centenary's television remembrances. Paget and Lipkin tie Dovey's identification of factual television's 'first person' address (2000) to New Docudrama's 'maximising of the act of witness both in performance and reception' (Paget and Lipkin 2009, 104). This pairing centres *Our World War*'s docudrama 'witness' within the formal and storytelling strategies of BBC Three's youth documentary.

Period drama is a potential ill-fit for a British youth channel, with *My Mad Fat Diary*'s 1990s setting being as far back as either E4 or BBC Three had previously travelled. *Our World War* seeks to align the First World War with the BBC Three audience's televisual experience of their own generation-defining war, embedding its stories in aesthetic elements familiar from *Our War*, aiming to create 'something gritty and immersive about a national experience usually memorialised in sepia' (Horth 2014). The drama uses fast-paced editing and dynamic camerawork (in what is markedly a post-*Saving Private Ryan* (1998) narrative), as well as some anachronistic late twentieth-century pop music to – clumsily at times – signify the energy of its youthful soldiers, attempting to paint 'history as current event' (Ebbrecht 2007, 221). From *Our War*, it borrowed the use of maps to plot troop movements in strategic overview and thermal imaging, highlighting swarms of enemy bodies. It also used limited perspective in camera movement and embodied camera to communicate the pace and confusion of the three different kinds of battle. The use of embodied cameras is skewed away from a direct repetition of *Our War's* helmet-cam; instead, small cameras are combined with lenses that concentrate perspective. At times these are strapped to bodies capturing characters' faces as they run, or are attached to guns or tight corners of tanks. Thus, rather than the technology-enabled soldier's-eye-view of *Our War*, the dramas offered an immersive camera that focused on the soldiers' face. This built dramas centred on emotion – in their foregrounding of moral quandaries as well as heroism – as much as the dynamic chaos of battle, with the latter significantly constructed through a perspective-based sound design. Emotional journeys are thus constructed through an embodied experience of war, seeking to communicate to the physical experience of the First World War to contemporary youth audiences.

This focus on immersive experience is presented through a frame of interactive innovation in the online 'fourth episode' of *Our World War*, hosted on the BBC's interactive learning platform iWonder. This shares a location with episode two, the fight for High Wood, and involves viewers in the decision making of a young corporal as he is forced to lead a small group of soldiers following the death of his commanding officer. Working through a three-act structure featuring two quick decisions to be made per act, viewers are statistically assessed at the close of each act, with charts identifying the success of their tactics and the effect of their choices on morale. The interactive episode combines action filmed by the *Our World War* team with animated, graphic novel-style shorts exploring the story of three of the men in the group, with storytelling that is built around voiceover and personal perspective. With this animation and the style of interaction evoking simple online games, the episode is distinct from the war-set first-person shooter games discussed by Debra Ramsay (2015) and in turn the soldier and gun-view aesthetics of both *Our War* and *Our World War*. Instead, the dramatic sections are shot relatively conventionally using a highly mobile camera, offering minimal point-of-view perspectives. Instead, the camera is focused closely on the young corporal's face as the viewer must make his decisions for him in seconds. Here the immersive experience of war is shifted from *Our War* and *Our World War*'s aesthetics and storytelling to the interactive nature of the platform itself, blended with an otherwise conventional aesthetic and a three-act story structure. Yet there remains care to craft a personalised experience of a historical event through the animations and the connection to the corporal's decision making in line with the central operating principle of British youth factual.

Our War and *Our World War* represent war, both contemporary and historical, through the youth voice and personal perspective favoured by BBC Three factual content. They render the complexity of military conflict as an intimate and immersive experience, presenting young soldiers as witnesses in order to offer a peer perspective on conflict. In its presentation of young soldiers as both a heroic brotherhood and traumatised victims, *Our War* continues the empathic nationalism of the grunt film, evacuating the impact of war on the occupied people. This tight aligning with the perspective of the young British soldier is achieved through the interweaving of self-filmed footage and its connotations of immediacy and transparency. This is supported and shaped by the testimony of soldiers in interview, with a focus on both what they have seen and their own faces as evidence of the trauma of war.

Agency and Immediacy in Online Factual Content

I close this chapter by leading from *Our World War*'s experiment with online interactive storytelling to consider youth factual platforms in the online spaces of public service broadcasters, specifically Channel 4. This final case study picks up the strand that has traced *Teens*' and *Our War*'s use of technological innovation to produce intimacy within youth factual content, extending this to the potential of multi-platform content. It explores part of Channel 4's online-based educational content, highlighting continuities with the centralising of youth voice and peer address in BBC Three documentary. The *Sexperience* and *Am I Normal?* platforms serve as public service digital spaces that offer a degree of interactivity in their provision of health, personal and social content for youth audiences, particularly the 14–19 year olds that the channel targets in its education content, claiming to fill the 'knowledge gap' between school and parental advice (Channel 4 2014, 61).

Sexperience

The last ten years have seen commitments to 360-degree commissioning at both the BBC and Channel 4 rolled back (Bennett and Medrado 2013; Chitty 2013), with interactive and multi-platform initiatives shifted to focus on key programme brands and the on-demand platforms of the iPlayer and All 4. Interactive content has been refocused around live play-along 'event' programming, which requires little post-broadcast maintenance to accommodate audience demand and future shifts in technology (Chitty 2013, 129). Channel 4's *Embarrassing Bodies* is such an 'event' programme brand which maintains a strong public service function (Bennett and Medrado 2013, 103). The programming is supported by multi-platform content that constructs a potential long-term post-broadcast commitment to educational interaction. *Embarrassing Bodies* encourages second-screen activity during broadcast via prompts to interact with website and app content; this online content extends the programme's identity beyond the television broadcast, offering a range of health-related content linked to NHS Choices. *The Sex Education Show* (Channel 4, 2008–2011) followed *Embarrassing Bodies*' embrace of a 'tabloid front-page, broadsheet content' focus (Bennett and Medrado 2013, 109), offering a combination of sensationalism and straight-talking in its address to a youth audience. The programme followed the lead of *Embarrassing Bodies* in presenting a 'hybrid form of public service media' that extended youth-focused factual into online spaces (Bennett and Medrado 2013, 105). This was delivered through the accompanying *Sexperience* platform, launched in 2008 as a 'video encyclopaedia of sexual experiences' (Bell 2008) featuring around 350 short videos which were later joined by clips from the programme. The site also centralised interaction and peer-to-peer education by inviting users to submit and provide crowdsourced answers to sex-related questions.

The development of *Sexperience* can be connected to Channel 4's 2008 decision to switch the £6 million budget of its education department to online digital media (Stuart 2010), which I explain further in relation to *Am I Normal?* It also formed part of the channel's ongoing use of sex education programming to teeter on the boundary between controversy and instruction; its 8pm pre-watershed slot targeted youth audiences but also played into the channel's reputation of troublemaking. Presented as response to the 'dearth of clear straightforward information about sex' (Luft 2009), *The Sex Education Show* addressed young audiences through a combination of frank-talking advice and shock tactics such as galleries of photographs of genitals and graphic imagery of STIs. The first of two explicitly teen-focused series of the programme, *Am I Normal?* was broadcast in 2010 and was linked to the government's reversal on plans to add compulsory sex education to the national curriculum. Here public service television positioned itself as stepping in for the absences of the state (Heritage 2010). However, Channel 4's sex education programming has seen consistent criticism from sex education experts over outdated or inaccurate information, together with a lack of address to key social and interpersonal concerns. This perception of the channel's sex education leaning too close to spectacularised, ratings-grabbing 'factual entertainment' culminated in a 2011 open letter of censure from respected sex-positive educators in relation to spin-off programme *The Joy of Teen Sex* (Channel 4, 2011). This letter was delivered to Channel 4 and also hosted on the blog of sex education researcher Dr Petra Boyd, who had previously consulted on *The Sex Education Show*. It expressed their concern that 'sexual and reproductive healthcare and education has been grossly misrepresented, leading to parents feeling anxious, young people's right to accurate information not being delivered, and professional advice being ignored at all stages of programme development' (Boyd 2011). This tension between professional medical concerns and the demands of factual entertainment demonstrate the complexity of producing prime-time factual content for young audiences. It echoed similar cultural censures around *Skins*' combination of spectacularisation and emotional realism (Woods 2016), only with potentially more costly educational consequences.

Sexperience had the potential to fill in the absences of *The Sex Education Show* and *The Joy of Teen Sex*. Its interactive, intimate address promised a greater depth and breadth of information – a stronger public service address – than could be provided within the prime-time, entertainment-led demands of commercially-funded television. Channel 4 countered criticisms of *The Joy of Teen Sex* by pointing to the success of the *Sexperience* platform as evidence of the intervention the programme had made. By positioning the site as a source of 'further advice or information' to be followed after the programme's conclusion (Butter 2011), Channel 4 framed interaction with *Sexperience* as offering a more impactful, explicitly educational experience than the programme itself. Developed from research with teenage focus groups, *Sexperience* was built around public voice and peer advice, blending original short videos and clips from Channel 4's sex education programming with a moderated forum that provided crowdsourced responses to user-submitted questions. The site saw significant engagement, attracting 'around 3 million page views in its first three weeks, with users posting 3,000 comments and questions a week' (Farber 2011) and 14 million page views over its first six months (Gee 2009). In 2011 it was bolstered by *Sexperience 1000*, an interactive digital visualisation of a national sex survey conducted in conjunction with season five of *The Sex Education Show*.

Sexperience's foregrounding of public voice contrasts with the institutional voice conferred by multi-platform content for *Embarrassing Bodies* and *Teenage Embarrassing Bodies* due to their links with NHS Choices (Bennett and Medrado 2013, 110). In the platform's offer of 'real-life stories without value judgements' *Sexperience*'s creators 'hoped to avoid the patronising, moralising attitude' they claimed excluded teenagers from other sex advice websites (Bell 2008). The platform's interactive interface is built around a question and answer format, illustrating Dovey and Rose's argument that Web 2.0 calls upon documentary producers 'to "stage a conversation", with a user community, with research subjects, with participants, coproducers and audiences' (2013, 374). User questions and crowdsourced answers are prominently featured on each page, and original video content features members of the public of a range of ages, ethnicities and sexualities. These participants answer questions such as 'When were you sure of your sexual identity?' and 'Have you ever had a problem using contraception?' direct to camera in a white studio. This material centralises 'the polyvocal nature of participatory content' (2013, 372), here built around first-person address, confessional speech and personal experience. The platform continues youth factual programming's tendencies towards first person and the personal, the 'foregrounding of individual subjective experience at the expense of more general truth claims' (Dovey 2000, 25) that this chapter has explored.

Am I Normal?

Channel 4 positioned its 2008 decision to provide its education content through online digital media as chasing the youth demographic – those moving away from terrestrial television towards social media and gaming. It should also be noted that the shift away from term-time daytime factual programming happened to free up scheduling space for more profitable, non-education programming. Under this new regime, internet-native projects such as educational games, interactive drama and multi-platform content covered topics such as politics, history, careers, citizenship and online privacy (Stuart 2010) and also contributed to the development of *Sexperience*. This placing of Channel 4 at the forefront of British online educational games development formed part of the corporation's ultimately failed experiment with the technology innovation fund 4iP (Bennett and Medrado 2013, 104). After 4iP was dissolved in 2010, education commissioning was progressively re-integrated into television, with digital education spending refocused towards companion content linked to programming (Khalsa 2012). This shift tied into the BBC and Channel 4's refocusing of multi-platform content towards event programming at the expense of core public service areas (Chitty 2013). Whilst this widened the potential audience for and awareness of educational content, it inevitably diffused the potential for innovation in multi-platform content. Arguably this move limited public service broadcasters' ability to intervene in the rise of short-form digital content, where they are now playing catch-up.

The re-integration of education content into the Channel 4 and E4 schedules across 2011 and 2012 saw the broadcaster's Annual Report position this content as smuggled in through the 'Trojan horse' of entertainment (Channel 4 2013). This included the online companion content for popular programme brands *Made in Chelsea* (E4, 2011–) and *Fresh Meat* (Channel 4, 2011–early 2016), with two sets of digital shorts using the former as a 'Trojan horse' for educational content around sex, relationships, friendship and ethics. *The Seven Deadly Sins* (2013) saw cast members discussing moral issues and 2014's *The Institute of Normal* focused on sex, relationship and internet concerns in *Normal for Chelsea?*. The latter series – based around 'therapy sessions' and group discussions presented with a comic edge in a white-walled, surveilled 'institute' – was the centrepiece of the 2014 launch of Channel 4's *Am I Normal?* platform (Campelli 2014). Pitched as the result of the channel's large-scale research project into its teenage audience's education needs (Bird 2014), the platform was intended as a single destination curating all such education companion programming from across Channel 4 and E4 – a space 'more in tune with the way young people consume and interact with content' (ibid.). At the time of writing in early 2016 it remains in soft launch stage with minimal new content presented since the summer of 2015, illustrating the issues involved in maintaining long-term commitments to digital educational platforms.

The platform features companion programming such as the *Institute of Normal* shorts and the *Hollyoaks* (Channel 4, 1995–) spin-off *Tom's Life*, alongside online original comic and documentary shorts focused on life skills, moral quandaries and internet safety. Short-form documentaries use YouTubers such as Emily Hartridge and Harry Hitchens as peer presenters, drawing on their established intimate engagement with a youth audience. Clips from youth-focused programming – from school documentary *Educating Essex* (2011) to soap opera *Hollyoaks* – are accompanied by polls focused on life and internet skills, tying educational content to youth audiences' favoured programme brands in a social media-friendly interface. The question-based structure of 'Is it normal to…', the poll-focused interface and the (sparsely used) Twitter hashtag seem to serve as discussion prompts. Yet the platform offers no embedded space or community for this discussion to develop at present. Rather than offering the opportunity to delve deeper into further information within the platform, the clip and poll structure seems intended to drive viewers to short- and long-form catch-up on All 4, with occasional links to Channel 4's centralised support site. Perhaps this will come with development, but more than a year after launch, this still remains limited.

Sexperience and (to an extent) *Am I Normal* offer educational online factual platforms that foreground peer voices, offering an intimate address to the personal through multiple perspectives on sexual and identity concerns. Kate Nash suggests that in web documentary, 'the creation of community itself becomes an explicit part of the production process, feeding into a process of collaborative content creation' (2014, 389). These platforms' spatial dynamics present a surface image of participatory, peer-focused public service media spaces; however, these remain largely top-down constructions, with limited opportunities for participatory experience.

A future path for online public service factual content is signalled by BBC Three's redevelopment as an online channel, which the BBC has positioned as a 'pathfinder' for the industry and the future of digital television (Gannagé-Stewart 2015b). Channel head Dominic Kavanagh has stated a desire to create an online youth-focused space that responds to the digital world's requirements for 'immediacy, a more personalised interactive experience, authenticity of voice and a tone that resonates with young people' (Gannagé-Stewart 2015b). These are all qualities that resonate with the central tenants of youth-focused factual explored in this chapter and thread throughout the British youth television discussed in this book as a whole. 'New BBC Three' offers a potential space for online innovation in interactive and short-form factual content.

As I discuss further in Chapter 7, BBC Three has taken itself to its audience's online social spaces, embracing the spreadability required to maintain a presence across these spaces. Its substantial Facebook presence (888,000 likes) hosts clips and short-form factual content that links out to iPlayer and YouTube. To return to where this chapter began, this includes short-form documentaries linked to 2015's 'Defy the Label' season. *My Autistic Twin and Me* (2015), *MS and Me* (2015) and *Stupid Questions Not to Ask Disabled People* (2015) embed the channel's focus on the personal, a youth voice and peer-address in an intimate exploration of physical and mental disability. This range of shareable, short-form factual storytelling signals a potentially healthy future for youth-focused factual content from 'New BBC Three'.

Notes

1. Programmes included *Don't Call Me Crazy* (BBC Three, 2013) a three-part observational series about a secure mental health unit, *Diaries of a Broken Mind* (BBC Three, 2013), a 90-minute single documentary made up of self-filmed footage with young people explaining the day-to-day experience of living with mental illness, and *Football's Suicide Secret* (BBC Three, 2013), an exploration of mental health problems amongst sportsmen presented by a professional footballer.
2. Programmes included *Life and Death Row* (BBC Three, 2014), a three-part documentary on the capital punishment system in the US, *Banged Up and Left to Fail* (2014), a peer presenter-led exploration of rehabilitation for young offenders, and *Can Criminals Say Sorry?* (BBC Three, 2014), an examination of the practice of restorative justice presented by actress and knife-crime advocate Brooke Kinsella.
3. This is a term used by BBC Three executives, creatives and in the press (Chapman 2014) to describe the channel's docudrama programming. It refers to dramas based on particular cases such as *Murdered by My Boyfriend* (BBC Three, 2014) or those built from a combination of cases such as *Don't Take My Baby*.
4. *Cherry Goes Drinking* (BBC Three, 2010), *Cherry's Parenting Dilemmas* (BBC Three, 2011) and *Cherry Healey's Property Virgins* (BBC Three, 2013).
5. *Kids with Guns: Stacey Dooley Investigates* (BBC Three, 2010), *My Hometown Fanatics: Stacey Dooley Investigates* (BBC Three, 2012) and *Stacey Dooley Investigates: New Drug Frontiers* (BBC Three, 2013).
6. A claim made in each episode's opening voiceover, which is also consolidated by production discourse in press coverage.

REFERENCES

Anden-Papadopoulos, Kari. 2009. 'Body Horror on the Internet: US Soldiers Recording the War in Iraq and Afghanistan'. *Media, Culture & Society* 31(6): 921–938.

Andrejevic, Mark. 2004. 'Visceral Literacy: Reality TV, Savvy Viewers, and Auto-Spies'. In *Reality TV: Remaking Television Culture*, edited by Susan Murray and Laurie Ouellette, 321–342. New York: NYU Press.

Arthur, Paul. 1993. 'Jargons of Authenticity (Three American Moments)'. In *Theorizing Documentary*, edited by Michael Renov, 108–135. London: Routledge.

Aufderheide, Patricia. 2007. 'Your Country, My Country: How Films about the Iraq War Construct Publics'. *Framework: The Journal of Cinema and Media* 48(2): 56–65.

Barr, Colin. 2011. 'Our War, BBC3'. *Broadcast*, 2 June. www.broadcastnow.co.uk/our-war-bbc3/5028353.article (accessed 25 May 2016).

'BBC Documentary to Show Helmand through Soldiers' Eyes'. 7 June 2011. https://www.gov.uk/government/news/bbc-documentary-to-show-helmand-through-soldiers-eyes (accessed 25 May 2016).

BBC Trust. 2014. 'BBC Three Service Licence'. www.bbc.co.uk/bbctrust/our_work/services/television/service_licences/bbc_three.html (accessed 25 May 2016).

Beckett, Stephen. 2014. 'Fly on the Facebook Wall: A Social Media Documentary'. *BBC News*. 23 July. www.bbc.co.uk/news/technology-28402656 (accessed 25 May 2016).

Bell, Andy. 2008. 'Sexperience Hits the Gee Spot – Mint Digital'. *Mint*, 12 September. http://mintdigital.com/blog/sexperience-hits-the-gee-spot (accessed 25 May 2016).

Bennett, James, and Andrea Medrado. 2013. 'The Business of Multiplatform Public Service : Online and at a Profit'. *Media International Australia* 145: 103–113.

Bird, Dominic. 2014. 'Our Programmes: Education & Older Children'. *Channel 4 Annual Report 2014*. http://annualreport.channel4.com/overview/education-older-children (accessed 25 May 2016).

Biressi, Anita, and Heather Nunn. 2005. *Reality TV: Realism and Revelation*. London: Wallflower Press.

Boyd, Petra. 2011. 'Channel 4 Sent Complaint from Practitioners re Problem Sex Broadcasting'. *Petra Boynton PhD*, 9 February. www.drpetra.co.uk/blog/channel-4-sent-complaint-from-practitioners-re-problem-sex-broadcasting (accessed 25 May 2016).

Bruzzi, Stella. 2006. *New Documentary*, 2nd edn. London: Routledge.

Burgess, Jean and Joshua Green. 2009. *YouTube: Online Video and Participatory Culture*. Cambridge: Polity Press.

Butter, Susannah. 2011. 'Joy of Teen Sex is a "Shocking Let-Down"'. *New Statesman*, 14 February. www.newstatesman.com/broadcast/2011/02/sex-channel-education (accessed 25 May 2016).

Campelli, Matthew. 2014. 'C4 Education Orders Youth-Skewing Slate'. *Broadcast*, 21 July. www.broadcastnow.co.uk/news/commissioning/c4-education-orders-youth-skewing-slate/5075381.article (accessed 25 May 2016).

Carruthers, Susan L. 2006. 'Say Cheese!: Operation Iraqi Freedom on Film'. *Cineaste* XXXIII(1): 30–36.

———. 2007. 'Question Time: The Iraq War Revisited'. *Cineaste* XXXII(4): 12–17.

———. 2008. 'Bodies of Evidence: New Documentaries on Iraqi War Veteran'. *Cineaste* XXXIV(1): 26–31.

Chanan, Michael. 2008. *The Politics of Documentary*. London: BFI.

Channel 4. 2013. 'Channel 4 Annual Report 2012: Engaging the Audience'. http://annualreport.channel4.com/engaging-the-audience (accessed 25 May 2016).

———. 2014. 'Channel Four Television Corporation Report and Financial Statements 2013'. Channel 4 Television Corporation.

Chapman, Alexandra. 2014. 'BBC3 Eyes Factual Dramas'. *Broadcast*, 21 August. www.broadcastnow.co.uk/news/commissioning/bbc3-eyes-factual-dramas/5076431.article (accessed 25 May 2016).

Chitty, Andrew. 2013. 'How Multiplatform PSB Stopped Trying to Change the World and Grew Up (But Got Smaller)'. *Critical Studies in Television: An International Journal of Television Studies* 8(1): 126–130.

Christensen, Christian. 2009. '"Hey Man, Nice Shot": Setting the Iraq War to Music on YouTube'. In *The YouTube Reader*, edited by Patrick Vonderau, Pelle Snickars and Jean Burgess, 204–217. Stockholm: National Library of Sweden.

Creamer, John and Colin Barr. 2012. 'Our War 2: Behind the Scenes'. *Televisual*, 21 August. www.televisual.com/blog-detail/Our-War-2-behind-the-scenes_bid-375.html (accessed 25 May 2016).

Dovey, Jon. 2000. *Freakshow: First Person Media and Factual Television*. London: Pluto Press.

Dovey, Jon and Mandy Rose. 2013. '"This Great Mapping of Ourselves" – New Documentary Forms Online'. In *The Documentary Film Book*, edited by Brian Winston, 366–375. Basingstoke: Palgrave Macmillan.

Duvdevani, Shmulik. 2013. 'How I Shot the War – Ideology and Accountability in Personal Israeli War Documentaries'. *Studies in Documentary Film* 7(3): 279–294.

Ebbrecht, Tobias. 2007. 'History, Public Memory and Media Event'. *Media History* 13(2–3): 221–234.

Ellis, John. 2000. *Seeing Things. Television in the Age of Uncertainty*. London: I.B. Tauris.

Farber, Alex. 2011. 'C4 Unveils Sexperience Site'. *Broadcast*, 18 July. www.broadcastnow.co.uk/news/multiplatform/c4-unveils-sexperience-site/5029930.article (accessed 25 May 2016).

Gannagé-Stewart, Hannah. 2015a. 'Kavanagh: BBC3 Can Be Digital Pioneer for the Industry'. *Broadcast*, 22 May. www.broadcastnow.co.uk/news/kavanagh-bbc3-can-be-digital-pioneer-for-the-industry/5088587.article (accessed 25 May 2016).

———. 2015b. 'BBC3 Given Greenlight to Move Online'. *Broadcast*, 30 June. www.broadcastnow.co.uk/news/bbc3-given-greenlight-to-move-online/5089935.article (accessed 25 May 2016).

Gee, Adam. 2009. 'Who Wants to Be a 20 Millionaire? – I Do'. *Simple Pleasures Part 4*, 13 May. https://aarkangel.wordpress.com/2009/05/13/who-wants-to-be-a-20-millionaire-i-do (accessed 25 May 2016).

Grajeda, Tony. 2007. 'Vietnam and Iraq War Documentaries by Tony Grajeda'. *Jump Cut* 49: 1–3.

Gray, Ann and Erin Bell. 2012. *History on Television*. New York: Routledge.

Heritage, Stuart. 2010. 'Sex Education is a Mess, So Can a TV Series Help Teenagers?' *The Guardian*, 7 July. www.theguardian.com/tv-and-radio/tvandradioblog/2010/jul/07/sex-education-show-tv (accessed 25 May 2016).

Hill, Chris. 2014. 'How BBC3 Changed the Future of War Reporting'. *Huffington Post UK*, 12 September. www.huffingtonpost.co.uk/christian-hill/bbc-3-our-war-war-reporting_b_6292740.html (accessed 25 May 2016).

Hochberg, Gil. 2013. 'Soldiers as Filmmakers: On the Prospect of "Shooting War" and the Question of Ethical Spectatorship'. *Screen* 54(1): 44–61.

Horth, Sue. 2014. 'Our World War, BBC3'. *Broadcast*, 7 August. www.broadcastnow.co.uk/features/our-world-war-bbc3/5075974.article (accessed 25 May 2016).

Ip, Chris. 2014. 'Not-So-Secret Lives on Smartphones'. *Columbia Journalism Review*, 24 July. www.cjr.org/reality_check/not-so-secret_lives_on_smartph.php (accessed 25 May 2016).

Kavanagh, Damian. 2014. 'Blazing a Trail for New BBC Three'. *About the BBC*, 10 December. www.bbc.co.uk/blogs/aboutthebbc/entries/fa632091-9a8c-304e-a479-e054dc368c47 (accessed 25 May 2016).

Khalsa, Balihar. 2012. 'C4 Education Switches Focus from Gaming to TV'. *Broadcast*, 15 March. www.broadcastnow.co.uk/news/multiplatform/c4-education-switches-focus-from-gaming-to-tv/5039276.article (accessed 25 May 2016).

Letort, Delphine. 2013. 'The War Tapes: Documenting the Iraq War with Digital Cameras'. *InMedia. The French Journal of Media and Media Representations in the English-Speaking World* 4 (November). http://inmedia.revues.org/729 (accessed 25 May 2016).

Luft, Oliver. 2009. 'Ofcom Clears Channel 4's Sex Education Show Despite 152 Complaints'. *The Guardian*, 11 May. www.theguardian.com/media/2009/may/11/ofcom-channel-4-sex-education-show (accessed 25 May 2016).

Morris, Steven and Richard Norton-Taylor. 2013. 'Marine Faces Life Term after Being Found Guilty of "Executing" Afghan Insurgent'. *The Guardian*, 8 November. www.theguardian.com/uk-news/2013/nov/08/military-royal-navy (accessed 25 May 2016).

Nash, Kate. 2014. 'What is Interactivity for? The Social Dimension of Web-Documentary Participation'. *Continuum* 28(3): 383–395.

Nichols, Bill. 1992. *Representing Reality: Issues and Concepts in Documentary*. New York: John Wiley & Sons.

No author. 2015. 'BBC Three's "Defying the Label" Season to Air This Summer'. *BBC Media Centre*, 6 July. www.bbc.co.uk/mediacentre/latestnews/2015/defying-the-label (accessed 25 May 2016).

O'Flynn, Siobhan. 2012. 'Documentary's Metamorphic Form: Webdoc, Interactive, Transmedia, Participatory and beyond'. *Studies in Documentary Film* 6(2): 141–157.

Paget, Derek and Steven N. Lipkin. 2009. '"Movie-of-the-Week" Docudrama, "Historical-Event" Television, and the Steven Spielberg Series *Band of Brothers*'. *New Review of Film and Television Studies* 7(1): 93–107.

Plunkett, John. 2015. 'Biggest BBC Shakeup in a Decade as Tories Put Corporation under Review'. *The Guardian*, 16 July. www.theguardian.com/media/2015/jul/16/bbc-review-government-green-paper-john-whittingdale (accessed 25 May 2016).

'Programme Information: Teens'. 2014. *Channel 4*, 18 August. www.channel4.com/info/press/programme-information/teens-w-t (accessed 25 May 2016).

Ramsay, Debra. 2015. 'Brutal Games: *Call of Duty* and the Cultural Narrative of World War II'. *Cinema Journal* 54(2): 94–113.

Rose, Bjorn. 2011. 'The Soldier's View'. *Broadcast*, 2 June. www.broadcastnow.co.uk/our-war-bbc3/5028353.article (accessed 25 May 2016).

'Ruhi Hamid – Producer/Director'. 2015. *The Talent Manager*. https://www.thetalentmanager.co.uk/talent/6580/ruhi-hamid (accessed 25 May 2016).

Stuart, Keith. 2010. 'Sex, Death and Government Oppression: How Channel 4 is Re-inventing the Educational Video Game'. *The Guardian*, 26 July. www.theguardian.com/technology/gamesblog/2010/jul/26/educational-games-channel-4-privates (accessed 25 May 2016).

Woods, Faye. 2016. 'My Generation(s): Cycles, Branding and Renewal in E4's *Skins*'. In *Multiplicities: Cycles, Sequels, Remakes, Spin-Offs, and Reboots in Film and Television*, edited by Amanda Ann Klein and R. Barton Palmer, 240–259. Austin: University of Texas Press.

CHAPTER 6

Structured Reality: Designer Clothes, Fake Tans, Real Drama?

Reality TV plays a central role in British youth television, shaping channel identities in its noisy, cheeky, intoxicated image. Its popularity with the 16–34-year-old demographic together with its relatively low budgets (particularly in comparison with the development of original drama) have made it valuable in developing audiences for emerging digital youth channels. The celebrity docusoaps chronicling the lifestyle of former glamour model Katie Price virtually built ITV2 and, as Chapter 2 demonstrated, BBC Three's sticky entanglement with reality TV in the mould of its reliable performers *Snog, Marry, Avoid* (2008–2013) and *Don't Tell the Bride* (BBC Three/BBC One, 2007–) has indelibly shaped perceptions of the channel. This chapter continues my tracing of the relationship between US teen TV and British youth television, exploring the early 2010s boom in 'structured reality' through analysis of ITV2's *The Only Way is Essex* (2010–) (hereinafter *TOWIE*) and E4's *Made in Chelsea* (2011–). Here the highly successful format of MTV's *Laguna Beach* (2004–2006) and *The Hills* (2006–2010) was appropriated and glocalised to suit British audiences and channel identities, forming part of the transatlantic flows traced in Chapter 4.

An earlier version of this chapter was published as 'Classed Femininity, Performativity, and Camp in British Structured Reality Programming' in *Television and New Media*, 2014. 15(3), pp. 197–214

© The Editor(s) (if applicable) and The Author(s) 2016
F. Woods, *British Youth Television*,
DOI 10.1057/978-1-137-44548-3_6

The ambivalent address of British youth television and its negotiations with authenticity continue with structured reality, which is particularly built around the former. The framework of intimacy and emotion that has woven through much of this book's discussion of British youth television is potentially ruptured by structured reality's heavily constructed nature and camp play. However, trace elements of intimate emotion remain in the complex audience pleasures produced by the form's negotiation of construction and emotional realism, particularly through the influence of soap opera. These soap connections combine with structured reality's distinctive aesthetics to link with my earlier discussions of British youth drama. This chapter draws out themes from across this book to place reality TV at the heart of British youth television.

Laguna Beach and *The Hills* melded docusoap's observational style with drama's high production values, continuity editing and carefully composed *mise-en-scène* (Schlotterbeck 2008). British structured reality continues to employ these elements, yet glocalises the US form through a focus on classed spaces and femininities, and a foregrounding of camp play, which helps to assimilate the form into the address of British youth television. Here the set of ambivalent investments that Helen Wood and Bev Skeggs argue are produced by reality TV (2012), together with the savvy audience charted across reality TV scholarship, map onto the ambivalence that forms an operating principle of British youth television. As I have noted at multiple points in this book, this ambivalence is built through British youth television's combination of an affect-driven emotional saturation and pleasure in melodrama with a savvy distance and sceptical gaze on television's construction. Ambivalence is central to the pleasurable tensions produced by structured reality's combination of emotional realism and construction. This chapter draws on Susan Sontag's (1967) work on camp, alongside recent scholarship on reality TV, to explore the form's embrace of a knowing comic tone and its engagement with camp. These elements seek to smooth its inherent tensions between intervention and 'authenticity', drama and reality TV.

British structured reality illustrates Misha Kavka's assertion that: 'At least since *The Hills*, reality television has busily been embracing a more obvious scriptedness, a winking artifice that meets media-savvy audiences halfway' (2014a, 460). The form is produced for a youth audience raised on the knowing address of celebrity gossip magazines (Holmes 2005) and *Big Brother*'s (Channel 4 2000–2010, Channel 5 2011–) celebration of performativity and intervention. Structured reality reads docusoap's crisis structure (Bruzzi 2006) onto interpersonal conflict and combines this with soap opera's serialised, emotion-led plotting. Its producers structure cast meetings and plan events that catalyse conflict arising from the existing personal problems of cast members, heightening the everyday into melodrama. With its strong storytelling links to soap opera, this programming can be seen as a descendant of both docusoap and *Big Brother*, with *TOWIE* initially pitched as '*Big Brother* without walls' (Frost 2011). In their focus on the labour and relationship issues of groups of twentysomethings, programmes such as *Made in Chelsea, Desperate Scousewives* (E4, 2011–2012) and *Taking New York* (E4, 2015) demonstrate a shift occurring in early 2010s British reality TV. This new form utilises the aesthetics and storytelling of drama, yet recognises and plays with issues of construction and performativity, targeting a sceptical, savvy, reality TV-literate youth audience.

My analysis aligns with Skeggs and Wood's assertion that 'British reality television is resolutely, spectacularly and unapologetically about class divisions' (2010, 94–95) and contributes to a British political climate where 'class relations are experienced affectively as well as structurally' (2010, 104). Both programmes discussed here are built around British regional and classed identities that inform both their aesthetic and tonal address and their individual modulations of glocalisation. *TOWIE* follows the friendship and relationship dramas of a group of twentysomething champagne-drinking, club-going glamour models, beauticians and entrepreneurs living in Brentwood, a relatively upscale town in the south-eastern county of Essex. Part of London's commuter belt, the county features a diversely classed citizenship located in wealthy enclaves and struggling working-class towns. *TOWIE* is built around a classed femininity that draws on the county's indelibly class-marked cultural archetype, the 'Essex girl'. The programme was a huge success for British youth-focused digital channel ITV2, winning the BAFTA audience award in 2011 and by its third season was attracting 1.7 million viewers and a ten per cent audience share – a significant achievement for a non-terrestrial channel (Plunkett 2011). This prompted other channels to develop their own structured reality programmes, the most popular and long-running being E4's *Made in Chelsea*, which has become one of the channel's central programme brands. It follows *TOWIE*'s charting of the interpersonal dramas of a group of twentysomethings, here focusing on the wealthy upper-class London boroughs of Chelsea and Knightsbridge. Socialites and heirs with double-barrelled surnames replace club singers and aspiring footballer's wives, offering an aspirational glimpse of a privileged lifestyle that utilises imagery of 'heritage' London to distinguish itself from its Essex-set competitor.

Both programmes employ the same formal aspects and production processes, but produce divergent aesthetics that serve to articulate their class divisions as well as the tonal address and demographics of their respective channels. This chapter's engagement with aesthetics redresses its surprising absence in reality TV scholarship (which tends to be dominated by ideological and audience analysis) beyond the discussions of surveillance found in Andrejevic (2003). *TOWIE* favours a bright lighting scheme and colour palette, maintaining a bouncing pace through its up-tempo pop soundtrack (the programme's title is a pun on the 1980s British dance hit 'The Only Way is Up'). Its title sequence – and in early seasons the onscreen banners that identified cast members – features profusions of sparkling crystals. These reference the cast's fondness for 'bling', their ostentatious accessories and the crystals used in the infamous bikini-line bejewelling practice of 'vajazzling', practised by the breakout star of season one, beautician Amy Childs.[1] *Made in Chelsea* used classed aesthetic markers to position itself as both successor to and foil for *TOWIE*, distinguishing itself from its predecessor's fondness for a camp, tongue-in-cheek artificiality. It offers a smooth, glossy, soft-toned aesthetic with carefully balanced compositions that dwell languorously on tear-filled eyes and judgmental looks, with lingering silent close-ups closing scenes. Characters are framed in pleasingly balanced wide-screen, picked out in shallow depth of field against their background, drawing on *The Hills'* aesthetic of centralising its privileged young women by digitally sharpening them in post-production against hazily focused backgrounds (Klein 2011). The programme uses a golden light that evokes the 'painterly glow' (McCarthy 2004) found in *Laguna Beach* and *The Hills*, together with a pastel-toned white grade that echoes the artfully composed Instagrams of beauty bloggers and stylists with their merchandising of commodified lifestyles (Figure 6.1). These are Britain's golden youth, shielded from life by parental wealth, honey-toned blondes and glossy brunettes who ostentatiously sport furs and pricey designer handbags in their lives of minimal labour and maximum leisure.

The uncertainty generated by structured reality's hybrid form is illustrated by the range of terms used to categorise these programs in US and British scholarship and press coverage: from 'staged documentary' (Raeside 2011) to 'unscripted drama' (Klein 2009), to 'dramality' (Khalsa 2012). However, I follow *The Guardian*, industry magazine *Broadcast*, and executive producer Sarah Dillistone – who has been the central figure in the form's UK devel-

Fig. 6.1 A shallow depth of field, golden light and pastel-toned grade aestheticise the privileged lifestyles of *Made in Chelsea*

opment – in the use of the term 'structured reality' as this best reflects the form's blending of fictional storytelling with reality TV (Khalsa 2011; Raeside 2011). Press and academic discourse at times uses structured reality interchangeably with the industry term 'scripted reality' to refer to programmes such as *Jersey Shore* (2009–2012), E!'s Kardashians franchise and Bravo's *Real Housewives* franchise. Similarly, *Geordie Shore* (2011–), MTVUK's glocalised version of *Jersey Shore*, is made by *TOWIE*'s production company Lime Pictures and is often linked with *TOWIE* and *Made in Chelsea*. The programme has been labelled as structured reality in press (Heminsley 2011) and academic accounts (Hill 2015), due to its classed regionality and low cultural status. These programmes all share a use of construction, docusoap serialised storytelling, and an embrace of performativity and transmedia tabloid gossip narratives. However, to follow Misha Kavka's positioning of reality television through a genealogical frame (2012), I place structured reality on a slightly different branching root from these programmes.

Jersey Shore and *Geordie Shore* sit on a branching root that connects clearly to MTV's *The Real World* (1992–), as they follow its casting of a group of strangers to live in accommodation provided by the production company, and use confessionals, a following camera and a surveillance aesthetic to chronicle the debauched antics of their casts. Structured reality – such as

Laguna Beach, The Hills, TOWIE, Made in Chelsea and *Taking New York* – differs through its use of a closed-world narrative that takes place in spaces presented as the cast's own homes and documents a version of their everyday lives. This closed-world narrative involves no interaction with the camera and the removal of the confessional interview that forms the central structuring presence of all the above-mentioned texts; this is replaced by expositional conversation and, in the US programmes, narration. Structured reality's distinctive aesthetic was introduced by *Laguna Beach* and further developed in *The Hills*; this evokes the 'dramatic look' of prime-time drama rather than the following camera of reality TV, rendering these docusoaps as aspirational drama. 'Cinematic' is at times used to describe the glossy beauty of *The Hills*' aesthetic (Klein 2011; Leppert and Wilson 2011), but I resist this term as it is loaded with legitimation and infers that television is not aesthetically appealing. In this chapter I use the (admittedly awkward) term 'drama-toned' to refer to the distinctive aesthetic of structured reality, as it is one derived as much from prime-time US drama as cinema.

This chapter explores British youth television's structured reality programming through a framework of storytelling, class and camp. It identifies key concerns of the form by charting *TOWIE*'s and *Made in Chelsea*'s glocalisation of *The Hills*, before setting out the production process and storytelling of the British programmes. It then looks at how class is coded through both space and place and through gender, with the latter pulled through to an articulation of the role of camp and performativity in British structured reality. This chapter unpicks the complex process that balances British youth television's investment in authenticity and structured reality's overt construction, which in some ways links back to British youth drama's interweaving of realism, melodrama and comedy. I demonstrate how in signalling its construction so clearly, structured reality somehow positions itself as authentic. This is programming that directly addresses the 'savvy voyeur' audience, those eager to demonstrate they are not duped by media spectacle, wanting to wrestle 'some shred of authenticity from the web of artifice' (Andrejevic 2004, 332). In doing so, I identify how the tensions at the heart of structured reality produce its pleasures.

GLOCALISING *THE HILLS*

The building of British structured reality through the translation and glocalising of *The Hills* model formed part of an ongoing influential relationship between US reality TV and British youth television. As early as 1993,

British television attempted to glocalise MTV programming with BBC Two's version of *The Real World, The Living Soap* (1993). Broadcast in the channel's youth slot *DEF II*, this offered an aborted attempt to bring together a group of Manchester students to live in a shared house and have their lives recorded for serialised broadcast. Channel 4's *Shipwrecked* (2000–2001, 2006–2009, 2011–2012) drew on CBS's *Survivor* (2000–) in leaving a group of attractive, bikini-clad teens and twentysomethings in paradise to fend for themselves and compete with each other in an elimination-based contest. Structured reality's roots can be traced to another transatlantic televisual journey in MTV's reworking of the docusoap mode that had dominated British television in the 1990s, producing a string of celebrity docusoaps that included *The Osbournes* (2002–2005) and *Newlyweds: Nick and Jessica* (2003–2005). The channel has progressively blurred the boundaries between docusoap and scripted storytelling as part of its self-conscious embrace of anti-naturalistic and openly interventionist techniques in its reality programming (Kavka 2012, 180). This borrowing of aesthetics and narrative techniques from fiction progressed from the positioning of *The Osbournes* within the framework of family sitcom to *Laguna Beach*'s blending of docusoap with the aesthetics and storytelling of teen TV.

Reality TV's embrace of a level of construction that edges towards drama (Piper 2004) has long blended John Caughie's delineation of the 'dramatic look' and the 'documentary gaze' (2000). *Laguna Beach* shifts docusoap's remnants of the documentary gaze even further towards a dramatic look in its erasure of any interaction between performer and camera (Schlotterbeck 2008). This lack of interaction could suggest a move towards the 'purity' of the observational ideal (Bruzzi 2006, 75), yet the programme's lack of a following camera and its carefully balanced widescreen compositions, picturesque locations, continuity editing and interwoven serialised narratives align it with the teen dramas then appearing on the WB and FOX. *Laguna Beach*'s original tagline 'The Real Orange County' purposely echoes *The O.C.* (Fox, 2003–2007) and it similarly chronicles the interpersonal dynamics of a group of wealthy Californian high school students in a beautiful affluent beachside neighbourhood.

The *Laguna Beach* spin-off *The Hills* refines this aesthetic to an even higher level of polish, following protagonist Lauren Conrad to Los Angeles, where she plans to study and work in the fashion industry. As Amanda Ann Klein argues, *The Hills* aims not for stylistic transparency, but for 'Hollywood fantasy':

> This polished, 'cinematic' style mirrors the programme's function as a 'projective drama', offering its viewers an escapist, consumerist fantasy of a world in which twentysomethings are financially independent and professionally successful, despite their obvious lack of marketable skills. (Klein 2011)

Capturing the zeitgeist at the peak of the 2000s boom years, the show was a huge basic cable hit. Its cast made the cover of *Rolling Stone* magazine and their conflicts spread across tabloid magazines and gossip websites. Yet despite their growing extra-textual fame, *The Hills* constructed a closed narrative world, ignoring its cast's celebrity in service of its fiction of their normality, a process that extends to the British iterations. Where the British programmes foreground classed privilege, *The Hills* seeks to disavow class. Despite her wealth and opportunities, the programme presents Lauren as an ordinary, all-American girl living an extraordinary life. In fusing heightened, beautiful aesthetics and soap opera conventions, '*The Hills* invites viewers to relate to Lauren as a soap opera heroine whilst simultaneously encouraging us to see her as exceptional, an image to be aspired to' (Leppert and Wilson 2011, 268). Despite *The Hills*' constructed aesthetic and its concealment of its characters 'real life' celebrity, Lauren's star identity is built around her 'authenticity' and transparent emotions, thus aligning the programme with US teen TV's blending of emotional realism and aesthetic aspiration.

Laguna Beach and *The Hills* defined MTV's channel identity in the late 2000s, yet fell into decline as boomtime gave way to a new recession. This led MTV to seek out a new 'authentic' and 'gritty' identity built around a return to a scrappier aesthetic with its connotations of transparency in *Teen Mom* (2009–2012, 2015–) and a shift from privilege to coarseness in the ribald antics of *Jersey Shore* (Stelter 2010). As MTV moved on, British youth television took up the form, reworking it to fit within its national sensibilities and cultural identities. *TOWIE* and *Made in Chelsea* offer closed narratives and utilise a dramatic look; however, they distinguish themselves from their US predecessors by pushing the self-awareness inherent in reality TV's recognition of its audience's literacy to the foreground, where it intertwines with emotional realism and a strong strand of comedy.

Structured reality internalises the pleasurable viewing practice Annette Hill identifies in the reality TV-literate audiences of *Big Brother*: the search for moments of authenticity when real people are really themselves in a constructed environment (2002, 324). Pitched by executive producer Tony

Wood as '*Big Brother* without walls' (Frost 2011), it takes *Big Brother*'s construction out into a real-world environment. In 2012 Sassy Film and Massive TV brought a claim of copyright infringement against both ITV and *TOWIE*'s production company Lime Pictures. They claimed they had pitched an Essex-set reality TV pilot starring some of *TOWIE*'s cast members to Lime in 2009, two years before *TOWIE* debuted. Lime's defence rested largely on the claim that *TOWIE*'s 'dramality' form (its phrasing) was distinct from the 'fly on the wall' reality form (its phrasing) the claimants had pitched, which was 'produced, lit and shot in a different way' (Khalsa 2012). Legal documents filed by Lime distinguished *TOWIE*'s production process from 'fly on the wall' techniques, claiming that in 'dramality' 'producers set up dramatic scenarios which are then filmed' (legal documents quoted in Khalsa (2012)). Thus, structured reality is built on producer intervention and an aesthetic distinct from the lingering observational connotations of docusoap.

British structured reality builds production teams with experienced backgrounds in British evening soap opera to support its combination of docusoap's crisis structure (Bruzzi 2006, 128) with soap opera plotting. When commissioning *TOWIE*, ITV2 executive Zai Bennett referred to it as a 'living soap' (Parker 2010) and the programme drew on the soap opera expertise of its production company Lime Pictures, which also produced Channel 4's early-evening youth soap *Hollyoaks* (1995–). Lime's chief executive Carolyn Reynolds and creative director Tony Wood had both been long-time *Coronation Street* (ITV, 1960–) producers, whilst *TOWIE*'s season one story producer Daran Little is a highly experienced soap writer whose credits include *Coronation Street*, *EastEnders* (BBC One, 1985–) and *One Life to Live* (ABC, 1968–2013). Little later moved on to work with *TOWIE* producer Sarah Dillistone on *Made in Chelsea*, forming the central creative team of British structured reality. Story producers such as Little have weekly meetings with cast members, then structure events that prompt conflict from their existing personal relationships, heightening the everyday into melodrama. To draw here from Laura Grindstaff, the story producer's skills as an experienced soap opera storyteller are employed to plot out 'contexts of interaction', which draw out the 'potential for drama' from the interpersonal tensions within friendship groups, whether they come pre-formed or are 'cast' (2011, 47).

Alongside the production presence of soap opera personnel, performance is central to the national distinction of British structured reality. Compared to the relatively artful naturalism of *The Hills*' Lauren Conrad –

whose emotional realism is central to the programme's success – the British casts often demonstrate an awkwardness and performativity. This pushes beyond even some of the more stilted cast members of *The Hills* such as Audrina Partridge. Their performance is not skilled and smooth enough to be read as pure drama, their stilted lack of 'naturalness' in turn denying any lingering documentary claims of real-life unfolding without intervention. As I discuss further below, in not papering over the cracks in its performances, *TOWIE* in particular showcases its cast as ultimately *more* authentic than a *Big Brother* contestant successfully 'playing the game'. Structured reality offers a complex interweaving of performativity and soap-like emotional realism, construction and transparency, with a pleasurable tension created between its glossy 'drama-toned' aesthetic and the British casts' inability to convincingly perform their everyday life. This tension produces a tone of cringing comedy familiar from British sitcoms (*The Office* (BBC One/BBC Two, 2001–2003), *The Inbetweeners* (E4, 2008–2010)) (Middleton 2014) and disrupts the emotional investment that is encouraged by the melodrama-infused content, offering the audience an ambivalent viewing position. This pleasurable tension allows for a simultaneously invested and detached viewing position that flatters their genre-literacy and links to the address of British youth television.

TOWIE smooths over yet simultaneously foregrounds this tension in its embrace of camp in aesthetic and tone. The wink to the savvy audience becomes aestheticised, the reality 'bubble' is not broken, yet at the same time the programme's constructed nature is clearly pronounced by its embrace of camp's 'love of the unnatural: of artifice and exaggeration' (Sontag 1967, 275). This signals its British difference from *The Hills'* Hollywood glamour, polished aesthetic and tendency towards melodrama. I draw here on Sontag's discussion of camp as sharing a delight in artifice and play, a refusal of seriousness yet having the potential for tenderness. *TOWIE*'s play with camp frames the programme as possessing an inherent reflexivity and lends its potentially problematic classed representations a tongue-in-cheek filter. In Misha Kavka's multi-layered articulation of 'flaunting' as a reality TV performance mode, she also evokes Sontag in linking camp and reality TV. However, Kavka positions camp and reality TV as 'kissing cousins', arguing that 'camp exhibitionism is not synonymous with the reality television performance' (2014b, 56). She distinguishes between camp's presentation of 'artifice as an ideal' and reality TV's mobilisation of artifice to offer 'authenticity as an ideal' (2014b, 52). Kavka instead offers 'flaunting' as a way to explore the gendered performances of reality TV as 'potentially playful as well as self-reflexive' (2014b, 56). Flaunting provides a valuable reading of gendered performance in reality TV; however, I believe that the national specificity and formal concerns of structured reality maintain a link with camp. This operates within the warmly arch tone of British youth television and draws on national comedy traditions.

TOWIE's playful camp and foregrounding of construction is signalled at the outset by its framing device. Each episode opens with a disclaimer stating that scenes have been created for entertainment purposes – the consequence of famous cases of 'faked' footage in late 1990s British television documentaries (discussed by Winston (2011)). *TOWIE* proffers its required acknowledgement of construction with a tongue-in-cheek humour that signals the programme's comic tonal address. Presented in glittering text as part of the titles and read in voiceover by Essex-born actress and presenter Denise Van Outen,[2] each episode's disclaimer offers a variation on 'this programme contains flash cars, big watches and some barefaced cheek. The tans you see might be fake, but the people are all real although some of what they do has been set up purely for your entertainment' (episode 2.10). *TOWIE* here connects the construction involved in both the cast's appearance and the programme's depiction of their lives, yet at the same time claims that despite their constructed aesthetic, their essence is 'real', that they offer emotional realism, foregrounding and diffusing the programme's pleasurable tensions from the outset.

Richard Kilborn has noted that many British docusoaps speak to their audience in a knowing manner, principally through narrative style and mode of address (2003, 108). British audiences are accustomed to a jauntily mocking voiceover, which serves to absolve them of the 'shame' Kavka suggests is borne of watching reality TV (2008). *The Hills* signals its melodrama and centralises Lauren Conrad's point of view by opening each episode with her earnest voiceover, opaquely recapping action and cueing up her current interpersonal concerns. *TOWIE* signals its British distinction and comic voice through its framing voiceover delivered by Van Outen, a voice external to the programme. Her performative reading of this disclaimer, together with the parodic, double entendre-filled 'previously on' and 'next time' segments that bookend episodes, sets out the programme's knowing tone. In 'foregrounding its modes of mediation', it teaches its 'viewers to be savvy about its status as cultural and technical construction' (Kavka 2008, 5).

In contrast, *Made in Chelsea*'s disclaimer is offered by E4's continuity announcer and remains wholly outside the text, leaving the programme's diegesis intact and signalling its less explicit engagement with a knowing address. A textually present disclaimer would be at odds with *Made in Chelsea*'s glamorously aspirational lifestyles and smooth aesthetic. The programme's title card uses a font and shimmering crown icon that references the then-ubiquitous 'Keep Calm and Carry On' poster and its connotations of stiff-upper-lipped British tradition. Anita Biressi and Heather Nunn suggest that the proliferation of the wartime phrase as a brand during the outset of the Coalition government's austerity ideology in the early 2010s (through both merchandising and parody) 'invoked both a dry British humour and a heads-down and let's get through this posture' (2013, 184). However, *Made in Chelsea* excises the phrase and retains only the font and crown, which shimmers in a defiance of frugality, repurposing the iconography of mass togetherness and tradition to signify a separate elite untouched by austerity. The programme's frame *does* signal its ambivalent viewing position, through the hint of mockery present in the quotes from cast members that follow the title card and operate as episode titles. These can indicate the episode's narrative trajectory; however, they often also showcase a foolish or pretentious remark, contrasting with the refined connotations of both the title card and the programme's aesthetic that follows, signalling the programme's ambivalence from the outset.

These two sets of programme titles signal the playfulness and comic voice of British structured reality together with its centralising of classed identities. Biressi and Nunn suggest that Essex girls and the privileged upper classes have a commonality in their tendency to be cultural underestimated for their intellect, labour power and economic power, often serving as targets of humour (2013, 39). The two dominant structured reality programmes of British youth television trace these commonalities, building their pleasures on a fond mockery of both Essex girls and the privileged upper classes.

The camp, comic play of *TOWIE* is driven by its engagement with the classed, excessive femininity of the 'Essex girl'. Biressi and Nunn note that Essex 'has become associated in the popular imagination with a train of largely negative, intensely classed associations' (2013, 23). The stereotype of the 'Basildon Man' or 'Essex Man' was coined in the 1980s to refer to the Thatcherite aspirational white working class – East End Londoners who moved out to Essex after benefiting from economic growth (May

2010). Thus, the county is culturally coded with both East End legacies of the working class and aspirational 'new money' – an often self-made new middle class viewed as lacking in culturally ratified taste codes.[3] Representations of Essex are dominated by regional working-class stereotypes, with class often unspoken yet clearly geographically coded (Skeggs 2003, 112). This characterization is compounded by reality TV, where the young white Essex girl or boy has become one of the staple casting 'types' (Biressi and Nunn 2005, 151). In much the same way that *Jersey Shore* embodies certain stereotypes of New Jersey inhabitants and Italian-Americans, *TOWIE* draws on cultural discourses that stereotype Essex girls as dim-witted and sexualised and Essex boys as loud and flashy. Focused on their appearance, consumption and status, the men of *TOWIE* offer variants on the brutish, swaggering, tasteless Essex boy of the 1980s and 1990s (Biressi and Nunn 2013, 31–38). They echo in part the ritualised production of compulsory masculinity that Amanda Ann Klein explores in *Jersey Shore*'s performance of guido subculture (2014, 162), yet many pursue a classic, refined model of masculinity built on well-tailored suits accessorised with 'bling' and often display a surprising emotionality. There is much to explore in these contemporary iterations of masculinity, but as discourses of class-based judgement operate primarily through femininity, this chapter focuses its gender-based analysis there.

Where *TOWIE* drew on the image of the Essex girl, *Made in Chelsea* drew on the figure of the ostentatiously wealthy young Sloane. Often depicted in mocking terms in popular culture as 'airheaded, braying, conceited, absurd' (Deacon 2011), the Sloane's privilege sees this stereotype lack the disgust-based mockery that shapes the Essex girl. The 'Sloane' was popularised in the 1980s by Peter York's *Sloane Ranger Handbook* (Barr and York 1982) and refers to residents of Sloane Square and the surrounding London boroughs of Chelsea and Knightsbridge. York produced a sequel in the late 2000s (York and Stewart-Liberty 2007) that identified the new breed of Sloane then experiencing a revival. This was connected with the lifestyles of the young royals and their club-going, polo-playing social circle – the socialite as celebrity. It formed part of a boom in British cultural fascination with wealth and heritage – which preceded and fed from the 2011 Royal Wedding of Prince William and Catherine Middleton – at a time when the Conservative-dominated Coalition government's austerity-based economic measures were coming into effect. Televisual examples of this fascination included *Downton Abbey* (ITV 2010–2016), with its sympathies for the woes of the aristocracy, and a series of BBC observational documentaries exploring life at elite institutions, from *Inside Claridges* (BBC Two, 2012), to *Chatsworth* (BBC One, 2012), to *Posh People: Inside Tatler* (BBC Two, 2014). This was aspirational-lifestyle programming consumed as spectacle in a time of economic downturn, reductions in social mobility and a widening income gap.

The *Made in Chelsea* cast is born into privilege and influence, which the programme luxuriates in while simultaneously undercutting; as a result, they initially lacked the populist appeal of *TOWIE*. The latter's cast quickly proliferated across the covers of tabloid gossip magazines, whereas the *Made in Chelsea* cast took more time to rise to the position of regular subjects of the *Daily Mail*'s website. The classed connotations of *TOWIE* connect with those of the working-class celebrity, whose appeal Biressi and Nunn suggest lies in a 'disconnection from traditional structures of influence (inheritance, education and so forth)' (2005, 145). This results in the nouveau riche featuring heavily in reality TV, in contrast to the relative absence of the upper class, who are connected to these traditional structures. Instead, the upper class serve as the subject of prestige observational documentaries or as the expert dispensing advice on lifestyle, property and makeover programmes, where they deploy their cultural capital to coach their lessers to class-pass (Biressi and Nunn 2013, 137–141). E4's preference for original British drama with 'edge', together with its youthful, slightly subversive channel identity, means it would be unlikely to develop a drama series offering a purely aspirational or sympathetic depiction of wealthy British society. Such representations are rarely present in British television outside of period drama. Instead, *Made in Chelsea* allows E4 to display the aspirational glamour and wealth found in its US teen TV imports, yet extend the mockery and suspicion with which the channel's middle- and working-class British youth dramas like *Skins* (2007–2013) and *Misfits* (2009–2013) treat upper-class outsiders.

Made in Chelsea offers up a glamorous aspirational lifestyle, led by consumption and leisure, yet it paints the upper class in a less sympathetic light than the BBC and ITV prestige markers. The series maintains an edge of amused mockery through its cast's awkward performance of self, linked to British traditions of satire of the upper classes and fed through its status as British youth television. Its glossy glamour is combined with comedy derived from the cast's lack of intelligence and awkward self-consciousness, suggesting an ambivalent relationship with class at play. It is tempting to frame the pleasures of class-centred reality television in terms of schadenfreude, but for me 'ambivalence' captures the complexity and pleasurable 'messiness' of British structured reality. This ties it to British youth television's address and structure of feeling traced in previous chapters, with its oscillation between investment and detachment. In their analysis of reality TV's affective audience relationships, Bev Skeggs and Helen Wood argue that the form's 'call to emotional investment may undermine traditional structures of representation and forms of subject position' (2010, 144), constructing an inherent ambivalence. Exploring the emotional management that reality TV calls its audience to perform, they suggest that the form prompts viewers to simultaneously perform affect-driven processes of investment and judgement (2010, 152–154), particularly around class. This echoes Lauren Berlant's reading of ambivalence within feminine intimate publics (2008, 181), which I have drawn on to position British youth drama's structure of feeling. Ambivalence offers a way to consider the pleasures of texts beyond the emotional distance that schadenfreude implies, offering space to hold multiple readings simultaneously and to pleasurably try on different subject positions. This can productively be applied to structured reality's complex relationship with class and gender, construction and emotional realism. Ambivalence is key to understanding the audience pleasure derived from *Made in Chelsea*'s offering of aspirational lifestyles, beautiful aesthetics and emotional realism intertwined with the knowingness that produces the mockery and cringe-comedy of its representations and performances. The pleasures of the form lie in these tensions.

The constructed nature of structured reality and its pleasure in artificiality could place the form at odds with British youth television's investment in authenticity and emotional intimacy. Ambivalence enables structured reality's construction – and the heightened awareness, distance and comedy it provokes – to sit alongside emotional realism; the real tears behind the fake eyelashes and glossy aesthetic. Retaining *The Hills'* investment in presenting Lauren Conrad as a soap-opera heroine (Leppert and Wilson 2011), the British form centralises emotion in its exploration of interpersonal conflict. This is particularly present in romantic struggles, be it Lydia and Arg in *TOWIE* or Binky and Alex in *Made in Chelsea*. As Arg is the least skilled performer of all the *TOWIE* cast members, his confrontations with on-off girlfriend Lydia have a stilted quality that signals the programme's construction. Yet Lydia's fragility cuts through this when she breaks down in her kitchen confronting him over his treatment of her in episode 4.6. The argument unfolds in a series of shot-reverse-shot medium close-ups that draw on the programme's use of the dramatic look; however, Lydia's raw emotion is communicated through profuse tears and swearing, her overly made-up face crumbling as she repeats and fragments her phrasing. Arg falters in his attempts to subdue her and is left sighing, grasping emptily for a suitable response. This moment lacks the saucy giggles or play of clueless machismo common to *TOWIE*, the 'playing straight' of the moment and its lack of a knowing distance increasing its emotional impact.

Similar moments of emotional realism appear in *Made in Chelsea*, with the season seven arc following gossip around Alex's infidelity culminating in a break-up scene in the rarely seen, intimate space of Binky's bedroom (episode 7.4). Twinkling fairy lights provide soft diegetic lighting and bring depth to the frame as the couple sit face to face, their conversation unfolding in a long series of tight close-up shot-reverse shots. The usually highly controlled aesthetic sees minor disruption. Alex's face is in moments obscured by Binky anxiously raking her hands through her hair, whilst the camera reframes more than is standard in order to maintain the intensity of Binky's trajectory from stony-faced determination, to angry tears, to weeping punctuated by swearing. Moments such as these highlight the appeal of 'structured reality' beyond its construction and knowing comedy, breaking apart the cast's glamour to offer moments of emotional realism that mirror the audience's own interpersonal problems.

We see here how British structured reality retains the drama-toned aesthetic and investment in emotional realism displayed by the US form, whilst glocalising it for British youth television. This assimilation is achieved through the use of soap opera production staff, the foregrounding of an awkward performativity, the embrace of camp play and the centralising of class. I tease out these aspects further as this chapter progresses, as well as continuing to explore how a pleasurable ambivalence is drawn from the tensions between its constructed nature, its glossy aesthetic and its investment in emotional realism. I now move on to identify how this is achieved through production processes and storytelling.

SHAPING BRITISH STRUCTURED REALITY

The rise of lifestyle and reality TV has been viewed as a side-effect of broad economic shifts in television production (Holmes and Jermyn 2004). Structured reality is shaped by the economic conditions of British youth television, enabling niche-focused yet low-budget digital channels like ITV2 and E4 to produce original British programming without the price tag of youth drama such as *Skins* and *Misfits* or a long-running soap like *Hollyoaks*. Structured reality draws on soap opera's serial form and youth drama's aesthetic, producing multiple seasons a year on a reality TV budget.

The production process of structured reality offers a prime example of Laura Grindstaff's self-service television, where 'producers construct the necessary conditions of performance and real-people participants serve themselves (more or less successfully) to these performances' (2011, 44). The story producer-as-writer plays a key role in the scaffolding (2011, 45) of long-form storylines and cast interactions in naturalistic settings, producing construction in the wild. This scaffolding draws from the cast's everyday lives to plan 'coincidental' meetings or large-scale events; these catalyse conflict and emotion or recap the gossip that serves as a structuring presence. The process uses the 'emotional labour' (Grindstaff 2011) of the cast to produce the melodrama and emotional realism (Ang 1985) central to this soap-informed storytelling. The resulting construction within 'real life' extends Kavka's assertion that 'viewers find truth not in the transparency or erasure of the media frame, but rather in the social or inter-subjective truths that arise out of the frame of manipulation' (2012, 94). Highly formalised in its aesthetic and structure and built by experts in serialised soap opera storytelling, the levels of construction in these programmes – whether signalled through tone, formal elements or performance – facilitate their production of emotional realism, the 'truth' of structured reality.

This is a form of 'pre-made' television, created 'out of particular contexts of performance rather than the content of scripts, rehearsals, etc' (Grindstaff 2011, 45). Structured reality is constructed by both production staff and experienced, savvy cast members who, as producer Sarah Dillistone notes, learn to withhold and reveal 'juicy' information on camera to produce affective moments of emotional impact (Kanter 2015). The unnaturalness of this scaffolded production process produces structured reality's inherent awkward performativity, which signals the form's artificiality and produces pleasurable tensions for its savvy audience. These viewers are highly literate in reality TV, and are able to hold an awareness of the genre's programmes, events and participants as 'simultaneously and legitimately real and fake, actual and artifice, performed and natural' (Weber 2014, 20).

Structured reality's scaffolding is facilitated by gossip, which serves as its story currency. This follows soap opera's use of gossip to serve both as a commentary on the action (Geraghty 1981, 22) and to formally bind together plots and characters, providing coherence and offering new information or detail for the audience (1981, 24). In an era of heavy competition for viewers, British prime-time soap opera now combines the pleasures of the everyday and the mundane with high-stakes events and moral quandaries – a murder, a rape, a car accident or a fire. In contrast, structured reality is driven by small-scale concerns rendered as high-stakes melodrama: romance, suspicion, cheating, friendship betrayals, backstabbing and judgement. Gossip plays a central role in the structuring of this storytelling around multiple moments of revelation.

The casts are entangled in a web of gossip, which is fed by their surrounding social circle and ricochets across social media and tabloid websites. Friends and strangers serve as real-life *Big Brother* cameras outside of the filming schedule, surveilling and documenting, discovering romances and infidelity, and feeding this information back to producers (Kanter 2015). Yet we rarely see the originating events on screen, as they often occur at parties that the cast attend in their role as celebrities, and recognition of this would puncture structured reality's sealed world; instead, we hear the aftermath, the gossip, focusing on revelation and reaction. Here it serves Geraghty's other articulation of gossip's role in soap opera – as a part of the action itself: 'Stories very frequently revolve round questions of knowledge or ignorance on the part of different characters, and the decision to tell a character about a previously unknown event is often a major issue' (1981, 24).

This is illustrated in a major storyline of *Made in Chelsea*'s seventh season, which operates around the rumours about and the impact of Binky's boyfriend Alex's infidelity. Binky's 'good girl' persona and performance of emotional authenticity position her as the Lauren Conrad of the later seasons of *Made in Chelsea*. Like Lauren, she is 'represented as a unified self, whose intentions and commitments ... remain transparent, sincere, and consistent' (Leppert and Wilson 2011, 266). Episode 7.3 is structured around the repeated reveals of proof of Alex's infidelity through scenes of gossip and revelation, building to the climax of Binky's reaction. Early on in the episode, acquaintances Stevie and Cheska meet for dinner where they discuss Cheska's obtaining of evidence of Alex's infidelity from a mutual friend; the revelation here is for the audience. Later in the episode, the cast attends a party at a club, where Stevie repeats the revelation to his friends Ollie and Jamie, prompting their dismayed reaction that Alex had lied to them all. These units of revelation and reaction build to the emotional set piece of the episode where Cheska apologetically reveals her confirmation of the rumours to Binky, producing a shaking and sobbing reaction. A nervous Alex then joins the women and Binky has Cheska repeat the gossip (now the fourth reiteration of the episode). The focus is here on Alex's reaction and his halting confession that he does not remember the event due to a drunken blackout. This produces Binky's confused emotional devastation that the camera lingers on to close the episode. Here the series of revelations form the episode's core action, the repeated reactions its dramatic beats, culminating in the melodramatic spectacle of Binky's public breakdown.

In the absence of the confessional interview, gossip plays a key role in structured reality's storytelling through expositional conversation – the exchange of narrative information as gossip – with 'recap conversation ... used to facilitate a forward movement in the narrative' (Klein 2009). This is illustrated in the series of revelations of episode 7.3 and the multiple scenes discussing both the infidelity and Binky's reaction that dominate episode 7.4, driving to a narrative peak at the episode's close when Alex breaks up with Binky in the scene discussed above. Here we see how gossip allows story producers to scaffold events to film, confident in their ability to produce moments of tension or emotion – seen in the holding back of Cheska's revelation for the party and witnessing cast members, producing a rare public breakdown from Binky. Thus, gossip drives structured reality's use of docusoap's crisis structure, which is here built on revelation and confrontation.

The loosely framed following camera of docusoap connotes its action as unfolding beyond the influence of the camera, which must constantly move to capture it, indexically signalling transparency. In contrast, structured reality employs a controlled aesthetic that is facilitated by its scaffolded narratives, featuring three-point lighting, large amounts of tripod shots, smooth dolly tracks, a shallow depth of field and steadicam. These aesthetics require the setting and lighting of the space for action, be it a Chelsea street corner or an Essex club, so production processes blend with those of drama. Sarah Dillistone sought to distinguish *Made in Chelsea* from her previous project *TOWIE* – which she suggested looked like a soap – by making the programme 'look like the closest we could to an American drama' (Kanter 2015). *Made in Chelsea* used Sony F3 digital cameras, which hadn't been used in reality TV at that point, gave directors time to 'craft the look' and had a lengthy post-production process for edit and grading (Kanter 2015), taking weeks where the quick-turnaround

TOWIE took days. This produced a glossy, beautiful 'look', one that necessitated the scaffolding of action rather than happening upon and capturing action in process. Dillistone's comments align with those made by *The Hills* production team linking their programme's aesthetic to drama and cinema (Klein 2011). Like the form it glocalises, this discourse aligns *Made in Chelsea*'s cultivated aesthetic with long-standing discourses of filmic legitimation and 'quality'; here the aspirational glamour of the US teen TV imports the programme sat beside in E4's schedule.

Structured reality evokes youth drama both through this push towards the dramatic look over the documentary gaze and through reality TV's use of 'the emotional and affective registers of melodrama' (Nunn and Biressi 2014, 478). Through reality TV's melodrama-informed investment in the 'dramatic intensity of the emotionally fraught face' (Nunn and Biressi 2014, 478), structured reality's emotion-led storytelling is dominated by the lingering close-up and reaction shot. Here it follows *The Hills'* reliance on close-ups to maintain the audience's identification with Lauren Conrad, providing 'unmitigated access to [her] emotions and thoughts' that counters the spectacularisation of her everyday life produced by its 'cinematic aesthetic' (Leppert and Wilson 2011, 270). The British programmes continue *The Hills'* practice of closing scenes with a lingering close-up – a device Elana Levine (2006) identifies as borrowed from soap opera – where it provides a contemplative moment or a beat for the audience to gasp at a dramatic moment. In British structured reality's stronger embrace of comedy, this can also serve as the sitcom's joke beat or laughter pause, particularly in the more performative moments of *TOWIE* and *Made in Chelsea*. Here this is a beat to giggle at a comic moment or an awkward conversational moment or a lingering pause. In the transmedia audience space of contemporary television viewing, the moment also provides a pause to live-tweet a reaction.

The transitional montages that move us between scenes serve a similar transmedia pause function, as well as establishing classed space. This practice is particularly strong in *Made in Chelsea*, due to its investment in the imagery of London heritage and luxury. Its episodes are built in a series of structurally cohesive repetitive segments with the 'beats' of its story tightly constructed. Each scene closes with a lingering reaction shot or a question that serves to propel the narrative onwards and create dynamism from minimal stakes. We then move through a narrative intersection consisting of a short montage establishing our next location or providing general imagery evocative of the spaces of Chelsea and Knightsbridge.

Although these sequences can end on a particular bar or shop location, they rarely serve to directly locate characters in space, but instead evoke their privilege through the classed connotations of these London neighbourhoods and architecture. These transitions offer heritage London as a spectacle of consumption and history, inherited wealth and new luxury brands. In contrast, *TOWIE*'s suburban Essex locations articulate class less clearly, offering anonymous high streets, bland new-build housing and spacious post-war suburban streets and parks. Both programmes are invested in classed spectacle and identity that mark their regionality; however, *TOWIE*, as I argue below, locates this in bodies and performance. *Made in Chelsea*'s use of locational montages as classed markers highlight the programme's coding of class through space and place.

Coding Class: Space and Place

Made in Chelsea revels in a classed articulation of Britishness presented through its use of 'heritage' London iconography. Transitional montages pick out the street signs and Georgian architecture of the Royal Boroughs of Kensington and Chelsea, and cast members sip champagne or tea at a parade of chic London bars and restaurants. Key confrontations occur at 'balls' and country house parties, and cast members gaze contemplatively over the River Thames from Chelsea Embankment. The programme offers a spectacle of privilege – in contrast with *TOWIE*'s spectacle of femininity – through British heritage and international commodity consumption. Heritage transitional montages interchange with those that pick out luxury shop brands from the neighbourhood's celebrated King's Road. Spaces of leisure dominate over spaces of labour, as whilst ineffectually performed labour plays a central role in *The Hills* and *The City* (Klein 2009; Leppert and Wilson 2011) and plays a minor part in *TOWIE*, the majority of *Made in Chelsea* cast members rarely speak of their professions. Freed from actual labour, the emotional labour of their interpersonal life is their central concern.

The programme presents four distinct spaces for interactions: communal leisure spaces (cafes, bars, shops, parks), the homes of cast members, the ballrooms and clubs that host spectacular parties, and the neighbourhood streets. The latter allow *Made in Chelsea* its signature slow-pans along the wrought iron railings of white Georgian townhouse terraces with the golden sun glancing across their points. These streets form the location of 'coincidental' meetings of cast members, where they happen upon a friend or enemy, chance upon a new couple or have a conversation that reveals a catalysing piece of gossip. These scaffolded 'street meets' take on an edge of ironic self-awareness at the 'coincidence' as the seasons progress. The cast members are aware that this intersection has been set in motion by production to occur at an aesthetically pleasing compositional moment and to produce narrative dynamics. When discussing the *Made in Chelsea* cast's move to the US for a 2014 summer season, Sarah Dillistone knowingly quipped: 'We're all in New York now, doing the same stuff, bumping into each other round corners!' (Kanter 2015).

One such sequence in episode 7.4 opens with an establishing pan across a sunlit curved terrace of white Georgian houses; we then cut to Andy and Lucy walking in separate shots along a similar road of grand Georgian houses. As they grow close, Andy calls out to Lucy who is engrossed in her phone, she gives an awkwardly performed double-take of surprise (as Lucy's usual performance style is one of a sarcastic, flat affect) before greeting him and fumblingly putting her phone away. They pause in front of the large white townhouses, which are ornate with moldings, wrought iron awnings and railings; the composition of the shot-reverse-shot positions their faces low in the frame to display their surroundings. Their expositional conversation reveals that Stephanie Pratt has returned to London as part of a European holiday and she and Lucy plan to surprise Spencer, Stephanie's former boyfriend, to Andy's delight. They part with Andy's over-loud, performative 'Okay neighbour, see you later', both stifling a smile as they leave. The sequence serves to place them alongside the grand Georgian terrace, offering a spectacle of beautiful British heritage that they are spatially connected with but never enter. Andy and Lucy's greeting has an over-performed edge of 'playing along' with the coincidence, whilst the expositional conversation sees Lucy awkwardly enduring her role of doling out reveals, speaking fast, almost tossing away the information. This expositional conversation signals future events – Stephanie's return, the plot to surprise Spencer – for the viewer to anticipate later in the episode.

Made in Chelsea's 'street meets' make the sprawling incestuous cast the borough's primary community; the Chelsea streets are otherwise largely deserted, presented as their playground. Pleasure is produced from the awkwardness of these meetings, either from the ironic edge displayed in the above scene or through the throwing together of enemies, crushes or new loves. In episode 10.1, Stephanie and Tiff 'bump into' JP and new cast member Harney on similarly wrought-iron railinged corner. In a conversation opened by JP's over-emphasised 'What are you guys doing here?', Harney haltingly performs a flirtatious banter with Stephanie that produces comedy from both his unskilled performance of self and the awkward pauses and laughter of the stumbling conversation. The women collapse into giggles after the men leave. In both 'street meet' conversations, the inelegance of the interactions is in tension with the architectural beauty they take place against, producing a pleasurable cringing comedy.

Restaurants and cafes serve largely as locations for gossip and expositional conversation, whereas parties are scaffolded as well-appointed stages for catalysing conflict or dramatic reveals. These are often located in grand heritage spaces: a shooting party or picnic in the grounds of a grand estate, 'balls' in spacious ballrooms with glistening chandeliers or dinner parties by candlelight in gilded private dining spaces. These serve as performance spaces for set pieces, offering good angles for composition and sight lines for spectators observing action. When Stephanie visits London from LA in episode 7.4, she confronts a surprised Spencer over his previous poor treatment of her, making a grand entrance in the centre of a lavish party. The cast are scattered around a brightly lit ballroom, amidst columns and candles, with classical music playing. The cast's blankly shocked or amused reaction shots are picked out during the confrontation, whilst pairs of extras shuffle in attempts at waltz moves in the corner of the frame. These opulent spaces often provide dead acoustics, lacking life and comfort, the shuffle of extras providing the primary accompaniment to heighten moments of awkward dead air.

Public spaces are often sparsely populated, emptied of London bustle to create uncluttered views of our protagonists. Series eight opens with part of the cast holidaying at Devon's Staunton Beach, depicted as the only inhabitants of pristine golden sands. In episode 8.1, a camera speeds alongside Louise and Binky as they gallop on their horses at pace through the surf in amber sunlight, against a blue sky spotted with fluffy clouds. We cut out to a wide-shot centring the racing riders against an expanse of beach and sky, with a crane shot arcing up over the horses as they race across the beach towards the headland. Privilege serves as spectacle, both through skilled horsemanship and the cast as sole inhabitants of spectacular emptied British landscape.

The cast's 'personal' spaces have the echo of the uninhabited, with living rooms and kitchens lacking signifiers of domesticity and the camera's shallow depth of field presenting cast members against a de-focused blank canvas of pastels and creams. These cleanly art-directed interiors could serve as signifiers of privilege, but also evoke a nowhereness, a cold compositional beauty that lacks a personal touch, contributing to the lack of warmth within the programme. This controlled aesthetic is at times presented with an edge of irony, particularly when we intrude on a couple's intimate 'morning after'. For instance, Spencer's lothario persona produces a string of white-robed morning-after bedroom scenes, including a hotel room one morning in series eight with new girlfriend Lauren Frazer-Hutton, a glamorous model (episode 8.11). The scene offers a performance of luxurious intimacy in wide-angled shots that track round a lavish wood-panelled hotel room. Spencer sits in the foreground organising a champagne breakfast, with Lauren in the rear of shot in a patch of soft light, reclining amidst artfully draped sheets with glossy tanned limbs and ruffled hair. A scene so artfully composed it is rendered airless and so suffused with picture-perfect privilege, it is pushed to a knowing comic edge.

When *Made in Chelsea* decamps to New York for a summer season, the city is rendered in echoing imagery and a lushly honey-toned colour-palate. Transitional montages feature luxury brands and iconic New York views, presenting a tourist vision of iconic streets and skylines, one familiar from myriad film and television depictions of the city. It is a space that our cast move through in comfort, from one life of privilege to another – Georgian heritage streets are exchanged for brownstone terraces, downtown lofts, rooftop bars and Central Park. It is a space of foreign yet familiar glamour, in which the usual storytelling spaces are deployed – cafes for gossip, bars for conflict, a river to contemplatively gaze over. *Made in Chelsea*'s use of classed space and place at home and abroad showcases an iconography of privilege. The spaces of structured reality illustrate the form's use of culturally coded signifiers of class to support storytelling and identity construction. *Made in Chelsea* offers everyday lives of luxury presented in well-appointed London landscapes. Yet these aspirational lifestyles and spaces are presented with such care and infused with such gloss that they ultimately produce an emptiness, which facilitates the awkwardness that creates structured reality's pleasurable tensions and ambivalence.

CODING CLASS: GENDER

In contrast to *Made in Chelsea*, *TOWIE* situates itself within spaces of the mundane middle-class everyday, against which the bright colours and 'bling' of its cast members stand out as comic spectacle. Fake tanned, plump-lipped Chloe is displayed in wide shots while sitting knock-kneed on her lounge's small chintzy sofa alongside her cousin Joey Essex, their dinner balanced on lap trays (episode 2.9). The cosy daytime domesticity is at odds with the glamorous excess of her heavy eye makeup, sky-high heels, tight dress and fake nails (Figure 6.2). Both *TOWIE* and *Made in Chelsea* are strongly shaped by British class concerns written through gendered identities. *TOWIE*'s pleasures are produced by its spectacle of excessive femininity, derived from the cultural identity of its Essex location. Biressi and Nunn argue that figures such as Liverpudlian scousers or Essex girls draw on folk knowledge about geographical areas that mark inhabitants with a 'lack of taste, poise or even of "class" itself' (2013, 38). *TOWIE* is culturally marked by classed stereotypes despite the middle-class backgrounds and lifestyles of its cast members. Laura Grindstaff argues that self-service television's scaffolding of production contexts for performance constructs 'particular roles for participants to inhabit' (2011, 51). These must be easily assumed for a non-professional working without script or rehearsal: thus, normative cultural scripts about gender, race, class and sexuality structure these roles (ibid.). *TOWIE* is built on social scripts surrounding the classed identities of Essex girls – the Essex of 'the cultural and political imagination' that 'has become a key motif for a far larger story of social transformation with attendant classed anxieties about politics, place, taste and social mobility' (Biressi and Nunn 2013, 24–25).

Fig. 6.2 *TOWIE* presents Chloe's glamorous excess as comic spectacle within the domestic everyday

TOWIE's classed pleasures are interlinked with the string of celebrity docusoaps that had built ITV2's early audience and its channel identity. These included a series of programmes following former glamour model turned entrepreneur Katie Price – *Jordan and Peter* (2005), *Katie and Peter* (2007–2009) and *What Katie Did Next* (2009–2011). In these she balanced celebrity life with the struggles of relationships and family, with their narratives articulating her ordinary-yet-extraordinary celebrity identity (Holmes 2005, 134).[4] Price's celebrity was built on a certain kind of working-class girl made good, succeeding despite many hard knocks and copious press criticism (Tyler and Bennett 2010). When Price left ITV2 in 2010 for a multi-million pound deal with satellite channel Sky Living, *TOWIE*'s success helped fill the commercial and representational gap she left behind. By replacing celebrities with 'ordinary' people, the programme spectacularised its cast's daily life, targeting a primarily female demographic with a mixture of hyper-glamour – their celebrity-inspired femininities – and the everyday – their mundane middle-class Essex surroundings, both familiar from representations of the 'celebrity chav'.

'Chav' is a derogatory term that labels a 'young, white, working class as lazy, tasteless, unintelligent, or criminal' (Tyler and Bennett 2010, 379). The 'celebrity chav' is a primarily female, formerly working-class celebrity who often achieves fame through reality TV, such as Jade Goody, Kerry Katona or Katie Price.[5] She is judged (by the press or public) as unworthy of her wealth or success due to her lack of education and consumption outside of middle-class taste codes. She is chastised for her inability to perform the 'correct' femininity associated with middle- and upper-class glamour and refinement (2010, 381). Pop star Cheryl Cole has managed to shed her celebrity chav image through her assimilation of these taste codes and a careful performance of vulnerability. The cultural discourse surrounding the women of *TOWIE* draws on similar coding, as despite their middle-class status achieved by their socially mobile Essex parents, their overtly constructed femininities still read as working class. When combined with their lack of language skills and general knowledge – they lack traditional cultural capital despite their financial capital – this can lead to observers coding them as 'chavs' (Cadwalladr 2011).

Drawn from similar class-based discourses as the working-class signifier 'Essex girl', the term 'chav' demonstrates an aggressive shift in tonality. In their analysis of the discursive construction of the Essex girl, Biressi and Nunn suggest that the aggression and misogyny of her cultural representations rely on shared social assumptions about 'class, consumerism and bad taste' (2013, 24). Drawing on Bev Skeggs (2003), they position this mockery as a reaction to the Essex girl's disruption of respectability and proper conduct, due to her adoption of 'a tough polished exterior' and her creation of 'economic and social worth through overt investment in [her] grooming, dress and personal appearance' (2013, 24). Whilst she may be the butt of class and gender-based mockery, the 'Essex girl' is rarely subjected to the vitriol thrown at the 'chav' and is an identity worn with pride by many of the women of *TOWIE*.

The coding of the *TOWIE* cast as 'chavs' is found in online discussions and broadsheet press discourse – illustrating the role of middle-class taste distinctions in cultural monitoring. The *Daily Telegraph* argued that 'the dismally moronic' programme contributed to Essex's 'chav-stained public image' (Christiansen 2011), whereas *The Observer* used *TOWIE* as its central case study of televisual representations of 'chavs', suggesting that the programme's success came at the expense of images of the 'respectable working class' (Cadwalladr 2011). Judgements of taste dominate these discussions, with *The Times*' Caitlin Moran suggesting the cast were offered up as 'the very worst of the working classes making good' (Moran 2011), whereas Owen Jones argued in *The Independent* that the programme 'caricatures the supposedly "tacky aspirational" working-class who can't spend money with the taste and discretion of the middle class' (2011). British structured reality illustrates the intricate coding of the British class systems around 'taste' and 'style', and the distinctions made between 'old' and 'new' money by the middle classes.

The particular articulations of femininity at play here are key to unpicking this discourse. The Essex girl has traditionally been figured as a 'monstrous figure of consumption' (Biressi and Nunn 2013, 24), which is evidenced in the press characterisations of the *TOWIE* cast as tacky and tasteless. This in turn echoes critiques of the chav's 'excessive consumption of consumer and branded goods' and '"bad", "vulgar" and excessive consumer choices' (Tyler 2008, 21). Postfeminist discourse positions contemporary femininity as inextricably intertwined with consumer culture (Tasker and Negra 2007); however, in these judgements, *TOWIE* represents a femininity constructed through *excessive* consumption.

This effortful femininity is built on a sexualised yet girlish aesthetic favouring pink and crystallised 'bling'. It is marked by an overt construction, including heavy makeup, ostentatious fake tan, hair, nails and lashes, and proudly displayed fake breasts. This is a femininity produced through conspicuous consumption and surgery, with fake breasts an everyday conversation piece. For example, at a pool party populated by many bikini-clad women, Chloe and Maria sit at the edge of the swimming pool. Chloe is clad in a hot pink bikini top covered in fake yellow flowers, which accentuates her large fake breasts, and she prods them unselfconsciously (episode 2.14). The friends casually discuss their fake breasts, giggling as they grab their own and identify the geographical provenance of those of the women surrounding them. They define their Belgian and 'Harley Street' versions, by inference elite, against the mass of the surrounding 'Essex tits'. Here, excessive constructed femininity is presented as everyday. The femininity displayed in *TOWIE* is a postfeminist glamour reliant on commercial beauty culture and is simultaneously sexualised yet girly (Tasker and Negra 2007). This is linked to the Playboy brand and glamour models, which is identified as an aspirational career by some of *TOWIE*'s female cast in early seasons, with Amy Childs viewing Chloe with admiration when she arrives in season two, due to her history as a Playboy Bunny.

This classed femininity feeds into the cultural stereotypes that position 'Essex girls' as unruly, vulgar and sexual (Skeggs 2003). The particular kind of hyper-sexual yet girlish femininity dominant in *TOWIE* is that personified by Katie Price and her hugely successful one-woman brand. Price's image combines the princess-industrial complex (Orenstein 2011) with a pornographic aesthetic – nothing about her femininity is refined. Her lips and breasts are pumped up through surgery and her brand is dominated by the 'girly' glamour of pink and crystals. Her wedding to fellow celebrity Peter Andre – documented in her ITV2 docusoap – saw her arrive in a crystallised carriage that echoed Disney's *Cinderella* (1950), clad in a huge pink tulle dress. Price's personality tends towards a coarseness that is rarely present in *TOWIE*. Despite the sexualised connotations of their appearances and the flinty toughness of some of the cast members, the women of *TOWIE* display behaviour that is markedly chaste and girlish. Amanda Ann Klein argues that in *Jersey Shore*, 'femininity is loud, messy, lusty, gluttonous, and self-serving. It is primary, abject, and visible' (2014, 161), a representation that extends to its glocalised British sister *Geordie Shore*. In *TOWIE* sex is gossiped about but happens off-camera, is rarely discussed in detail and is often referred to in child-like terms – with genitalia described as 'nu-nu' and 'willy'. Dramatic set pieces at parties often display a slurring delivery that suggests the alcohol needed to support public emotional display, yet the constructed nature of the production process lends itself to control, never pushing into the on-camera abject display of *Jersey Shore*. *TOWIE*'s narrative focus is on comic set pieces and the social impact of sex and off-camera hedonism, hook-ups, new relationships and infidelity.

Bev Skeggs argues that femininity is distinctly classed, as appearance and conduct act as markers of respectability. She draws on Bourdieu to illustrate how women's bodies have historically been used as markers of taste cultures, noting that across a range of social and cultural representations, vulgarity and excess are coded as working class (2003). *TOWIE*'s revelling in glitz and 'bling' through its femininities and aesthetic exhibits a playful defiance of 'respectable' taste. This is connected with the 'class cross-dressing' of the working-class celebrity, whose 'sartorial and material signifiers of class transformation mark both [their] working class origins and the move away from them' (Biressi and Nunn 2005, 145–146). Despite their present middle-class distance from their families' roots in the East End of London, the *TOWIE* cast's valuing of artifice and the demonstrable effort involved in their appearance connects them to working-class femininity. They are positioned as financially solidly middle class, with transitional montages positioning them within new-build estates and mock-Tudor detached suburban houses. Yet they employ and celebrate a form of glamour and femininity that highlights excess and artifice and which they repeatedly define as central to their Essex identity. Although this 'excessive' brand of glamour is coded as 'vulgar' by middle-class taste codes, its practitioners connect it with a pleasurable display of status. As Chloe notes: 'In Essex, like, all the guys and all the girls, they all like, make an effort, even if they're going somewhere simple, like in competition' (episode 4.2). This pleasurable, effortful depiction of working-class femininities can be found across a range of British televisual representations. In sitcoms from *The Liver Birds* (BBC One, 1969–1979) to *Bread* (BBC One, 1986–1991), in the long history of soap opera's naive bombshells and ageing vamps, and in the ITV2 celebrity docusoaps of Katie Price. The fondness present in many of these television representations – and in Britain's attitudes towards Essex itself (May 2010) – speaks to British culture's ambivalence over the excessive femininity employed by *TOWIE*.

Skeggs suggests that class-based articulations of femininity categorise the appearance of naturalness with a higher cultural value than artifice, as the latter's display of labour is 'de-valued for being made visible' (2003, 101). The glamorous femininity of *TOWIE* is, as Chloe noted in the above quote, about making an effort. In contrast, the glamour displayed by the women of *Made in Chelsea* offers a pose of studied effortlessness. The labour needed to maintain it is hidden – a gossip session at a blow-dry bar will be the only evidence. The majority of cast members display expensively cut yet artfully dishevelled hair or carefully cultivated loose waves, subtle yet meticulously applied makeup, 'natural' tans and discreet cleavage. This refined glamour operates around an effortful display of 'naturalness' that seeks to present them as both normalised, yet elite. The audience are well aware of the money needed to maintain it – the furs tell us that. This glossy 'effortless' femininity is thrown into relief by the few cast members who do not conform to the model, often disruptive outsiders like Gabrielle in the early seasons and Stephanie Pratt from season six onwards. An aspiring pop star and notably the only member of the privately educated cast to go to state school, Gabrielle displays a more explicitly constructed and thus 'vulgar' femininity: her fake tan in tones of orange, dark makeup and large amount of bare skin offers an imagery of artificiality more familiar in the world of *TOWIE*. Stephanie was previously a cast member of *The Hills*, yet within *Made in Chelsea* her Hollywood-informed American femininity – achieved by a degree of plastic surgery – does not pass muster; her style and her assertive bluntness initially position her as an outsider. She makes a dramatic entrance strutting into the ballroom to confront a shocked Spencer at the party in episode 7.4 (discussed above), with the exchange delighting his onlooking friends. However, her outsider status is signalled by her hot pink dress in stark contrast with the sleek black Dolce & Gabbana gown of Emma, Spencer's new love interest, who is stood at his side during the confrontation. Stephanie's sweeping triumphant exit is undermined by a cut to Rosie stood at the back of the room, stifling a giggle as she dismissively whispers about the quality of the pink dress.

The first season of *Made in Chelsea* was structured by a series of love triangles connected to Caggie Dunlop, who fit smoothly into the programme's aspirational aesthetic and whose wide-eyed pouting stares, soft tan and glossy blonde hair strongly recalled *The Hills'* Lauren Conrad. Yet, the most popular cast members were the supporting trio of Ollie, Binky and Cheska, who while still positioned as upper class were outsiders to Caggie's central group. All three sport heavy eye makeup, an often unrefined fashion sense and a tendency toward camp squeals, flamboyant gestures and a pose of wide-eyed cluelessness. Binky and Cheska's aesthetic is smirkingly critiqued by the more conventionally tasteful Amber and Rosie in the opening episode, helping to establish the social dynamics of the cast. The pair dismiss fake tan as 'possibly the most offensive thing in the world', a distinctly classed judgement on artificial beauty. Their passive-aggressive, conspiratorial agreement that Binky and Cheska's tans and short dresses are 'just not my style' serves to articulate their belief in their own refinement and higher social rank. They communicate their own status through their carefully low-key yet moneyed style and their studiedly 'natural' yet expensively maintained beauty. The unspoken levels of status within *Made in Chelsea*'s upper-class society demonstrate Skeggs' argument that class is articulated through cultural practices as much as economics (2003).

Ollie, Binky and Cheska are private educated, their families own country cottages and they live in well-appointed period buildings, but in early seasons, their at times excessive appearance together with their play with camp's 'theatricalization of experience' and its refusal of traditional seriousness (Sontag 1967: 287) distinguishes them from the other cast members. They seem more suited to Essex than Chelsea. As the seasons have progressed, Binky has become assimilated into the central group, taking on the role of the unlucky-in-love, emotionally authentic heroine rather than the comic relief. This process was facilitated by her refining of her glamour in line with the dominant femininity of *Made in Chelsea*, yet she retains a slight dishevelled edge tied to her air of guileless naiveté; these contribute to her facility to perform emotional authenticity.

Like *Made in Chelsea*'s articulation of space and place, the femininities centralised in both this programme and *TOWIE* work to code class. Here we see British structured reality glocalising *The Hills* by foregrounding class-based identities, contrasting with the US programme's disavowal of its cast's upper-middle-class privilege. This disavowal of class aligns with US television's normalising of white upper-middle-class privilege and served *The Hills*' status as boom-time consumerist fantasy. The British programmes instead align with British youth television's engagement with class and regionality. Their regional representations have the potential to slip into stereotype, but this is countered by the ambivalent audience position encouraged by structured reality. This ambivalence is displayed in the British form's shaping of its classed identities through camp play and performativity.

Camp Play and Comic Voice

The rejection of middle-class taste codes and foregrounding of artifice in *TOWIE*'s femininities, combined with its knowing tone and awkward performances, could encourage a mocking audience position that pokes fun at its cast's inarticulate excess. However, the programme's infusion of its narrative and aesthetic with a tongue-in-cheek camp suggests that structured reality offers multiple access points for viewers beyond derogatory mockery. Here structured reality displays reality TV's 'play-off between performance and authenticity' (Hill 2015, 53), a tension that Hill suggests drives its audiences' investment in questions of performance, identities, truth and artifice (2015, 54). British structured reality's highly self-aware nature is fed by a centralising of camp's 'love of the unnatural: of artifice and exaggeration' (Sontag 1967, 275), particularly in *TOWIE*'s positioning of its performances and excessive femininities as knowingly comic. In framing its excesses through this knowing tonal address, the programme seeks to defuse potential charges of negative stereotyping. Whilst some observers question whether the cast demonstrates enough self-awareness to avoid exploitative caricaturing (Raeside and Flynn 2011), this critique is largely built on a somewhat patronising class-based assumption that cast members are not as savvy as the audiences for whom they perform.

The cast's giggling pride in their unnatural and artificial femininity contributes to *TOWIE*'s camp tone, as it enacts a knowing performativity of the social scripts surrounding the figure of the Essex girl. Whereas the 1990s British docusoap subject was required both to retain their ordinariness and to perform it (Kavka 2012, 70), the artificiality inherent in the production process of structured reality prompts a performance that creates tension with any remaining desire to ascribe documentary naturalism to reality TV. The process produces an image that is simultaneously ordinary and extraordinary. *TOWIE*'s framework of camp serves to 'naturalise' its cast's self-conscious performativity and to smooth the tensions created by their imperfect performances by embedding playfulness into the programme.

Cast member Amy Childs – who left the programme after two seasons – is highly performative in her manner, drawing on camp's favouring of the strongly exaggerated, illustrating Sontag's 'Being-as-Playing-a-Role' (1967, 280). Like all *TOWIE* cast members, Amy wears full makeup and blown-out hair whether at a club or at work, or gossiping in a friend's living room, where this excessive femininity is often at odds with the suburban domestic space (as noted above with regards to Chloe's sofa perch). Fellow cast members such as Lydia or Sam display emotional realism despite their constructed appearances; however, Amy plays the role of 'Amy Childs', the celebrity she desired to be but not yet was.[6] At her bubblegum pink home-salon, she offers a pose of straight-talking airheadedness fragmented by giggles, seriously yet clumsily talking through the treatments she gives to her friends as she 'performs' her role as beautician. She wears impractically high heels and her brightly dyed red hair clashes with her pink, tight-fitting uniform, which prominently displays the cleavage of her fake breasts. These she discusses at the beginning of season two with new arrival Chloe while giving her a spray tan, having playfully set out her choice of shades through a set of swatches ranging from 'oompa loompa' to 'cornbeef' (sic) to 'why bother', in a self-aware commentary on the tanning excesses of herself and her community (episode 2.1).

The artificiality present in *TOWIE*'s performances contributes to its comic voice and play with camp, yet it also informs an authenticity. Karen Lury considers whether watching ordinary people perform in reality TV creates anxiety in television audiences because 'if real people convincingly "put on an act" where can sincerity, authenticity and real emotion be located with any conviction?' (1995, 126). In not papering over the cracks in its performances, *TOWIE* showcases its cast as ultimately *more* authentic than a *Big Brother* contestant successfully 'playing the game', as they unable to 'put on an act'. They are brought closer to us the audience through their inability to perform convincingly – they are made 'real'. The awkwardness of popular *TOWIE* cast member Gemma's performance of self – her dialogue and attempts at a saucy sexuality almost comical in their stiltedness – make her all the more real and identifiable for the audience due to her striving for, yet failing to perform, Essex femininity. Whilst sporting the prominent cleavage and fake tan, hair and nails of the other *TOWIE* ladies, she is older and much heavier, her look less polished. The awkwardness of Gemma's performativity thus signals her attempts to imperfectly fit into 'acceptable' models of femininity in Essex culture and makes her all the more accessible to audiences.

TOWIE's 'unrefined' and larger-than-life glamour is played for gentle comedy, particularly when positioned within the everyday locales of suburban or rural Essex. When Amy and her friends go 'glamping' (glamorous camping), comedy is derived from the sight of their constructed aesthetic set against the natural beauty of the Essex countryside – as Sontag notes, 'nothing in nature can be campy' (1967, 279). A montage of the group unpacking the car is accompanied by a big band version of Dean Martin's 'Powder Your Face with Sunshine', featuring a close-up of a snail on a white fluffy blanket, Sam dragging pink suitcases across the grass, Gemma struggling to put on zebra-print wellington boots, and Amy standing powdering her nose as the rest unpack the Land Rover (episode 2.10). The sequence offers a playfulness and works to build a comic contrast between untamed nature and the group's attempt to maintain an inappropriate glamour. As the women attempt to put up their boldly coloured gazebo, Amy is framed in wide shots against the sun-dappled green fields as she feigns ignorance and performatively pouts at the task. The juxtaposition of the natural landscape with her bright blue puffed-skirt party dress paired with Ugg boots and chandelier earrings signals her appearance as comically inappropriate and excessive.

This juxtaposition of the women's heightened constructed glamour with everyday British locales helps to position *TOWIE* within the sensibilities of British youth television. Here, *TOWIE*'s knowing sensibility, its recognition of its distance from naturalism – camp's 'theatricalization of experience' and its refusal of traditional seriousness (Sontag 1967, 287) – aligns it with the ambivalent address of British youth television. It hails the savvy subject 'who isn't taken in by the performance of others, who insists for all to see that he or she "gets it"' (Andrejevic 2004, 322). Structured reality's aesthetic and performances centralise pleasurable tension, ensuring its audience 'gets it' by foregrounding imperfect performance. This use of irony and camp to negotiate the tensions between structured reality's construction and the emotional realism of its interpersonal storytelling mirrors the address Su Holmes identifies in British gossip magazine *Heat*, which shares British youth television's youth demographic. Holmes suggests that *Heat*'s irreverent and ironic address acknowledges the fabrication of celebrity culture, but in the process works to smooth over the magazine and reader's involvement in this process (2005, 36). *TOWIE* takes up this address, foregrounding the awkwardness of its own construction and artificiality of its femininities through its framework of comic camp. This allows the programme to flatter its savvy audience, recognising their genre literacy – the cast's femininities are artificial and inauthentic, so the programme's artificial nature is naturalised. Thus, constructions of femininity are aligned with production and narrative construction.

The performativity of the women of *TOWIE* signalled their ease with reality TV and their awareness of its performance demands; in contrast, *Made in Chelsea*'s heirs and socialites were initially more self-conscious, although as the seasons have progressed, the majority have relaxed into their roles as they became more experienced reality TV participants. This has led to an increase in playful performativity for some cast members, such as Spencer, Rosie, and particularly Marc-Francis and Victoria. The latter pair have a comic scene each episode where they drawlingly perform their privileged cultural capital and moneyed taste as a pair of grande dames, be it trying on lavish jewellery or surveying a sculptor's studio. This camp play exists alongside a pursuit of emotional authenticity for other cast members, such as Lucy's cold straight-talking and Binky's open-heartedness. The cast's initial tentativeness and lack of performativity appeared as an attempt to maintain a class-based aloofness over the project itself, a desire to retain dignity and power over their reality TV representation. Yet, the resulting performances were often stiff and awkward, playing into stereotypes of the cold aloofness of the British upper class; the cast were too self-conscious to embrace the 'playful, anti-serious' nature of *TOWIE*'s camp (Sontag 1967, 288). *TOWIE*'s revelling in its cast's slightly unnatural performances of their everyday life serves the programme's camp tone in the same way as its artificial femininities do, working to highlight a pleasurable lack of naturalness in line with the cultural associations of its regionality. In contrast, *Made in Chelsea*'s initially stilted performances – and the air of hesitancy and awkwardness that still remains – clashes with the cast's otherwise glamorously refined femininities and the programme's artful aesthetic to pleasurably uncomfortable effect.

This stiltedness punctures the programme's aspirational glamour, creating tensions between the flawless setting and the cast's awkwardness that serve as one of the programme's central ambivalent pleasures. The cast's elite position is undercut and their pretension exposed by an inability to convincingly perform their own lives. British structured reality may mimic the glossy, dramatic look of *The Hills*, but it pushes the awkwardness that poked through this gloss in the US programme to the foreground. It seems uninterested in smoothing out the rough edges of its cast's performances and this is perhaps its clearest contribution to a camp sensibility: 'It's good because it's awful' (Sontag 1967, 292). Yet this awkwardness also signifies the cast's authenticity within this constructed process; in displaying their lack of professional skills, particularly the self-conscious giggle prevalent in the *TOWIE* cast, the programme brings them closer to us. Conversely, British youth television's ambivalent relationship with privilege derives pleasure from the discomfort of *Made in Chelsea*'s awkward performances against a backdrop of covetable elite lifestyles.

TOWIE and *Made in Chelsea* appropriate *The Hills'* blurring of drama and reality TV, yet glocalise the US form to fit within the ambivalent address of British youth television. It assimilates the US form's melodramatic storytelling and aspirational consumption-oriented lifestyles into British television by acknowledging the construction and artificiality that *The Hills* often sought to obscure. *TOWIE* and *Made in*

Chelsea continue British reality TV's fascination with class, articulating the role of classed hierarchies within British society, fed through aesthetic distinctions and femininities. Their celebration of excess can tilt towards caricature, yet they seek to defuse their problematic representations by employing a knowing comic address and camp performativity. The savvy detachment encouraged by British youth television sees these programmes employ culturally divisive representations, yet frame them as untroublingly comedic through their camp play. Their constructed production process produces awkward performances, with the resulting pleasurable tensions informing these programmes' differing comic voices. *TOWIE*'s camp-informed comic voice brings pleasure from artificiality in terms of both performance and femininity, particularly when set against its suburban everyday. *Made in Chelsea*'s comic voice is drawn from British youth television's ambivalent relationship with privilege, presented in a pleasurable clash between awkward performances of self and the programme's refined glossy aesthetic. Structured reality's ambivalence allows its simultaneous presentation of highly constructed aesthetics and emotion-led storytelling, producing intimacy through the emotional realism that is catalysed by its constructed production process. These programs demonstrate the centrality of ambivalent comic play, classed representations and emotion-based storytelling to the pleasures of British youth television.

Notes

1. 'Vajazzling' refers to the decorating of the area around a woman's bikini line with decorative crystals.
2. Van Outen's identity as both a television presenter and actress is built around her claiming of her Essex identity and an embrace of a broad comedy voice at odds with her blonde glamour.
3. See Biressi and Nunn (2013) for a detail charting of the development of Essex stereotypes.
4. Katie Price is a former highly successful topless model 'Jordan', whose celebrity is built on her plastic surgery, the tabloid coverage of her string of broken relationships and the resulting children. She parlayed this celebrity into a string of docusoaps and autobiographies and successfully commodified her personal brand across an extensive range of products, from children's books to beauty products to horse accessories.
5. Although Price has a middle-class background, her Estuary accent, toughness and glamour model past code her culturally as working class.

6. Childs ultimately became a celebrity via *TOWIE* and subsequent tabloid newspaper coverage, though she left the programme in 2011 to take part in *Celebrity Big Brother* (Channel 5, 2011–) and later her own docusoap *It's All About Amy* (Channel 5, 2011).

References

Andrejevic, Mark. 2003. *Reality TV: The Work of Being Watched*. New York: Rowman & Littlefield.

———. 2004. 'Visceral Literacy: Reality TV, Savvy Viewers, and Auto-Spies'. In *Reality TV: Remaking Television Culture*, edited by Susan Murray and Laurie Ouellette, 321–342. New York: NYU Press.

Ang, Ien. 1985. *Watching Dallas: Soap Opera and the Melodramatic Imagination*. New York: Methuen.

Barr, Ann and Peter York. 1982. *The Official Sloane Ranger Handbook: The First Guide to What Really Matters in Life*. London: Ebury Press.

Berlant, Lauren. 2008. *The Female Complaint: The Unfinished Business of Sentimentality in American Culture*. Durham, NC: Duke University Press.

Biressi, Anita and Heather Nunn. 2005. *Reality TV: Realism and Revelation*. London: Wallflower Press.

———. 2013. *Class and Contemporary British Culture*. Basingstoke: Palgrave Macmillan.

Bruzzi, Stella. 2006. *New Documentary*. 2nd edn. London: Routledge.

Cadwalladr, Caroline. 2011. 'Vajazzled! How Chavs Have Replaced Working Class People on Britain's TV'. *The Guardian*, 5 June. www.theguardian.com/tv-and-radio/2011/jun/05/how-chavs-replaced-working-class (accessed 25 May 2016).

Caughie, John. 2000. *Television Drama : Realism, Modernism, and British Culture*. Oxford University Press.

Christiansen, Rupert. 2011. 'Firstsite Gallery: Golden Banana or White Elephant?' *Daily Telegraph*, 3 October, 30

Deacon, Michael. 2011 'Shut Uuuuup! How TV Reinforces Regional Stereotypes'. *Daily Telegraph*, 13 July, 19.

Frost, Vicky. 2011. 'From *The Only Way is Essex* to *Made in Chelsea*: Has Reality TV Been Reborn?' *The Guardian*, 9 May. www.theguardian.com/media/2011/may/09/the-only-way-is-essex-made-in-chelsea (accessed 25 May 2016).

Geraghty, Christine. 1981. 'Continuous Serial – A Definition'. In *Coronation Street*, edited by Richard Dyer, 9–26. London: BFI.

Grindstaff, Laura. 2011. 'Just Be Yourself – Only More So: Ordinary Celebrity in the Era of Self-Service Television'. In *The Politics of Reality Television : Global Perspectives*, edited by Marwan Kraidy and Katherine Sender, 44–58. London: Routledge.

Heminsley, Alexandra. 2011. 'Is *The Only Way is Essex* Still Compulsive Viewing?' *The Guardian*, 26 September. www.theguardian.com/tv-and-radio/tvandradioblog/2011/sep/26/the-only-way-is-essex (accessed 25 May 2016).

Hill, Annette. 2002. 'Big Brother: The Real Audience'. *Television & New Media* 3(3): 323–40.

———. 2015. *Reality TV*. London: Routledge.

Holmes, Su. 2005. '"Off-Guard, Unkempt, Unready"?: Deconstructing Contemporary Celebrity in *Heat* Magazine'. *Continuum* 19(1): 21–38.

Holmes, Su and Deborah Jermyn. 2004. 'Introduction: Understanding Reality TV'. In *Understanding Reality Television*, edited by Su Holmes and Deborah Jermyn, 1–32. London: Routledge.

Jones, Owen. 2011. 'It's Time for a Debate on the C Word'. *The Independent*, 6 June, 4.

Kanter, Jake. 2015. '18: Talking TV: BBC Arts & *Made in Chelsea*'. *Broadcast: Talking TV Podcast*. 28 March. www.broadcastnow.co.uk/talking-tv-bbc-arts-and-made-in-chelsea/5070146.article (accessed 25 May 2016).

Kavka, Misha. 2008. *Reality Television, Affect and Intimacy: Reality Matters*. Basingstoke: Palgrave Macmillan.

———. 2012. *Reality TV*. Edinburgh University Press.

———. 2014a. 'A Matter of Feeling: Mediated Affect in Reality Television'. In *A Companion to Reality Television*, edited by Laurie Ouellette, 460–477. Chichester: John Wiley & Sons.

———. 2014b. 'Reality TV and the Gendered Politics of Flaunting'. In *Reality Gendervision: Sexuality and Gender on Transatlantic Reality Television*, edited by Brenda R. Weber, 54–75. Durham, NC: Duke University Press.

Khalsa, Balihar. 2011. 'Structured Reality: The New Reality'. *Broadcast*, 26 August, 34.

———. 2012. 'ITV and Lime Strike Back in TOWIE Legal Dispute'. *Broadcast*, 14 June, 1.

Kilborn, Richard. 2003. *Staging the Real: Factual TV Programming in the Age of Big Brother*. Manchester University Press.

Klein, Amanda Ann. 2009. 'Postmodern Marketing, Generation Y and the Multiplatform Viewing Experience of MTV's *The Hills*'. *Jumpcut*. www.ejumpcut.org/archive/jc51.2009/HillsKlein (accessed 25 May 2016).

———. 2011. 'The Hills, Jersey Shore, and the Aesthetics of Class'. *Flow* 13(12). http://flowtv.org/2011/04/the-hills-jersey-shore-and-the-aesthetics-of-class (accessed 25 May 2016).

———. 2014. 'Abject Femininity and Compulsory Masculinity on the Jersey Shore'. In *Reality Gendervision: Sexuality and Gender on Transatlantic Reality Television*, edited by Brenda R. Weber, 213–243. Durham, NC: Duke University Press.

Leppert, Alice and Julie Wilson. 2011. 'Living *The Hills* Life: Laurne Conrad as Reality Star, Soap Opera Heroine, and Brand'. In *In the Limelight and under the Microscope: Forms and Functions of Female Celebrity*, edited by Diane Negra and Su Holmes, 261–279. London: Continuum.

Levine, Elana. 2006. 'The New Soaps? *Laguna Beach*, *The Hills*, and the Gendered Politics of Reality "Drama"'. *Flow* 4(10). http://flowtv.org/2006/08/the-new-soaps-laguna-beach-the-hills-and-the-gendered-politics-of-reality-drama (accessed 25 May 2016).

Lury, Karen. 1995. 'Television Performance: Being Acting and "Corpsing"'. *New Formations* 27 (June): 114–127

May, Pete. 2010. 'Essex Man: The Bonds of Basildon'. *The Independent*, 10 June. www.independent.co uk/life-style/health-and-families/features/essex-man-the-bonds-of-basildon-2098663.html (accessed 25 May 2016).

McCarthy, Anna. 2004. 'Laguna Beach'. *Flow* 1(5). http://flowtv.org/2004/12/laguna-beach (accessed 25 May 2016).

Middleton, Jason. 2014. *Documentary's Awkward Turn: Cringe Comedy and Media Spectatorship*. Abingdon: Routledge.

Moran, Caitlin. 2011. 'This is Life or Death - and it's the Purest Form of Drama There is'. *The Times*, 14 May, 17.

Nunn, Heather and Anita Biressi. 2014. '"Walking in Another's Shoes": Sentimentality and Philanthropy on Reality Television'. In *A Companion to Reality Television*, edited by Laurie Ouellette, 478–498. Chichester: John Wiley & Sons.

Orenstein, Peggy. 2011. *Cinderella Ate My Daughter: Dispatches from the Front Lines of the New Girlie-Girl Culture*. New York: HarperCollins.

Parker, Robin. 2010. 'ITV2 and Lime to Make "Living Soap" Set in Essex'. *Broadcast*, 20 May. www.broadcastnow.co.uk/itv2-and-lime-to-make-living-soap-set-in-essex/5014213.article (accessed 25 May 2016).

Piper, Helen. 2004. 'Reality TV. Wife Swap and the Drama of Banality'. *Screen* 45(4): 273–286.

Plunkett, John. 2011. '*The Only Way is Essex*'s Return Dazzles 1.7m Viewers'. *The Guardian*, 26 September. www.theguardian.com/media/2011/sep/26/the-only-way-is-essex-tv-ratings (accessed 25 May 2016).

Raeside, Julia. 2011. 'A Different Kind of Reality TV'. *The Guardian*, 1 June. www.theguardian.com/tv-and-radio/2011/jun/01/reality-tv-only-way-essex (accessed 25 May 2016).

Raeside, Julia and Paul Flynn. 2011. 'Do TV's "Scripted Reality" Shows Fuel Regional Prejudice?' *The Guardian*, 17 July. www.theguardian.com/commentisfree/2011/jul/17/scripted-reality-tv-shows-debate?INTCMP=ILCNETTXT3487 (accessed 25 May 2016).

Schlotterbeck, Jesse. 2008. 'What Happens When Real People Start Getting Cinematic: *Laguna Beach* and Contemporary T.V. Aesthetics'. *Scope* 12. www.

scope.nottingham. ac.uk/article.php?issue=12&id=1081 (accessed 25 May 2016).
Skeggs, Beverley. 2003. *Class, Self, Culture*. London: Routledge.
Skeggs, Beverley and Helen Wood. 2012. *Reacting to Reality Television: Performance, Audience and Value*. Abingdon: Routledge.
Sontag, Susan. 1967. *Against Interpretation and Other Essays*. London: Eyre & Spottiswoode.
Stelter, Brian. 2010. 'MTV Reinvents itself for the Millennial Generation'. *New York Times*, 24 October. www.nytimes.com/2010/10/25/business/media/25mtv.html?_r=3 (accessed 25 May 2016).
Tasker, Yvonne and Diane Negra. 2007. 'Introduction: Feminist Politics and Postfeminist Culture'. In *Interrogating Postfeminism: Gender and the Politics of Popular Culture*, edited by Yvonne Tasker and Diane Negra, 1–25. Durham, NC: Duke University Press.
Tyler, Imogen. 2008. '"Chav Mum Chav Scum"'. *Feminist Media Studies* 8(1): 17–34.
Tyler, Imogen and Bruce Bennett. 2010. '"Celebrity Chav": Fame, Femininity and Social Class'. *European Journal of Cultural Studies* 13(3): 375–393.
Weber, Brenda R. 2014. 'Trash Talk: Gender as an Analytic on Reality Television'. In *Reality Gendervision: Sexuality and Gender on Transatlantic Reality Television*, edited by Brenda R. Weber, 1–34. Durham, NC: Duke University Press.
Winston, Brian. 2011. *Lies, Damn Lies and Documentaries*. London: BFI.
Wood, Helen and Beverley Skeggs. 2010. 'Reacting to Reality TV: The Affective Economy of an Extended Social/Public Realm'. In *The Politics of Reality Television: Global Perspectives*, edited by Marwan M. Kraidy and Katherine Sender, 93–106. London: Routledge.
York, Peter and Olivia Stewart-Liberty. 2007. *Cooler, Faster, More Expensive: The Return of the Sloane Ranger*. London: Atlantic Books.

CHAPTER 7

Conclusion: A Short-Form Future?

This book has set out British youth television as an ecosystem, consisting of the niche digital channels of BBC Three, ITV2 and E4 (with some overspill into Channel 4). A voice emerges from its programming that is both defiantly British, shaped by national televisual traditions, but also coloured with perhaps a hint of an American accent. From this analysis emerge different visions of British youth, from superheroes under ASBOs, to soldiers in battle, to Essex girls at play. If this television builds an image of British youth, then this is a shifting identity that contains multitudes, just as no one genre can define British youth television. This study has forced a space for British voices in the academic documentation of youth narratives, a realm previously dominated by the American teenager and their high school stories, their college campuses and their first steps into an adult world. It has marked out the territory, pushed British youth programming to the foreground and argued for its importance.

Looking across the last 15 years of British television, this study has explored a significant moment in the digital era – an industry spreading its reach through new channels and online spaces, but on constantly shifting sands of viewing behaviours and technological change. British youth television would not exist without digital television; what were once fragments of provision scattered across the schedules of the five main channels became defined into three distinctly different free-to-air digital youth channels, informed by the identities of their parent companies BBC, ITV and Channel 4. Both youth strands on main channels and niche digital channels illustrate British television's attempt to articulate national specificity whilst also negotiating the role of popular US imports. These channels built their youth voices through reality TV and companion programming, supported by American imports, but all eventually produced a wealth of original British youth programming. This handful of small channels has made a significant cultural impact, producing a raft of BAFTA winners and introducing a new form of reality TV to the British industry. This is television distinct from US teen TV, as it is indelibly shaped by public service broadcasting and its competition with the commercial market, supported by remits to provide programming for young adults and to inform, educate and entertain. The demands and address of youth television – noisy, awkward, risk-taking, coarse, populist, entertainment-led – sit in constant tension with certain cultural expectations of 'legitimate' public service broadcasting. This is particularly evident at the BBC, where BBC Three serves as a synecdoche for the corporation's ongoing struggles, critiques and tensions. The target of censure and mockery from media elder statesman, journalists and politicians alike over its tricky balance of education and entertainment, BBC Three cuts through this noise. It brings both the world and hitherto ignored parts of Britain to light in a breadth of youth-focused documentary not seen elsewhere in the British or US markets. Here youth is not a problem to be solved, but serves as a window on social and cultural issues. At the same time, the channel develops and supports new voices in comedy, offering the time and funding to develop, innovate and take chances with a safety net (if at times cleaving a little too close to the comedy industry's white male image).

An underlying mission of this book has been to demonstrate the breadth of British youth television in its analysis of a range of genres. Like British youth itself, British youth television is too often dismissed – by press and politicians alike – misrepresented and marginalised; the victim of discourses of legitimation and the first to be sacrificed to BBC budget cuts. But this programming offers a view from the ground and from within, not of British youth as a problem to be solved. However, the intention was not to assert the value of British youth television through legitimation, highlighting BAFTA-winning drama and documentary at the expense of the populist and pleasurable (although these are often the same). And it is unfortunate that there is not the space to think further about comedy, to look at reality TV beyond structured reality, particularly the often-dismissed lifestyle formats – *Don't Tell the Bride* (BBC Three/

BBC One, 2007–)), *Snog Marry Avoid* (2008–2013) – that are the highly popular, yet 'bad objects' of British youth television.

So, what has emerged from this book's analysis; what *is* British youth television? It is no one thing, not one single voice; the range of areas covered in this book – drama, comedy, documentary, reality TV – makes connections trickier than a single genre study. This illustrates, perhaps, why hour-long drama has dominated academic discussions of US teen TV. However, connections can be made across genres by identifying themes that emerge. These are concerns that in no way should be painted as exclusive to British youth television, as many are also present in US teen TV and the wider British televisual landscape, but they kept rising to the surface as this book progressed. One is the search for and assertion of that tricky, elusive quality: authenticity. This connects with the negotiation of self that is part of adolescent identity formation and links with British televisual traditions of realism; from this emerges youth television's pleasure in the mundane and the everyday, yet also a starkness of language and emotion. A quest for authenticity is seen in the focus on peer-address and first-person in documentary content, where complex issues are read through the framework of the personal and autobiographical experience. It is present in the blunt language and freedoms of sexuality in British youth drama, and drawn on in discursive attempts to normalise spectacles of nihilistic pleasures. It is there in the pleasurable tensions and sceptical address of structured reality where a play with camp frames programmes – particularly *The Only Way is Essex* (ITV2/ITV Be 2010–) – as possessing an inherent reflexivity, a winking awareness of their own construction.

Authenticity also plays a role in British youth television's complicated relationship with US teen TV. British youth drama was born amidst and positioned itself against the dominance of US imports in youth strands and channels. Here it pushed back against tendencies towards aspirational, melodrama-led storytelling, fearing the taint of sincerity, yet also seeking its own emotional investment. This is a transatlantic intertwining, a relationship made of borrowings, challenges and continuities, demonstrating a push and pull that has catalysed British television's creativity and assertion of voice. I have sketched similarities and delineated difference in this relationship, demonstrating that it is not merely one built on opposition, a binary of the US as fantasy and UK as realism. At times, US teen TV has been painted in quite broad strokes to assert boundaries, but it is clear that melodrama also runs deep in British youth television and that US teen TV can be sharp, sceptical and at times nuanced around class. And yet they *are* nationally distinct forms and, as Chapter 2 has demonstrated, US teen TV that leant heavily on aspirational lifestyles and melodrama-led storytelling had to be framed in particular ways to smooth its assimilation into British youth television schedules. In turn, Chapter 6 highlighted the need to glocalise MTV's model of structured reality to fit the address of British youth television, producing a form read through with class, comedy and camp. Travelling in the opposite direction, MTV's transatlantic translations charted in Chapter 4 saw a messy and ultimately failed attempt at appropriating British youth drama and its attendant discourses of 'authenticity'. MTV tried to build a confrontational and disruptive youth voice for its new scripted programming identity by drawing on British youth drama's difference from US teen TV, yet it struggled to assimilate a form so closely bound to national televisual identity through space, language and storytelling.

Ambivalence also emerged as a recurring theme throughout this book, a way for me to articulate British youth television's audience address and its structure of feeling – its ability to simultaneously offer an emotional investment and a sceptical detachment. This built on Karen Lury's articulation of the oscillation of cynicism and enchantment in an early pocket of British youth television in the late 1980s, where entertainment and music programming targeted Generation X (Lury, 2000). What Lury positioned as an uneasy play is now normalised and embedded in British youth television, although this is stronger in some areas, such as drama, comedy and reality TV, than others. Ambivalence is central to the pleasurable tensions produced by structured reality's combination of emotional realism and construction, yet is minimised in youth documentary. British youth television's ambivalence towards sincerity is why youth documentary is at times in a tricky position, built as it is around truth claims, intimacy and personal connections, centralising investment, investigation and education.

This ambivalence is related to a desire to display knowledge of television's construction, addressing the savvy media-literate viewer – one who is reluctant to take the delegitimated position of invested engaged viewer. We can link this ambivalence to scepticism around sincerity, traceable back to British youth television's desire to present itself as 'not teen TV'. Yet this sits alongside a desire for emotion-based storytelling, the articulation of the melodrama inherent in explorations of the intensity of youth experience, coming of age and the negotiation of identity. This is notably present in the second wave of British youth drama which contributes to the 'celebration of high emotion' that Louisa Ellen Stein identifies in the 'millennial feels culture' that flourishes within the micro-blogging platform Tumblr (2015, 8). British youth drama offers a distinctive blend of televisual traditions of realism with the pleasurable excesses of melodrama and comedy. In turn, the emotion-led storytelling of soap opera has a significant influence on structured reality, where emotional realism emerges from construction and performativity.

This ambivalence is also linked to British youth television's position as a 'bad object' within British culture, in line with the cultural dismissal and fear of youth. For all its critically acclaimed documentary and drama, British youth television's connection with genres deemed feminine or low status – from melodrama to lifestyle and reality TV to the broader edges of sitcom's comic tastes – sets it in a culturally delegitimated position (Newman and Levine 2011). British youth television lacks traditional cultural capital, but takes pleasure in this, in its disruption and 'messiness'. Embodying ambivalences' ability to serve as 'an inevitable condition of intimate attachment and a pleasure in its own right' (Berlant 2008, 181). I have taken Berlant's assertion on board and throughout have pushed the pleasures of British youth television. I wanted to think about the warmth and emotion found across this programming, to separate this analysis from the cultural – and at times academic – worrying *about* youth audiences.

Of course, British youth television is not without its problems and I have not touched enough on the lack of diversity – the at times wearying dominance of the white male point of view in drama and comedy narratives, and the lack of diverse creative voices in British youth television. 2015 and 2016 have showed some promise, but not enough. *Chewing Gum* (2015–) and its creator and star Michaela Cole followed in the footsteps of *Youngers* (2013–14) to finally give black British femininity a comic voice and authorial space on E4; the flagship drama of BBC Three in its new online guise is its first from a female writer with a solo female protagonist, *Thirteen* (2016) But these join BBC Three's schoolgirl sitcom *Some Girls* (2012–) and E4's twentysomething slacker sitcom *Drifters* (2013–) amidst a veritable sea of white males. British youth identity is diverse in race, class, gender and sexuality, and British youth television needs to make more space for developing voices that can articulate this.

Across its life, British youth television has had to make noise, to draw attention and court controversy, to cut through all the other competitions for the attention of youth audiences, to position the identities of its new digital channels and to force a space for its original drama and comedy. British youth television has needed to be canny, sharp and fresh, to push through youth audiences preferences for the budgets, spectacle and glamour of US television. With youth audiences at the forefront of shifting behaviours in media consumption, British youth television needs to push to diversify itself, to develop its interaction with its viewers and to innovate in its storytelling forms. But is there space for national specificity in a media landscape increasingly dominated by US-based multinational media companies or in the permeable geographical boundaries of streaming, downloading and digital video? Is there a future for licence fee-funded public service broadcasting if its audience has grown up expecting its media to be free? The latter is a larger and more complex question than can be answered here, but I want to conclude this book by looking to British youth television's place in this shifting media landscape. With online short-form video now a significant part of the entertainment consumption of its target demographic, I want to claim portions of short-form for British youth television. To do so, I draw on recent Ofcom research to sketch a picture of youth audiences, television and digital media in the mid-2010s, before charting the industrial contexts of two short case studies and suggesting what they signal for the place of British youth television in televisual futures.

THE SWIFTLY SHIFTING MEDIA LANDSCAPE

The mid-2010s have seen significant changes in viewing behaviours, facilitated by a growth in on-demand streaming platforms, the increasing availability of broadband, and technological developments in smartphones and tablets. In 2014 a fifth of UK drama was viewed on catch-up through on-demand platforms (Glennie 2015) and industry regulator Ofcom reported that live television had fallen to 50 per cent of 16–24s' and 61 per cent of 25–34s' audio-visual consumption (2015, 1). The 16–24 year olds were less likely than all adults to use a television set daily (Ofcom 2014, 74), with 16–24s (59 per cent) and 25–34s (50 per cent) choosing a mobile phone as the technology they would miss the most, compared to television's dominance in other age groups (2014, 77). Ofcom noted that catch-up services and internet-originated content have become increasingly important to audiences, especially younger audiences. The latter have grown up in a media environment that includes digital television, broadband internet and easier access to paid-for content online, and Ofcom suggested that their needs and behaviours may be indicative of future patterns of consumption (2015, 19).

In press and industry discourses proclaiming the 'changing face of television', the dominant image of the youth audience is the digital native abandoning linear television. In proliferating press portraits, the (white, middle-class) television-free millennial is cast as a figure to be feared, alongside the under-16s who have grown up with YouTube.[1] Youth audiences are regularly touted as the death of the medium, abandoning the television set for tablets, laptops and the interactivity of social media and YouTube (Steel 2015; Steinberg 2015). *Variety* warned that '"television" may be a word from a lexicon no longer relevant to people who watch YouTube in large quantities' and suggested: 'The rising generation of video viewers ... has already established habits unlikely to be broken' (Steinberg 2015). British industry analysts BARB, noting declining viewing of children's television, questioned: 'What will happen ... if people never get the chance to fall in love with TV in the first place?' (2015, 34). Such doom-laden narratives have increased in frequency in the past few years and are indicative of the tendency of the (particularly US) industry press to respond to shifts in media consumption with apocalyptic rhetoric, but they are nothing new. Concerns around television's need to attract a distracted youth audience abandoning it for competing media was a narrative already at play in the 1980s (Frith 1993). This has also been part of press discourse around British youth channels in the past 15 years, with a 2009 profile of E4's then-channel head Angela Jain questioning: 'Is this a magic formula to attract young people back to television?' (Burrell 2009).

However, the rise of short-form video does indicate a distinct shift in media tastes, with Ofcom reporting that short-form video is growing significantly as an area of consumption for youth audiences, making up eight per cent of all audio-visual viewing by 16–24 year olds (in contrast to two per cent amongst 25–34 year olds) (2015, 20). Central to the BBC Trust's approval of BBC Three's move online was the acknowledgement that the channel's audience was more likely than other age groups to use online video services, although it took pains to highlight the impact of the digital gap on the access of poorer households, an issue widely ignored in the press and industry evangelising (Kanter 2015). But this is not a wholesale shift, as BARB's 2015 viewing report suggested that content on streaming platforms such as YouTube and Netflix was evolving in parallel as part of a diverse media diet, not as a replacement (BARB 2015).[2] With the development of smartphone and tablet technologies, short-form content is more dominant in mobile viewing (2015, 10). To situate British habits within an international generational picture, the *New York*

Times suggested 16–24 year olds' entertainment-focused smartphone use (music, video, games) had doubled between 2014 and 2015 to 40 hours a week (Steel and Marsh 2015). So *is* the future of youth television short-form? Or, more comfortably, is a *strand* of the future of youth television short-form?

This question is explored through two short case studies of internet-native content distributed by both British public service broadcasters and international media companies. I consider public service broadcasters' on-demand platforms and touch on the presence of British youth channels' identity on the BBC's iPlayer and Channel 4's All 4, as well as their spread into the social media spaces of their youth audiences' everyday. I then discuss some of the youth-focused original short-form content produced for these platforms as 'bite-size', spreadable programming. I then highlight the presence of British youth voices on YouTube, using makeup vloggers to explore the place for British youth identity within a multinational media platform. I close by taking a brief look at the face of the new, online-only BBC Three in its launch-week, a sign of British youth television's future.

YOUTH CHANNEL IDENTITY AND SHORT-FORM CONTENT ON DIGITAL PLATFORMS

With youth audiences blending live linear viewing with on-demand platforms across multiple screens, the digital platforms of public service broadcasters take on greater importance as the gateways to British youth television. Here the role of branding echoes the development of digital niche channels discussed in Chapter Two, with the UK's main broadcasters extending their corporate brand identities to their online on-demand services (Johnson 2012, 79). With viewing occurring across multiple screens via apps, BBC iPlayer, ITV Player and All4 could potentially become the central brands of their broadcasters, privileged over the specific channel identities of BBC Three, ITV2 and E4. Similarly, as broadcasters spread their short-form content across Facebook, YouTube and Tumblr in order to reach youth audiences, how will channel identities be retained? Short fragments of the BBC Three ident preface the channel's content on iPlayer at present and closing bumpers identify the provenance of its short-form content streamed via YouTube and Facebook. However, E4 programming becomes just another piece of Channel 4 content when streamed via All

4. Rather than the E4 ident discussed in Chapter 2, programmes are here fronted by an ident that spans all the corporation's content. Similarly, the short-form content targeted at youth audiences is currently positioned under the identity of All 4 rather than the niche youth space E4. 'New BBC Three' can potentially bring short-form more strongly under its channel branding rather than iPlayer's. Both the BBC and Channel 4 are relative newcomers to original short-form content, but are increasing their investment – with £6 million of New BBC Three's budget going to digital content – attempting to catch up with US media companies' dominance of the market (Gannagé-Stewart 2015a).

In their ongoing attempts to reach youth audiences, public service broadcasters are embracing the social media spaces that are the domestic everyday for this screen-agnostic demographic. BBC Three and E4 promote programming via behind-the-scenes content or storytelling teasers on Snapchat and Instagram, or embed trailers and clips on YouTube, Twitter and Facebook.[3] They also spread short-form content beyond the branded spaces of their own streaming platforms. In a spreadable media economy (Jenkins, Ford and Green 2013) based on the share, like and click-through (Gehl 2013), Facebook is in a renewed ascendency as a powerful platform for sharing news and media content (Herrman 2015). In April 2015 the platform claimed it was receiving four billion video views per day, a figure that had quadrupled since September 2014. This statistic was decidedly suspect as it counted a Facebook video 'view' after three seconds of a muted, auto-played video, in contrast with the 30 seconds taken to count as a YouTube view (Green 2015b; Wagner 2015). Yet this claim is indicative of Facebook's power in the spreading and sharing of video content. The increasing centralising of media consumption – be it news items, long-form journalism and commentary or video content – through Facebook (and YouTube) blurs ascription of authorship. Is a news item Facebook's or the BBC's if one doesn't have to click through to the broadcaster's website to read or view it? The diffusion of viewers' attentions across multiple screens and platforms – with versions of the same content potentially viewed 'on BBC Three', 'on iPlayer', 'on YouTube' and 'on Facebook' – sees a broadcaster's brand identity and in turn its nationality potentially subsumed to that of a multi-national media giant. If short-form content produced for 'New BBC Three' is spread to, embedded in and viewed on a platform separate to the iPlayer, does the viewer still recognise this as public service content, funded by the licence fee? Ofcom's 2015 review of public service broadcasting raised questions over how far 'young people distinguish public service content from other content' (2015, 3). Public service broadcasters must balance the need to reach out to youth audiences through short-form content spread to social platforms with the retention of the brand identities that are central to asserting their public service value.

Channel 4 showcased a decisive move into short-form video with the 2014 launch of 'Shorts', short-form content offered via its streaming platform All 4. At less than five minutes, these are pitched as 'bite-sized', distinct from the broadcaster's full-length programming hosted on the platform. At the time of writing in 2015 All 4's Shorts were dominated by lifestyle and interpersonal topics (dating, sex, relationships) and were targeted at a youth audience, with 75 per cent of viewers aged below 35 (Campelli 2015a). Shorts joined the pre-existing comic shorts initiative Comedy Blaps, which had run since 2011 on All 4's predecessor 4OD. Channel 4's short-form commissioner Isaac Densu has emphasised the importance of spreadability and immediacy in the success of All 4 Shorts, suggesting they are sold to their audience with an arresting image and a synopsis that should be crafted like a tweet (ibid.).

All 4 Shorts include both companions to linear programming and original series. *Made in Chelsea*'s (E4, 2011–) associations with luxury lifestyles and interpersonal conflict have resulted in sponsored short-form spin-offs *Chelsea Style Secrets* (2015) and *Misbehaving in Chelsea* (2015), together with the educational content such as the *Normal For Chelsea* (2014) series discussed in Chapter 5. The short-form storytelling opportunities offered by All 4 Shorts could further develop the corporation's currently limited youth-focused documentary content. Currently Shorts are dominated by a profile-based structure that uses interview and direct address. The latter demonstrates the confessional, conversational 'aesthetic intimacy' of vlog-based online video (Creeber 2013, 134), whilst also connecting with youth factual's tendency towards personal perspectives and first-person aesthetics discussed in Chapter 5. For example, *Circus Girls* (2015) offers profiles of acrobatic women who perform with silks and hoops, continuing British youth television's tendency to mix spectacle with the mundane. Interview audio unfolds over images of the women demonstrating their skills in atmospherically lit industrial spaces, which is intercut with their domestic and everyday spaces. The lifestyle-focused Shorts series' continue the aspirational lifestyles and ambivalent address of the reality programming discussed in Chapter 6. *Rich Kids Go Shopping* (2014) explores luxury consumption and *Young & Minted* (2015) profiles young lottery winners, whilst *Internet Famous* (2014–) profiles YouTube creatives who explain how they developed successful careers from their passions.

Internet Famous is produced by the YouTube multi-channel network *Style Haul* and features some of the company's most popular British creatives, highlighting the funding issues tied to short-form. A significant percentage of All 4's Shorts blur the line between sponsored content and advertorials, including the *Made in Chelsea* spin-offs sponsored by makeup company Rimmel and technology giant Samsung and the Foster-sponsored series *Helluva Tour* (2015). This echoes the native advertising model of media companies such as Vice and Buzzfeed (Bell 2014), but also links back to advertising models of 1950s television (Gillan 2014). The budgetary limitations of All 4's Shorts potentially limit both their content and the development of a sustainable short-form production ecology in the UK. A Channel 4 digital executive conceded that Shorts were likely to produce minimal profit and instead positioned them as 'an opportunity for fledgling producers to land projects with the broadcaster, and for more mature indies to enter the growing digital content market' (Campelli 2015b). In turn, an early lack of transparency around budget tariffs in BBC Three's move online was also a concern for the independent television production sector (Gannagé-Stewart 2015a). The further development of and innovation within British short-form video need to be supported by greater investment from broadcasters, both to create a sustainable production culture and to differentiate this programming from the vastness of content offered on YouTube and proliferating platforms.

The BBC's iPlayer has progressively showcased a range of original shorts – both comedy and drama – as part of the BBC's online-first strategy, which seeks to position the platform as the 'front door' to the corporation's programming (Deans and Conlan 2014). The years 2014 and 2015 saw an increased investment in iPlayer's long- and short-form original content, including a range of comedy shorts from high-profile comedians such as Meera Syal, Vic and Bob, and Frankie Boyle; arts series *Private View* (2014–); and an Adam Curtis documentary *Bitter Lake* (2015). As Chapter 2 has highlighted, BBC Three has been at the forefront of the corporation's streaming innovations over the past decade: it was the first BBC channel to stream live online in 2008, iPlayer has hosted pre-air debuts of BBC Three sitcoms since 2014 and the channel's Comedy Feed project has seen iPlayer stream a yearly set of comedy pilots since 2012 (Rushton 2008; Kanter 2014; Rigby 2014).

These pilots were joined by two rounds of iPlayer Original Drama Shorts in 2014 and 2015, all offering a youth focus and showcasing writers and directors who were often new to TV. These displayed a welcome emphasis on racially diverse and female writers, in contrast to the dominance of white males in BBC Three's Comedy Feeds. The project indicates the potential for BBC-supported short-form online drama, a form whose budgetary requirements have seen it relatively underdeveloped in digital media outside of primarily US-based independent web series (Christian No date). The first round of Original Drama Shorts resulted in a commission for 'Muslim rom-com' *My Jihad* (2015) as a four-part series of 15-minute episodes, hosted on iPlayer. The attention-grabbing title referred to an all-consuming spiritual quest, here Nazir's search for a wife through an arranged marriage. The series embraced its timing and budgetary limitations by building its narrative largely around a series of conversations that charted the tentative romance between two devout twentysomething British Muslims. Working with a small cast and limited locations – the original short took place at a table at an arranged-marriage speed dating event and on a night bus – it sketched its narrative in time jumps and vignettes, building an intimate picture of a potential romance between two wary strangers.

With BBC Three's short-form content as yet limited to comedy and documentary, *My Jihad* signals the potential for the channel to develop the British market for short-form drama. Currently two BBC Three short-form drama projects from female and BAME writers[4] are in development for the channel's new online 2016/2017 slate, showing promising signs. Yet some things remain the same, as in October 2015, the BBC made the surprise announcement that it had commissioned a spin-off from *Doctor Who* (BBC One, 1963–1989, 2005–) as the flagship drama for 'New BBC Three' (Sweney 2015b). *Class* was to be set at the school which the Doctor's then-current companion Clara Oswald taught and written by young adult novelist Patrick Hess. The series continued the BBC's use of spin-offs and transmedia content linked to its powerful programme brand to support emerging platforms, following on from the use of *Torchwood* (BBC Three/BBC Two/BBC One, 2006–2011) to draw audiences for BBC Three.[5] Yet this was a strange move for a project that had until then been couched in a discourse of supporting and developing new voices and faces, only for a venerable old institutional product to colonise an already limited drama budget.

CONCLUSION: A SHORT-FORM FUTURE? 237

To return to content discussed at the close of Chapter 6, BBC Three short-form factual content illustrates the challenges inherent in reaching audiences online. The period 2014–2015 saw the channel begin to commission short-form documentaries linked to its factual seasons. These are hosted on both iPlayer and YouTube, and are embedded on the channel's Facebook page and Twitter streams, with the social platforms boosting spreadability. The 2015 disabilities season 'Defying the Label' offered short-form documentaries including *MS and Me* (2015), *My Autistic Twin* (2015) and *Stupid Questions Not to Ask Disabled People* (2015). The latter is constructed as a 'viral' short and is five minutes long, comic, snappy and confrontational in style, built around the direct address of a range of disabled subjects in domestic settings. To date this has received over 350,000 views and 2,150 shares on Facebook[6] together with 44,000 views on YouTube. In contrast, *MS and Me* is a ten-minute documentary filmed in an observational and interactive style, structured as a short-form version of the season's hour-long documentaries that investigated young lives lived with disabilities. This was not hosted on BBC Three's Facebook page and to date has only 1,500 views on YouTube. In commissioning content for different platforms, the 'Defying the Label' season evidenced a multi-pronged approach to reaching BBC Three's target audience and signalled the future for 'New BBC Three'. Yet the different fortunes of the channel's more challenging short-form content illustrates potential difficulties ahead in modifying its core documentary storytelling for short-form – the challenges of reaching its youth audience with the public service content that is the heart of BBC Three.

BRITISH YOUTH VOICE ON YOUTUBE: BEAUTY VLOGGERS

If a key theme within this book's narrative of British youth television is the quest for and claims of authenticity, then YouTube is perhaps the ultimate conclusion to this. The cultural narrative that has solidified around the video-sharing platform is one of a democratic, participatory temple to user-generated content, full of amateur creatives reaching a vast international youth audience. Tales are told of teenagers in their bedrooms striking it rich with a video camera, youth media created seemingly without industrial intervention, content created by for youth by youth. To chart the processes and spread of YouTube is beyond the scope of this conclusion – Jean Burgess and Joshua Green (2009) offer a valuable study of the shape of YouTube circa 2009 – so I focus here on one subsection of YouTube creators[7]: beauty vloggers. There is a significant British presence in this category, including Zoe Suggs (Zoella), Tanya Burr, Sam and Nicola Chapman (Pixiwoo) and Fleur DeForce, vloggers who blend beauty, fashion and lifestyle content.[8] Beauty vloggers are a fragment of a vast range of British YouTube creators working across different YouTube subgenres, and these women indicate the significant presence of British youth voice on the multi-national, Google-owned media platform. I will briefly trace the business model that supports their content as these women are all part of international multi-channel network Style Haul and are managed by British-based Gleam Futures talent agency.

Online video entrepreneur and long-time vlogger Hank Green – an elder statesman of YouTube – has noted that genres of scripted content prevalent on television have struggled to work within the budgets of online video. Low advertising revenue puts 'a dramatic emphasis on getting the most views possible, not just per video but per day' (Green 2015a). Green highlights how YouTube's three most prominent 'genres' of video content are both cheap to produce and hugely popular: video game 'Let's Plays', style tutorials and direct-to-camera monologues or 'Vlogs' (ibid.). The vloggers mentioned above combine the beauty tutorial format – built around instruction in a conversational direct address – and the vlogging monologue. Their accounts blend beauty and fashion tutorials, which include showcasing and discussing products; lifestyle and entertainment vlogs, which include interactive Q&As and personal advice drawn from autobiographical experience, games and conversations with fellow YouTube creators; and on-the-fly self-filmed vlogs charting their day-to-day activities.

As a form, vlogging is built around an aesthetic of intimacy (Creeber 2013, 134), a confessional, conversational address with the figure in medium shot or close-up, often in a bedroom space. Both audiences and celebrity are built through the vlogger's interaction with viewers through their videos, YouTube comments and across social media. These elements construct a 'parasocial' interaction that allows viewers to feel as if they are being directly addressed, in an intimate and personal space (Creeber 2013, 134). Alice Marwick suggests that online communities expect such community-based creatives to be available and accountable to their audience, qualities 'frequently contrasted with the distance maintained between readers/individuals and the creators of traditional media content' (Marwick 2013, 5).

YouTube's participatory potential is driven by the accessible and interactive features of Web 2.0, the ability to upload, share and comment on video content. The resulting democratisation of opportunities for digital authorship (Stein 2015, 22) sees narratives of 'authenticity' built into industrial, peer and promotional discourses surrounding YouTube and threaded through academic work on the platform. As Marwick notes, the centrality of the ideal of authenticity seems contradictory to online fashion and beauty communities that are built around commodities; however, she suggests that 'the authentic is not something that exists apart from commercial culture, but a set of affective relations between individuals, audiences, and commodities' (2013, 2). Burgess and Green's study of YouTube argues that its 'affective economy' is built on interaction, participation and the sharing of 'authentic' emotion (2009). This is reflected in research charting youth audiences' relationship with YouTube creators, here phrasing that connotes authenticity is prevalent – 'real', 'genuine' and 'relatable' (Peterson 2015; Spangler 2015). This is often contrasted with the inaccessibility of film and television programming and celebrity. Such research is often commissioned by digital media companies, so should be treated with a degree of scepticism; however, Heather Mendick, Laura Harvey and Kim Allen's research project on British youth and celebrity (funded by the Economic and Social Research Council (ESRC)) also found a strong engagement with YouTube creators. Their focus groups of British teenagers presented YouTube 'fame' as 'more authentic than other forms of celebrity', positioning YouTubers as self-made, skilled labourers in contrast to other celebrities who were viewed as more 'manufactured' (Harvey 2013).

Ordinariness is a key discourse surrounding YouTube creators, with being 'real' central to their exchange value and success with youth audiences (Smith 2014, 264). Beauty vloggers' production of user-generated education and advice, their direct address and their bedroom or living room locations centralise the everyday, the mundane experience of daily lives made entertainment. The domestic space is perhaps the central space of YouTube (Ford 2014) and is retained as a location even when young British beauty vloggers such as Zoella and Tanya Burr have gained millions of subscribers. Rachel Moseley has highlighted the role of the bedroom in teen narratives as a space where 'identity is expressed in conversation, action and in the *mise en scène*' (2015, 39), and this connects with Sian Lincoln's work on the bedroom as a space of female creativity and expression (2012). As the location for much teenage and twentysomething beauty vloggers, the bedroom's intimate role in identity formation and expression is shared with and extended to the audience, mirroring the probable location of their consumption of these videos. This domestic intimacy is maintained in to their twenties as Zoella and Burr progress from the teenage bedroom in the parental home to their own spacious houses shared with partners. With the most successful of women in this beauty vlogging sphere, this domestic ordinariness becomes intertwined with the glamour associated with the commodities displayed to produce the ordinary extraordinariness of celebrity. Notably, when Zoella and her boyfriend and fellow vlogger Alfie Deyes (PointlessBlog) were immortalised in wax in Madame Tussauds, they were posed on a replica of the double bed which they perch on to film their videos.

Authenticity claims and connotations of transparency are central to the discursive construction of successful YouTube creators as amateurs-turned-entrepreneurs. This authenticity exists in tension with the commercial aspects of YouTube, both as a massive international media company and a target for advertisers seeking access to youth audience (in 2014, the UK became the first market in which half of all advertising spend went to digital media (Sweney 2015a)). Burgess and Green suggest that YouTube can be understood as a '"patron" of collective creativity, controlling at least some of the conditions under which creative content is produced, ordered, and re-presented for the interpretations of audiences' (2009, 54). In a bid to draw more advertising money away from television, YouTube has encouraged the professionalisation of its creators' content, with a refinement in form and style supported by regional production facilities – in LA, New York and London – that offer equipment, studio space and training free to creators with over 5,000 subscribers (J. Ford 2014). Here we can see how YouTube supports and shapes the productions of its more successful freelance creators in order to procure a higher level of advertising revenue from its distribution.

YouTube's advertising money is shared with creators through the YouTube Adsense programme, which installs pre-roll advertising and pays creators an average rate of \$2 per 1,000 views (a \$2 CPM^9) of their channel (Green 2015a). This price point necessitates low-budget content outside of the million-subscriber echelons of creators such as Zoella. As a result, many YouTube creators develop relationships with brands in order to draw a sustainable income. This exists in tension with beauty and lifestyle vloggers, whose relationship with viewers is built around personal recommendations and endorsement of products (Marwick 2013, 6). In 2014, the Advertising Standards Authority ruled that paid-for content in You Tube videos must be clearly marked as advertising in a video's title or description box (Sweney 2014). These brand partnerships are facilitated by multi-channel networks, which are often obscured in discourses of YouTube's democracy and 'authentic' celebrity. The multi-channel network Style Haul focuses on fashion and beauty, with its viewership and stable of YouTube creators primarily the commercially valuable demographic of women between the ages of 14 and 30. It aggregates hundreds and thousands of individual creators' channels, educates creators about video content and their internet presence through tutorials and workshops, promotes creators' videos and provides commercial services. The latter includes taking control of creators' AdSense accounts in order to sell advertising by bundling the audiences of multiple accounts, providing 'affiliate links' to online stores selling the products featured in videos, and building deals with brands. This includes sponsored content (paid advertorial videos on creators' own channels) and 'collaborations' with large global beauty companies on branded content (Crocker 2014), such as Proctor & Gamble's 'Beauty Recommended' channel. This features makeup tutorials from prominent British Style Haul beauty vloggers Fleur DeForce, Ruth Crilly ('A Model Recommends') and Anna Gardner ('Vivianna Does Make-up'), displaying products from Proctor & Gamble-owned beauty companies.

The years 2014 and 2015 saw several large media companies purchase multi-channel networks, including Disney's purchase of Maker Studios for $500 million (Kafka 2015) and European media company RTL purchasing a controlling interest in Style Haul. The latter facilitates production deals with RTL subsidiaries such as television and digital media super-indie FremantleMedia (Bloom 2014). Such deals support the ambitions of multi-channel networks to capitalise on their creators' draw with youth audiences and move into television development. The Style Haul-produced All 4 Shorts series *Internet Famous* showcased the company's own YouTube creators – including Fleur DeForce – and illustrated the slippage between promotional and entertainment content in much of All 4's short-form content. Yet it also demonstrated the potential blending of YouTube creators and British youth television in short-form content and beyond.

These beauty vloggers work with an international multi-channel network and their content is hosted on a platform owned by an international media company. But connections can be made with British youth television and the themes and concerns traced in this book. YouTube has a greater online reach to audiences under 25 than the BBC – 75 per cent compared to the BBC's 50 per cent – and accounts for 15 per cent of time spent online in this age group, compared to three per cent for all the British public service broadcasters (Enders Analysis 2014). Thus, it is a significant media space for British youth audiences, with Ofcom highlighting the ability of YouTube vloggers to educate young audiences on social and personal issues, aspects central to public service broadcasting (Enders Analysis 2014).

In these British beauty vloggers we can trace connections with British youth television's investment in authenticity, with the peer-address and first-person structuring of BBC Three documentary, together with the intimacy displayed in British youth drama. In their centring of young British creatives in a mode that is formed by youth voice and a sharing of personal experience – although one framed by larger corporate structures – we can link these vloggers with *Skins'* investment in young creatives and youth voice as means to assert the authenticity of the programme's depiction of British teen lives. However, these qualities are by no means limited to British creators, just as these qualities are not limited to British youth television. Like British television's intertwining with US teen TV, these women style themselves with the international language of beauty vlogging built by US vloggers. Whilst they foreground British voices in videos often filmed in domestic space and speak of the British everyday, of high street shops Primark, Boots and Superdrug, they describe these high street chemists using the US phrase 'drugstore'. In turn, these videos' soft, white and pastel-toned backgrounds, bright frontal lighting and shallow depth of field position them within an aesthetic that dominates the international beauty vlogging subgenre. Detailed discussion of aesthetics and form is surprisingly absent from the small amount of existing studies of YouTube vlogging, which is primarily produced by sociologists focused on language and identity (Tolson 2010; Smith 2014; Morris and Anderson 2015). Further close-textual-analysis study – which is beyond the space available here – could help to define whether national identity is strongly articulated across the development of beauty vloggers' careers. It must also be noted that while British Afro-Caribbean beauty vloggers and prank-based comics (on both YouTube and social media platform Vine) have carved out their own niche (Adewunmi 2015; Campelli 2015b), a particular kind of Britishness dominates on YouTube. As Burgess and Green explain, 'the dominance of vlogging in shaping what counts as the means to participate actively in the [YouTube] community may privilege some identities over others' (2009, 74), particularly those with the time and finances to devote to the labour of building an audience. This results in the most visible image of British youth being white, middle class and well-spoken, with beauty vloggers demonstrating an upbeat, supportive 'nice girl' persona that facilitates their appeal to brands. As Marwick (2013) and Sarah Banet-Wieser (2012) note, these are youth with the financial support to acquire the camera, lighting, computer and broadband required to produce the level of content that appeals to both audiences and advertisers. This suggests that YouTube does not offer quite the revolutionary democratising challenge to television that is often claimed of it. Here certain models of Britishness, ones that British youth television has had a negotiated relationship with and at times pushed back against, potentially dominate, closing down articulation of a broader British youth identity.

'New BBC Three': A British Youth Platform?

In the post-midnight hours of Tuesday 16 February 2016, the plans documented in Chapter 2 became concrete with BBC Three's closure as a linear television channel and its rebirth as a navigational database of on-demand streaming content (Bennett 2011, 1). After an evening showcasing the channel's biggest hits, from factual entertainment *Don't Tell the Bride* to sitcom *Gavin & Stacey* (2008–2010), 'New BBC Three' moved from the abstract to become BBC Three, the online-only channel. It sported a colour scheme of bright deep pink with green accent and new logo '!!' to signal this new identity. 'Channel' seems an inappropriate descriptor for this BBC Three, as it exists as a branded platform within the BBC's online space. This BBC Three also has its eyes set on its audience's online social spaces, reaching out through Facebook, Twitter, Snapchat, Tumblr, Instagram and YouTube to draw audiences in, reassuring them that it had not closed, but had been reborn.

The new home for BBC Three was the channel's BBC website, which had previously echoed all the broadcaster's channel-specific pages and served only as window to iPlayer, showcasing current programme links with no other content. This was redesigned as 'Best of Three', the channel's online face, collecting programmes and short-form content in a scrollable stream of boxes. These paired key imagery with limited text descriptors, linking through to iPlayer or blog entries. The 'Best of Three' page served as a branded gateway to BBC Three's 'stuff', to use the collective term the page's interactive guide used to refer to programmes, short-form video and other digital content. 'Television' no more.

Fig. 7.1 The top of the new BBC Three homepage showcased the channel's focus on comedy and factual programming, offering shareable links to the BBC iPlayer.

On launch day, the top of the page showcased two new programmes – the second season of documentary *Life and Death Row* (2014–) and the third season of sitcom *Cuckoo* (2012–)– popular and critical successes for BBC Three in its former life (Figure 7.1). This pairing also handily set out the channel's 'make you think' and 'make you laugh' organisational principles. Scrolling down the page, a series of 'topic' buttons offered an updateable menu to the channel's content. These allowed viewers to 'filter' their genre interests (Comedy, Docs, Drama, News, Sport), highlighted 'trending' programmes (promoted and popular shows) and seasons such as 'One Click Away' (devoted to online culture), as well as accessing 'box sets'. The 'box set' archives hosted on iPlayer showcased a limited selection of episodes from BBC Three sitcoms from *Little Britain* (2003–2006) to *Some Girls,* dramas from *The Fades* (2011) to *Our World War* (2014), and factual from *Life and Death Row* to *Don't Tell the Bride*. This allowed BBC Three to highlight the successes of its previous 13 years and retain a connection to its channel brand and linear past.

Short-form content had a presence across this BBC Three: on the main 'Best of Three' scroll, on the Daily Drop page and under the 'The BBC Brief' topic button. The latter collected contextual and 'behind the scenes' short-form video linked to current programmes and seasons, particularly documentary, showcasing the channel's continued commitment to education and the expanded potential of online storytelling. Short-form comedy and documentary rolled out across the first week post-launch, creating a regularly updated stream of fresh BBC Three. The three-part documentary *The Man Who Witnessed 219 Executions* (2016) unfolded in three five-minute episodes across the week, linked to and expanding the worldview of the flagship documentary *Life on Death Row* from the point of view of Texas' execution chamber spokesman. The potential for short-form comedy was signalled by mockumentary series *The Ladventures of Thomas Gray* (2016). All of BBC Three's short-form content was also posted to YouTube – around three videos a day in launch week – signalling this as a central distribution outlet alongside iPlayer (Figure 7.2). This followed the success of the BBC's youth-focused music station Radio 1 in its development of a strong video-based footprint on the platform. This brought the BBC's youth-focused content to the online spaces frequented by its target audiences. Yet the challenge here will be the maintenance of the BBC Three identity as a public service broadcaster within this multi-

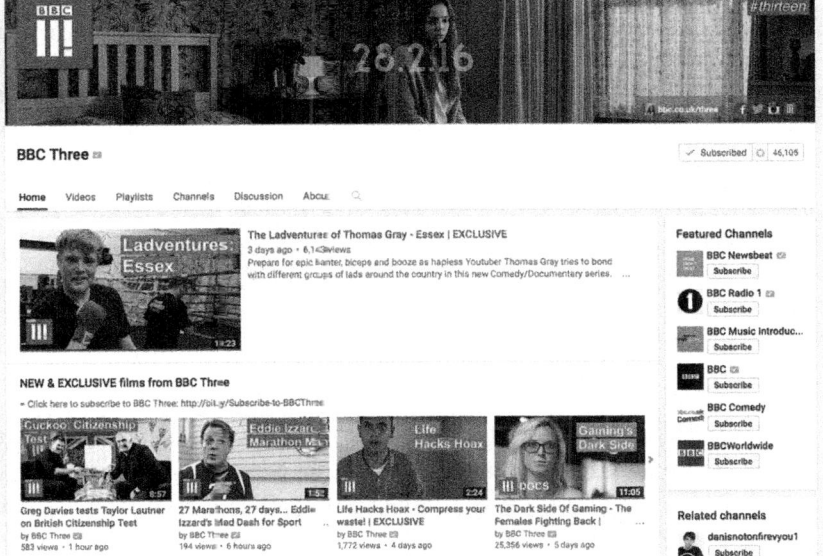

Fig. 7.2 BBC Three's YouTube channel showcased a range of short-form content, and also advertised the arrival of new drama *Thirteen*.

national media giant. Will freely available content drive viewers back to iPlayer? Will it retain the relationship with the BBC needed to create the licence fee-payers of the present and the future?

If 'Best of Three' was relatively static, supplemented daily with new programmes or short-form content, its companion page Daily Drop served as a micro-blogged rolling stream similar to a Tumblr page. This sought to maintain the 'liveness' of the linear channel, as it was updated multiple times a day with original shot-form video, trailers and curated content from across the BBC's news and sports sites. The Daily Drop allowed BBC Three to be reactive to and interact with the minutiae of internet and popular culture through memes, gifs and clips, as well as serving as a home for its original short-form and blog-based content. It also serves as an attempt to retain the cheeky, comic, gossipy BBC Three 'voice' which had previously been constructed through the interstitial elements of continuity announcers, idents and adverts. BBC Three's Twitter account – augmented with Facebook and Tumblr – now becomes even more important in integrating this voice into the everyday social media lives of its potential viewers. Serving as both as the 'live' face of the channel and the guide to its new online identity, BBC Three's Twitter identity now shifts from a live-tweeting companion to a guide to and facilitator for the online spread of its content. It takes the place of the televisual linear flow, linking to the website and iPlayer, sharing new and recent programmes, short-form video and promotional content, keeping the relatively static database of on-demand programmes 'live'.

In 2015, when Damian Kavanagh set out the BBC's plans for this 'New BBC Three', he signalled the potential future of British youth television for the BBC and beyond. He needed to position the corporation's plans within the existing successes of British youth television, whilst reflecting the changing media behaviours of its audience. He argued for the importance of 'New BBC Three' as an on-demand and platform-agnostic channel, one that offered 'immediacy, a more personalised interactive experience, authenticity of voice and a tone that resonates with young people' (Gannagé-Stewart 2015b). As this book has demonstrated, these are qualities – immediacy, authenticity and the personal – that have always been at the centre of British youth television's success. The special conditions that produced this blossoming of youth-focused, nationally specific television in these first two decades of the twenty-first century are changing and it remains to be seen whether this wealth of programming continues and in what form.

Notes

1. It should be noted that, like many think pieces or trend reports on millennials, a great deal of these profiles are based around anecdotal evidence of journalists' white middle-class children and acquaintances.
2. Under-16s do not form part of BARB's measurement and their distinct viewing practices could be obscured within the practices of the whole household.
3. According to Ofcom's report on public service broadcast and online media, over 35 million people in the UK use Facebook, with social media the most popular internet activity amongst 16–24 year olds (Enders Analysis 2014, 20).
4. BAME is the shorthand term the British cultural industries use to refer to people of colour – Black Asian Minority Ethic.
5. Elizabeth Evans (2011) discusses the range of ways in which *Doctor Who* transmedia content has developed the BBC's multi-platform offering.
6. As Facebook measures 'views' at the three-second mark, this is an unreliable marker of actual viewers, whereas the share figure signifies a degree of active involvement.
7. Whilst You Tube 'celebrity' is sometimes used to refer to the most popular YouTubers, I use YouTube's chosen term 'creator' to highlight the creative labour involved in the role.
8. Their popularity is indicated by their subscriber numbers – as of late 2015, Zoella at 9.5 million, Tanya Burr at 3.3 million, Pixiwoo at 1.9 million and Fleur DeForce at 1.3 million.
9. CPM is the term used by YouTube, advertisers and throughout online sales in relation to an advert displayed on a web page. It refers to the cost to an advertiser of a thousand ad impressions (or views).

References

Adewunmi, Bim. 2015. '14 UK YouTubers Who Will Transform Your Fashion and Make-Up Game'. *BuzzFeed*, 21 April. www.buzzfeed.com/bimadewunmi/for-black-girls-who-have-considered-youtube-when-diversity-w (accessed 25 May 2016).

Banet-Weiser, Sarah. 2012. *Authentic(TM): The Politics of Ambivalence in a Brand Culture*. New York: NYU Press.

BARB. 2015. 'The Viewing Report'. www.barb.co.uk/trendspotting/analysis/annual-viewing-report (accessed 25 May 2016).

Bell, Emily. 2014. 'Native Advertising is the New Paywall in Media Economics - But is it Here to Stay?' *The Guardian*, 5 January. www.theguardian.com/

media/media-blog/2014/jan/05/native-advertising-paywall-transparency (accessed 25 May 2016).
Bennett, James. 2011. 'Introduction: Television as Digital Media'. In *Television as Digital Media*, edited by James Bennett and Niki Strange, 1–27. Durham, NC: Duke University Press.
Berlant, Lauren. 2008. *The Female Complaint: The Unfinished Business of Sentimentality in American Culture*. Durham, NC: Duke University Press.
Bloom, David. 2014. 'RTL Buys StyleHaul YouTube Network for $107 Million'. *Deadline*, 3 November. http://deadline.com/2014/11/rtl-buys-stylehaul-youtube-network-for-107-million-1201272475 (accessed 20 May 2016).
Burgess, Jean and Joshua Green. 2009. *YouTube: Online Video and Participatory Culture*. Cambridge: Polity Press.
Burrell, Ian. 2009. 'Is This a Magic Formula to Attract Young People Back to Television?' *The Independent*, 7 December. www.independent.co.uk/news/media/tv-radio/is-this-a-magic-formula-to-attract-young-people-back-to-television-1835376.html (accessed 25 May 2016).
Campelli, Matthew. 2015a. 'Channel 4 Shorts Strategy Revealed'. *Broadcast*, 13 August. www.broadcastnow.co.uk/news/channel-4-shorts-strategy-revealed/5091566.article (accessed 25 May 2016).
———. 2015b. 'ITV2 Orders Diverse Comedies ahead of Mobos'. *Broadcast*, 26 August. www.broadcastnow.co.uk/news/itv2-orders-diverse-comedies-ahead-of-mobos/5092037.article (accessed 25 May 2016).
Christian, Aymar Jean. No date. 'Web TV Networks Challenge Linear Business Models'. *Carsey-Wolf Centre: Media Industries Project*. www.carseywolf.ucsb.edu/mip/article/web-tv-networks-challenge-linear-business-models (accessed 25 May 2016).
Creeber, Glen. 2013. *Small Screen Aesthetics: From Television to the Internet*. London: BFI.
Crocker, Lizzie. 2014. 'Inside StyleHaul, the Largest Fashion Network on YouTube You've Never Heard of'. *The Daily Beast*, 24 August. www.thedailybeast.com/articles/2014/08/24/inside-stylehaul-the-largest-fashion-network-on-youtube-you-ve-never-heard-of.html (accessed 25 May 2016).
Deans, Jason and Tara Conlan. 2014. 'BBC iPlayer: Major Upgrade to Include Exclusive Content from Boyle and Curtis'. *The Guardian*, 11 March. www.theguardian.com/media/2014/mar/11/bbc-iplayer-revamped-adam-curtis (accessed 25 May 2016).
Enders Analysis. 2014. 'How Online Media Services Have Fulfilled the Public Service Objectives: YouTube Star Vloggers'. http://stakeholders.ofcom.org.uk/consultations/psb-review-3/supporting-documents/enders-report (accessed 25 May 2016).
Evans, Elizabeth. 2011. *Transmedia Television: Audiences, New Media, and Daily Life*. Abingdon: Routledge.

Ford, Jonathan. 2014. 'Is YouTube the New Television?' *Financial Times*, 14 November. www.ft.com/cms/s/2/3591cb26-6abf-11e4-a038-00144feabdc0.html#axzz3rwK6Iyyl (accessed 25 May 2016).
Ford, Paul. 2014. 'The American Room'. *The Message*, 30 July. https://medium.com/message/the-american-room-3fce9b2b98c5#.1hwhia1jt (accessed 25 May 2016).
Frith, Simon. 1993. 'Youth/Music/Television'. In *Sound and Vision: The Music Video Reader*, edited by Simon Frith, Andrew Goodwin and Lawrence Grossberg, 57–72. London: Routledge.
Gannagé-Stewart, Hannah. 2015a. 'Indies Voice Concerns about BBC3 Bid'. *Broadcast*, 27 March. www.broadcastnow.co.uk/news/indies-voice-concerns-about-bbc3-bid/5035805.article (accessed 25 May 2016).
———. 2015b. 'Damian Kavanagh, BBC3'. *Broadcast*, 26 August. www.broadcastnow.co.uk/features/damian-kavanagh-bbc3/5091982.article (accessed 25 May 2016).
Gehl, Robert W. 2013 'A History of Like'. *The New Inquiry*, 27 March. http://thenewinquiry.com/essays/a-history-of-like (accessed 25 May 2016).
Gillan, Jennifer. 2014. *Television Brandcasting: The Return of the Content-Promotion Hybrid*. London: Routledge.
Glennie, Alasdair. 2015. 'UK TV Drama Budgets "Slashed by 44% in Six Years"'. *The Guardian*, 2 July. www.theguardian.com/media/2015/jul/02/uk-tv-drama-budgets-slashed-bbc-itv-channel-4 (accessed 25 May 2016).
Green, Hank. 2015a. 'The $1,000 CPM'. *Medium*, 6 April. https://medium.com/@hankgreen/the-1-000-cpm-f92717506a4b#.rywj9peli (accessed 25 May 2016).
———. 2015b. 'Theft, Lies, and Facebook Video'. *Medium*, 3 August. https://medium.com/@hankgreen/theft-lies-and-facebook-video-656b0ffed369#.1xytya3o9 (accessed 25 May 2016).
Harvey, Laura. 2013. 'YouTuber Celebrities – Expertise, Discovery and Legitimate Work'. *CelebYouth.org*, 19 September. www.celebyouth.org/youtuber-celebrities-expertise-discovery-and-legitimate-work (accessed 25 May 2016).
Herrman, John. 2015. 'Mutually Assured Content'. *The Awl*, 30 July. www.theawl.com/2015/07/in-no-charts (accessed 25 May 2016).
Jenkins, Henry, Sam Ford and Joshua Green. 2013. *Spreadable Media: Creating Value and Meaning in a Networked Culture*. New York University Press.
Johnson, Catherine. 2012. *Branding Television*. Abingdon: Routledge.
Kafka, Peter. 2015. 'Disney and Maker Studios' Big Deal May Be Smaller Than They Thought'. *Re/code*, 14 August. http://recode.net/2015/08/14/disney-and-maker-studios-big-deal-may-be-smaller-than-they-thought (accessed 25 May 2016).

Kanter, Jake. 2014. 'BBC Eyes Online-Only Future for BBC3'. *Broadcast*, 5 March. www.broadcastnow.co.uk/bbc-eyes-online-only-future-for-bbc3/5068278.article (accessed 25 May 2016).

———. 2015. 'Unpicking the "Finely Balanced" BBC3 Decision'. *Broadcast*, 30 June. www.broadcastnow.co.uk/news/unpicking-the-finely-balanced-bbc3-decision/5089936.article (accessed 25 May 2016).

Lincoln, Siân. 2012. *Youth Culture and Private Space*. Basingstoke: Palgrave Macmillan.

Lury, Karen. 2001. *British Youth Television: Cynicism and Enchantment*. Oxford University Press.

Marwick, Alice. 2013. '"They're Really Profound Women, They're Entrepreneurs": Conceptions of Authenticity in Fashion Blogging'. *Tiara.org*. www.tiara.org/blog/theyre-really-profound-women-theyre-entrepreneurs-conceptions-of-authenticity-in-fashion-blogging (accessed 25 May 2016).

Morris, Max and Eric Anderson. 2015. '"Charlie is So Cool Like": Authenticity, Popularity and Inclusive Masculinity on YouTube'. *Sociology* 49(6): 1200–1217.

Moseley, Rachel. 2015. 'Teen Drama'. In *The Television Genre Book*, edited by Glen Creeber, 3rd edn, 38–43. London: Palgrave Macmillan.

Newman, Michael Z. and Elana Levine. 2011. *Legitimating Television: Media Convergence and Cultural Status*. London: Routledge.

Ofcom. 2014. 'Adults' Media Use and Attitudes Report 2014'. http://stakeholders.ofcom.org.uk/market-data-research/other/research-publications/adults/adults-media-lit-14 (accessed 25 May 2016).

———. 2015. 'Public Service Broadcasting in the Internet Age'. http://stakeholders.ofcom.org.uk/consultations/psb-review-3 (accessed 25 May 2016).

Peterson, Tim. 2015. 'Why Female YouTube Stars Carry More Clout Than Mainstream Celebs'. *Advertising Age*, 29 October. http://adage.com/article/digital/female-youtube-stars-carry-clout-mainstream-celebs/301119 (accessed 25 May 2016).

Rigby, Sam. 2014. 'BBC Three to Debut 9 Comedy Pilots on iPlayer for Comedy Feeds'. *Digital Spy*, 20 June. www.digitalspy.com/tv/news/a579131/bbc-three-to-debut-9-comedy-pilots-on-iplayer-for-comedy-feeds (accessed 25 May 2016).

Rushton, Katherine. 2008. 'BBC3 Launches Multi-Platform Rebirth'. *Broadcast*, 22 January. www.broadcastnow.co.uk/bbc3-launches-multi-platform-rebirth/525166.article (accessed 25 May 2016).

Smith, Daniel. 2014. 'Charlie is So "English"-Like: Nationality and the Branded Celebrity Person in the Age of YouTube'. *Celebrity Studies* 5(3): 256–274.

Spangler, Todd. 2015. 'Millennials Find YouTube Content More Entertaining, Relatable Than TV: Study'. *Variety*, 3 March. http://variety.com/2015/digital/news/millennials-find-youtube-content-more-entertaining-relatable-than-tv-study-1201445092 (accessed 25 May 2016).

Steel, Emily. 2015. 'TV Transformed: How We Watch'. *New York Times*, 3 October. www.nytimes.com/interactive/2015/10/01/business/media/TV-Transformed-Viewer-Profiles.html (accessed 25 May 2016).

Steel, Emily and Bill Marsh. 2015. 'Millennials and Cutting the Cord'. *New York Times*, 3 October. www.nytimes.com/interactive/2015/10/03/business/media/changing-media-consumption-millenials-cord-cutters.html (accessed 25 May 2016).

Steinberg, Brian. 2015. 'To Lasso Runaway Kids, TV Networks Test New Rope'. *Variety*, 2 September. http://variety.com/2015/tv/news/kids-tv-digital-measurement-streaming-video-1201583885 (accessed 25 May 2016).

Stein, Louisa Ellen. 2015. *Millennial Fandom: Television Audiences in the Transmedia Age*. University of Iowa Press.

Sweney, Mark. 2014. 'Vloggers Must Clearly Tell Fans When They're Getting Paid by Advertisers, ASA Rules'. *The Guardian*, 26 November. www.theguardian.com/media/2014/nov/26/vloggers-must-tell-fans-paid-adverts-asa-rules (accessed 25 May 2016).

———. 2015a. 'UK First Country in World Where Half of All Ad Spend is on Digital Media'. *The Guardian*, 27 March. www.theguardian.com/media/2015/mar/27/half-ad-spend-digital-media (accessed 25 May 2016).

———. 2015b. 'BBC to Make *Doctor Who* Spin-off for Hunger Games-Loving Teens'. *The Guardian*, 2 October. www.theguardian.com/media/2015/oct/02/bbc-to-make-doctor-who-spin-off-for-hunger-games-loving-teens (accessed 25 May 2016).

Tolson, Andrew. 2010. 'A New Authenticity? Communicative Practices on YouTube'. *Critical Discourse Studies* 7(4): 277–289.

Wagner, Kurt. 2015. 'Facebook Users are Notching Four Billion Video Views Every Day'. *Re/code*, 22 April. http://recode.net/2015/04/22/facebook-users-are-notching-four-billion-video-views-every-day (accessed 25 May 2016).

INDEX

A
ABC, 5, 13, 16, 31, 32, 76, 111, 116, 193
ABC Family, 5, 12, 13, 111
Accused, 8, 71
adolescence, 9, 10, 74, 76, 86, 90
advertising, 6, 7, 36, 38, 40, 41, 43, 49, 125, 235, 238, 240, 241
aesthetics, 5, 10, 13, 14, 18, 32, 34, 37, 44, 58n4, 70, 71, 73, 75, 84–6, 90–3, 119, 121, 126, 131, 134–6, 153–5, 159, 163–6, 168, 171–3, 186–96, 199–201, 203, 204, 206, 208, 211–14, 216–220, 234, 238, 242
A Face of War, 159
affect, 7, 9, 10, 19, 43, 84, 85, 87, 89, 92, 93, 100, 121, 164, 186, 199, 206
Afghanistan, 20, 51, 100, 146, 151, 156, 157, 159–64, 169, 170
After School Special, 12
alcohol, 115, 129, 130, 132, 212
All, 4, 46, 57, 174, 178, 232–4
    Shorts, 46, 235, 241
All in the Family, 117, 118, 131

Ally McBeal, 93
amateur, 4, 85, 90, 147, 149, 151, 152, 237
Amazon, 7, 54
ambivalent/ambivalence, 6, 10, 11, 13, 15, 20, 43, 44, 46, 70, 71, 77, 83, 84, 101, 186, 194, 196, 198–200, 208, 213, 215, 218–20, 228, 229, 234
American Pie, 120, 127, 131
Am I Normal, 173–9
An American Werewolf in London, 97
anarchic, 32, 43, 46
Anden-Papadopoulos, Kari, 161, 167, 168
Andrejevic, Mark, 154, 188, 190, 218
Ang, Ien, 13, 86, 87, 201
annotation, 87, 91, 156
anti-social behaviour, 74, 78
anti-social behavioural order (ASBO), 45, 77
app, 174
armed forces, 158
artifice, 186, 190, 194, 201, 213, 215, 216
As If, 34, 75

aspirational, 10, 12, 13, 16, 35, 69, 71, 72, 75, 84, 88, 101, 115, 121, 123, 130–2, 135, 188, 196–9, 204, 208, 211, 212, 214, 219, 227, 228, 234
assimilation/assimilate, 12, 15, 20, 27, 28, 33, 35, 41, 44, 57, 95, 98, 100, 107, 109–11, 113, 114, 118, 120–4, 128, 135, 186, 200, 210, 215, 219, 228
Attack the Block, 81
Aufderheide, Pat, 159, 162, 163
authenticity, 9–11, 18, 56, 69–102, 108–10, 112, 115, 117–28, 133–5, 136n2, 146, 149, 158, 159, 163, 166, 178, 186, 190, 192, 194, 199, 202, 215–17, 219, 227, 228, 237, 239, 240, 242, 246
autobiographical, 119, 147, 148, 151, 152, 166, 227
Awkward., 136
awkwardness, 194, 206, 208, 217–19

B
Bad Education, 54, 76
Baltimore, 133
Band of Brothers, 170
Banet-Weiser, Sarah, 9
Banged Up and Left to Fail?, 148, 152, 179n2
Banks, Miranda J., 13, 70, 83, 88, 126, 135
BARB, 29, 43, 231, 247n2
Barr, Colin, 161, 171
BBC. *See* British Broadcasting Corporation (BBC)
Beaver Falls, 3
bedroom, 91, 132, 155, 200, 237–40
Beesley, Damon, 116
Being Human, 4, 41, 50, 69, 72, 77, 80, 84, 94, 96, 107, 114, 115, 128

Bennett, Zai, 36, 54, 193
Berlant, Lauren, 10, 199
Berridge, Susan, 15, 38, 122
Big Bang Theory, 41
Big Brother, 18, 28, 36, 40, 41, 153, 154, 186, 187, 192–4, 202, 217
Big Brother's Little Brother, 40
Biressi, Anita, 158, 196
Bitter Lake, 235
bling, 188, 197, 208, 211, 213
Blood, Sweat and T-Shirts, 50
Blossom, 32
bodies/body, 3, 9, 12, 29, 30, 70, 81, 82, 85, 87, 88, 91, 93–5, 98–101, 108–10, 119, 123–7, 131, 132, 135, 136, 149, 151–3, 156, 158, 159, 162–8, 170, 172, 174, 176, 205, 213, 229
borders, 3, 5, 130, 136
Born, Georgina, 30, 46
Boyz Unlimited, 75
brand
    branding, 27–58
    channel brand, 19, 27, 28, 30, 36, 38, 40, 46, 56, 72, 77, 233, 244
    identity, 28, 30, 34, 35, 37, 38, 43, 46, 57, 112, 114, 118, 233
Brassed Off, 96
Bread, 213
Bristol, 80, 114, 128, 134
Britain, 3–21, 27, 30, 50, 56, 78, 108, 188, 213, 226
British Broadcasting Corporation (BBC)
    America, 111, 112, 114–16, 118, 120–2, 124, 127
    Choice, 49
    Four, 49, 53, 149
    iPlayer, 4, 7, 232
    One, 6, 8, 16, 18, 28, 31, 34, 36, 47, 49, 50, 52–4, 71, 73, 75, 111, 112, 116, 117, 126, 129,

171, 185, 193, 198, 213, 227, 236
Switch, 52, 53
Three, 4, 7, 17, 19, 28, 30, 31, 36, 39–41, 46–58, 69, 76, 77, 107, 145–52, 157–60, 163, 165, 170, 171, 173, 178, 179, 185, 225, 226, 229, 231–3, 235–7, 242–7
Trust, 46, 51, 52, 54, 55, 145, 147, 231
Two, 6, 31–4, 47, 52, 54, 72, 74, 76, 107, 116, 129, 171, 191, 194, 198, 236
Britishness, 8, 72, 82, 120, 205, 242, 243
British new wave, 96
Brittain, Jamie, 38, 44, 118
broadband, 29, 51, 55, 230, 243
Broadcasting Act 1990, 38
Broken Britain, 78
Brookside, 8, 17, 75
Brunsdon, Charlotte, 80, 82
BSkyB, 6, 39, 40
Buffy the Vampire Slayer, 11, 12, 77–9
Burgess, Jean, 147, 237, 239, 240, 242
Burr, Tanya, 238–40, 247n8
Butterflies, 129
Buzzfeed, 56, 235
Byker Grove, 16

C
Cables from Kabul, 150
Call of Duty, 165
camp, 3, 20, 36, 37, 44, 158, 166, 188, 190, 194–196, 200
Canada, 128, 133
Carruthers, Susan, 157, 159
Casualties of War, 159
Caughie, John, 9, 72

celebrity, 18, 28, 36, 37, 44, 50, 58n3, 148, 149, 151, 152, 185, 186, 191, 192, 197, 198, 210, 212, 213, 216, 218, 220n4, 221n6, 238–41, 247n7
Celebrity Juice, 36, 37
Chalaby, Jean K, 109–12
Channel, 4, 6–8, 14–19, 28–35, 38–43, 46, 58n2, 71, 72, 74, 75, 77, 96, 114, 126, 129, 146, 148, 150, 152–4, 173–8, 180, 186, 191, 193, 225, 226, 232–5
Channel 5, 6, 18, 28, 41, 153, 186, 221n6
Chatsworth, 198
chav, 78, 79, 102n4, 210, 211
Chelsea, 20, 41, 177, 185, 187–90, 192, 193, 196–200, 202–6, 208, 209, 213–15, 219, 220, 234, 235
Chelsea Style Secrets, 234
Cherry Healey: Old Before My Time Reggie Yates: Extreme South Africa, 149
Chewing Gum, 8, 78, 229
children's television, 15, 17, 75, 76, 80, 231
Childs, Amy, 188, 212, 216, 221n6
Christensen, Christian, 161, 168
Circus Girls, 234
citizenship, 7, 21n2, 29, 39, 177, 187
Clocking Off, 73
Cohen, Danny, 47, 50, 52, 54
Cole, Cheryl, 210
college, 76, 127, 148, 225
Comedy Blaps, 234
Comedy Feeds, 52, 236
comic, 17, 36, 38, 43, 44, 69, 70, 73, 76, 83–7, 89, 90, 98, 101, 110, 123–7, 135, 177, 178, 186, 195, 196, 204, 208, 212, 215–20, 229, 234, 237, 239, 242, 246
coming of age, 5, 76, 127, 128, 160, 228

commercial broadcaster, 6, 46, 49
Communication Act 2003, 6
Company Pictures, 115, 133
Conrad, Lauren, 191, 193, 195, 199, 202, 204, 214
conservative, 7, 12, 15, 78, 83, 99, 114, 116, 121, 122, 145, 197
construction, 6, 9, 10, 13, 15, 18, 20, 33, 44, 72, 77, 117, 119, 149, 151, 156, 158, 160, 163, 165, 178, 186, 187, 189–91, 193–5, 199–201, 208, 210, 211, 218, 219, 227–9, 240
consumer, 5, 13, 28, 29, 37, 108, 111, 211
continuity announcer, 37, 41, 196, 246
convergence, 111
Coronation Street, 8, 17, 193
council estate, 8, 81, 128, 129, 136n3, 150
Coupling, 107, 116, 119, 134, 155
Creative Future, 50, 51
Creeber, Glen, 71, 73, 88, 121, 123, 234, 238
crime, 8, 71, 78, 133, 145, 147, 150, 151, 179n2
cringe comedy, 115, 127, 199
crowdsource, 174, 176
Cuckoo, 244
cult, 44, 77, 83, 112, 114, 116, 120
cultural capital, 37, 47, 108, 112, 198, 210, 218, 229
cultural discount, 108

D

Dallas, 86
Dance Energy, 32
Daniels, Susanne, 12
Dapper Laughs, 37
Davis, Glyn, 4, 11, 13, 14
Dawson's Creek, 10–12, 14, 34, 76, 88, 114
28 Days Later, 94, 95
Dead Set, 41
DEF II, 32, 33, 191
DeForce, Fleur, 238, 241, 247n8
Degrassi Junior High, 32
Delivering Quality First, 52, 55
demographic, 5–8, 14, 16, 18, 19, 27, 29, 31–3, 35, 36, 38, 39, 41, 46, 47, 49–51, 53, 55, 57, 58n4, 76, 85, 112, 113, 115, 145, 163, 176, 185, 188, 210, 218, 230, 233, 241
desire, 11, 29, 30, 40, 57, 73, 83, 86–9, 93, 97, 118, 122, 126, 127, 134, 159, 164, 178, 216, 219, 228
Desperate Scousewives, 187
Devil's Whore, The, 8
Dickinson, Kay, 4, 11–14
didacticism, 10, 17
digital camera, 157, 164, 203
Digital Economy Act 2010, 39
digital-rig, 153, 156
digital switchover, 6
digital television, 3, 4, 6, 27, 35, 49, 57, 178, 225, 230
digital youth channels, 28, 35, 37, 39, 46, 72, 74, 185, 225
Dillistone, Sarah, 188, 193, 201, 203, 204, 206
direct address, 12, 20, 147, 167, 168, 170, 234, 237–9
Disney, 212, 241
Doctor Who, 28, 112, 114, 236, 247n5
documentary, 9, 20, 30, 32, 33, 39, 46, 47, 49, 136n2, 145–9, 151–60, 164–7, 169–71, 173, 176, 178, 179n2, 188, 191, 194, 204, 216, 226–9, 234–7, 242, 244, 245

docusoap, 36, 185–7, 189–91, 193, 195, 203, 210, 212, 213, 216, 220n4, 221n6
domestic, 70, 72, 80, 81, 94, 97, 99–101, 111, 128, 153, 155, 166, 207, 216, 233, 234, 237, 239, 240, 242
Don't Blame Facebook, 148
Don't Call Me Crazy, 148, 157, 179n1
Don't Take My Baby, 145, 179n3
Don't Tell the Bride, 49, 53, 185, 226, 243, 244
Dooley, Shaun, 148–50, 158, 161, 165, 179n5
Dovey, Jon, 147, 149, 151, 152, 158, 163, 164, 176
download, 4, 7, 29
Downtown Abbey, 197
dramality, 188, 193
dramatic look, 190–2, 200, 204, 219
drama-toned, 190, 194, 200
Drifters, 229
drugs, 15, 17, 69, 78, 115, 119, 122, 125, 129, 148, 179n5
Dunlop, Caggie, 214
DVR, 4

E

E4, 3, 4, 7, 8, 16, 18–20, 28, 30, 31, 33, 35, 38–46, 48–50, 57, 69, 70, 72, 73, 75, 77, 78, 83, 85, 86, 107, 111, 113, 115–17, 124–6, 136, 147, 148, 156, 171, 177, 185, 187, 194, 196, 198, 204, 225, 229, 231–4
E20, 17
East End, 196, 197, 213
EastEnders, 8, 17, 28, 49, 71, 88, 89, 193

eco-system, 3, 20
Educating Essex, 153, 178
education, 7, 14, 21n2, 29, 31, 39, 54, 74, 76, 148, 174, 175, 177, 180n7, 198, 210, 226, 239, 245
elite, 112, 196, 198, 212, 214, 219
Ellis, John, 37, 38, 43, 166
Elsley, Brian, 118
Embarrassing Bodies, 174, 176
embed, 85, 179
embodied, 149, 158, 159, 162–6, 170, 172
emotion, 13, 19, 20, 70, 74, 83–6, 89, 92–4, 99–101, 146, 152, 155, 157, 172, 186, 187, 199–201, 203, 204, 217, 220, 227–9, 239
emotional labour, 201, 205
emotional realism, 13, 71, 88, 112, 175, 186, 192, 194, 195, 199–201, 216, 218, 220, 228, 229
ER, 40, 150, 151
Essex,, 4, 16, 20, 36, 37, 153, 178, 185, 187, 188, 193, 196, 197, 203, 205, 208–13, 215–17, 220n2, 220n3, 225, 227
Essex Girl, 187, 196, 197, 210, 211, 216
ethnic minorities, 8
Evans, Elizabeth, 54, 247n5
everyday, 15, 17, 36, 37, 43, 69, 71, 75, 77, 80, 82, 84, 89, 92, 95, 99, 101, 114, 115, 124, 130, 146–8, 152–4, 157, 187, 190, 193, 194, 201, 202, 204, 208, 210–12, 218–20, 227, 233, 234, 242, 249
excess, 69, 73, 83, 84, 87, 93, 95, 123, 127, 166, 209, 213, 215, 220
exposition, 190, 193, 206, 207

F

Facebook, 7, 37, 51, 56, 148, 153, 179, 232, 233, 237, 243, 246, 247n3, 247n7
factual, 4, 17, 19, 20, 39, 40, 46, 47, 49–51, 53, 54, 56, 109, 110, 145–79, 234, 237, 243, 244
factual entertainment, 47, 49, 53, 175, 243
Fades, The, 50, 77, 79, 92, 94, 244
fake breasts, 211, 212, 217
fake tan, 36, 185–221
Fallout, 8, 71, 73
Family Guy, 49
fandom, 12, 84
fantasy, 3, 12, 70, 73, 75, 81, 87, 89, 91, 95, 101, 121, 123, 191, 192, 215, 227
Fawlty Tower, 116
Feasey, Rebecca, 79
Felstead, Binky, 199, 200, 202, 203, 207, 214, 215, 219
femininity, normative, 86, 88, 126
FilmFour, 38
First-person, 20, 146, 152, 158, 163–5, 169, 173, 176, 227, 234, 242
Fish Tank, 119
fixed-rig, 153, 156
Florida, 131
flow, 4, 28, 32, 33, 35, 44, 56, 107–10, 246
format, trade, 110–13
Fosters, The, 13
Fox, 10, 12, 34, 35, 41, 49, 72, 77, 91, 134, 191
Freaks and Geeks, 120
free-to-air, 6, 27, 30, 40, 124, 225
Freeview, 6, 27, 40, 41
Fresh Meat, 77, 177
Fresh Prince of Bel Air, The, 32
Friday Night Dinner, 129
Friday Night Lights, 12
Friends, 40, 41
Frith, Simon, 5, 27, 32, 38, 79, 115, 127

G

Game of Thrones, 124
Gateley, Liz, 125
Gavin & Stacey, 48, 50, 76, 243
Generation X, 14, 228
Geordie Shore, 189, 212
Geraghty, Christine, 88
Gilmore Girls, 11, 12, 82
Girlhood, 119
Girls on the Frontline, 157
girly, 37, 212
glamour, 10, 36, 37, 72, 115, 124, 185, 187, 198, 200, 204, 208, 210, 212–15, 217–19, 220n2, 220n5, 230, 240
Glee, 12, 41
globalisation, 110–13
glocalisation/glocalising, 20, 37, 110, 111, 134, 135, 185–7, 189–200, 204, 212, 215, 219, 228
glossy, 10, 35, 71, 72, 188, 190, 194, 198–200, 204, 208, 214, 219, 220
Glue, 69, 77
Going Out, 14, 17, 74, 75
Good Life, The, 129
Good Wife, The, 134
Gorton, Kristyn, 85, 92, 93
gossip, 18, 36, 58n2, 78, 88, 95, 121, 156, 186, 189, 192, 198, 200–3, 206–8, 213, 218
Gossip Girl, 12, 76, 88, 121
government, 7, 95, 98, 168
Grajeda, Tony, 159, 161–3
Grandma's House, 129
Grange Hill, 16, 17, 31, 74, 75

Great War: The People's Story, The, 170
Green, Hank, 134, 238
Green, Joshua, 237
Grindstaff, Laura, 193, 201, 209
gritty, 118, 133, 192
Grownups, 76
grunt
  grunts eye view, 159
  noble grunt, 159
Gunner Palace, 159

H

Hall, Tony, 53, 122, 124, 126, 159, 192, 193
Hangover, The, 127
Happy Days, 32
Harry Brown, 78
HBO, 30, 40, 124, 170
Heartbreak High, 32, 76
Heat magazine, 33, 36
Helmand, 157, 160, 161
helmet-cam, 164–6, 168, 170, 172
heritage, 188, 197, 204–8
Hex, 77
Higson, Andrew, 96
Hills, The, 20, 37, 71, 97, 115, 117, 185, 186, 188, 190–2, 199, 204, 205, 214, 215, 219
Him & Her, 76
Hogg, Christopher, 108
Hollyoaks, 17, 32, 34, 75, 178, 193, 201
Hollywood, 12, 120, 191, 194, 214
Holmes, Su, 18, 58n3, 186, 200, 210, 218
Home and Away, 16, 75
hoodie, 45, 78
House of Cards, 54, 111
housing estate, 73, 129, 136
Hulu, 111

I

icon, 42, 196
idents, 30, 32, 33, 37, 40–4, 51, 232, 233, 246
IED, 166, 168
Ill Manors, 78
I'm a Celebrity Get Me Out of Here, 28
immigration, 73, 98, 99
import, 16, 32, 35, 37, 39, 41, 49, 72, 79, 109, 111, 113, 118, 119, 121–3, 127
Inbetweeners, The, 4, 19, 37, 41, 70, 72, 73, 76–8, 83, 102n2, 107, 109–17, 120, 123, 126–31, 135, 136n1, 194
Inbetweeners US, The, 107, 113, 116, 117, 127, 128, 131, 135
Independent Television Council (ITC), 40, 49
industrial, 4, 5, 9–11, 15, 19, 20, 27, 28, 30, 32, 43, 58n3, 72, 107–9, 111, 113, 114, 117, 123, 133, 212, 230, 234, 237, 239
inner-city, 8
Inside Claridges, 198
Inside North Korea, 150
Instagram, 233, 243
institution, 18, 47, 149
interaction/ interactive, 29, 33, 35, 51, 52, 55, 56, 145–80, 190, 191, 193, 201, 205, 207, 230, 231, 237–9, 243, 246
  in documentary, 164
  online, 173
interiority, 85, 86, 91–3, 100, 101, 152, 156
Internet Famous, 235, 241
intervention, 94, 152, 153, 164, 171, 175, 186, 191, 193, 194, 237
interview, 34, 38, 56, 122, 150, 156, 158, 160, 162, 163, 165–70, 173, 190, 203, 234

In the Flesh, 19, 48, 50, 69, 70, 77, 80, 84, 94–101
intimacy, 13, 19, 20, 69–102, 147, 150, 153–5, 157, 159, 163, 164, 166, 173, 186, 199, 208, 220, 228, 234, 238, 240, 242
iPlayer Original Drama Shorts, 236
ironic, 35, 43, 46, 206, 218
issue-led storytelling, 17
ITV, 6, 8, 14, 16, 18, 28, 31, 34, 35, 38, 57, 58n6, 71, 74, 75, 80, 112, 126, 148, 170, 193, 197, 198, 225, 227, 232
ITV2, 4, 19, 28, 30, 31, 36, 37, 40, 49, 51, 77, 147, 185, 187, 193, 200, 210, 212, 213, 225, 227, 232
ITVBe, 37

J

Jack: A Soldier's Story, 50, 157
Jain, Angela, 41, 231
Janollari, David, 122
Jersey Shore, 114, 117, 189, 192, 197, 212
Johnson, Catherine, 28, 30, 38, 41, 81, 197
Jones, Owen, 211
Jordan and Peter, 36, 210
Jowell, Tessa, 49
Joy of Teen Sex, The, 175, 180

K

Karlyn, Kathleen Rowe, 87
Kavanagh, Damian, 48, 53–6, 147, 178, 246
Kavka, Misha, 186, 189, 194
Keep Calm and Avoid the Undead, 97
Kids, 119–21, 129, 148, 179n5, 234
Kids Behind Bars, 148

Kidulthood, 78
Klein, Amanda Ann, 191, 197, 204, 212
Knightsbridge, 187, 197, 204

L

Ladventures of Thomas Gray, The, 245
Laguna Beach, 20, 185, 186, 188, 190–2
landscape, 4, 5, 8, 15, 20, 27, 29, 30, 40, 43, 51, 57, 70, 74, 78, 80, 81, 94, 96–7, 101, 102, 123, 133, 156, 207, 208, 218, 227, 230–2
language, 9, 17, 19, 70, 77, 82, 83, 92, 101, 107, 108, 112, 114, 117, 119, 124, 136, 167, 168, 210, 227, 228, 242
Law & Order: UK, 71
legitimation, 13, 47, 49, 50, 190, 204, 226
Letort, Delphine, 161
Levine, Elana, 204
licence-fee, 6, 46, 47
Life After Beth, 95
Life After War: Haunted By Helmand, 157
Life and Death Row, 48, 179n2, 244
Likely Lads, The, 126
Lime Pictures, 189, 193
liminal, 31, 74, 75, 127
Lincoln, Sian, 239
linear, 4, 7, 27, 29, 46, 48, 52, 54, 56, 145, 156, 231, 232, 234, 243, 244, 246
Little Britain, 50, 244
Little, Daran, 193
live, 7, 29, 40, 51, 70, 88, 150, 153, 174, 189, 191, 193, 204, 215, 230, 232, 235, 246
Liver Birds, The, 213

livestreaming, 52
Living Soap, The, 191, 193
local, 75, 80, 82, 83, 95, 110, 111, 115, 116, 129, 148, 150
location, 6, 128, 129, 132, 134, 158, 164, 172, 204, 205, 209, 239
locational specificity, 129, 134
Lock Up, The, 157
London, 43, 78–80, 82, 97, 129, 131, 150, 187, 188, 197, 204–8, 213, 240
Lotz, Amanda, 4, 191, 197, 204, 212
Lunch Monkeys, 76
Lury, Karen, 4, 31, 43, 217, 228
luxury, 204, 205, 208, 234

M

Made in Chelsea, 20, 41, 177, 185, 187–90, 192, 193, 196–200, 202–6, 208, 209, 213–15, 219, 235
Mad Men, 134
Maggie, 31, 74
Maker Studios, 55, 241
Man Who Witnessed 219 Executions, The, 245
Marwick, Alice, 238–40, 243
masculinity, 83, 87, 110, 123, 126–8, 162, 167, 169, 197
Masters of Sex, 124
Me & My New Brain, 145, 152
melodrama, 9–11, 13, 34, 44, 70, 73, 74, 76, 77, 80, 83–5, 87–95, 99–102, 112, 114, 121, 135, 186, 187, 190, 193–5, 201, 202, 204, 227–9
Men Behaving Badly, 126
mental health, 39, 84, 93, 98, 157, 179n1
middle class, 12, 18, 45, 53, 71, 75, 77, 78, 101, 127–9, 131, 132, 166, 197, 208–11, 213, 215, 220n5, 231, 243, 247n1
Middle-East, 146, 157
Mighty Boosh, 48, 50
millennial, 5, 12, 84, 117, 154, 229, 231
Miller, Jeffrey, 108, 117
Ministry of Defence, 158, 161
Misbehaving in Chelsea, 234
Misfits, 16, 19, 41, 50, 69, 70, 72, 73, 77–85, 94, 96, 126, 128, 198, 201
mobile phone, 230
Monty Python's Flying Circus, 116
moral, 17, 73, 122, 123, 162, 163, 172, 177, 178
Moran, Caitlin, 211
Morris, Ian, 116, 129, 164, 242
Moseley, Rachel, 6, 8, 9, 12–15, 17, 18, 31, 70, 74, 75, 78, 239
MS and Me, 179, 237
MTV, 5, 11, 14, 19, 30, 32, 70, 78, 107, 109–11, 113, 115–18, 120–2, 124, 125, 131, 133–5, 136n1, 191, 192, 228
multi-channel networks, 55, 241
multi-platform, 27, 29, 51, 52, 55, 146, 150, 173, 174, 176, 177, 247n5
mundane, 3, 43, 69, 70, 75, 77, 80, 84, 89, 92, 94, 95, 101, 114, 128–30, 202, 208, 210, 227, 234, 239
Murdered By My Boyfriend, 48, 54, 171, 179n3
Murphy, Stuart, 49, 90
music television, 15
My Autistic Twin and Me, 179
My Boyfriend the War Hero, 157
My Jihad, 236
My Mad Fat Diary, 4, 19, 39, 41, 69, 70, 77, 83–94, 98, 100, 156

262 INDEX

My Murder, 171
My So-Called Life, 12, 16, 90

N

narration, 70, 87, 89, 90, 152, 161, 168, 190
national distinction, 4, 72, 77, 126–8, 133, 193
national identity, 19, 43, 69, 77, 97–9, 109, 242
natural, 10, 96, 112, 201, 214, 215, 217, 218
NBC, 40, 44, 72, 117, 119, 120
Neighbours, 16, 75
Netflix, 4, 7, 54, 231
new-build estate, 129
Newlyweds: Nick and Jessica, 191
Newman, Michael, 11, 229
New York, 117, 122, 125, 131, 134, 187, 190, 206, 208, 231, 240
NHS, 98, 174, 176
niche, 6, 8, 27, 31, 34, 37, 47, 48, 53, 111–13, 115, 200, 225, 226, 232, 233, 242
9/11, 94, 95, 159, 160
90210, 72
nudity, 114–16, 123–5, 127
Nunn, Heather, 158, 196, 239

O

observational, 145–9, 153, 154, 157, 159, 164, 179n1, 186, 191, 193, 198, 237
O.C., The, 10, 34, 35, 72, 88, 191
4OD, 234
Ofcom, 6, 7, 20n1, 21n2, 29, 58n2, 230, 231, 242
Office, The, 116, 194

on-demand, 7, 27, 30, 46, 54, 56, 57, 174, 230, 232, 243, 246
One Born Every Minute, 153
One Life to Live, 193
One Tree Hill, 10, 34, 44, 72, 114
Only Way Is Essex, The (TOWIE), 4, 16, 20, 36, 37, 185, 227
On the Edge and Online, 148
oral testimony, 171
ordinariness, 80, 129, 216, 239, 240
ordinary, 4, 10, 18, 43, 72, 80, 101, 192, 210, 216, 217, 240
Osbournes, The, 191
Osgerby, Bill, 6, 7, 14, 18
Our War, 4, 20, 48, 146, 148, 156–73
Our World War, 146, 170–3, 244
Outlander, 124
Overman, Howard, 72, 73, 78, 79

P

Pacific, The, 170
paratext, 8, 9, 35, 97, 160, 167
Parents Television Council (PTC), 121, 122, 125
participation, 29, 51, 239
party, 78, 98, 130–2, 202, 203, 207, 212, 214, 218
Party of Five, 12
pay-TV, 39, 40, 124
PBS, 112
Peep Show, 126
peer-led, 146
peer presenter, 149–57, 179n2
peer-to-peer sharing, 5, 113
Peirse, Alison, 80
performativity, 9, 19, 20, 84, 186, 187, 189, 194, 200, 201, 215–20, 229
personal exploration, 148, 152, 160
personalised, 16, 56, 170, 173, 178, 246

INDEX 263

Peters, Andi, 34
Peterson, Latoya, 118, 133, 239
Pixiwoo, 238, 247n8
place, 10, 16, 19, 20, 27, 30, 35, 38, 45, 47, 49, 55, 57, 69–102, 109, 110, 121, 126, 128, 132, 134–6, 145, 149, 164, 169, 186, 189, 190, 199, 205–9, 215, 230–2, 236, 246
platforms, 4–7, 17, 27, 29, 30, 40, 46, 51–3, 55–7, 84, 98, 111, 112, 146, 147, 149, 150, 156, 172–8, 229–46
platoon, 158–60, 162, 163, 165, 167
playful, 35, 84, 88, 195, 196, 213, 216–19
pleasure, 10–13, 20, 34–7, 46, 47, 69, 70, 73, 80, 93, 101, 123, 126, 135, 186, 190, 196, 198, 199, 202, 206, 209, 210, 219, 220, 227, 229
Plebs, 37
point of view, 16, 19, 75, 83, 89–91, 146, 158, 160, 162, 163, 166, 170, 173, 195, 229, 245
Pop Idol, 18, 28, 36
Popworld, 34
Porky's, 120, 127
pornography, 122, 125
portal, 7, 97
post-apocalyptic, 94, 96
Postfeminist, 211–212
post-network television, 4
Posh People: Inside Tatler, 198
Pratt, Stephanie, 206, 207, 214
presenter, 18, 32–5, 44, 148–57, 178, 179n2, 195, 220n2
Press Gang, 16, 19
prestige, 8, 16, 40, 49, 54, 112, 120, 124, 134, 148, 198
Pretty Little Liars, 12

Price, Katie, 36, 185, 210, 212, 213, 220n4
prime-time, 8, 13, 17, 32, 33, 86, 111, 113, 148, 150, 175, 190, 202
Prince Harry: Frontline Afghanistan, 157
Prisoner, The, 112, 148
Private View, 235
Probyn, Elspeth, 93
profanity/obscenity, 82
publicly-owned, 6, 38
public service broadcasting, 5–8, 10, 11, 14, 15, 19, 21n2, 27–30, 35, 39, 47, 48, 57, 58n2, 58n6, 146, 226, 230, 242
public service remit, 6, 7, 17, 29, 36, 38, 58n2

Q
quality television, 13, 71

R
Ramsay, Debra, 160, 165, 173
Rapido, 32
Ratcatcher, 97
Ready Steady GO, 18, 31
Real Housewives, 189
realism, social realism, 9, 69, 71–3, 75, 81, 88, 94, 101, 123
realist, 9, 10, 41, 72, 73, 80, 81, 88, 89, 96, 100, 118–20, 123, 124, 132, 133
reality TV, 4, 9, 11, 12, 15, 18–20, 34, 36, 37, 111, 113, 134, 156, 185–95, 197–201, 203, 204, 210, 216–20, 226–9
Real World, The, 114, 154, 189, 191, 193
Red Bee Media, 51

Redmond, Phil, 17, 74, 75
Red Riding, 96
Reggie Yates: Extreme Russia, 151
Reggie Yates: Extreme South Africa, 149, 150
regionality, 80, 189, 205, 215, 219
remake, 5, 107, 108
reportage, 32, 150
representation, 3, 5, 8, 9, 11, 15, 17–20, 45, 57, 69–3, 78, 107, 117, 118, 123, 134, 135, 159, 162, 165, 180, 194, 197–9, 210–13, 215, 219, 220
Returned, The, 95
Rich Kids Go Shopping, 234
Rixon, Paul, 34, 35, 40
romance, 15, 17, 87, 89, 202, 236
Ross, Sharon Marie, 11, 71
Roswell, 12, 126
Rough Guide to…, 32
Run, 8, 73
Ryan, Mo, 114, 122, 133, 172

S

Sanford and Son, 117, 131
Sanson, Kevin, 107, 109, 119
satellite, 6, 14, 27, 30, 33, 37–40, 77, 210
Saving Private Ryan, 172
savvy audience, 186, 194, 201, 218
scaffolding, 41, 201, 204, 209
sceptical/scepticism, 10, 20, 33, 98, 126, 187, 227, 228, 239
school, 4, 16, 44, 54, 76, 77, 79, 114, 115, 119, 127, 129, 131, 136, 153, 155, 159, 174, 178, 191, 214, 225, 236
Sconce, Jeffrey, 94, 95, 98, 100
Secret Life of Students, The, 152–4
self-filmed footage, 146, 147, 156–8, 161, 171

self-service television, 201
set-top boxes, 6
sex, 3, 15, 53, 87, 114, 115, 117, 119, 122, 124–8, 136, 156, 174–7, 180, 212, 213, 234
Sex Education Show, The, 174–5, 180n7
Sexperience, 173–8
sexuality, 15, 69, 86, 99, 117, 125–7, 131, 209, 217, 227, 229
Shameless, 71, 73, 114
shareable, 37, 179
Shaun of the Dead, 72, 80, 81, 94
Shipwrecked, 191
short form, 20, 46, 56, 58n9, 177–9, 225–47
sitcom, 4, 32, 33, 37, 41, 44, 54, 69, 70, 76, 77, 107, 115–19, 126, 128, 191, 229, 243, 244
Six Feet Under, 40
Skeggs, Bev, 186, 187, 197, 199, 211–13, 215
Skins, 9, 11, 12, 15, 16, 19, 41, 50, 69, 70, 72–7, 79, 80, 84–7, 102n2, 107–26, 128–35, 175, 198, 201, 242
Skins US, 79, 107, 110–23, 125, 128, 131–5
Sky Living, 37, 210
Sky One, 33, 39, 51
Sloane, 197
Smallville, 34, 77–9, 126
Smith, Greg M., 91
Snapchat, 17, 153, 233, 243
Snog Marry Avoid, 49, 185, 227
soap opera, 15–17, 19, 20, 35, 37, 58n5, 71, 75, 76, 86, 88, 178, 186, 187, 192, 193, 199–202, 204, 229
social exclusion, 73
socialite, 197

social media, 17, 30, 37, 51, 84, 146, 147, 153–7, 161, 164, 167, 176, 178, 202, 231–3, 238, 242, 246, 247n3
social surrealism, 14, 17, 73, 88, 121, 123, 135
soldiers (squaddies), 20, 157–71
Some Girls, 4, 76, 77, 229, 244
Sontag, Susan, 186, 194, 215–17, 219
Sopranos, The, 40
Spaced, 75
spreadability, 56, 179, 234, 237
Stacey Dooley in the USA, 150
Stacey Dooley Investigates,, 149, 179n5
Stein, Louisa Ellen, 5, 11, 12, 71, 84, 228
Stelter, Brian, 5, 114, 117, 125, 192
Steptoe and Son, 117, 131
streaming, 4, 5, 7, 29, 52, 54, 55, 111, 112, 230, 231, 233–5, 243
street meets, 206, 207
structured reality, 9, 11, 18, 20, 36, 110, 111, 115, 185–221, 226–9
structure of feeling, 10, 11, 15, 69, 84–6, 89, 93, 101, 163, 199, 228
Stupid Questions Not to Ask Disabled People, 179, 237
Style Haul, 235, 238, 241
subscription, 40, 53, 124
suburbia/suburb, 80, 110, 128–32, 155
Sugar Rush, 75
Sun, Sex and Suspicious Parents, 53
Superbad, 120
supernatural, 33, 37, 50, 69, 77, 78, 95, 96, 98, 99, 134, 135
supertext, 33, 44
surreal, 43, 45, 48, 51, 73, 75, 80, 101, 114
surveillance, 152–4, 188, 189
Survivor, 191
Switch, 4, 77, 80, 94

Switched at Birth, 13
SyFy, 107

T
T4, 19, 28, 31, 33–5, 38, 44, 57, 75
Taking New York, 187, 190
Taliban, 160, 162
teen film, 12, 120, 128, 131, 135
Teen Mom, 117, 192
Teens, 146, 152–6
Teen TV, 4–6, 10–13, 19, 27, 32–5, 37, 44, 57, 58n5, 69–72, 74, 76–80, 82, 83, 88, 90, 101, 102n5, 107–36, 145, 185, 191, 192, 198, 204, 226–8, 242
Teen Wolf, 78, 135
telefantasy, 32, 41, 69, 70, 77, 79, 80, 82, 84, 94–7, 100, 101, 107, 114, 126, 135
telenovelas, 111
terrestrial, 6, 21n3, 27, 28, 30, 32–5, 40, 57, 176, 187
Thamesmead, 78, 80, 81
Thirteen, 229
This is England (film), 97
This is England (television trilogy), 8
'Till Death Do Us Part, 117, 118
Toddler's truce, 31
tone, 5, 6, 31, 34, 37, 41, 43, 44, 56, 70, 73, 77, 85, 87, 136, 168, 178, 186–8, 194, 195, 201, 215, 216, 219, 246
Top Boy, 8, 71, 73
Top of the Pops, 18
Torchwood, 114, 236
Toronto, 128, 133, 134
tower block, 81
trailers, 30, 43, 44, 233, 246
transatlantic, 5, 9, 20, 70, 107–10, 120, 131, 132, 135, 136, 185, 191, 227, 228

translation, 84, 107–28, 130–3, 135, 136n1, 190
transmedia, 17, 18, 98, 189, 204, 236, 247n5
transnational, 19, 109, 111, 113, 118, 127
transparency, 10, 11, 18, 111, 147, 149, 152–4, 158, 159, 164, 170, 173, 191, 192, 194, 203, 235, 240
True Life, 146
truth claims, 9, 136n2, 149, 164, 176, 228
Tube, The, 18, 31
Tucker's Luck, 31, 74
Tulisa: My Mum and Me, 148
Tumblr, 84, 153, 229, 232, 243, 246
tutorial, 238
tweet, 156, 204, 234
twentysomethings, 4, 76, 126, 187, 191, 192
Twitter, 153, 154, 178, 243, 246
Two Pints of Larger and a Packet of Crisps, 76

U

Ugly Face of Disability Hate Crime, The, 145
Unbreakables, The, 145, 148
uncanny, 70, 80, 81, 94–7, 99, 101, 128
Underage and Gay, 148
underclass, 73, 78, 79, 81, 114
unemployment, 14, 74
universality, 39, 46, 120, 129, 132, 155, 156
university, 75, 76, 154
Unreported World, 150
unruly woman, 86–8
upper class, 160, 187, 198, 210, 214, 215, 219
utopian, 3, 12

V

Vampire Diaries, The, 37, 77, 78
Vermeulen, Tim, 129, 131
Veronica Mars, 12, 76, 82
Vice, 55, 56, 150, 235
Video Diaries, 147, 158, 160
video diary, 147, 163, 166
Video Nation, 147
Vietnam, 159
viral, 237
vlog, 234
vlogger, 238, 240
voice, 10, 15, 17, 19, 20, 27, 35, 40–1, 44, 51, 53, 56, 58n3, 70, 83, 84, 86, 89, 90, 93, 102, 107, 110, 115, 116, 119, 121–3, 134, 135, 146, 152, 154, 156, 160–3, 166, 167, 173, 176, 178, 179, 195, 196, 215, 217, 220, 225, 227–9, 237, 238, 242, 246
Voiceover Man, 44
vulgar, 211–14

W

Walking Dead, The, 94
war, 4, 20, 48, 94, 98, 129, 146, 148, 151, 156–73, 205, 244
Warm Bodies, 95
War Tapes, The, 166, 167
WB, the, 10–13, 34, 35, 72, 76, 77, 79, 82, 114, 126, 134, 191
web 2.0, 176
web series, 12, 236
What Katie Did Next, 36, 210
WhatsApp, 153, 154
Wheatley, Helen, 80, 81
Wicker Man, The, 97
Williams, Linda, 5, 10, 33, 84, 95, 100
Williams, Raymond, 10
Wire, The, 133

witness, 20, 146, 151, 152, 158, 162, 167–71
Wolfblood, 16
Women, Weddings, War and Me, 151, 160
Wonder Years, The, 16
Wood, Helen, 186, 199
Wood, Tony, 193
Word, The, 18, 32, 83, 232
working class, 18, 45, 73, 78, 80, 98, 129, 131, 133, 158, 160, 187, 196–8, 210, 211, 213
World's Worst Place to Be Disabled, The, 145
World War One, 146, 171
World War Z, 94

X

X Factor, The, 18, 28, 36, 148
X-Files, The, 77, 134

Y

Yates, Reggie, 149–51
Youngers, 8, 39, 77, 78, 229
Young & Minted, 234
A Young Person's Guide to Becoming a Rock Star, 75
young soldiers, 51, 156–8, 161, 162, 170, 173
youth
  audiences, 4, 5, 7, 13, 15, 17–19, 27, 29–31, 38, 47, 48, 50, 51, 75, 111, 145, 172, 174, 178, 229–34, 239, 241, 242
  culture, 14, 18, 111
  drama, 9, 13–17, 19, 31, 58n5, 69–102, 107–9, 112–14, 117–21, 123, 124, 126, 128, 131, 134–6, 156, 186, 190, 198, 199, 201, 204, 227–9, 242
  strand, 19, 27–58, 226, 227
YouTube, 4, 7, 55, 56, 114, 147, 168, 179, 231–3, 235, 237–43, 245

Z

Zoella, 238–40, 247n8
zombie, 41, 94–100, 102n7
'zoo' aesthetic, 34

Printed by Printforce, the Netherlands